NEW CONCEPTS IN LATINO AMERICAN CULTURES

A series edited by Licia Fiol-Matta and José Quiroga

Cosmopolitanisms and Latin America: Against the Destiny of Place,
  by Jacqueline Loss

Ciphers of History: Latin American Readings for a Cultural Age,
  by Enrico Mario Santí

Remembering Maternal Bodies: Melancholy in Latina and Latin American Women's Writing,
  by Benigno Trigo

NEW DIRECTIONS IN LATINO AMERICAN CULTURES

Also edited by Licia Fiol-Matta and José Quiroga

New York Ricans from the Hip Hop Zone,
  by Raquel Rivera

The Famous 41: Sexuality and Social Control in Mexico, 1901,
  edited by Robert McKee Irwin, Edward J. McCaughan, and Michele Rocío Nasser

Velvet Barrios: Popular Culture & Chicana/o Sexualities,
  edited by Alicia Gaspar de Alba, with a foreword by Tomás Ybarra Frausto

Tongue Ties: Logo-Eroticism in Anglo-Hispanic Literature,
  by Gustavo Perez-Firmat

Bilingual Games: Some Literary Investigations,
  edited by Doris Sommer

Jose Martí: An Introduction,
  by Oscar Montero

New Tendencies in Mexican Art,
  by Rubén Gallo

The Masters and the Slaves: Plantation Relations and Mestizaje in American Imaginaries,
  edited by Alexandra Isfahani-Hammond

The Letter of Violence: Essays on Narrative and Theory,
  by Idelber Avelar

Intellectual History of the Caribbean,
  by Silvio Torres-Saillant

Forthcoming titles

None of the Above: Contemporary Puerto Rican Cultures and Politics,
edited by Frances Negrón-Muntaner

Puerto Ricans in America: 30 Years of Activism and Change,
edited by Xavier F. Totti and Félix Matos Rodríguez

Ciphers of History

Latin American Readings for a Cultural Age

Enrico Mario Santí

palgrave
macmillan

CIPHERS OF HISTORY
© Enrico Mario Santí, 2005.

First published in 2005 by
PALGRAVE MACMILLAN™
175 Fifth Avenue, New York, N.Y. 10010 and
Houndmills, Basingstoke, Hampshire, England RG21 6XS
Companies and representatives throughout the world.

PALGRAVE MACMILLAN is the global academic imprint of the Palgrave Macmillan division of St. Martin's Press, LLC and of Palgrave Macmillan Ltd. Macmillan® is a registered trademark in the United States, United Kingdom and other countries. Palgrave is a registered trademark in the European Union and other countries.

ISBN 1–4039–7046–7

Library of Congress Cataloging-in-Publication Data is available from the Library of Congress.

A catalogue record for this book is available from the British Library.

Design by Newgen Imaging Systems (P) Ltd., Chennai, India.

First edition: November 2005

10 9 8 7 6 5 4 3 2 1

Printed in the United States of America.

For Nivia

Pity would be no more
If we did not make somebody Poor;
And Mercy no more could be
If all were as happy as we.
William Blake, "The Human Abstract"

To see ourselves as others see us can be eye-opening. To see others as sharing a nature with ourselves is the merest decency. But it is from the far more difficult achievement of seeing ourselves amongst others, as a local example of the forms human life has locally taken, a case among cases, a world among worlds, that the largeness of mind, without which objectivity is self-congratulation and tolerance a sham, comes.
Clifford Geertz, *Local Knowledge*

The poet is the reader of himself: the reader who discovers, in what he writes, while he writes it, the presence of the unsaid, the absence of saying which is saying all. The work is form, the transparency of language upon which a shadow—untouchable, illegible—is drawn: the unsaid. I, too, suffer from unreality.
Octavio Paz, "Sólido/insólito"

CONTENTS

viii   Contents

PREFACE

Ciphers of History argues for the study of local contexts as keys to literary interpretation. Its seven readings were fifteen years in the making, but their coalescence into a single organic argument was a matter of one year's intense work. Over the years in which I worked on these essays, I have benefited from the support and dialogue of a number of dear friends and colleagues, among them: Alfred J. MacAdam, Jorge Edwards, Georgette Dorn and Everett Larsen; Efraín Kristal, Gustavo Pérez Firmat, the late Manuel Moreno Fraginals and Teresita Pedraza; José Pascual Buxó, Adriana Méndez Rodenas, William Luis, Graciella Cruz–Taura, José M. (Manolín) Hernández, and the late Enrique Baloyra; Klaus Müller-Bergh, Araceli García Carranza, Suzanne Jill Levine, Danubio Torres Fierro, Nedda and Enrique Anhalt; Suleiman Darrat, Emil Volek, Lydia Rubio, Marie José Paz and, last but not least, my beloved teacher, the late Octavio Paz.

Eduardo González, Richard McKirahan and Voula Tsouna read the Introduction and made very useful comments. Maarten van Delden gave the whole book a sharp, fair reading. My dear friend Miriam Gómez was a source of recondite information I wouldn't have otherwise known, as was the Cuban poet Orlando González Esteva. Carlos and Mina Ripoll Aurelio and Sara L. de la Vega and Elias and Georgina Sabat Rivers are couple friends my family and I cherish.

I publish this book while mourning the loss of three friends who contributed greatly to my thinking about all these issues: Roberto Esquenazi-Mayo, Antonio Benítez Rojo, and Guillermo Cabrera Infante.

My students Lilliam Oliva-Collmann and David Bird valiantly tackled first-draft translations of chapters one and seven and I thank them for it. I also thank my friend, *maestro* Ramón Alejandro, for allowing his cryptic "*Le Philosophe paralysé par le doute*" to grace our cover.

I was able to work on this book while on a leave from the University of Kentucky, where I now teach. I thank former Arts and Sciences Dean Howard Grotch and Edward Stanton, Chair of the Department of Hispanic Studies, for allowing me this time off. I owe another debt of gratitude to my friend, Professor José Quiroga, whose interest in this editorial project made it a reality, and yet another one to my editor, Gabriella Pearce.

I owe the greatest debt to my family: my children Alexis, Venissa, and Camila, and my wife Professor Nivia Montenegro. The "local knowledge" I gain from them everyday is the source of love and strength that keeps me going.

Claremont, California
December, 2004

Introduction

I

My favorite Borges poem of all time is *La cifra*, the title work of one of his last books (1981). The poem's overt subject is the inconstant moon, about which Borges wrote so often throughout his career, perhaps as a response to Leopoldo Lugones, Borges's famous precursor who, following Laforgue, had turned it into a staple of modern Hispanic poetics. But for this old poet, whose *persona* permeates the bulk of Borges's late works, the poem is not so much about the moon as what the moon has meant poetically and paradoxically, being both present in memory and inconstant physically. It reads:

The Limit

The silent friendship of the moon
(I misquote Virgil) has kept you company
since that one night or evening
now lost in time, when your restless
eyes first made her out for always
in a patio or a garden since gone to dust.
For always? I know that someday someone
Will find a way of telling you this truth:
"You'll never see the moon aglow again.
You've now attained the limit set for you
By destiny. No use opening every window
Throughout the world. Too late. You'll never
                                        find her."

Our life is spent discovering and forgetting
That gentle habit of the night.
Take a good look. It could be the last.[1]

I provide Trueblood's translation not because I like it, necessarily, but because its flaws will help me come round to introducing the subject of this book. Those flaws begin, of course, with the title: "*cifra*" is cipher and not just "limit." With the latter, Trueblood fixed upon the meaning of Spanish *suma* (English amount, or quantity) in the eleventh line of the original, but thereby restricted the word's resonance. He may also have attempted, with all good reason, to evoke Borges's earlier poem "Limits" [Spanish "Límites"] (collected in *El otro, el mismo* [1964]), whose theme is strikingly similar. Its core lines:

If there is a limit to all things and a measure and a
      last time and nothing more and forgetfulness,
who will tell us to whom in this house
we without knowing it have said farewell? (179)

In both poems, awareness of temporality causes fear and trembling; one never knows which moment will be our last. But the later poem goes beyond existential thematics, I think, to broach additional perils, such as those of what I call ciphered reading.

In the poem's fiction, the young poet, perhaps the very author of *Moon Across the Way* (1925), Borges's second book, had read, deciphered, and understood the moon—that the paragon or *cifra* of poetry par excellence, as the further allusion to Virgil (and Ezra Pound) suggests. All this constitutes the material context, or historical background, for Borges's poem. And yet the old poet has now outlived not only those early "limits," but also his own juvenile interpretation. "Borges," the poetic *persona*, whose fascination for number theory was as great as his fear of labyrinths, fears he's used up his quota (Trueblood's *limit*) of poetic ariants—his apportioned repertoire, if you will. Still he responds, "*our life is spent discovering and forgetting/that gentle habit of the night,*" and concludes that it only takes the self-same moon to reinterpret anew: it's only a matter of forgetting it.

The semantic trick, which Trueblood didn't catch, was that the moon is both there *and* not there, both present and absent, not only because Borges could literally not see it ("Borges," person and *persona*, is blind), but because the (full) moon's very physical shape is a circle: 0, zero, *la cifra*.

The final warning: "Take a good look" (Spanish: "*Hay que mirarla bien*") is, in this further sense, doubly ironic and does not fully capture the impersonal construction of the original, which underscores the enigma of a look that doesn't actually take place except perhaps in the mind's eye.

Could we then say that here the cipher, like Robert Frost's "poetry," is "lost in translation"? Another favorite text of mine, this time from the musical *Chicago* is when Roxie, signaling a fingered 0 to Billy Flynn, remarks: "Amos, in the bed department, was . . . zero." True to form, the elder Borges, showing he, too, understands ciphers, not to mention ciphered reading, warns: "The moon, in the poetic department, is . . . zero." That is, the moon like Roxie's "marital bliss," is both there and not there; it is there to be read, as Trueblood certainly does, in the historicist context of the Borgesian canon; but it is also, paradoxically, and *at the same time, not* there as a fresh object—as soon as the poet (or poetic language) "forgets" it and then isolates it in a timeless present. Only by viewing the moon as cipher, or metaphor, does it acquire full value. The "last" in the poem's last line, is, in that sense, both ironic and significant: Spanish *última*, especially without the restrictive article (*la*) can mean "last in a series," but also "the most recent"—both "the end" and "the last one seen." Thus by attributing to *cifra* a meaning other than the literal one, the translator misread, and therefore restricted, the poem's argument about ciphered reading. Had such mistranslation not occurred, however, bilingual readers could not have ascertained the cipher's enigmatic logic.

Ciphers of History collects a series of readings of Latin American texts where such play between presence and absence both guides and diverts interpretation. Its broad subject is the relationship between literature and history, although how that relationship is established in each of these readings remains anything but constant. By calling these readings ciphers I intend to cast them as engaged, at times even enigmatic, interpretations of historical issues, events, and sometimes concepts, however marginal they may appear to be. Thus by *cipher*, about which I shall have more to say, I mean an interpretive dynamics in relation to historical or material phenomena. Cipher means for me something antithetical and literally cryptic: the ways in which texts provide interpretive codes that allow for retrieval, and, at the same time, abscond historicist evidence that produce other margins of interpretation. Ultimately, my purpose in pursuing these readings is to join a growing debate, urged in part by the challenging rise of Cultural Studies as a field of inquiry, on the teaching of literature, the fate of research, and the ongoing crisis of the humanities.

One good way further to introduce this book would be to follow the logic of my whole title, beginning with its ironic tail. Indeed, my Latin

American readings all appear during an age we are wont to call
"cultural." All ages are, of course, cultural, in the sense that they are all
constituted by a fabric of sundry social expressions. But our own postmodern age wills itself as "cultural," especially, in a heightened sense my
quotation marks express imperfectly, because of the way "culture" today
suffuses all social constructs, a suffusing that in the academic world, and
particularly in the field of literary studies, often works to exclude attention to other, perhaps less current but still beneficent analytical tools.
Such suffusing is part of what Fredric Jameson, noting what he calls the
current "dissolution of an autonomous sphere of culture," describes as
its dialectical result, namely how "everything in our social life—from
economic value and state power, to practices and to the way the very
structure of the psyche itself—can be said to have become 'cultural' in
some original and yet untheorized way."[2] Thus "culture," for the postmodern age Jameson reads darkly, and reflecting a pervasive critical
hegemony, has become the unwitting avatar of Pascal's "nature," which
"being lost, becomes its own nature."[3] Yet as much as I agree with the
urgency to theorize culture today, it is not my intention to pursue
that here. I view this book, rather, as a more modest contribution to what
Borges once called "the halting and rudimentary art of reading." For
reading, I believe, is what most often becomes relegated, or repressed, in
the hyper-theorized, and therefore abstract, discourses of this, our
"culturally"—suffused age.

Today relegating or repressing reading is most evident in cross-cultural
analysis, as in the treatment of foreign texts that are taught and
interpreted in the Western academy with an eye toward an understanding
we call "theoretical" but which often ends up blinded to textual, or
indeed cultural, particularity. Robert Alter once described, in a book that
deals with some of the issues that interest me, this normative "disappearance of reading" as part of what he calls an "emotional alienation from
the imaginative life of the texts under discussion" that obtains from our
critical climate and which, to him, "often seems in its bristling concep-
tuality empty of an experiential ground in reading."[4] The crisis Alter
described appears doubly compounded, in my view, in the inevitable distance that is created by reading across cultures and languages. In the case
of reading literary texts from Latin America in the U.S. university, the
context I am most familiar with, one common strategy that is evident in
scholarly books that now constitute a new genre is simply to lump
together texts and figures from different generic, historical, and geographical settings under a single overarching theme, usually derived from
current critical and theoretical trends. Cutting across epistemological

borders in *bricolage* form thus provides, for the academic reader, the spectacle of a novel arrangement of the Latin American past, perhaps even an allegory of the theory at work, but gives little in the way of discussion of the contexts that gave rise to each of the texts in question, or how those contexts contain codes to deciphering those texts. More alarming still is that sundry arrangements like these often come justified with advocacy to a particularist cause, defenses of national and local knowledge that are supported with arguments that border on demagogy, while allowing theoretical fawning to displace material knowledge of the texts they purport to analyze.

From the above it should be clear that my interest lies in practicing Latin American readings rather than simply reading Latin American texts. Shifting the key term from verb to noun form allows me to underscore one of my chief concerns, which is to bridge, however imperfectly, the built-in epistemological gaps between archive and academic context that constitute all cross-cultural interpretation. In reading Latin American texts, I have sought to reconstruct their sundry material and historical contexts, not so much in order to illuminate those contexts exclusively, as a positivist literary history used to prescribe, nor to read texts as they would have been upon original publication, as an orthodox historical critic would perhaps insist, or even to relate base to superstructure, as diehard Marxists are wont to demand, so much as to interplay text and context dialectically as a means to interpretation. In this sense, my readings set out to accomplish a relatively limited task: to retrieve the archive of the Latin American Other in order to pay heed to its voice. While I do not pretend to represent that "Other," or for that matter to retrieve the totality of the Other's archive, each exercise does attempt to interpret from the Other's point of view by reconstructing contexts that can aid us in that "halting and rudimentary art of reading." And because the reconstruction of those contexts requires, in my view, exhausting the pertinent bibliography, in the end I hope not only to practice informed interpretations, but also to provide summary statements, *états présents*, of the critical questions particular texts pose.

My concern for reading as a practice that has either been lost or is en route to being so, thus comes on top of a normative concern for the equivalent loss of the historical archive, otherwise known as "context," which, existing in languages other than English, has been further removed from our hermeneutic horizon. What Gayatri Spivak calls, writing about contexts much different from mine, "the foreclosure of the native informant," affects as well a field as commercially popular and apparently accessible as so-called Latin American Studies.[5] In this, my own response to what I view as the unfortunate decline of reading departs from those of other critics, like Alter himself, who advocate the solution of a simple return to the "language of literature," yet sidestep the more complex issues of what this same critic called "the eccentric and at times tendentious use of history" (20). I subscribe, rather, to what yet another historian of literature has averred: while the "environment (i.e., context) to which a text refers remains fixed," that text's "subsequent generations of readers is subject to change," and in ways such that past works of literature "come to refer to one environment while its readers refer to another," thus constituting "the most serious obstacle to understanding what past works of literature meant."[6] Yet on top of this obstacle, which of course pervades all critical work, or at least all readings, lies what I think is the more insidious one that frames the specific reception of Latin American literature in the United States, where texts are often read stereotypically, that is, as decorative reflections of current events, or else as mystified projections of current U.S. minority issues.[7] There is of course plenty of reason to sustain, write about, and advocate political positions on racial, ethnic, gender, and power struggles, in the United States and elsewhere. I doubt, however, that writing or reading about these issues by themselves will help us understand a given poem or novel, less so the specific contexts from which poem and novel arise, and not at all the political issues one could thereby sustain.

Thus, one graver obstacle still to informed reading has to do with what I view as the intrinsically contradictory nature of much of the work currently billed as cultural, evident at least when confronted with the task of interpreting literary texts. While concern for "culture" is most often upheld by an overriding moral call to retrieve archives far removed from the present, the abstract, de-historicized way in which many such retrievals often takes place works to violate the integrity of particular texts that are part of the Other's archive, indeed of the Other's "culture," and whose concrete knowledge a minimal literary interpretation requires. Against such trends, a return to contextual reading can, I believe, offer a healthy correction. For it is only through context that the Other's archive can be known; it is through concrete knowledge that the Other can be fully respected.

Some of the concerns of this book thus intersect in part those of the current school known as "subaltern studies," though I nowhere use the label, at least explicitly, and my readings sometimes take me far afield. With subaltern studies I do share a concern for tuning an ear to what Ranajit Guha has called "the small voice of History."[8] But it is not enough, I think, simply to listen to that voice. It is also important to decipher its intonation, which for someone like Mikhail Bakhtin was not simply the voice's material context, but the realm where one could find "the purest expression of the values assumed in any utterance," while at the same time lying "on the border between the verbal and nonverbal, the I and the other." That is, intonation, for Bakhtin, and in readings such as the one I attempt, "clearly registers the other's presence, creating a kind of portrait in sound of the addressee to whom the speaker imagines she is speaking."[9]

I would like to think, then, that my readings, emerging from a peripheral culture in relation to the Western metropolis, engage the very problematics of representation that Spivak's burning question—"Can the subaltern speak?"—poses so disturbingly.[10] Such at least is the goal of my chapter 3, arguably the moral or theoretical core of this book, on Octavio Paz's "restitution" of Sor Juana Inés de la Cruz, the seventeenth-century Mexican nun whose work is being constantly rediscovered as an exemplary Latin American subaltern. There is, of course, much ongoing debate within subaltern studies on the nature of such research, and in the Latin American field in particular there brews an open polemics that I do not mean to pursue or chronicle here.[11] I also realize that most of the canonical authors and works I deal with in these readings are not, strictly speaking, "subaltern." But the position I assume throughout these readings is a relative one in regard to subalternity and the periphery, such that the central Latin American canon I assume is actually peripheral in respect to the Western canon, which encompasses it. Suffice it to say that, in my efforts to retrieve the Other's context and voice, I have come to identify with historian Florencia Mallon's critique of the slippages into theoretical mystification that, in the realm of subaltern research, violate an alleged concern for the subaltern subject, even as they also protest a commitment toward his or her defense. Mallon's solution, which I share, is to advocate an antithetical type of reading that reclaims "the centrality of the archive and the field [work]," which can "no longer be done in isolation from textual analysis or literary sources," yet still recognizes how "the archive and the field are constructed arenas in which power struggles—included those generated by our presence—help define and obscure the sources of information to which we have access."[12] Such defense of contextual research is, in this sense, exemplary. It not only redresses the general political aims of subaltern studies, but also underscores the more specific goals of a critical reading that avows cross-cultural integrity through respect for context, historical, and other. In my own readings antithetical recourse surfaces, for example, in my treatment of Pablo Neruda's *Canto general* and my penchant for reading through, sometimes against, but always abiding closely with, the specific contexts of Neruda and his times; elsewhere, in locating the specifically "Cuban critique" of Spanish historical pathology in my reading of 1898 intellectual discourse; or else, in the local knowledge (the *Cristero* rebellion) of "national allegories" like Juan Rulfo's and Elena Garro's.

It is precisely such antithetical critical practice that Jerome McGann, writing specifically on the subject of historical method in literary studies, has described as "trans-historical," in the sense that poetry and poems acquire perpetuity "by virtue of the particular historical adventures which their texts undergo from their first appearance before their authors' eyes through all their subsequent constitutions."[13] Without avowing any strict adherence to McGann's prescriptions, which are more relevant for studies that deal specifically with textual history, my own concern for varieties of transhistorical perpetuity becomes evident, in some of these readings, in the attention paid to accidental features, such as the "errors," including typographical ones, that appear in texts as different as Neruda's *Canto general* (1950) and Ortiz's *Cuban Counterpoint* (1940); or in the mediated reception, through French and Italian sources, of Walt Whitman's work and figure among Latin American poets.[14] Not all my readings pursue such accidents, or deem them relevant; but their pursuit, notably at the beginning and end of the book, does constitute one of the more salient features of the kind of "contextualist formalism" that makes up the backbone of this book.

The latter seeming oxymoron is my borrowing from Hayden White's discussion of the formalist and contextualist strategies that lie at the heart of all historical explanation. White addresses, specifically, "the dead end at which structuralist hyperformalism appears to have arrived" and the critical turn that that dead end determines toward "wedding a formalist analysis with a historically informed sensitivity."[15] His overall aim, in this essay at least, is to elucidate the implicit strategies of social science analysis. But I believe his observation applies as well to any reading, including the literary, which is self-critically aware of both limits and available tools. (White's further defense of the strategies of the so-called New Historicism suggests as much.) And yet, for all its relevance and usefulness, what I still miss in White's discussion, and seems crucial for readings like mine, is a fuller awareness of the cross-cultural divide that affects critical reading as much as or more than the division between formalist and contextualist advocacies, a divide which can be bridged, I think, at least partially, by a return to a relativist positioning on the part of the critical reader.

I mention "positioning" because recently it has become a matter of considerable debate in the annals of Cultural Studies, to the point that practitioners like Peter Hitchcock advocate now what he calls "principles of dialogic exchange." Among such principles figure prominently that "cultural identities in 'other' cultures are in the process of becoming in dialogic interaction and not static as subjects," along with the idea, which strikes me as plain common sense, that "the knowledge produced through this activity is always already contestable, and by definition is not the knowledge of the other as the other would know herself or himself."[16]

Such is, in fact, the moral core of the question I should like my readings to pose: how can one maximally reduce the distortions inherent to cross-cultural reading, including the mystifications of a Western theoretical narcissism, as we read literature from Latin America? I settle for the melancholy "maximally" while aware that full or total coincidence with the Other is both desirable and impossible, at least under the particular circumstances in which I happen to read, write, and publish. Whether we are "imagining Argentina" or "dreaming in Cuban," the abiding risk, from the vantage point of a U.S. academic reader, remains to fantasize about Latin America, as opposed to dealing with its material historical reality, a "cultural exchange" that Gareth Williams defines as "a movement of apprehension and domestication implicit in the repressive establishment of 'shared values.' "[17] I therefore harbor no illusions about my readings, which remain interpretive *approximations* through and through. Yet, I underscore these epistemological quandaries because I find them posed too infrequently in current critical practice, even as that practice continues to proclaim, under the threat of an absorbing globalization, unprecedented philosophical awareness and undying political sympathy.

One misses in such practice, for example, discussions of Pike's useful distinction, available since at least the mid-twentieth century, between "etic" and "emic" views, or how this distinction has often worked to clarify the interpreter's work across cultural and epistemological divides. Pike coined these terms in reference to linguistics, and specifically from the endings of phon*etics* and phon*emics*, and later generalized them onto a theory of human knowledge that has found wide resonance in fields like Anthropology and Psychology.[18] Thus etic, for Pike, is the detached observer's view, while emic is the participant's. As such, etic is alien and cross-cultural, in the specific sense that it compares systems and abstracts from them units that are then synthesized and homogenized; while emic, by turns, is domestic and monocultural, which relates units internally. And so, while the etic view is classificatory, typological, and absolute, the emic view is structural and relative to the specific place where units are found. Thus, and finally, etic systems are "the creation of the analyst," while emic ones "are discovered by the analyst, as units reacted to or constituting the reaction of native participants in events." As such, the generalized version of the emic–etic distinction is meant as a logical, or more specifically, dialectical, hermeneutic tool that, used in tandem, makes up a "stereoscopic window" onto human behavior. That is, in an ideal scheme, analysts would use etic and emic views together, dialectically; observer and participant views joined together as a double-barreled tool of hermeneutic accuracy. My own use of the etic–emic distinction, or else its stereoscopic ideal, is rather implicit in my recourse to both theoretical grids and attention to local context. Yet, as the foregoing should suggest, the bias of my readings on an imaginary etic–emic scale falls squarely on the side of the emic. That is, it is emic or "participant" content, so to speak, what I find lacking in much of the work that today goes under the name of Latin American "cultural studies," a practice which, in its theoretical excesses, too often amounts, in my judgment, to bad faith abuses of the etic view.

"To set forth symmetrical crystals of significance," wrote Clifford Geertz three decades ago, in his own complaint against the Grand Theory excesses of his time, "and then attribute their existence to autogenous principles of order," amounts, in Geertz's informed opinion, to pretending "a science that does not exist and [to] imagine a reality that cannot be found."[19] Geertz was reacting then to the grand paradigms of anthropological theory, such as those of Parsons (Geertz's teacher), or Lévi-Strauss, that impeded ethnographic interpretation and only served, in the words of one of Geertz's more sympathetic critics, "to inhibit understanding local knowledge by shrouding local idioms."[20] Even as I am far from espousing an explicit anthropological method in these readings, I find in Geertz's critique of the universalist claims of much recent ethnography another refreshing precedent for my own work. That is, as I have reworked these essays in the form of chapters for this book and searched for cognates for my own thinking, I have found Geertz's notions of "thick description," "local knowledge," or indeed his idea of ethnographic description as contextually "microscopic," so as to substantiate interpretation, the most useful, most surprising, formulation of the kinds of detailed contextual readings I attempt. Geertz's semiotic view of culture, in the Weberian sense of a net of significance that humans themselves spin, allows him to postulate an interpretive anthropology that relies upon "thick descriptions" of local materials as its hermeneutic basis. Geertz borrowed the concept of "thick description" from Ryle to signify the object of ethnography as the "stratified hierarchy of meaningful structures," what Ryle himself calls "established codes."[21] For someone in literary studies like me, "thick description" resonates closely on our traditional "close reading," in the same way that "established codes" harks back to the concept of text. In fact, Geertz himself has insisted often that the interpretive ethnographer works pretty much like "a literary critic," and that cultures can be read in the same way texts are. Thus, describing thickly (or else, doing ethnography), "is like trying to read (in the sense of 'construct a reading of') a manuscript—foreign, faded, full of ellipses, incoherencies, suspicious emendations and tendentious commentaries . . ." (*The Interpretation of Cultures*, 10). What Geertz does add, and the formalist inventors of "close reading" lacked, is the notion that thick descriptions, or at least those worth their salt, involve a detailed knowledge of the local context in which those "texts" reside; that is, that those contexts provide a web of signification through which texts can be substantially decoded. Hence the need to view culture, however imperfectly, "from the native's point of view"; and to understand that "the form and pressure of natives' inner lives is more like grasping a proverb, catching an allusion, seeing a joke," or Geertz adds, "reading a poem—than it is like achieving communion" (*Local Knowledge*, 70).

I am of course aware of the various critiques to which Geertz's ideas have been subjected over the years, including the far-fetched accusations of a reactionary ethnocentrism.[22] Yet I find that, not unlike White's "contextualist formalism," Mallon's commitment to scouring the local archives, or Pike's emic view, Geertz's program (if it can indeed be called that) strikes me as a useful corrective to our newest forms of scholasticism, estranged as they often are from local knowledge. Geertz has been criti-cized often, in fact, for his choices of context, which, to quote one of his more sympathetic readers, he reads "largely in terms of local cultural idioms rather than global forces and interaction," such that by often excluding "issues of political power, colonialism, domination, and the modern world system, his interpretive readings seem constrained."[23] Geertz himself would counter, however, that what counts most for the specific interpretations he is after are local idioms or local knowledge, in the sense of microscopically specific rather than just globally relevant. While I do not discount, in some of my own readings, the relevance of so-called global forces and interaction, in most of them my bias does remain "Geertzian" (emic, in Pike's distinction), in the sense of observing a penchant for reconstructing local archives. And I do so while also aware that, as Derrida's debate with Searle demonstrated long ago, contexts, and thereby the meaning-structures that depend on them, are fluid rather than absolute. For as Jonathan Culler once glossed that particular debate, it is not, in any deconstructive strategy, simply a matter of denying that historical contexts determine meaning, as much as realizing that discourse and meaning "are produced in processes of contextualization, decontextualization and recontextualization."[24]

To admit that the outcome of interpretations—and not just those resulting from deconstructive strategies—depends on such plural and unstable process, means, however, also to face that no context, no matter how detailed or exhaustive our retrievals may be, can saturate texts totally. Up to now, that is, I have been arguing on behalf of contextual retrieval; now I wish to call attention to the inevitable limits of that procedure. For all texts, and particularly aesthetic ones, such as the ones I read here, ultimately escape contextualization, in the sense that context alone cannot explain them. Such is the paradox that no one less than Karl Marx confronted in his *Contribution to the Critique of Political Economy*, as he articulated the antithetical relationship he found between history and art, or else (in Marxian terms) between base and super-structure:"The difficulty," Marx wrote, "does not lie in understanding that Greek art and the epic are associated with certain social developments. The difficulty is that they still give us aesthetic pleasure and are in a certain respect regarded as unattainable models."[25] Writing more than a century later, Octavio Paz himself remarked, at the end of his own historicist reading of Sor Juana Inés de la Cruz and her times, how he refused to "see culture either as the reflection of changing social forces *or* as the imperfect imitation of immutable ideas." Thus unwilling to choose between a strict historicism and an orthodox formalism, Paz opted instead for what he called a "poetic solution" which views "harmony or correspondence among a society's tools, institutions, philosophies and works of art." Paz added then that "the autonomy of works of art and their inevitable correlation with history and society seem to be contradictory or even incompatible ideas," but if so, he explained, it must be because "reality, too, is contradictory. The culture of a society at a given moment is also a fluid system of interconnections" as "events are the product not only of so-called causes but also of chance."[26]

Both Marx and Paz were actually describing, as critical readers dealing with literary texts, the limits of a historicist hermeneutics. If our knowledge of context, regardless of how microscopic, can never saturate totally the figurative nature of texts, then this circumstance must account for the (often contradictory) wealth of interpretations each text summons throughout its reception. That is, because context can never saturate text, there always remain margins for further interpretation, as if there always remained residues of resistance to historical retrieval. Roland Barthes' dream, exposed in a book like *S/Z* (1970), of total retrieval through the teasing and identification of the cultural codes of which texts are made, is just that: a dream whose boldness does not make it any more real or acceptable. Barthes, in *S/Z* and elsewhere, alerted us to the existence in texts of codes whose "accumulated cultural knowledge . . . enabled a reader to recognize details as contributions to a particular function or sequence."[27] But even as Barthes (and, through him, Structuralism) acknowledged such codes, he also refused to interpret them. "In the multiplicity of writing, everything is to be *disentangled*, not *deciphered*," Barthes wrote; for "by refusing to acknowledge an ultimate meaning, to the text (and to the world as text), liberates what may be called an anti-theological activity."[28] For Structuralism, that is, codes were there to be recognized and disentangled, though not interpreted; interpreting, assigning a meaning, meant deciding on a specific pattern that arrested the freeplay of those codes. And yet, if codes do restrict freeplay and fix meaning, it must be because the plural, elastic nature of such codes has been misunderstood in the first place.[29]

Thus in preferring to speak of ciphers, which leave open a margin of error or unknowability, instead of codes, available for stable contextual retrievals, I wish to focus and acknowledge the supplementary nature of all interpretation, an acknowledgment that chapter 3, on Paz's reading of Sor Juana, itself reads under the concept of restitution. The intriguing problem for me, in that chapter specifically, but also throughout the book's focus on what I call ciphered reading, lies in restitution's supple-mentary nature. That is, all restitution exceeds, or changes, the object in the process of making right the alleged wrong. Indeed, my reading there begins by clarifying that there is a crucial difference between restitution and restoration. For in setting out "to restore voice," or else, "to speak in the name of," critical restitutions, by their very supplementarity, exceed the object and thus do everything except see things "from the native's point of view." Cipher is therefore the metaphor I use for both the object of contextual retrieval, which for me is always partial and incomplete, and the general enigmatic relationship between text and context. The phrase "ciphers of history" in this book thus invokes both the literary text that contains statements about historical contexts and the critical restitution that wages an interpretation about that text.

The thrust of my argument may be further gathered from the difference between Barthes' (and Ryle's) *code* and the word *cipher*, which I rather favor. Both refer to signs that are hidden or disguised. But whereas cipher and code are close in meaning, they differ subtly in the force of their respective concealments. Accepted definitions of *code* (from Latin *codex*) stress a decisive and systematic hermeneutic anchoring, an inflexible norm or set of rules that expressions like "code of honor" capture vividly.[30] *Cipher*, on the other hand, (from Arabic صفر the word for zero) stresses the sign's uncertain, enigmatic content. Latin *codex* (or *caudex*) originally meant "tree trunk" and, by metaphorical extension, a ledger or account book whose registry, solid as a trunk's, was meant to avoid or exclude inconsistencies. Cipher, by turns, invites such inconsistency and even outright paradox. Unlike code, which carries the inflexibility of Roman law, cipher evokes the sinuous flow of Islamic (or Hindu) metaphysics in its signifying, at the same time, *both* the arithmetical symbol zero (0) *and* any Arabic numeral. Cipher thus means *both* nothing and something, presence *and* absence.[31] There is, in English at least, no "cipher of honor," except perhaps to denote how precarious, or mysterious, honor can be; and a "ciphered ledger" is a bookkeeper's nightmare. Spanish *cifra*, as opposed to *código*, appears just as paradoxical as its English cognate, if not more so; it magnifies semantic instability in its triple meaning (not available in other languages) of "number," "secret sign" and "paragon" (as in: "*El Cid, cifra de la caballería*"; "The Cid, paragon of chivalry"). That is, in Spanish, *cifra* means both the paradoxical absence of zero and a paragon's hyperbolic presence. Spanish *código*, usually reserved for sets of laws (as in "*código de tránsito*" or "*código napoleónico*") disallows any such ambiguity.[32]

My general point here is that whereas the word *code* stresses hermeneutic certainty, *cipher* denotes the ultimate ambivalence of interpretation. To invoke ciphering thus means to navigate a margin of error or uncertainty, even as one retrieves material evidence that tends to neutralize, or displace, the effects of such error. Like the linguistic sign, which consists of a present material signifier and an ideational absent signified, a cipher is simultaneously present and absent. Thus, on the surface, *Canto general* deals with the cold war; however, it contains aesthetic and personal codes that refer, at once, to issues of poetic genre and Neruda's personal enemies. On the surface, *Strawberry and Chocolate* is a film about Cuban homophobia; otherwise, it deals with the current State's policy of national reconciliation. It could be said that in each of my readings my aim has been to go beyond the text's surface argument, its figurative statements, and to decipher its implicit level. But rather than do this through a structuralist method, as in Lévi-Strauss, or through ideological analysis, as in Jameson, I have favored a dialectic of historical and formal elements whose end result I call ciphered reading. One could also say, in general, that in this I proceed according to the method of the School Paul Ricoeur has named "of Suspicion": the trio of Marx, Nietzsche, and Freud. "Beginning with them understanding is hermeneutics: henceforward, to seek meaning is no longer to spell out the consciousness of meaning, but to decipher its expressions . . . What all three attempted, in different ways, was to make their 'conscious' methods of deciphering coincide with the 'unconscious' work of ciphering which they attributed to the will to power, to social being, and to the unconscious psyche."[33] Cipher is the metaphor I use, following Ricoeur, for the process of understanding how texts embody false consciousness, the contents of which can be deciphered, if only incompletely, through hermeneutic interpretation.

II

Ciphers of History begins and ends with pedagogical exercises. The dual occasion is the English versions of introductions to Spanish critical editions of Pablo Neruda's *Canto general* (1950) and Fernando Ortiz's *Cuban Counterpoint: Tobacco and Sugar* (1940). Both of these readings go through contexts, biographical and historical, in detail before tackling the far subtler task of interpretation. I begin and end the book this way not because I find it provides an ideal chapter format but because it lays out a method that perhaps appears too compact in the sandwiched five chapters. Yet the origin of the tenor, if not actual substance, of all these essays goes back farther, to 1992, in a paper now gathered here in an appendix. Back then I had called attention to the fact that, like the "Orientalism" studied by the late Edward Said, Latinamericanism created its own object of study in the name of so-called Latin America— so-called, in fact, because the name itself, the result of bureaucratese, is seldom if ever used in Latin America by "Latin Americans," and its abuse exposes, rather, an outside or exogenous gaze that constitutes that disciplinary discourse. (My own use, in the title of this book, can therefore be viewed as self-canceling, or *sous-rature*; as ironic as the word cultural in the subtitle.) In retrospect, I can see now that this 1992 piece sealed my renewed historicist conviction, set me on the course of other defining essays, like the present chapter 3, and sparked other critical responses.

While my reading of *Canto general* and the cold war marks my return to the subject of my first book, the chapter on Ortiz (now Chapter 7) represents a head-on engagement with some issues, like transculturation, recently made current in Cultural Studies. By the late 1980s, when I returned to work on Neruda and began the period when I wrote these essays, I sensed that I was already too historicist to be satisfied with close readings that avoided political aperçus, yet also too formalist to abandon the obvious benefits of a formalist training. By returning to topics such as Neruda's big Book, or Walt Whitman's Latin American reception (here chapter 2), I engaged the kind of work—what I now call ciphered reading—I had been unable or unwilling to undertake earlier in my former orthodox formalist life. I therefore opted to produce, in the first instance, a critical introduction that would, at once, be specific enough about Neruda's circumstances (1940s Mexico and Chile) and broadly theoretical to encompass the book's formal and ideological complexity. The touchstone was the context of my research. As opposed to my first book, research for which I did entirely in U.S. libraries, and was made up exclusively of close readings of the poems, the later edition was the result of actual field work in Santiago de Chile, which I visited while the country was still under military rule. But the other circumstance—Washington, D.C., where I was then living, during the fall of the Berlin Wall and the so-called end of the cold war—was just as momentous. If *Canto general* had been the quintessential cold war book of poetry, then what could or should I say about it at the end of that conflict, whose impact at the time I was feeling closely at the heart of a victor empire? While I felt that Neruda's communist bias had to be exposed, and criticized, in detail, something still missing by and large from extant Neruda criticism, I also learned that his Book, or else its formal poetic accomplishment, escaped such discredit. What I did end up saying reflected such a cross-roads: a gathering of first-hand material and historical sources, a close reading of the way the book violated fruitfully its Historical–Materialist argument, and a telescoping of its broad argument on poetic genre.

My reading of Fernando Ortiz's *Cuban Counterpoint* reflects, by turns, a different set of concerns made current 20 years later. Over the years I became struck by the way this classic had become too facile a reference in both postmodern criticism and Cultural Studies, neither one of which displayed much familiarity with the actual historical polemics (the abuse of the sugar single-crop economy in Cuba, and thereby, the power politics behind it) the book actually engaged. As I set out to reconstruct that context, however, I learned that yet another gap in the Ortiz archive was its tense relationship with Functionalism, the brand of ethnographic research espoused during the early twentieth century by, among others, Bronislaw Malinowski. The latter had been Ortiz's friend and collaborator, and at Ortiz's request had written the book's introduction and there propped-up the latter's coinage of "transculturation," the term and concept that was meant to foil, and ultimately discredit, "acculturation," favored then by U.S. anthropologists. As I discovered that Malinowski had distorted the facts about acculturation for interested professional reasons with an embarrassing political edge, it became clear that Ortiz's book, and, particularly, its uninformed abuse in ideological discussions stemming mostly from second-hand references (such as Angel Rama's most influential book), provided a test case for that "foreclosure of the native informant" that in my view makes up much of the bad faith of our cultural age.

Whitman's haphazard image in Latin America provided a similar test case, this time on the reception of a U.S. poet whose figure provided a rhetoric of prophecy for Latin American peers. My interest on the subject had begun, again, with my work on Neruda, yet I soon found myself reacting against a trend, led by Doris Sommer's essay on the same subject, that studied such reception as pretext for de-historicized theoretical speculation.[34] That is, even as I found myself taking a lead from Sommer's suggestive frame, I felt increasingly that the devil lay, rather, in the bibliographic details, the sheer archival work that attested to such a reception; and that the use of theory, in such a reading at least, was not only insufficient but cross-purposed. Such details reveal, for one thing, that Whitman's Latin American reception was mediated not only by French sources (a fact established by Fernando Alegría as early as 1954), but also by Italian translations of Whitman, which his early admirers plundered. Establishing such plural mediation was important, if only because it showed a complex reception that could not be reduced to the political blandishments of the critical canon. That is, beginning with Alegría perhaps, critical commentators of the Whitman reception, as opposed to his first Spanish translators, opted to read his influence as an unmediated block phenomenon, a kind of Pan-American chorus whose pseudo-mystical unison was strangely at odds with the initial rhapsodic transmission of his poetry. The truth is that the politics attendant to Whitman's reception—first used to criticize U.S. imperial power, later manipulated during the Good Neighbor Policy years, and finally exploited by leftist causes—was part of a complex of continental influence that made of polar opposite poets like Borges and Neruda, among others, strange bedfellows of the American Bard.

With chapter 3, on Paz's reading of Sor Juana, and what I call the "poetics of restitution," we arrive, as I have noted, at the book's moral core. I emphasize moral because it is here that I engage the problem of a compensatory hermeneutics, such as abounds in much current criticism, which intends to restore "voice to mute classes of people," to cite Geoffrey Hartman's formula. Paz himself, in his own brilliant reading, had wanted to *restitute* (his verb, used in all its legal force) not only Sor Juana's stature in the canon of Golden Age Spanish poetry—relatively lost, or devalued, among her better-known male peers—but also the significance of what Paz called Sor Juana's "defeat" before the forces of a bureaucracy like the Catholic orthodoxy of her time. He accomplished as much, but in so doing reproduced, unwittingly, the signature mode of most canonical interpretations of Sor Juana—the critical restitution of her lost archive, be that Liberal, Feminist, or Catholic. The fundamental problem for me lies in this epistemological doubt: how can we read Sor Juana without betraying Sor Juana? That is, how can we read her without risking restitution through a given interpretive grid that is often not hers or her times'? Are ciphers avoidable? Thus my reading confronts antithetically the details of Paz's ideological reading along with Sor Juana's own use of restitution as a term and concept in her poetics, and specifically in the proem of her first and only self-edited collection.

Taking a cue from the essay version of this one chapter, my friend Alberto Moreiras objected recently in a fine book to the political implications of my reading, whose links to Hartman he recognizes, in what he calls its "operation of arbitrary closure." This closure is evident, accordingly, in my critique of the customary critical translation of Sor Juana into something other than herself, which in my reading becomes generalized as one of the forms of contemporary "identity politics." Moreiras prescribes for its partial resolution what he also calls a practice of "self-restitutional excess," available in one of two forms: either "metadisciplinary reflection," what I take to mean self-awareness of the perils of restitution, or outright self-negation—"it can look for its own point of closure in an attempt to come to the end of itself." I confess that of the two I prefer the first—not seeing much of a point in simply negating the discipline—but would add contextual "thick description" as a further, and I believe more effective, means of self-restitution. And while I would agree "there is also restitutional excess in self-restitution," I also believe that contextual or archival fieldwork and its thick description provide empirical checks against such excess, even if they do not eliminate it completely. Moreiras' objections, finally, come in the context of a welcome, lucid discussion of Latinamericanism as a discipline, thus picking up the discussion that I initiated in my 1992 piece. For although I did not state so explicitly then, restitution happens to be the mechanism whereby a latinamericanist discourse constitutes itself—pretending to speak "in the name of," but never actually doing it "from the native's point of view."[35]

My defense of similar local knowledge runs all through the remaining chapters, but is a matter of particular contention in chapter 4, on the question of national allegory in Juan Rulfo's *Pedro Páramo* and Elena Garro's *Recollections of Things to Come*. Here I am interested in contesting two myths. First, the alleged emptying-out of historical content in so-called magical–realist texts, such as in these two signature novels; and second, the alleged failure of twentieth-century Latin American novels at providing national allegories. The two are, in my view, related, as I attempt to vindicate, and resituate, the novels' historical content while reading through Fredric Jameson's useful, if ultimately flawed, concept of "national allegory." I coincide, for example, with Jean Franco's identification of the *Cristero* rebellion as the contextual archive for the partial decipherment of both novels; but I also disagree with Franco's indictment of the contemporary novel's failures at allegory. I argue, instead, for situating its index at a formal, and specifically narratological, level rather than a strictly anecdotal one. Yet the key to such allegory lies, I believe, in the further ways both texts manipulate rhizomatic narratives, available in the form of gossip and rumor, whose formal versions are intercalation and digression. Both ultimately point back, I submit, to a statement about the power critique marginal writers like Rulfo and Garro developed in response to the failures of modern state-building in post–revolutionary Mexico.

Cuba is the common theme of the book's latter three chapters, with the reading of Ortiz at the tail end, and beginning with the postcolonial reading of 1898 Spanish intellectual discourse in chapter 5. Aside from my own personal stake on the subject, evident in part in the tone of this particular chapter, here I am interested, admittedly, less in detailing the "native point of view" than in speculating on the reasons, some of them deep-seated, why it is so seldom discussed in the critical canon. As I see it, the issue has been given scant attention, even in this allegedly postcolonial age, because of the neocolonial narcissism that still dominates much of Spanish Peninsular thought on the Cuban question, including that of major Spanish historians. The subject of Cuba is still treated, in much of that discussion, as if the entire conflict still revolved exclusively around Spain's damaged relationship with the United States, the formal victor in the "splendid little war," and the "Cuban" or subaltern viewpoint (extensive to Puerto Rico and the Philippine and Mariana Islands) of sovereignty and independence simply got lost in the shuffle. The underside of this question is the pathological melancholy stemming from an incomplete, perhaps never existent, mourning of colonial loss, evident in much of the writing by some of the most prominent 1898 figures (like Ganivet, Maeztu, and Unamuno), and which, even today, accounts for the harmful repetition of neocolonial attitudes, both political and psychic, in Spain's attitude toward the former "ever loyal" island.

As I attempt to restore that "Cuban point of view" in an inaugural event like the 1898 conflict, at the birth of the Cuban Republic, so I am also intrigued, in chapter 6, by the politics of national reconciliation dramatized in a film like *Strawberry and Chocolate*, rhetorically situated "after" the Revolution. When this film, Tomás Gutiérrez Alea's next-to-last, was first released close to a decade ago, Cubans, both within and abroad, became excited about the political winds it blew, as it purportedly made a bold public statement, unheard-of in Cuba until enactment of the so-called special period, right after the collapse of the Soviet Union, about the renewed need for a culture of tolerance and reconciliation. While the tolerance the film summoned explicitly was for homosexual rights (and, obversely, against Cuban homophobia) in the sympathetic figure of Diego, the film's cipher argued for the broader *difference* between two friends—the gay, traditional Diego and the straight, revolutionary David—and thus, by extension, for political plurality, including the political rights of the Cuban exile community that at the end of the film Diego is about to join. But while a thick description of the film's context reveals that the local popularity of the story on which the script was based did provide a defense of homosexuality, a close reading of the film and its script shows they both perform a ruse on the theme of national reconciliation, what I call a "ritual of repentance," and has Diego, the gay character, assume the burden of apology for the national standoff.

Professor Marvin d'Lugo, reacting to the first, essay version of this chapter, has criticized such a reading, stemming from his opinion that my "explicit politics" "detemporalizes" Cuban post-revolutionary history, and reduces it "to a condition that has seemingly not changed in four decades." While I make no apology for my so-called explicit politics, I find such a reaction, at once, puzzling and relevant. Puzzling indeed because my argument rests upon the premise that *Strawberry and Chocolate* introduces a debate on a new subject (national reconciliation), and nowhere do I argue that the Castro regime has not changed in 40 years. On the contrary, what I believe has changed, and I underscore throughout that chapter, is how a new so-called Cuban special period, now more than a decade old and with no signs of being declared closed, enacted a state policy emphasizing an *ideology* of reconciliation, which, like all ideologies, are fictional power constructions.

Yet I also find Professor d'Lugo's reaction most relevant. It demonstrates, once again, how an expert, outsider gaze can attempt to "foreclose the native informant's" to the point of confusing state-sanctioned interpretations with the film's actual language, not to mention obviating the Cuban exile point of view.[36]

That, precisely, is what this book is all about.

PART 1

CHAPTER ONE

Poetry and the Cold War: Pablo Neruda's Canto General

I

No single Latin American book of the twentieth century engaged more a historicist imagination than Pablo Neruda's *Canto general* (1950). I take up it up first in this series of readings not just because of its exemplary treatment of historical data. Describing it "thickly" will also allow me to illustrate the complexities of what I call ciphered reading, my own version of Geertz's idea, as the book maneuvers historical and biographical clues under its sweeping encyclopedic scope. In this I proceed inductively, taking up first general descriptions, particularly those Neruda offered up about the book successively and over a 30-year period. Indeed, Neruda began describing *Canto general* even before he wrote it, when it was still a draft that grew in time and took several years to complete. And because he often charged those descriptions with ideological content, as he engaged in polemics that forced him eventually to flee his native Chile, their sum-total provides an unwitting context, a screen against which the reader can judge the extent to which the resulting book carried the original project to fruition.

Although specific circumstances of the cold war will surface variously throughout my reading, I shall not pursue strictly that contextual marker of my title. Instead, I'll view that context merely as the general signpost for the kind of local knowledge I wish to explore. My reconstruction of Neruda's political and personal contexts do link up, in the chapter's last section, with a reading of what I call encyclopedic form, what I view as the material equivalent of Neruda's "cyclic ambition" or lifelong poetics.

Tedious though it may be to detail such contexts at the outset, they provide a database for my full reading later, where context weaves into text. I choose this time a more generalized reading that emphasizes the role of context in the text's decipherment, less focused, admittedly, than the one I attempted years ago in my book on Neruda's prophetic imagination.[1]

Neruda's tenth organic book, one of his longest, most crafted and the one he avowedly loved best, was also his best-known, owing in great measure to the scandal amidst which he finished writing it while being pursued by the Chilean police for publicly challenging his country's president. Its contents range from masterpieces (*The Heights of Macchu Picchu*) to sectarian doggerel (*Let the Woodcutter Awaken*). He once referred to it as "my most important book."[2]

The synoptic, monumental features of *Canto general* have often earned it comparison with masterworks from religion (*The Bible, Popol Vuh*), literature (*The Divine Comedy, Leaves of Grass*), and painting (Renaissance frescoes, Mexican Muralism), with all of which it shares expansive range. Indeed, *Canto general* is a poetic encyclopedia that gathers together multiple themes, genres and techniques, its sole formal unity deriving from the theme of America. As such, it caps a venerable tradition, dating back to the nineteenth century, that Gordon Brotherston once called "the Great Song": a poem of hemispheric dimensions that identifies morally and geographically with the entire American continent.[3]

Were one to concentrate solely on the book's first five sections, a linear sequence spanning from prehistoric origins to the rise of twentieth-century dictatorships, one could conclude that *Canto general* is simply a verse narrative of political history. Beginning with its Section VI, however, a series of poems foreign to that design interrupts the sequence, and the reader is led elsewhere. In fact, it could be said that not even its first five sections follow that sequence: while Section I (*The Lamp on Earth*) refers to prehistory, Section II (*The Heights of Macchu Picchu*) fast-forwards to a modernity that looks upon the ruins of an indigenous past. We are therefore dealing with more than just a historical narrative whose sheer length (289 poems) does not make it any less partial. Its contents include sections on a nostalgic song about Chile (VII); dramatic monologues of victims of political oppression (VIII); a diatribe against the cold war (IX); chronicles of political persecution (X), union strikes (XI), and partisan attacks (XII); the poet's letters to poet-friends (XIII), along with his autobiography (XV); and, in between the latter two, a love song to the sea (XIV). This repertoire responds to Neruda's description: "a jagged mountain range, like our geography."

Although *Canto general* covers five-and-one-half centuries of historical life—"1400" and "1949" are its two end-dates—Chronicle, not History, is what holds the book together. We understand a History to be a homogeneous narrative of a series of events with a reflexive, distanced and objective point of view, official character, and closed form; a Chronicle, on the other hand, encompasses all the sundry materials that are *previous to* a History. Chronicles display a circumstantial, immediate, and subjective viewpoint, a marginal character, and an open form. And so, Chronicles are, in effect, the seldom acknowledged source of History. Like the "Chronicles of Indies" it so frequently evokes, though written from the point of view of the vanquished, *Canto general* is a marginal History of Latin America.

Neruda's book had two almost identical first editions in 1950: an official one in Mexico and an underground one in Chile. Since then, it has been reprinted often with little change.[4]

II

Barely a few months after *Canto general* first appeared in Mexico, Neruda told Alfredo Cardona Peña in a long interview: "The first idea was to write a *Canto general de Chile* . . . his country's extraordinarily poetic geography, its burned-out deserts, snow-capped peaks, fiords: a mixture closely linked to the Chilean people."[5] *Canto general de Chile: Fragments* was published in 1943, its subtitle suggesting it was part of a longer sequence.[6] Two years before, in his first-ever comments on the entire book-project, he also told Maurice Halperin he was writing then "a long epic poem about his country. 'It will have descriptive and lyrical elements . . . and it will attempt to reveal the deep process of historical transformation, which Chile has undergone. I want to offset the great poetry of the classics, such as Ercilla and Pedro de Oña. But I feel humble in this task.' "[7] Neruda went on to describe how, first limited to Chile, the book project had evolved: "When he returned to his country, he made two discoveries. First, the struggles of the Chilean people, which became all-too-real during his travels to mines, the pampas, and the desert. Second, after his famous visit to Macchu [*sic*] Picchu in Peru, he witnessed the roots of American history, 'confused and as if underground' . . . 'I then changed plans,' " he told me, 'and turned it into a *Canto general* with the aim of writing a poem about 'Our America' " (36). Finally, he recited the following description:

> I should warn you that if many proper names, events, both important and insignificant, were made, it's because I've tried to portray our continental struggle by means of a revolutionary romanticism that accords with the book's aspiring realism. It may thus seem strange to read names of no historical importance, like González

Videla's and his accomplices; I've done so deliberately so as to blend them symbolically. I know the people will punish them, but my poem accuses their human cast: they're all the diplomats, pimps, perverted journalists and hounds of a corrupt dictatorship. I know this is hard stuff, and that many readers will be shocked and disturbed, but I want you to think how bitter it has been for me to make all the realities of our time concrete.

I believe my book, despite the sadness surrounding it . . . is happy, healthy and optimistic from the start. During the entire year of embattled work [it took me to write it], I felt a dizzying happiness, because life was giving me the chance to defeat the people's enemies at a time when I saw myself at the nadir of defeat. This I gathered from two great sources of happiness: one, was my book; the other was the intangible reality of the materials for the struggle. (36)

Two points surfaced then. First, the book aspired to broad historical span. Neruda called it the book's "realism" within "revolutionary romanticism"—or else, in our own terms, Chronicle, immediate and subjective, within History, distanced and objective. Second, a visit to Machu Picchu in October 1943 had influenced the book's length, breadth, and tone. "Throughout all these visions I've wished to materialize the portraits of America's struggles and victories as well as our fauna and geography—*Canto general* is perhaps my most poetic book, my attempt at a lyricism capable of facing our entire universe" (54).

Barely three years later, in a 1953 speech, Neruda returned to the same themes by highlighting the book's style. "I faced a number of problems, the greatest of which was perhaps the one related to opacity and clarity. Writing simply was my hardest job." Hence, his kindred spirit: "Andrés Bello, whose name graces this hall along with Sarmiento's, actually wrote *Canto general* before I ever did. Many were the writers who felt a duty bound to America's geography and citizens—To unite our Continent, discover, build it, recover it: that was my goal." He added further on the book's range and genre:

I struggled in my conscience and in my burgeoning book against the darkness of those days. Each day that goes by I intend to be simpler in my new songs. I also set out to embrace our American hugeness without the spark of our heroes, or avoiding the crimes that have bloodied us. I had doubts on whether to name the petty villains who stain our heritage from time to time alongside our founding fathers. I decided I could and did, even though I know my book lacks neither heroes nor scoundrels.

Thus I kept working at the chronicle or memoir, which at one point seemed to me pebble-like and inhospitable. Yet I soon learned that this poetic chronicle had been built by all. When it comes to our reality, there's no such thing as non-poetic material, and we must carry on that task. Our plants and flowers ought for the first time to be counted and sung. Our volcanoes and rivers have been relegated to dry texts.[8]

The book's kinship onto a specifically Latin American tradition, which included "scoundrels and villains" and "founding fathers," therefore made it resemble a Chronicle. The very concept of Chronicle ("pebble-like and inhospitable") whose distant origin was set against cultural tradition, thus bore the encyclopedic strain close to Andrés Bello's, Spanish America's foremost Neoclassical poet and encyclopedist par excellence.

Hardly a year later, in a fiftieth-birthday speech, the subject arose again by way of Neruda's discussion of a "new stage" in his poetry. He described then a shift in his poetics, when he "began to think not only about social poetry" and felt "indebted to my country and people.

My first idea of *Canto general* had been only a Chilean song, a poem for Chile. I then wished to cover my country's physical and human landscape, to define its people and production, its living nature. But soon I felt myself disturbed because Chilean roots spread underground and sprouted elsewhere . . . O'Higgins had roots in Miranda, Lautaro in Cuauhtémoc, Oaxaca pottery had the same black shine of Chilean textile. 1810 was a magical year, common to everyone, a year of insurrection, like a red poncho flying over all American lands.

Lastly, he described his experience at Machu Picchu thus:

Years before, I had visited India and China but I found Macchu Picchu (*sic*) more magnificent still. History books told us about Assyria, the Aryans, the Persians, and all their fabulous buildings. After seeing the ruins of Macchu Picchu, the fabulous cultures of antiquity all seemed to me to be made of papier maché. India itself seemed minuscule, gaudy, banal, a popular fair of gods, as opposed to the proud solemnity of those abandoned Inca towers. I could no longer set myself apart from these constructions. I understood then that if we trod the same hereditary ground, we had something to do with the tall efforts of the American community, we could no longer ignore them; our ignorance or silence was not only a crime, but the continuity of a defeat. Aristocratic cosmopolitanism had made us revere the past of the most distant peoples and had blinded us to our own treasures. Ever since I visited Cuzco, I thought often about ancient American man. His struggles were linked to our own. That's where my idea of an American *Canto general* was born. Before that, I had gotten the idea of a *Canto general of Chile*, in the manner of a chronicle. But that visit changed my idea entirely. Now I could see the whole of America from the heights of Macchu Picchu. That was the title of the first poem with my new conception. I began to see what was necessary. It had to be an extraordinarily local, partial poem. It had to have jagged coordinates, like our geography. The earth had to be constantly present. I wrote this poem about Macchu Picchu much later. Because it preceded a new stage in my style and new concerns, the poem came out drenched of my self. The first stanzas, for example, are a series of personal memories. I also wanted to touch there for the last time on the theme of death. Amidst the solitude of ruins, death cannot be that far off. I wrote Macchu Picchu at Isla Negra, facing the sea.

My contact with popular struggles was growing then. I understood the need for a new epic poetry, different from old forms. The idea of a rhymed long poem seemed to me unsuited for American themes. Verse had to acquire the features of a confused earth, and rise and fall in the plains.[9]

Such seeming rejection of "social poetry," the type Neruda had been writing since the Spanish Civil War, was therefore set against a "new stage," deliberately national and popular. This was the result of discovering in Machu Picchu historical roots that were common to the entire continent. Thus from the ruins' "heights," Neruda "saw" "the whole of America," a vision that defined his book: "an extraordinarily local, partial poem" of "jagged coordinates, like our geography," as if unmediated poetry erupted out of soil and history.

It was also in that 1954 speech where Neruda referred, in a defensive tone that betrayed he was responding to criticism, to the poetry's prosaic quality.

Life is made up of more than just high stuff and noble characters. A people's developing current is made up of infinite different grains, unknown feats, obstacles that at times seem petty and evil but are actually part of everything else . . . I was forced to change, as life and the continent itself did, and I had to begin taking stock of the smallest things. For this, I chose the chronicle, a deliberately prosaic style that contrasts with splendid visions. I wrote step by step, like someone walking through crooked shrubs, counting stones and street accidents. Rather than diminish my poetry, I wanted to hand it over to life. I don't mean this as a defense. A huge book like *Canto general* will be liked by some; others will like only parts of it, and perhaps many won't like it at all. I did my job leaving it as a vast landscape. (16; *OC*, IV, 937)

Eight years later, in his 1962 Memoirs, he described the experience again:

But before getting back to Chile, I made another discovery that was to add another layer to my poetry. I stopped in Peru and made a trip to the ruins of Macchu Pichu (*sic*). There was no highway then and we rode up on horseback. At the very top I saw the ancient stone structures hedged in by the tall peaks on the verdant Andes. Torrents hurtled down from the citadel eaten away and weathered by the passage of centuries. White fog drifted up in masses from the Wilkamayu River. I felt infinitely small in the center of that navel of rocks, the navel of a deserted world, proud, towering high, to which I somehow belonged. I felt that my own hands had labored there at some remote point in time, digging furrows, polishing rocks. I felt Chilean, Peruvian, American. On those difficult heights, among those glorious, scattered ruins, I had found the principles of faith I needed to continue my poetry. My poem *The Heights of Macchu Picchu* was born there.

And in yet another passage, he referred to the whole book: "What was happening to me and all the old American themes became dramatically intertwined, and in that year of danger and hiding, I finished writing *Canto general*, my most important book."[10]

The 1962 comments, which the posthumous *Memoirs* (1974) expanded upon, were, as one can see, suffused with organic imagery. Eight years before, the book had begun "to germinate" in Machu Picchu within "a new conception" (in its dual sense of idea and procreation); now they were the womb or "navel of an uninhabited world" from whose connection the poem "was born." Similar organic metaphors surfaced in descriptions of Neruda's life underground, during which "historic struggles," endured during "a year of danger and hiding," and were dramatically intertwined onto the "ancient American themes" the poems reflected, as if the poet embodied collective historical experience in his own person. Or else, again in generic terms, Chronicle was fast becoming a personal and immediate version of History. Clearly, as the book receded in time, Neruda's recollections began to focus less on the book's verbal art and more on its life-content.

Two years later, in a 1964 speech on his 60th birthday, Neruda broached the subject for the last time, at least publicly. It was then he described his life-long wish to be "a cyclical poet who moves from a moment's emotion or vision to a broader unity," and explained further that a "cyclical will" determined in him a drive to write "poetry that encompassed man along with Nature and hidden forces; an epic poetry that fathomed the universe's great mysteries and man's possibilities"; poems "of broad range and totality." And after acknowledging his troubles with the Chilean government ("my long illegal and difficult life, provoked by political events,") he again raised what for him had been the book's chief formal trait:

> In the loneliness and isolation I lived in and aided by the aim of giving great unity to the world I needed to express, I wrote *Canto general*, my most passionate and vast book. This book crowned my ambitious attempt. It's long as a good chunk of time and in it there's light and shadow. I attempted to embrace the great spaces in which lives and peoples move, work and die . . . Although I used many techniques, from classical ones to folk poetry, I'd like to state one of my purposes. I refer to its prosaic nature . . . Prose is closely linked to my concept of Chronicle. The poet ought to be, in part, the chronicler of his time. Chronicles ought not to be distilled, refined or cultivated. They ought to be rocky, dusty, rainy, and everyday, and bear the poor track of useless days and all of man's damnation and complaints.
>
> I've often been surprised at how these simple aims, which actually meant great changes in my work, and cost me a lot, have been misunderstood. Because my poetry had always tended to mysterious, inward visions, as in *Residence on Earth* or *Attempt of Infinite Man*, it was actually very hard for me to reach the prosaic abasement of certain passages in *Canto general*. . . .[11]

The principle underlying Neruda's poetry, of which *Canto general* was to be the crowning achievement, was therefore "cyclical will." It was to be a poetry of both moment and succession; "epic" by logical opposition to "lyric," whose most overt goal was to create "unity." "Prosaic style" was therefore linked to what Neruda then called Chronicle. Ten years before, he had thought the book's "jagged coordinates" mirrored geography; now he redefined it further through poetic genre, and in the process redefined himself as a "chronicler of his time," a kind of narrator of immediate circumstance. Adoption of a chronicle style had, accordingly, been misunderstood; hardly a reproachable decision, he argued, since all along it was a crafted effect.

Neruda's last comments on *Canto general* appeared in his posthumous *Memoirs*, where he either compiled or rewrote earlier statements. The two exceptions were passages where, amidst recollections of his 1938 return to Chile, he noted: "I had struck a vein, not in rocks underground, but in the pages of books. Can poetry serve our fellow man? Can it find a place in man's struggles? I had already done enough tramping around over things negative and irrational. I had to pause and find the road to humanism, outlawed from contemporary literature but deeply rooted in mankind . . . I started work on my *Canto general*" (139). That had been the time Neruda had bought a beach house in Isla Negra with money earned from book royalties. The remark not only allows us to date 1938 as the book's origin, but also note his commitment to a project "that brought together the historical events, the geographical situations, the life and struggles of our peoples" (140).[12]

III

I turn now to biographical context in an effort to retrace the steps Neruda took in writing *Canto general*. From all we know, the book appears to have been composed in three stages during a 13-year period. The first took place in Chile (1937–1940); the second, in Mexico (1941–1943); and a third, the longest, after Neruda's return to Chile (1943–1949), interspersed with brief trips to Europe and to Mexico, where the first edition was launched.

Chile, 1937–1940

Following the Civil War in Spain, where he lived between 1934 and 1938, Neruda returned to Santiago and soon jumped into its cultural and political fray. Nine of the previous 11 years he had spent living overseas; having left at 23, he returned at 34. In between, his poetry had changed from the hermetic surrealism of *Residence on Earth* (1933, 1935) to the social poetics of *Spain at Heart* (1938). The new poems (particularly, the famous "Meeting Under the New Flags") showed a gradual change, a "conversion" that could be traced to Neruda's experiences during the war and his increasing social conscience.

Barely a month after returning to Santiago, Neruda organized an "Intellectual Alliance for the Defense of Culture," along with *Aurora de Chile*, its official journal. This was to be the Chilean branch of the European anti-Fascist "Alliance" that had sponsored, the year before, the legendary conference of intellectuals in wartime Spain.[13] He began working as well in Pedro Aguirre Cerda's Popular Front campaign for president. Under the slogan of "Bread, Roof and Coat," the Front had organized a broad center-left coalition of Radical, Socialist, and Communist parties against an increasingly powerful Right. Its victory in the October 1938 elections earned Neruda another political appointment as Special Consul for Spanish Emigration, whose mandate was to bring to Chile 3,500 stranded Spanish refugees. In Paris, where he was posted, Neruda became a colleague of Gabriel González Videla's, then the Front's ambassador, later a candidate for the Chilean presidency. Despite threats of a Nazi sabotage, and after many a glitch, the Spanish refugees finally made it to Valparaíso on January 2, 1940 aboard the S.S. Winnipeg.

Both before and amidst Aguirre Cerda's campaign (between May and August 1938), Neruda endured the personal setback of both of his parents' deaths. It was during his first trip south from Santiago, the evening after his father's burial, he wrote what was to be the first poem of *Canto general* (cited as *CG*). First called "Almagro" and then "Discoverers of Chile" (*CG*, 59–60; *OC*, I, 466), it was the initial poem of *Canto general de Chile: Fragmentos* (1943), later part of *The Conquistadors*. According to most Neruda biographers, the poem must have released an inner emotional spring. Yet whatever internal change it reflected, it would not become apparent until "The Cup of Blood," another text written during the same period, surfaced later in 1943; it was there Neruda began to acknowledge, after his two trips south, his deep-seated conflicts with his native land.

> I belong to a piece of poor southern land, towards Araucania; my acts have arrived from the most distant clocks, as if that forested and endlessly rainy land guarded a secret of mine that I don't know; that I don't know and must learn, and that I search for, desperately, blindly, while looking through long rivers, inconceivable vegetation, wood stacks, south seas, burying me in botany and rain, without

ever reaching that privileged froth that waves both deposit and break, without ever getting to that measure of special earth, without ever touching my true sand.[14]

Two events converge in this haunting text. The first shows a childhood memory: the narrator enters donning a "poet's tie" when his uncles are about to "cut open a lamb's pulsating throat and bring a burning cup of blood to my lips." The incident impacts on the child-poet as a revelation, an epiphany of earth: "for, I, too, wish to be a centaur, and pale, uncertain. Lost amidst the deserted childhood, I raise and drink up the cup of blood." The second event, also an epiphany, occurs during his father's funeral.

At noon, we went with my brother and some rail workers, friends of the deceased, we pried open the sealed niches and took out the mildewed urn, and on it there was a frond with wilted black flowers. Humidity had split open the coffin and while lowering it, not believing our eyes, we saw great amounts of water flowing out, unending liters that fell within its own substance . . . that terrible water, water coming out of an impossible bottomless, extraordinary hideout, so as to show me its tormented secret, that original and terrifying water warned me, once again, with its mysterious flow, about my own endless connection with a specific life, place and death. (*OC*, IV, 417)

The two events, told in dream-like fashion, share a common thread: the symbolic rituals that tie regressions onto earth. In the first, the "cup of blood" stands for communion among centaurs, half-beasts bound to Nature; in the second, rain shows the communion of bodies with geography. Both texts dramatize the poet's closeness with the elements.

What Neruda later called the "new stage" of his poetry was therefore not entirely political; it was actually a meditation on the local or regional setting, soon to acquire symbolic significance. We can also date the origin of that meditation in 1938, the same year on the printer's mark of *Canto general de Chile: Fragmentos* (1943), and the same year Neruda began working on Aguirre Cerda's campaign. Clearly situated beyond politics, the "new stage" made Neruda think in terms of a wholesale popular mythology.[15]

Mexico, 1940–1943

Aguirre Cerda soon reappointed Neruda as Consul General to Mexico City, where writer Luis Enrique Délano joined him as second-in-command. His three years in Mexico left deep impressions, as they coincided with the end of Lázaro Cárdenas' administration, itself marked by populist nationalism and an anti-Fascist politics. Mexico was at the time a cauldron of refugee intellectuals and artists of various tendencies where one could find as many Republican exiles from the Spanish War as fleeing Stalinist heretics, like Leon Trotsky. Moreover, the Cárdenas government itself constituted a climax to Mexico's nationalist revolution, as demonstrated by the increasing "institutionalization" that had taken place during the latter two decades.

It was in Mexico where Neruda was to broaden his "new stage," and it was there he renewed contacts with friends from Spain (José Herrera Petere, Lorenzo Varela, Juan Rejano), Mexico (Octavio Paz, Carlos Pellicer), and Europe (Ludwig Renn, Anna Seghers). It was also in Mexico where he made new friends, and notably, "the three greats" of muralist painting: Diego Rivera, David Alfaro Siqueiros, and José Clemente Orozco. "Mexican painters," he wrote in his *Memoirs*, "covered the city with history and geography, with civil strife, with fierce controversies." For Neruda, Orozco's work was "a revelation of our cruelty"; Rivera's "a kind of historian's calligraphy" that tied "together Mexico's history and brought out in high relief its events, traditions, and tragedies"; and Siqueiros'—of the three, the closest ideologically to Neruda—"a volcanic temperament that combines astonishing technique and painstaking research" (153–155). And yet Mexico itself remained, as Neruda himself put it, both "flowery" and "thorny." In a 1941 speech, at a ceremony welcoming back from Chile two Mexican exchange students, he allowed himself one candid critique: "A new mythology of speaking leads us to facile flattery. We think we flatter each other by highlighting the similarities between our two countries. I, for one, can assure you that no two countries are more different than Mexico and Chile." Within the contours of the "new stage," surface differences thus hid deeper affinities. He added:

> But if we descend from the same cup and flower, if we shed all surface appearance, if we defeat all good sentiment, if we go from leaf to trunk and from trunk to origin, there we all meet. Mexicans and Chileans meet in the roots, searching for bread and truth in the same needs, the same anxiety . . . in this bloody hour, war and the invaders advance towards Our America. They want to lock us up between blood and gold. I don't know, and neither do you, what the future holds amidst this terrible storm. Old and new pirates are apportioning the world's booty. Europe's old hands, which molded, painted and wrote everything we learned, now rise up

under a bloody moon so that Our America can learn from it the complete art of annihilating life.[16]

World War II, then at its bloodiest, no less than the American circumstance Neruda had newly discovered, was providing the background to his book project.

Perceived flippancy created greater tensions still. By then, Neruda was telling a reporter from *El Nacional*, Mexico's most popular newspaper: "You have some great poets in Mexico; I'd certainly like Chilean poets to partake of that peculiarity that stems from form . . . I can't tell Chilean poets anything of the sort, mostly because I have tried to undo the very form that is Mexico's."[17] The remark forebode another storm, this time over *Laurel*, the famous 1941 anthology of "modern poetry in Spanish," edited by poets José Bergamín, Xavier Villaurrutia, Emilio Prados, and Octavio Paz, in which Neruda refused to participate. He had broken earlier with Bergamín, also *Laurel*'s publisher, apparently over petty literary squabbles.[18] The sole allusions that surface in *Canto general* attribute the whole matter to the exclusion of Spanish poet Miguel Hernández from the tome. But Neruda's own self-exclusion had far more serious repercussions, for it also caused eventually a rift with Octavio Paz, a close friend since the two had met in Spain, with whom he broke publicly and violently in 1941.[19]

By then, the global anti-Fascist struggle had made of Neruda a *cause célèbre* all his own, as shown in a series of public events: a reading of "Canto for Bolívar" at the University of Mexico's Amphitheater; a recital on the occasion of his honorary doctorate from Michoacán University, in October 1941; or else, when he was physically attacked, a year later, by Nazi protesters in Cuernavaca.[20] Such incidents explain in part why Neruda chose to leave Mexico for extended periods on two occasions to visit both Guatemala and Cuba, two of three overseas trips (the third one was to New York City) he made during his stint as Mexican consul.[21] Tensions had already come to a head on September 30, 1942 when Neruda read publicly, at a rally organized by the "Society of Friends of the USSR," his famous "Song to Stalingrad," where he praised openly Soviet resistance to the Nazi invasion. A few days later the poem was "published" in poster form and plastered all over Mexico City in what was to be the first of Neruda's open homages to muralist painting. Indeed, to public outcry against the poem and its subject, he responded by producing a "New Song of Love to Stalingrad," in which he both justified himself and answered his critics.[22]

By then it was clear Neruda was the embodiment of "political poetry." But he was also trying to set his political or social poetry apart from what he called his "new stage." In fact, none of the more or less polemical poems Neruda wrote during this period (not even the clearly pertinent "Canto for Bolívar") was to be included in *Canto general* and instead all made their way to the last section of his *Third Residence* (1947). It was as if by displacing them onto a different book Neruda had wanted further to separate immediate politics from the new "chronicle" of Americanist tone, even as the distinction between the two was becoming harder to sustain.

Such at least was suggested in the debate that Juan Ramón Jiménez and José Revueltas held over the very topic of Neruda's "new stage." "He wasn't always as nativist [*lo indígena*] as he now wants to be," wrote Jiménez in the August 1943 issue of *Repertorio Americano*. Jiménez's own strained relationship with Neruda harked back to pre–Civil War years in Madrid, when the literary battles of the time over "impure poetry" had pitted one against the other, and to Jiménez's earlier caricature of Neruda. This time, however, Jiménez opted to pass judgment as a rejoinder to Revueltas, then a young Mexican novelist and Communist Party member, who had responded to Jiménez' earlier "Open Letter to Pablo Neruda." According to Revueltas, Jiménez condescended to Neruda and his "Americanist" sensibility, a reaction which for Revueltas showed "the problem of Europe itself . . . as it faces new realities." For Jiménez, on the other hand, Neruda's "new stage" betrayed "too much of an Indigenism learned in an international travel experience."[23]

In March 1943, Neruda got news of the death of his only daughter (Malva Marina) in Holland, after what appears to be a long period of miscommunication with his first wife.[24] This personal tragedy was offset days later by publication of *Canto general de Chile*, the first preview of the big book that included four poems, with "Almagro," the poem written the night of his father's burial, as the opening piece. By summer, however, the polemics had not ceased, and by the end of August Neruda would leave Mexico altogether.

On June 18, and as a show of solidarity with Luis Carlos Prestes, a jailed Brazilian Communist leader, Neruda read the poem "Hard Elegy" (*OC*, I, 409–410) at Prestes's mother's wake. The reading made the Brazilian ambassador in Mexico react in protest. The reading had itself been a public protest to Prestes not being allowed to travel to Mexico to attend the wake. But rather than respond to the ambassador through diplomatic channels, Neruda chose public rebuke. He wrote: "Chilean writers carry on a tradition: in accepting a public or government post, no matter how high or low, we don't mortgage our freedom or our dignity."[25] His statement so shocked the Chilean Foreign Office that, according to Wilberto Cantón, "in August it was announced Neruda had asked for a six-month leave from his Mexican post, although he quit the diplomatic service altogether after his return . . ."[26] Days later, amidst plans for a massive farewell banquet, the polemic literally exploded in an interview with Spanish journalist Alardo Pratts: "For me, the best things in Mexico are its agronomers and painters . . . In poetry there's a total misguidance and an impressive lack of civic morality . . . The novel, in four of its younger representatives-Juan de la Cabada, Laureano Gómez, José Revueltas and Andrés Henestrosa—reaches the level of a new classicism . . . The essay, on the other hand, has been spoiled by an anemic generation."[27] As part of the banquet speech, Neruda read for the first and last time "On Mexico's Walls" (*CG*, 384–387; *OC*, I, 819–821), the poem where he refers to his entire Mexican tryst as "a small mistaken eagle/ circulating in my veins. . . ." Years later, in his *Memoirs*, he'd remark further: "when I decided to return to my country I understood Mexican life even less than when I got there . . ." (151).

September–November 1943

It took Neruda two months and four days to make his way back to Chile in a journey marked by stops in Panamá, Colombia, and Perú. Everywhere he went he gave recitals and lectures, met writers and politicians, and, especially, got to know people firsthand. As a young man, Neruda had spent time in Europe and the Far East, and in his early adult years had lived in Buenos Aires and Madrid. By the time he returned to Chile in November 1943, he had toured a total of eight Latin American countries, including Argentina, Mexico, Guatemala, and Cuba. Still, according to Teitelboim, Mexico was the one place that "truly gave him the disturbing sense of an almost unknown America."[28]

In Panamá (September 3), Neruda urged his writer-peers to join the anti-Fascist struggle without detriment to national identity; all the while the new continent "gathers, like an open cup, the fresh fragrance that comes to us from the wide world." In this view, contemporary Chronicle was fast becoming the History of the entire American continent, not just of regional, national identity: "We are not frightened by the old singsong of exotic ideas. We ourselves are exotic, descendants of races alien to these naked lands. Exotic was our servitude and exotic is our liberation."[29]

From Panamá, Neruda flew to Colombia, where he visited Cali, Medellín, and Bogotá. Besides giving recitals and lectures, he engaged then a spirited polemic with Laureano Gómez, future president and arguably the country's most powerful politician.[30] But it was Perú, as he visited Lima, Cuzco, Machu Picchu, and Arequipa in October, which affected him deepest. At a dinner organized by the local Alliance of Artists and Intellectuals, he described Perú as the "watchtower of America, enclosed within high, mysterious stones." He had not yet visited Machu Picchu, but the idea he had of Perú envisioned it: "There's something cosmic in your Peruvian lands, something so powerful and sparkling that no fashion or style has ever been able to cover it, as if under your territory, like a buried statue, mineral and phosphorous, monolithic and organic, still covered by cloths and altars, time and sand and its strong structures would peek out of abandoned stones upon the deserted grounds we have yet to discover." Once again, an emerging historical view forecast the continental vision Neruda was proposing: "The sons of American freedom, like Sucre, Bolívar, O'Higgins, Morales, Artigas, San Martín, Mariátegui, are hated equally by caveman reactionaries and sterile demagogues. Freedom in Latin America will be the daughter of our deeds and thoughts."[31]

From Lima, Neruda traveled to Cuzco, and from there, on October 31, he began his trek up to Machu Picchu on horseback. He was joined by a posse that included host José Uriel García, a Socialist senator from Cuzco whom Neruda had met years before. A follower of José Carlos Mariátegui's (1895–1930), the legendary Peruvian Socialist, Uriel García had published that same year a second edition of a book about "the new Indian" in which he followed closely his mentor's ideas; namely, that the "real" Perú lay in the highlands, the Spanish Conquest had arrested the country's development; and only by recovering the Incas' primitive Socialism could the country be saved.[32] Neruda himself was slowly absorbing all those ideas. Upon his return from Cuzco, he stopped off in Arequipa, and from there flew on to Santiago on November 3.

A full month later, in a long interview with Volodia Teitelboim, he talked for the first time about his travels. Waxing hyperbolic, he told of how Machu Picchu "made up the most important archeological group in the whole world . . . It's wonderful to sit on its stone banks, surrounded by an amphitheater of huge dimensions among America's highest mountains. There precisely, among the condors, which nest in the lonely ruins, some archeologists have dated them 12,000 years old."[33]

Chile, 1943–1949

Returning to Chile for the second time in five years, Neruda faced a different country. He himself would soon be different. It had been two years since the Popular Front had disappeared. Aguirre Cerda had died in office and the Radical Party's Juan Antonio Ríos had succeeded him as president. If Neruda's literary fame was on the rise (barely had he arrived in Santiago when he received two national awards for his life's work), he also began to participate in Chilean politics, as the local Communist Party was filling in the Popular Front vacuum. Like many at the time, the Chilean party was not only pro-Soviet; it was also orthodox Stalinist, and Neruda soon closed ranks. Though not yet an official Communist (he would get his card on July 8), he did run under its banner for the northern senate seats of Antofagasta and Tarapacá. He also spent practically the entire year campaigning in the mining north along with Elías Lafferte, the Communist labor leader with whom Neruda eventually shared the northern provinces. For a native of the humid Chilean south like him, campaigning in the desert north literally meant scouring the antipodes: "Coming into those lowlands, facing those stretches of sand, is like visiting the moon . . . I come from the other end of the republic. I was born in green country with huge, thickly wooded forests" (167).

The beginnings of Neruda's political career can therefore be viewed as a vindication of sorts. Just as he was being awarded the "National Literature Prize" in May 1945, Adolf Hitler committed suicide and the Allies declared victory in Europe. Two months later, days after officially joining the Party, he traveled to Brazil to read a poem ("Said in Pacaembú," *CG*, 144–146; *OC*, I, 560–562) in a massive homage to the recently pardoned Luis Carlos Prestes, the same Brazilian leader whose defense had cost Neruda his job in Mexico. The journey east, which also included a tour of Uruguay and Argentina, must have also vindicated him, as he was newly inserted into Chilean life: enjoying unprecedented prestige, buoyed by a political party, and having reached life's midpoint— *nel mezzo del camin di nostra vita.*

It was amidst such success that Neruda began writing *The Heights of Macchu Picchu*. Indeed, in his speech accepting the National Literature Prize he invoked its ominous symbol ("I have not lowered my head to dream empty dreams amidst fire and ruins,") and had ended his first Senate speech (May 30) invoking them again: "Today, he [Hitler] lies, along with his nation's ruins and the millions of casualties he took with him to the grave, like a twisted, anonymous carcass."[34] Two months in the making, the poem was published in Caracas' *Revista Nacional de Literatura* in July 1946.

That same year, Chilean President Ríos died in office. Special elections were called and González Videla became the Radical Party's candidate as part of a so-called Democratic Alliance that included Liberals and

Communists. The Alliance called for a pact between Right and Left. According to a local political scientist, it was a "marriage between Manchester and Moscow." González Videla's platform was offering to revive the old Popular Front, and as publicity manager of the new campaign Neruda reprised his old job under Aguirre Cerda. The relationship between Neruda and González Videla dated back to 1939, when they had worked together on behalf of Spanish refugees. In his role as publicity manager, the poet came up with a catchy slogan: "*El pueblo lo llama Gabriel*" (The people call him Gabriel), itself part of a set of doggerel he would read at a campaign rally. According to Teitelboim, Neruda tore up the poem after reading it; but González Videla saved two stanzas for posterity:

> From sand to heights
> From salt to thickness,
> The people call him Gabriel
> both simple and sweet.
>
> Like a brother, loyal brother
> and among all the pure things,
> there's nothing like this laurel:
> The people call him Gabriel.[35]

Victory at the polls for González Videla was therefore Neruda's too, as the new president formed a cabinet that included no less than three Communists. One of the last events in his gradual metamorphosis would come at the end of that year (December 28) when he legally changed his name to *Pablo Neruda*. Days barely passed before he became disillusioned with the new president, who proceeded to deny him a coveted appointment as Chilean ambassador to Italy.[36]

Indeed, by then the political cauldron had boiled over. The temporary alliance between Radicals and Communists, which had received only 40.1 percent majority, broke apart. It was the start of the cold war, and Chile was one of the first Latin American countries to be affected. The United States was by then the biggest buyer of Chilean copper, to the point that it stockpiled to gouge prices. By favoring industrial interests and urban elites, González Videla broke all political alliances and rebuffed the provinces, where he happened to have received the most votes. From then on, the Chilean president made earning U.S. trust a priority, as the latter was eager to win allies in the undeclared cold war. Domestic discontent with González Videla's politics spread rapidly and was hardly limited to the Left. In addition, the Communist Party's rapid expansion and influence in Chile (from 10.2 percent of the vote in the 1945 municipal elections to 16.5 percent in 1947; double the votes received by Socialists in 1947) began to worry the other political parties. Its greatest support (71 percent of the coal vote, 63 percent of the nitrate, as opposed to 55 percent of the copper sectors) came from the mining regions, whose Senator Neruda was. "The Communists," according to Drake, "were tolerated as government participants where they served as safety valves for working class discontent, but they were unacceptable when they used their government positions to rally the masses and pressure the administration from below."[37] In the context of cold war politics, Chile became a literal time bomb.

During all this time, Senator Neruda pursued partisan work. Domestically, he favored the north's mining interests; on foreign policy, he was a Pan-Americanist. In the year and a half between January 1946 and June 1947, Senator Neruda wrote or spoke on the senate floor about unstable political situations in several countries, among them the Dominican Republic, Uruguay, Paraguay, Nicaragua, and Ecuador.[38] But by September 1947, Neruda was also asking the Party for a year's leave to finish writing *Canto general*, a request that betrayed two unspoken facts: the urgency of the book project, and his relative uselessness in the Senate. Nobody could forecast the gathering storm.

Lightning first struck in October 1947. On the twenty-first, González Videla demanded the resignation of three of his cabinet members, all Communists, ordered the arrest of the entire party leadership, and declared practically the whole mining north in a state of siege. In reaction, the Party organized massive protests, including labor strikes, which the government repressed by calling out the army. Soon after, González Videla ordered a break in diplomatic relations with the USSR, Czechoslovakia, and Yugoslavia. In response, Neruda fired off in Caracas's *El Nacional* (thus sidestepping Chilean censorship) a long "Intimate Letter for Millions" in which he accused González Videla of "political betrayal."[39] The next day, the president, his anti-Communist campaign in full swing, had his government begin legal proceedings to cease Neruda's Senate immunity. In his own memoirs, González Videla argued the charge had become necessary because Neruda had "insulted my government and Chile's prestige abroad. . . ."[40] Actually, the "Intimate Letter" had only accused González Videla of backstabbing; the president himself had cast the first stone by declaring open season on the Communists. Because of his personal collaboration during the campaign, Neruda must have felt especially responsible. Hence he became the president's most outspoken opponent.

Making full legal use of his Senate prerogative, Neruda fired off again at the start of the new year. On the Senate floor, he read another long speech, now known as his "*J'accuse*," toward the end of which, and bringing forth no less than 13 charges, he specified that if "I had wanted to insult the President, I would do so through my work. But should I be forced to take up his case in my *Canto general of Chile*, which I'm now writing, I'll do so, too, with the same honesty I have shown in my politics."[41] By then, both Neruda and the Party must have foreseen the February 3 Supreme Court ruling that ceased his senate immunity. A few days before (January 27), he and his wife had asked for asylum in Santiago's Mexican embassy. Unable to grant asylum on his own, Mexican ambassador Pedro de Alba then drove the couple himself to the Argentine border, where the Chilean police stopped the party and forced them to return to the capital. Two days later, in an interview with Chilean Foreign Minister Vergara Donoso, De Alba was able to secure guarantees regarding Neruda's personal safety. In a published interview with Teitelboim, Neruda himself confirmed he had requested asylum, arguing that the Chilean government had "pressured against it through Enrique Gajardo," the Chilean ambassador in Mexico.[42] Jaime Torres Bodet, then Mexico's Foreign Minister, and himself a well-known poet, recalled in his memoirs that Gajardo had gone as high up as Mexican President Miguel Alemán to make his case, during which Torres Bodet was assured "nothing would happen to the famous poet and he'd be granted all legal guarantees when he left our Embassy."[43]

Neruda was hardly the only Communist on the run. The Chilean government had arrested a number of party leaders, closed down *El Siglo* (its official newspaper), and opened a detention camp in Antarctic Pisagua. Persecution of communists became widespread with passing of the so-called Permanent Law in Defense of Democracy ("the Wicked Law," according to its victims), which declared the Party illegal, and even went so far as to strike members' names from voting lists. In the face of defeat, the Party opted to go underground in order to maintain cadres intact, win support among other political parties, and regain eventual legality. The same day Chile's Supreme Court ruled to cease Neruda's immunity, *Ercilla*, Santiago's leading magazine, published an interview where he told that Senate President Alessandri had authorized him a leave "for more than a month and less than a year."[44] (Having his immunity ceased, Neruda was therefore effectively suspended as Senator, though the ruling could always be appealed.) In the same interview Neruda also said he was fleeing Chile "not out of fear, but rather following carefully thought-out orders," a statement that hardly excluded personal caution. Still, the court ordered Neruda's arrest. He had become "*The Fugitive*."[45]

For the following 13 months (until February 24, 1949) Neruda remained underground for strictly practical reasons: there was simply no way to slip out of the country without risking capture. In fact, the same day the arrest warrant went out, 300 police officers were sent after him.[46] In his *Memoirs*, González Videla discounted all such reports. But he never referred to the way his government had chosen further to embarrass Neruda in other ways, as when it brought bigamy charges against him, to the point of flying Maria Antonieta Haagenar, Neruda's first wife, from Holland to testify against him.[47] The government's campaign eventually reached the tabloids. On August 14, *Zig-Zag* magazine ran an editorial titled "The People Used to call him Chilean"—the echo was obvious— reminding everyone of the changed winds.[48]

In 1954, years after the whole scandal was over, details of Neruda's life underground finally surfaced:

Freedom in our continent is a luxury, a tiny piece of the flag that people barely and infrequently grasp and soon blow off into the wind.

In order to escape I couldn't leave my room and had to change venues often. Prison has something definitive about it, a certain routine and finality. Underground life is more disquieting and one never knows when it will end. From the first moment I understood that the time had come to write my book. I started studying themes, ordering chapters, and I didn't stop writing, except perhaps to move.[49]

The *Memoirs*, published years later, gave further details still: "I moved from house to house every day. Doors opened to receive me everywhere. It was always people I didn't know, who had somehow expressed their wish to put me up for a few days. They wanted to offer me asylum even if only for a few hours, or for weeks. I passed through fields, ports, cities, camps and was in the homes of peasants, engineers, seamen, doctors, miners" (173).

Life as "The Fugitive," it turned out, provided the leave of absence Neruda had sought all along. In 1963 he told Teitelboim: "My contact with popular struggles was getting closer . . . I cherished the idea of writing a long poem that reflected it. But my work had kept me from doing it. Then came the crackdown and underground life, and in a matter of a year and two months, the book was done." He also talked then about his work method: "For the first time in my life I wrote poems for eight or more hours a day. I had few comforts: I had to write on wooden boards, tree trunks, rocks. I also lacked the books I needed to gather facts about Latin American history, Chile's birds and plants . . . but sometimes my hosts went out and got them for me."[50] But years before, in 1954, he had already told what those sources had been:

> Halfway through, I started needing books. As I became acquainted with history, I wanted to have reference sources, and it was marvelous how they always turned up. At a comfortable farmhouse I once stayed in, I happened to find a Spanish American Encyclopedia. I hate to see those large tomes stored in lawyers' shelves. This time I had found a treasure! All kinds of things I didn't know: names of cities, historical events, plants, volcanoes, rivers. At a beach house where I also stayed a couple of months I asked if they had any books. They had only one: Barros Arana's *Summary of Spanish American History*. Just what I needed![51]

He also told then he had read through *The Birds of Chile*, by J.D. Goodall, A.W. Johnson and R.A. Philippi. It would appear, however, that neither these books nor their availability were as random as Neruda made them out to be. For according to Teitelboim, who was keeping close tabs: "a historian friend who was in charge of his night moves got him the reference works."[52]

I shall take up soon the extent to which Neruda drew upon those sources. Suffice it to note that it was indeed a time of feverish production. Close examination of the bibliography allows me to calculate that by October 1947, when his Senate leave came to a halt, 15 percent of the poems that in time would make it into *Canto general* had been published. Further inspection allows me to classify those poems as destined for the book's first seven sections. A few (*The Heights of Macchu Picchu* and *America, I do not invoke your name in vain*) make up entire sections; others, like *Canto general of Chile*, almost half. It is even conceivable that by the time the red scare began, Neruda had written a good portion of those first seven sections.[53] All this means that *Canto general* was a much different book before November 1947. The events surrounding the red scare changed both the book and its author.

It was only in February 1948 that Neruda began writing the book's latter half. Accordingly, the dividing line between the two halves would be Section VIII (*The Earth's Name is Juan*), which contains the monologues of victims of political oppression, the moral parallels to Neruda's underground victimage. Section IX (*Let the Woodcutter Awaken*) was finished, according to the underground printer's mark, as early as May 1948, barely three months into underground life. My view of the book's gradual, if haphazard, composition is further supported if we consider that it is divided into two halves, each containing seven sections and sharing a core section (number VIII). The first seven sections make up a unit of their own, with a sustained linear design that spans from primitive origins to the age of modern dictators, and is followed by a lyrical summary that peaks in *Canto general of Chile* (section VII). The second half, sections VIII through XV, lacks such a linear design and is more varied. The stark difference between the book's two halves could be broadly explained by Neruda's radically different circumstances while writing them: calm, systematic and therefore linear in the first; unstable ("disquieting," said the poet) in the second.

While underground, Neruda kept publishing section after section; uncensored previews circulated widely. *Let the Woodcutter Awaken*, for example, his tirade against the cold war, spawned a number of underground editions beginning in July 1948. Both *New Year's Chorale for the Country in Darkness* and "González Videla, Chile's Traitor" followed suit.[54] When at one point plans for Neruda's escape route through Valparaíso and onto Ecuador fell through, the Party decided it was high time to spirit him out. Owing to the cold climate, the escape plan called for a southern route sometime during the South American summer, December to March. Jorge Bellet Bastías, a Party militant, was put in charge of the operation. Neruda donned the alias of "Antonio Ruiz Lagorreta, ornithologist," and took with him the book manuscript under the guise of a tome with a false cover bearing a turgid title: *Laughs and Tears* "by Benigno Espinoza." Joined by Raúl Bulnes Cerda, a mutual friend, Bellet and Neruda drove south at the start of February 1949.[55] According to Margarita Aguirre, just before leaving Chile he stayed a few days at Julio Vega Godomar's house in Santa Ana de Chena. This is an important fact, as it was precisely in that village where Neruda chose to date the last poem of *Canto general: "Today, 5 February, in this year/of 1949, in Chile, in Godomar/de Chena, a few months before/I turned forty-five"* (*CG*, 400; *OC*, I, 836). *Godomar de Chena* was therefore a composite signature that made up, rather than registered, a place, a fiction reinforced further when we know Neruda kept adding poems to the book even after signing off on it.

By mid-1949 Neruda had left Argentina for Paris. While there, as well as later in Mexico, he took part in several of the "peace conferences" the two sides were hotly organizing at the start of the cold war. As the two editions were readied for publication, he then traveled to the Soviet Union, Poland, and Hungary. The official Mexican edition, for which a sponsoring committee collected 343 subscribers, donned two flyleaves by Rivera and Siqueiros, which Neruda himself asked the artists to design based on poems from *Canto general*. (The underground edition, which the Party published in Chile, carried illustrations by printmaker José Venturelli.) As if to emphasize the Book prototype, it was decided to produce two separate bulky editions ("six kilos of poetry," according to Luis Enrique Délano): the official one measured 36 centimeters and was 567 pages long; the underground one, 27 centimeters and 468 pages.[56]

According to Teitelboim, Neruda "kept adding poems to the very end." Indeed, it was only in Mexico, where he returned in August 1949, that he wrote "González Videla, Chile's Traitor (epilogue)" (*CG*, 200–230; *OC*, I, 624–626) and "To Miguel Hernández" (*CG*, 316–319; *OC*, I, 745–747), who had recently died in a Franco prison in Spain. The underground edition even included an appendix that included the poems Neruda kept churning out poems as the book was being printed. The official launching took place April 13, 1950, at a signing ceremony held at the home of Carlos Obregón Santacilia, an architect friend of Neruda's. Two months later, Neruda left again for Europe to begin a three-year exile period, until González Videla stepped down as president.

IV

As we have seen, *Canto general de Chile* (1943), a preview devoted to Chilean history and landscape, was the textual origin of *Canto general*. In his 1941 comments to Halperin, Neruda described his early project as a "long epic poem" made up of "descriptive and lyric elements" whose aim was "to reveal Chile's deep historical transformation." He also said then he wanted "to offset" the effect of Chilean epics, such as Ercilla's and Pedro de Oña's. Later in 1954, he added the "need for a new epic poetry that would go beyond an older formal concept," since "the idea of a rhymed long poem in royal sextets" seemed "unsuitable for American themes." Indeed, the slightest reading of *Canto general* can identify many epic traits, though the actual finished book showed little of the precursor epics Neruda had wanted to offset. Among these traits, two in particular stand out. First, its historical theme, past and contemporary, which more than three-fourths of the poems in *Canto general* share; second, its long narrative form, the contents of which trace broadly the continent's history and moral destiny. No muse is invoked in any of the first poems, as prescribed by one of the epic's chief conventions; and yet, all of Section II (*The Heights of Macchu Picchu*) does call forth the continent's ancient peoples: "*I've come to speak through your dead mouths*" (*CG*, 41; *OC*, I, 447). Heroes and heroines certainly abound, and yet the book lacks a single individual one, as prescribed further by epic tradition. Every one of its 15 sections provides detailed catalogs—rivers, plants, birds, surnames, heroes, ports—as if underscoring yet another epic convention. Thus faced with all this evidence, Durán and Safir summarized what by now has become a critical commonplace: "It is the scope and attitude of the poem that classify it as epic, rather than any adherence to classical rules of epic form."[57]

Despite all its epic elements, then, *Canto general* overflows the genre; it is an epic and something more. Neruda himself referred in 1964 to the "many techniques, from classical ones to folk poetry" he used, and claimed for it other concepts, like "cyclic poetry" and "chronicle." No sooner do we begin reading the virtual Genesis of Section I, *The Lamp on Earth*, than we realize that, rather than the epic, its privileged model is the Bible as reinforced by various means, including subtle allusions, the rhetoric of prophecy, and even hints at an apocalypse.[58] If to all this we add the book's sheer range as a catalog of natural, and not just political, history, in addition to dramatic monologues by simple folk, letters to the author's friends, and even the poet's autobiography, we soon realize that all this sundry textuality clearly exceeds the epic model.

Canto general is therefore, and quite literally, *a* Book; or rather, *The* Book. Its first editions emphasized its huge physical dimensions. Neruda himself described it as "a vast landscape," and its last poems even highlighted the Book as prototype: "*And so this book ends, / here I leave my Canto general written / on the run . . .*" (*CG*, 400; *OC*, 836). Neruda's Book follows broadly the principles of "encyclopedic form," what Northrop Frye defined once as a massive literary model that collects episodes around central themes. Encyclopedic forms have as prototype the Sacred or Mythic Book, be that the Western Bible, the Hindu *Mahabharata*, or the Mayan *Popol Vuh*. Every literary era creates its own version of The Book, beginning with the ideal prototype of sacred scripture, and up to "increasingly human analogies of mythical and scriptural revelation."[59]

Like Whitman's *Leaves of Grass*, Hugo's *Légende des siècles*, or Pound's *Cantos*, then, *Canto general* is a modern, secular analogy of encyclopedic form, held together by a comprehensive vision of history and nature. Neruda's own name for it was "cyclical poetry," a term he used to describe all his major books, but especially this one. He never said why he chose to call his poems cyclical, but the concept itself harks back to Giambattista Vico, who in his *New Science* (1755), and years before the German Romantics had taken up the entire "Homeric question," had referred jointly to the *Odyssey* and the *Iliad* as "the encyclopedia of gentile antiquity," "limitless archives of the dialects, customs, laws and history of

Greece." Vico's "cyclical poet" was not, to be sure, the individual author that Modernity was well on its way to inventing. Instead, s/he was an anonymous popular source, found typically in ancient Greek festivals, fairs, and marketplaces. "Authors of this sort," wrote Vico, "are ordinarily called *Kykloi* and *enkykloi*, and their collective work was called *kyklos epicos, kyklia epe, poiema enkyklikon* (epic cycle, encyclopedic poems)."[60]

In *Canto general*'s case, "cyclical poetry" harked back not only to generalized prototypes, like the Bible, but to a specifically Latin American poetic tradition, what Gordon Brotherston has called "the great song of America": long poems whose breadth and expanse constitute the continent's symbolic analog. They include Bello's unfinished *Silvas Americanas* (1823), Darío's fragmented *Cantos de vida y esperanza* (1902), and José Santos Chocano's *Alma América* (1906); all failed attempts at the "Great Song" that coalesced eventually in Neruda's. What links Neruda to all, but particularly to Bello, Latin America's foremost neoclassical poet, is not so much encyclopedic form as its implicit goal: the reader's enlightenment. Education, pedagogy, didacticism, a scientific literary model, had all been Bello's encyclopedic aims. Indeed, encyclopedism is what explains the "double root"—"Neoclassical form and passionate, Romantic nature"—that Rodríguez Monegal perceived in Neruda's book project, and it is what explains the "explicit goal to explore America's greatness and thus prepare its destiny," and how the "mixture of geographical vision, epic chronicle and political blame" provided sundry forms and genres that constitute the "encyclopedia" Neruda borrowed from Bello.[61]

A taste for a poetic/scientific encyclopedia was therefore the common denominator between Bello and Neruda, underlaid in both by a shared modern concept of history as progress. Their difference, however, was ideological. Bello was an Enlightenment poet and intellectual who wanted to examine, as stated in his "Prospect" to *Repertorio Americano*, the journal Bello founded in London in 1823, "the progress of arts and sciences in the new world so as to complete its civilizations." Neruda wrote *Canto general* not only as a fervent Americanist, but as a Communist guided by Historical Materialism, the "new science" that, filtered as it was in his case through biased personal lenses, nonetheless attempted to "perfect civilization." Bello had wanted not only to educate people, but to give political unity to Latin America, which at the time was spatially dispersed and politically fractured; or else, as he claimed in *Repertorio Americano*, "to preserve the names and actions that appear in our history, assigning them each a place in time's memory." Neruda, too, wanted to educate ("Our Epic is Education" was the title of one of his 1938 speeches) and to "unite our continent, discover, build it, recover it." In 1949, on the verge of publishing *Canto general*, he had even called for "building in our America a world to come, as we're not the forlorn shipwrecks of a horrible island, but the joint components of a building force." Ultimately, Bello's and Neruda's encyclopedic imagination shared one important source: the Chronicles of Indies which, beginning in the sixteenth century, had brought "news" to the Old World about the New.[62] As such, *Canto general* purports to provide a map to shared Latin American roots. Its motto could well have been: *there's strength in Encyclopedias.*

The basis for such strength lay in the very idea of the encyclopedia. All encyclopedias provide internal coherence to knowledge through logical principles; and their common reformist purpose involves educating the general public. At the same time, however, tapping such coherence requires a concept of authorship beyond the subjective. Thus, in the collaborative endeavor all encyclopedias demand, individual authors become superseded by a group of editors who organize and compile their work—encyclopedias are actually authored by plural and anony-mous editors. The earliest precursor to that concept was, arguably, Vico's own "cyclic poet," to whom Neruda alluded. But it stems, too, from Bello's encyclopedic principles, to which Neruda linked up through none other than Diego Barros Arana (1830–1907), the well-known Chilean historian, arguably Bello's most important disciple, and author of that rare *Summary of America's History* that Neruda claimed he had found once in a farmhouse closet, and that in 1954 he referred to as one of three main sources he had used for *Canto general.*

Barros Arana's *Summary*, whose "basic" version was the history primer for generations of Chilean students, was itself the pioneer *compendium* (his word) or encyclopedic summary of all the history of Latin America that was known at the time. His work had also included a massive *Historia Jeneral de Chile* (1884–1907) in five volumes, which title could in fact have inspired Neruda's own.[63] Barros Arana's scholarship was itself infused by not only well-known pedagogical values ("a text aimed at teaching American history," according to its "Introduction") but also by a variety of sources, as required by the scope of his research. He thus credits, for precisely that reason, studies of "different periods of New World history" and "historical scholarship," as well as the testimony of "primitive historians, witnesses and authors" which constitute the core of his *Compendium* or digest of historical knowledge.[64]

Simply by collating poems Sections II to IV and Barros Arana's descriptions of the same historical events, one can gather the degree and extent to which Neruda used this primer of Latin American history as source-text.[65] But even as we witness those parallels one cannot claim that *Canto general* is simply a political history in verse. To this one must add the mediation of fields as disparate as Natural History, Ornithology, Geography, Geology, and even travel literature. As told to Cardona Peña, Neruda portrayed America's "fauna and geography," along with its "struggles and victories," and took pleasure in collecting—not unlike Bello had done—descriptions of rivers and birds, volcanoes and shells. One has only to browse through Neruda's personal library at the time, which today constitutes a separate collection in Chile's National University, to realize his life-long passion for Natural History. Hence the presence of classical naturalists—Aldrovandi and Buffon, Lamarck and Linneaus, Cuvier and Robinet, Philippi and House, among others— in *Canto general*'s structure and contents. Shelved alongside these there's even one important Chilean precursor: Juan Ignacio Molina, S.J. (1740–1829), author of a *Saggio sulla storia naturale del regno del Chili* (1782), who devoted a number of Natural History works, written in exquisite eighteenth-century Italian, to the study of the Chilean fauna and flora he had yearned for during his nostalgic exile in Bologna.[66]

Thus the Book that is also an Encyclopedia is many more things: Museum and Botanical Garden, Archive and Cabinet. But rather than just another naturalist work, it is a book of poems that *imitates* the breadth and objectives of Natural History; a poetic semblance of scientific discourse. The object of that imitation is none other than the reader's education regarding the uniqueness of the American "phenomenon." Much like a new Lucretius, Neruda attempted to synthesize science and poetry by singing "the nature of (American) things." Such a distant, "naturalist" link betrays the poetry's deepest sense. For instead of simply embodying Nature, the discourse of this "general song," in a manner not unlike that of Natural History's, actually records its absence: it sings to Nature's remoteness. For if, as Michel Foucault once observed, "until the time of Aldrovandi, History was the inextricable and completely unitary fabric of all that was visible of things and of the signs that had been discovered or lodged in them," then "Natural History" as a field of study emerges from the chasm between Nature and Representation which Modernity caved open. And if "until the mid-seventeenth century the historian's task was to establish the great compilation of documents and signs—of everything, throughout the world, that might form a mark, as it were," then

> the documents of this new history, are not other words, texts or records, but unencumbered spaces in which things are juxtaposed: herbariums, collections, gardens; the locus of this history is a

non-temporal rectangle in which, stripped of all commentary, of all enveloping language, creatures present themselves one beside another, their surfaces visible, grouped according to their common features, and thus already virtually analyzed, and bearers of nothing but their own individual names.[67]

The poetics of *Canto general* arises precisely out of that "clear space" where "things are juxtaposed," as its opening poem is the first to alert us:

> Man was dust, earthen vase, an eyelid
> of tremulous loam, the shape of clay—
> he was Carib jug, Chibcha stone,
> imperial cup of Araucanian silica.
> Tender and bloody was he, but on the grip
> of his weapon of moist flint,
> the initials of the earth were
> written.
>   No one could
> remember them afterward: the wind
> forgot them, the language of water
> was buried, the keys were lost
> or flooded with silence or blood.
>   (*CG*, 13–14; *OC*, I, 417)

Further in the same section, the Book's "Chronicler" literally introduces himself to the reader (*"I'm here to tell the story"*) though the task of telling will devolve onto a post-Diluvian reconstruction; that is, the telling begins to take place once "the earth's initials" have been literally forgotten, buried and lost, and the poet, thanks to a literally encyclopedic effort, works to restore them.

V

One key question thus arises at every step of our reading: who authors these poems? Neruda? Barros Arana? Natural historians? Perhaps an impersonal agent called History? The question arises each time the book's chameleon speaker, who rules over the text, surfaces overtly and shifts just as quickly from one poem to the next. One glaring example appears in the 15 dramatic monologues of Section VIII (*The Earth's Name is Juan*). But there are far subtler cases, such as "Pedro de Valdivia's Heart"

(*CG*, 85–86; *OC*, I, 494), where the speaker turns, from one poem to the next, from chronicler to Lautaro's feats (Poems VIII to XI in Section IV) to Lautaro's very voice: *"I sank my teeth into that corolla, / fulfilling the rites of earth"* (*CG*, 86; I, 495). The touchstone of all such transformations may well be Canto XI of *The Heights of Macchu Picchu*, where, having identified with the ruins, the speaker envisions his ancient forebears and takes up the cause of speaking *"through your dead mouths"* (*CG*, 41; *OC*, I, 447).

The mask-making or *persona*-crafting Rodríguez Monegal showed was a constant in all of Neruda's poetry appears more overtly in *Canto general* than in most of his other books. It surfaces, as we have seen, in the speaker's plural, multiple nature. It is hardly an accident, then, that Section VIII (*The Earth's Name is Juan*) should consist of 15 dramatic monologues (precisely the book's total number of sections) and occupy the book's physical core, as if emphasizing by such coincidence the plural nature common to both speaker and text. Indeed, this heteronymic, "chorus principle," so evident in Section VIII, seems to have been inspired not only on Edgar Lee Masters' *Spoon River Anthology*, masters' collection of epitaphs which Neruda owned and read. It was also essayed in a rare *Antología popular de la resistencia* (Popular Anthology of Resistance), a gathering of anti-government poems (including satires of González Videla), and attributed to ten fictitious Chilean popular poets, which Neruda himself authored in 1948 and published in the Chilean underground.[68]

All of this demonstrates the extent to which the book's "chorus" of voices is homologous to its "library" of sources. Both chorus and library constitute implicit critiques of the bourgeois concept of single or sub-jective authorship—private, individual, isolated—that was brandished aggressively by the Communist Neruda of those years. Indeed, the Marxist notion of trans-individual authorship bears strong conceptual links with Vico's "cyclical poet," Bello's encyclopedic author, and even with that "popular artist" who in 1938 had reminded Neruda of "fresh, spontaneous creation," close to "a bee's or a child's." Suffice it to recall Neruda's thesis, in his 1953 speech, on how "poetic chronicle is made by all," since "there's no such thing as non-poetry as long as it deals with our reality." The poetic speaker we know as "Pablo Neruda" will not, to be sure, vanish entirely from *Canto general*, either into the marketplace, or behind the poem's mask. Nor will he imitate either Vico's "Homer" or Ezra Pound's disembodied voices. Pablo Neruda, the real author, as opposed to the book's Chronicler, will himself come and go all throughout the book, slipping in dialectically between poet and mass. In formal

terms, this will amount to a pendulum movement between lyric meditation and epic narrative. "Man, much as he may therefore be a *particular*
individual," seems to be the Marxian dictum *Canto general* virtually
quotes between the lines, "(and it is precisely his particularity, which
makes him an individual, and a real individual social being), is just as
much the totality—the ideal totality—the subjective existence of thought
and experience that society presents for itself. . . . ."[69] Only in the book's
very last poem does the speaker choose to take off his mask to reveal
the author's "true" identity, or at least his autobiographical signature.
But even that signature, as we shall see, is ultimately destabilized by the
arbitrariness of chronicle and fiction.

What one can therefore call the Marxist content of *Canto general* seems
more closely linked to the book's enunciation, its sheer discursive practice,
than to its ideological content, which upon close scrutiny appears questionable. Indeed, one can gather how questionable that message turns out from
the ambivalence with which Marxist critics have reacted to it. Making this
important point will take me some time but it is worth working through.

One must agree with Alain Sicard, for example, when he notes that the
book's description of "anti-imperialist struggles" and "lessons of historical
materialism" refer ideologically and as a whole to a "clear joint conscience of historical movement and the forces acting upon it."[70] It would
be difficult not to sympathize with such a thesis: contemporary events,
such as the economic and ideological invasions the Great Powers have
regularly foisted upon Latin America, are structurally related to earlier
historical events, such as the Spanish Conquest. To convey that thesis,
Canto general assumes a narrative attitude with respect to History (what
Sicard calls "joint conscience") that is peculiar to Marxism, a kind of
"master narrative," or vast and incomplete plot, that narrates the history
of class struggle. Within such "narrativization of history" (the term is
Hayden White's) proposed by Historical Materialism (the Marxist philosophy of history), past events prefigure future ones: U.S. Imperialism
appears as a belated version of the Spanish Conquest; today's revolutionary leaders, avatars of the heroes of Spanish American Independence. As
White puts it: "every present is at once a realization of projects performed by past human agents and a determination of a field of possible
projects to be realized by living human agents in their future."[71] Hence
the defense of the poor (the proletariat) in *Canto general*, as Neruda, along
with Marx, views this class, in Sicard's words, "the expression of the dissolution of all classes and the embodiment of all humanity's interests."

And yet, the precise reading of Latin American history *Canto general*
sets forth actually falls short of any such dialectical rigor. In fact, one

could even say that it does not follow strictly Historical Materialist principles. For one, it fails to provide a critique of social conditions in Latin America based upon socioeconomic groupings. That is, the book shows neither how historical situations respond to the types of societies Historical Materialism describes (Primitive, Slave, Feudalist, Capitalist, or Socialist), nor how those conditions can be achieved. *Canto general* is therefore not a strict Historical Materialist treatise, at least not in the same way Volodia Teitelboim's *The Dawn of Capitalism and the Conquest of America* (1943), for example, certainly is. Teitelboim's historical essay analyzed, among other things, the subtle financial dealings between Charles the Fifth and European bankers, and speculated how this historical background could explain the rise of Fascism in twentieth-century Germany. By contrast, Neruda's book chronicles a vast array of exploiters and exploited, yet appears far more interested in the anecdotes regarding Valdivia and Lautaro than in the facts about Fugger or the Rothschilds. Teitelboim and Neruda shared a narrative attitude toward history but were far apart in their objectives. Teitelboim analyzed abstract causes; Neruda described concrete consequences.[72]

Neruda's lack of dialectical approach is what contributes most, perhaps, to the book's narrative inflexibility, as it excludes entire sections of historical reality. Shot through by sectarian passion, and thus eager to outline the major features of a history torn apart by class struggle, it fails to show, as Rodríguez Monegal once pointed out, "prehistoric feudalism as carried out by Aztecs in Mexico and the Incas in Perú." Nor does it deal with "European imperialists who were no less rapacious than the Spaniards, such as the Dutch, the French or the British." (In fact, it leaves out one far harsher, group: the Portuguese colonialists.) Neruda heaps praise upon Father Bartolomé de Las Casas for his defense of the Indians, yet forgets that Las Casas was himself partly responsible, so as to spare the native Indians from further cruelty, for promoting the African slave trade. Neruda's wholesale lack of dialectical rigor causes, in turn, stark historical errors, not to mention moral flaws. While the book condemns slavery and defends Africans (as shown in poems like "Toussaint L'Ouverture" and "The Wind over Lincoln," *CG*, 116, 119–120; *OC*, I, 529, 532–533), it also shows a serious lapse with respect to the Black substratum: "the word Africa does not appear in *Canto general.*" Its sheer sectarian nature is often so extreme as to make for difficult reading, particularly given the turgid tone of some poems. Years after the Moscow Trials were known, at a time when the existence of Soviet concentration camps was being debated and Stalin's collectivization campaign was a global scandal, the book turns a blind eye to all these terrible events and heaps praise upon the Soviet leadership. Barely 100 of its more than 15 thousand lines have women as their subject. And, as no less than Borges complained once, its long, detailed catalog of Latin American dictators skips over Perón's unavoidable monument.[73]

Thus, if historical dialectic in *Canto general* "relies (unlike Brecht's) less on Marx than on cold war politics," it simply cannot endure a rigorous critique.[74] Not unlike the work of the Mexican muralists Neruda so admired, his book idealizes pre-Columbian societies and is horrified by the Spanish Conquest, itself portrayed as the triumph of reactionary evil. If, on the one hand, some of its poems (the one on Lautaro, for example) glorify cannibalism, they also "caricature," on the other, "all of the conquistadors' negative, shady traits," to quote Octavio Paz on the Mexican muralists' Manichean treatment of history. And yet, a far stricter dialectical reading would underscore instead, as Marx and Engels themselves did, that the Conquest had been a necessary evil that bore ultimately positive results, since it meant the triumph of a superior mode of production (nascent Capitalism) over the primitive one prevalent among Aztecs and Incas. "Whatever may have been the crimes of England," wrote Marx about the 1853 Hindu revolt, "she was the unconscious tool of history in bringing about the revolution."[75] Marx's comments on the British Raj can be extrapolated onto the Spanish empire. "The imperialist expansion of the West," notes Paz again on Marx, "was positive because it imposed on backward and static societies the new and dynamic economic rationality of capitalism."[76]

All of which brings me roundabout to my point: the strange failure of Marxist criticism to do justice to *Canto general*. It is perhaps significant that Sicard himself, in his own substantial Marxist study of Neruda should plead for comparisons of "the presence . . . of all those factors that owe themselves to historical materialism," as opposed to what he called "a type of criticism all too ready to exclude them," and yet, the weight of such option notwithstanding, Sicard himself would choose to skip over an "inventory" of all such elements in order to concentrate, instead, on what he calls "specific modes of the poetry's materialist praxis." In my view, this laconic statement fails to engage the book's questionable treatment of history.[77]

More significant still is that Neruda himself in his many comments on the book never did add anything useful to this ideological debate. On the one occasion when he did—his long interview with Cardona Peña— he put the matter in terms so blurry as to render them contradictory. While a poem like "Despite the Fury" (*CG*, 68–71; *OC*, I, 476–477) does make an important concession to dialectical reading ("it tells how, in addition to the crimes, Renaissance ideas and industrial capacity came to our America,") hardly had Neruda finished providing a description of the

Independence period in Spanish America than he proceeded to distort the contents of Section IV (*The Liberators*): "Immediately after the Conquest, a caste seized power over the liberation movement and imposed a new dominant regime . . . creole oligarchies betrayed the Indian heroes, and few memorials have been dedicated to the great heroes of the first American struggle." Such remarks seem entirely appropriate as historical and moral commentary—particularly with respect to racial attitudes in Southern Cone countries like Chile; but they actually distort the contents of Section IV. For one, it confuses "the caste" that takes power along with "the liberation movement" with the nascent colonial bourgeoisie, which poems like "The Colony Covers Our Lands" (*CG*, 88; *OC*, I, 497–498), for example, analyze in detail. The poems in section IV that do portray the Independence period ("Bernardo O'Higgins Riquelme [1810]" or "San Martín (1810)," *CG*, 94–99, *OC*, I, 505–509) are actually odes to Latin American founding fathers, and the reader must await, in the same sequence, to read "Balmaceda from Chile (1891)" (*CG*, 122–125; *OC*, I, 535–539) for any word on that kind of judgment. A similar distortion recurs in yet another of Neruda's comments on Chilean "new aristocrats' " disdain for Lautaro and his indigenous legacy, though none of the poems bear this out; and recurs once again when he reduces all of section V, *The Sand Betrayed*, to the frustration of what he calls "Araucanian Independence."[78]

One could therefore conclude that Neruda's original plan seems indeed to have made *Canto general* a verse narrative of Latin American history according to Historical Materialist principles. This is borne out, in great measure, in the book's published previews, almost all of which follow that particular line. To write such an ideologically charged narrative must have been, moreover, the motivation behind the Party's granting Neruda a year's leave. And yet the political crisis that erupted appears to have changed that original plan, and Neruda ended up writing a different book altogether. Which of course didn't prevent him, even after publication, from describing it according to his original idea, or perhaps even the way he wished it had turned out. For the book Neruda did end up writing does contain a historical vision, though one on the far side of Historical Materialism.

VI

I mentioned before that *Canto general* is divided into two long halves of seven sections each (I–VII, IX–XV), joined together by a core (VIII). The first half is ruled by a historically linear concept; the second lacks linearity and is both more heterogeneous and sectarian. In between the two, one central section (*The Earth's Name is Juan*), the book's physical core, is made up of 15 dramatic monologues, plus two poems of various themes. The monologues, whose number coincides with the book's total number of sections, are voiced by poor people, real and historical, who tell of their own plights. The centrality of *The Earth's Name is Juan* is not only textual; it stems as well from its transparent allusion to "The People Call Him Gabriel," the unfortunate doggerel Neruda wrote for candidate González Videla. The allusion is a palinode, a poetic correction: it replaces "traitor" with "people" and thus suggests the latter are the book's true "authors."[79] Focusing the book's core upon such a plural drama underscores the author's trans-individual character, the ideological implications of which I have already reviewed. Before reaching this core, however, the reader must work through the book's first seven sections, all of which are ruled by an apparently linear character. I say apparent now because linearity does not, strictly speaking, begin in Section I, as one would expect, but rather in Section III, with the arrival of *The Conquistadors*, and ends with *Canto general of Chile* (Section VII).

But if all this is true, and as we focus on the book's first half, then how do Sections I and II relate to the next five? Within the book's fictional narrative time, the latter five sections actually occur between the first two. Section I (*The Lamp on Earth*), for example, is a New World Genesis that describes a time *"before the wig and dresscoat"* (*CG*, 13; *OC*, I, 417)— that is, historically, before Discovery and Conquest; it celebrates not only the "genesis" of an American natural environment—birds, rivers, and minerals—but also the continent's historical dimension: indigenous tribes and civilizations, Caribs to Araucainians, who inhabit such a world. Section II (*The Heights of Macchu Picchu*) contains, in turn, a conversion poem that professes solidarity with an American reality within the historical present. Clearly, we are no longer within the same time frame, since the appearance of ruins assumes metaphorically that a time-lapse has taken place between construction and decay. Such sudden emergence of ruins within the narrative proceeds to inform us, in other words, that ages have actually elapsed between Sections I and II and that a narrative ellipsis separates them. That is, the reader is not shown what actually transpired between the birth of indigenous civilizations, at the end of Section I, and the ruin of those same cultures in Section II. What does seem obvious is that "a fall" has taken place: *"you tumbled / as in autumn / to a single death"* (*CG*, 35; *OC*, I, 440), a literal collapse that underscores the Latin etymology of ruin (*ruere*: to fall). Thus the speaker looks onto the past, both historical and personal, from the ruined present; professes to speak *"through your dead mouths"* and to *"tell the story"* he had promised earlier in *"Amor América"* (1400) (*CG* 13–14; *OC*, I, 417).

The question therefore remains: whatever happened between the "Genesis" of Section I and the "ruins" of Section II? What exactly constitutes the "history" that must be "told"? It befalls sections III to VII to tell, or rather reconstruct, all those historical events: Discovery, Conquest, Violence, Opression, Rebellion, Betrayal, Dictatorship, Revolution, Reflection, and Discovery of the Poet's country of birth; in other words, everything that transpired during the almost five centuries between 1493 (the date inscribed atop *The Conquistadors*) and 1949 (date of the "Epilogue" in *The Betrayed Sand*). Condensed and telescoped, all those events make up the ellipsis between Sections I and II. The ruined present, the point from which reconstruction is undertaken, not only embodies the physical remains of the indigenous past; it also shows the spiritual desert of a global circumstance that elicits the poet's song and historical reconstruction. When at the end of Section II, after the prophet surveys the meaning of the ruins and asks the dead to *"speak through my words and my blood"* (*CG*, 42; *OC*, I, 447), his demand summons the historical events that are to be narrated next and toward which he points. In turn, the ruins symbolize a collapsed history. Ruins is all that remains, in the present, of the grandeur human beings built in the New World between Genesis and that present.

Thus, *Canto general* starts off combining biblical allusions and epic conventions. While Section I is a secular Genesis, Section II sets forth an *in medias res*. It is precisely from that epic present the speaker returns to the past events that Sections III to VII review in detail. Reams surely have been written about the meaning of *The Heights of Macchu Picchu* but in the context of the book it is clear that this magnificent poem has two formal functions. First, it invests the speaker with the *persona* of a prophet—in its strict sense of mouthpiece or spokesperson—and, thus, with the mandate to carry out a historic mission. And second, it tells us this historic mission is cast in legal terms. That is, in addition to a fall, the ruins constitute evidence of a historical and physical violation. The discovery of that violation takes place in the course of the poet's ascent to the ruins, from which he proceeds to reconstruct details of the crime, to bring the criminals to justice, and to restitute victims' rights. *"Who seized the cold's lightning / and left it shackled in the heights . . .? / What are your tormented sparks saying? / . . . who once again entombs farewells?"* (*CG*, 36–37; *OC*, I, 441–442) are but some of the lyrical questions the prophet-turned-prosecutor wields, as if interrogating witnesses and anticipating those questions that will follow in the rest of the narrative.

The litigious framework provides the book with a legal argument whose rhetoric is derived from the Chronicles of Indies—Las Casas's

Brevísima relación (1552), for example, or Poma de Ayala's *Nueva corónica y buen gobierno* (1612–1616). For, as is well known, such chronicles arose throughout the sixteenth and seventeenth centuries as part of an institutional debate about the nature of the New World and its inhabitants, as well as the rights of native-Americans. As texts of a legal and moral nature, chronicles make *"titanic materials . . . out of reason,"* to quote Neruda's poem about Father Las Casas (*CG*, 76; *OC*, I, 482–484), a well-known "chronicler" in his own right. It is precisely such legal argument that accounts as well for the book's narrative character. For if, as Hayden White has shown, all narrative "presupposes the existence of a legal system against which or on behalf of which the typical agents of a narrative account militate," and, as such, all narrative presumes "topics of law, legality, legitimacy, or more generally, authority," then *Canto general* must be the narrative text par excellence.[80] It is from such narrative power—that is, from the book's drive to moralize the American continent's reality and identify with its own social system—that the book's profound historicity derives. Historical verse narrative and search for justice become parallel, contiguous tasks, as the book invokes at every step sources of authority that might support the speaker in his quest—be it the dead viewed from the ruins' heights, a privileged reading of the historical past, or the monologues of witnesses whose words make up the book's physical and dramatic core.

And so, the prophet's discourse blames two betrayals at two separate levels: historical treason, perpetrated against Latin America; and political treason, against poet "Pablo Neruda." The legal framework becomes transparent as soon as we consider the autobiographical implications. And small wonder: since 1925, when he left Chile for the Far East, Neruda held a number of diplomatic posts. Upon his return in 1944, he was elected Senator, during whose tenure he took up again the task of writing the book he had begun six years earlier. And he finished writing that book precisely in the middle of a political crisis that revoked his citizen rights. Far from being an unrelated context, then, Neruda's biography is part and parcel of the book's fiction, a biography that Sections X (*The Fugitive*) and XV (*I am*) even dramatize explicitly. So much so, in fact, that it justifies the very act of writing in a poem justly called "They Shall be Named":

> With milk and flesh you gave me the syllables
> that will also name the pale worms
> that crawl in your womb,
> that prey on your blood, plundering your life.
> (*CG*, 330; *OC*, I, 759)

Thus it is no exaggeration to say that *Canto general* dramatizes the survival of Representation, in the dual political and literary senses of the word. While Pablo Neruda's legal representation may have been annulled in the Chilean Senate as a result of an anti-Communist campaign, his poetic and narrative Representation nevertheless survived precisely out of opposing the same repression that had victimized him.

<h1 style="text-align:center">VII</h1>

And so, the text about political and natural history Neruda ended up writing—endowed with a panoramic, cyclic vision, and broadly ruled by Marxist principles—became, as he called it, a Chronicle. On the one occasion he discussed this subject he was quick to link it to the book's prosaic character—"it ought to be rocky, dusty, rainy and everyday"— and to its reflection of immediate reality: "the poor trace of useless days and all of man's damnations and sorrows." Chronicle for Neruda was evident in two ways: testimonial content, sheer closeness to immediate circumstance, as in the style of a newspaper or a personal diary; and linearity, as shown in the sections of the first half of the book. Not everything in *Canto general* is Chronicle, of course—a good part of it does veer away from immediate testimony. And yet, we must inquire further into why Neruda insisted so much that we read the book this way.

We should recall Neruda had pointed out to Cardona Peña "all those proper names," as well as "important and insignificant events" he had chosen to include "so that a symbolic stigma might befall them." What Neruda then called the book's "realism," which in his view was hardly at odds with its "revolutionary romanticism"—constitutes what I have called the emergence of Chronicle, immediate and subjective, within History, distanced and objective. The overlap between the two, which in another context might appear arbitrary, is closely related to the "narrativization of history" I discussed earlier in relation to the book's ideology. For if, as we have seen, Marxism in *Canto general* works as a master code that links events and actors that are distanced in time with the implicit purpose of showing they belong to the same vast historical plot, then it is possible as well, within the same principle, to bring in to this plot more immediate events and actors that are further related to the poet's biography. For example, just as Recabarren, the legendary Chilean union leader, appears in the book as a new version of Father Las Casas, so "Fernández Larraín" (a conservative opponent of Neruda's in the Chilean Senate) can show up in a list of names of lowly landowners

(*CG*, 90; *OC*, 500); "Raúl Aldunate Phillips" (a journalist and personal enemy of Neruda's) can, too, be called "conquistador of magazines" (*CG*, 168; *OC*, I, 588); and "Rosario" (the poetic name Neruda gave to Matilde Urrutia, then his lover and future wife) can surface at the end of *Let the Woodcutter Awaken* (*CG*, 271; *OC*, 699). Not even "Reyes," Neruda's real family name, escapes that technique, as it surfaces in lists of both conquistadors and native heroes.[81]

Chronicle traits such as these point to yet another feature beyond ideology. For if Neruda's insertion of a biographical cipher within historical discourse meant wielding a "symbolic stigma" against his enemies (much like Victor Hugo's did against Napoleon III in *Les Chatiments*), then a whole ironic dimension takes hold as we move further away from immediate context. That is, beneath the fiction of the historical chronicle lies yet another cipher: the autobiographical fiction of "Pablo Neruda" and his times that we, as informed, cooperative readers, recognize each time he "winks" at us through the text. The total effect is close to our knowing that in *The Last Supper* Leonardo da Vinci made Judas's face resemble a personal enemy of his; or, conversely, that in *The Great Tenochtitlán*, his mural of ancient Mexico, Diego Rivera paid homage to his wife, the painter Frida Kahlo, by using her face as *La Malinche*'s. In all such cases, irony stems from such scenes of recognition, the "secret" pacts between implicit author and implicit reader who thereby become accomplices in the cipher, keys to a code. The irony also bears a message: History may be subject to change, but many other things remain constant—personal betrayal, a woman's mysterious beauty, political opportunists, the exploitation of the poor, and their ongoing, necessary defense.

Both levels surface at every one of the book's turns as the text works through the distinction between, on the one hand, *the chronicler* or speaker, in all chameleon splendor, who rules over the historical chronicle; and, on the other, *Pablo Neruda*—the "author" who controls the biographical cipher that lurks beneath. As in Brecht's *Vervremsdungseffekt* (estrangement or alienation), which creates a distance between reader and work by inserting self-conscious comments, the overt display of autobiography creates an even greater awareness of the text's deliberate construction, its *fabrication*, yet another sign of its material historicity. Among the features of such self-conscious construction are the implicit quotations (from the *Bible* in Section I), the book's sundry secular sources (Barros Arana), and even the appearance of a speaker who is not totally trustworthy, analogous to what narrative theory calls the "unreliable narrator."[82] I am not of course drawing a strict analogy to the type of suspicion created by a Henry James-type narrator, whose limited knowledge of the plot has a moral effect on the reader. The reader's distrust, in this case, arises especially when we realize that the "errors" the chronicler makes on a number of historical details impact our *mediated* relationship with the history being narrated. That is, the "mistakes" the chronicler makes are all, in a sense, justified, for such happens to be the imperfect quality of all chronicles ("rocky, dusty, rainy, everyday") at least as this poet wills them to be. We gather that impression from such "errors" as the book's version of *"materna Oello,"* instead of the real Inca "Mama Ocllo" (*CG*, 57; *OC*, I, 464); the pidgin Quechua in a quotation attributed to Tupac Amaru I, which the chronicler appears to derive from a Western, secondary source (and in translation) and then uses as epigraph (*CG*, 43; *OC*, I, 448); or else, the howlers in *"La Guayra," "Morínigo," "Anaconda Cooper,"* and *"Rodríguez de la Crota"* (*CG*, 177, 169, 164; *OC*, I, 579, 583, 598), whose "correct" versions are: *La Guáira, Moríñigo, Anaconda Copper,* and *Rodríguez de la Sotta*.[83] All of these "errors" coalesce at the end of the book onto the false "signature" borne by the last poem:

> Today, 5 February, in this year
> of 1949, in Chile, in "Godomar
> of Chena," a few months before
> I turned forty-five.
> (*CG*, 400; *OC*, I, 837)

All the facts conveyed in this signature fuse onto the autobiographical cipher, save for one: *"Godomar de Chena"* happens to be a fictional composite of the real place *Santa Ana de Chena*, where Neruda hid from the Chilean police on his escape route out of Chile, and *Julio Vega Godomar's* (his host there) second last name. The "invention" of this signature, in turn, cannot simply be explained away as a ruse to lead Neruda's hunters astray. Here is where a contextual explanation breaks down, is clearly insufficient. The "error" actually opens the text up to the relative formal freedom of the chronicle, and suspends, or at least renders suspicious, all referentiality. At the same time, however, the apocryphal signature constitutes a window onto "the invention of America" the book proposes throughout. For as Hayden White has observed: "The Chronicle typically promises closure but does not provide it."[84] It is precisely such open character that explains, within the book's heterogeneous second half, the wholesale absence of a historical apocalypse, be it Christian or Communist, and despite the many instances throughout the book where it is prophesied or at least hinted at. And its formal openness, or at least lack of closure, is what makes even the book's most sectarian poem admit: *"I don't want to solve anything/I came here to sing/so that you'd sing with me"* (*CG*, 272; *OC*, I, 700).

Of all the book's instances of error, perhaps the chronicler's most aberrant alteration appears in the misspelling of *Machu Picchu* (which the chronicler always writes *Macchu Picchu*, with an extra *c*), as all published editions observe. That is, the chronicler changes, or rather improves upon, the traditional spelling (adding a *c* to *machu*, which means "old" in Quechua) to create a typographical symmetry between the name's two elements. Typographical symmetry is meant to mirror the poem's structure: the title's twelve letters correspond to the poem's twelve cantos, and both in turn to the day's twelve hours, or the year's twelve months, within a cyclical structure and cosmic design. Symmetrical "improvement" in both poems and ruins would hardly be significant were it not for the fact that it happens to contradict the poem's argument, which advocates the very opposite: an unmediated encounter with American reality within a structure of conversion. In other words, the supplement in the poem's title (the extra letter *c*) reveals an implicit exogenous or exotic perspective, since neither the Inca clock nor calendar was based on a Western duodecimal system. The very search for such symmetry betrays a complicity to that perspective, even when there actually is, strictly speaking, no "correct" spelling for the ruins' name—Quechua is not an alphabetical language and it exists only in phonetic transcriptions that are subject to the arbitrariness of Western linguistics. For the chronicler, whose Spanish writing itself is a form of cultural mediation, the additional letter thus signifies the crucial difference between the actual ruins and their allegorical reconstruction. Far, then, from an archeology that restitutes the original meaning of Machu Picchu (*sic*) in Inca culture, the poem sets out to do something else: to subvert the Western Library. It does so not by means of indigenous texts, as a strict anthropological reading would insist, but rather through allusions to a Western poetic canon that is as "foreign" to the physical ruins as are Dante, Romantic poetry, Rubén Darío, and even Neruda's own poetry prior to *Canto general*.[85] In other words, the supplemental *c* in "Macchu Picchu" (*sic*) is not a mere typo. Its persistence signals the imprint of a viewpoint midway between external self and internal "American love" (*CG*, 36; *OC*, I, 441), the very spirit the prophet invokes in the poem's central canto (VIII). It is this same viewpoint that the chronicler's mediated nature and the poem's scandalously Western interpretation happens to expose. "Exotic was our servitude, and exotic is our liberation," was Neruda's rallying cry in 1943 in Panamá, Latin America's geographical center, amidst a debate on his poetry's polemical relationship to Latin American origins and identity. Jiménez may therefore not have been that far off when he remarked that Neruda was not "as much of an indigenist as he now claims to be." Neruda's poetics was, in fact, more *indigenist* than indigenous: he wrote *about*, rather than *from*, the Indian point of view.

VIII

Such *indigenist* imagination is what ultimately links *Canto general*, among other art works, to Mexican muralist art, to which it is often compared. As we know, Rivera and Siqueiros contributed original flyleaves to the first, public edition. Years before, Siqueiros had himself illustrated an anthology of Neruda's poems.[86] In 1940, as Consul General in Mexico, Neruda had even helped Siqueiros, accused at the time of plotting to kill Leon Trotsky and his family, out of jail and into Chile, where Siqueiros went on to paint the murals of Chillán's "Escuela México." According to Cardona Peña, who was partly in charge of the Mexican first edition, Neruda sent the galleys to Rivera and Siqueiros and asked them to choose the poems for their flyleaves. At the time, all three shared a telluric vision of the New World, not to mention a mystical Marxist faith. Muralist painting was clearly the model for Neruda's "new stage," and it is very likely that Neruda witnessed Diego Rivera at work on the frescoes for the Mexican National Palace, whose sheer historical expanse he set out to imitate in his own Book. In his *Memoirs*, Neruda captured Rivera's work in a statement that recalls his own: a "calligraphy of history" with which he "tied together the History of Mexico, shaping events, customs and traumas."

Indeed, comparing *Canto general* to muralist painting has by now become fairly commonplace.[87] Both are, after all, types of "public art." As muralist painting, according to Serge Fauchereau, "is done by only one person, but is often produced in a group," this means that it wields a concept of authorship similar to that anonymous and plural author which operates in *Canto general*.[88] Not unlike encyclopedias—"*Common book/ of mankind, broken bread/ is this geography of my song*" (*CG*, 399; *OC*, I, 836),—muralist painting itself attempted trans-individual expression, destined to all, as if responding to what José Vasconcelos, Secretary of Education during the Mexican Revolution, and arguably the muralists' most important mentor, had demanded: an organic and total art inspired on the great historical periods of Byzantium and the *Quattrocento*. Fixed upon grottoes or immovable church walls, muralist "public art" took its inspiration from anonymous primitive and medieval painting with the express goal of reaching the greatest amount of spectators, who were often illiterate. Clearly, it was not meant to be a faithful reproduction of such ancient models, but rather—as in the case of the uses of Natural History in *Canto general*—of modern works that imitate those models. Modern works like Neruda's or Rivera's are, of course, hardly anonymous. What sustains their common discourse is the fiction of collective creation; we believe that fiction despite our knowing full well the authors' identities. Finally, even when poet and muralist do coincide in objectives and ideology, a subtle but important difference separates them. Muralist painting is accessible to all, even the illiterate; the Book, subject to writing, limits its readers.

Neruda's was but one instance of the American prophetic imagination that was fueled in part, beginning in the 1880s, by the erratic reception of Walt Whitman's life, work, and mythology throughout the southern continent. I devote the next chapter to that reception as yet another version of the historicist ciphers I find, at once, fascinating and cryptic. The shift in focus, briefly, will be from the macro-politics of social and historical forces at work in one particular text to the micro-politics of aesthetic reception in a number of texts and authors over a full century's span. My view there, as I engage a particular instance of reception theory, will be that the Whitman myth that proliferated among the works of many a Latin American poet, including two of our greatest, Borges and Neruda, concealed a poetic contest, or conquest—a kind of breathless race for the Laurel crown—rather than the pious political myth that U.S. influence projected onto the world since the turbulent 1930s and that, since then, took hold, mysteriously and pathetically, of some of the sharpest Latin American literary critics at the time.

CHAPTER TWO

This Land of Prophets: Walt Whitman in Latin America

The American poets are to enclose old and new, for America is the race of races. Of them a bard is to be commensurate with a people. To him the other continents arrive as contributions.

Walt Whitman, 1855 Preface to *Leaves of Grass*

But because we live not in a continent but in islands, so terribly isolated, we know so little of each other that we don't even hate one another.

Octavio Paz, "Is America a Continent?"

Does this Aleph exist in the heart of a stone? Did I see it there in the cellar when I saw all things, and have I now forgotten it? Our minds are porous and forgetfulness seeps in.

Jorge Luis Borges, "The Aleph"

I

In 1943, amidst a year ridden by crisis—personal, political, and poetic—Octavio Paz wrote a proposal to the John Simon Guggenheim Memorial Foundation for one of its yearlong research fellowships. Paz's proposal called for a study of "America and its Poetic Expression," by which he meant poetry in both North and South, Anglo and Latin America, and taking at face value the Foundation's stated criteria for "strengthening interamerican cultural relations and fostering greater continental intelligence." In that study, which set out to answer one single question: "Do the Americas have a common soul?" Paz sought to isolate, in the history of Western Hemispheric poetry, "those traits that single it out, give it an original native profile, accent, and direction," though not so much, he warned, in order to show "the forms in which that poetry has crystallized" as "to find in its language the history of a sensibility." While surveying the span of continental poetry from Sor Juana and Emily Dickinson to Alfonso Reyes and Robert Frost, the proposal did single out three names—Poe, Darío, and Whitman—as sundry cases split into two tendencies: one (Poe's and Darío's) universal or cosmopolitan, the other (Whitman's) a native strain expressing the "burgeoning American soul." Indeed, Whitman's name punctuated Paz's entire proposal, and although he never did complete it (mercifully, perhaps), and instead spent his fellowship year at Berkeley writing his own poetry, the proposal does stand as a key document in the history of what one could call, for lack of a better name, the Whitman question in Spanish America.[1]

That Whitman, rather than Poe or Darío, was the real focus of Paz's proposal was confirmed several years later, in the first edition of *The Bow and the Lyre* (1956), Paz's tome on "the poem, poetic revelation, poetry and history." There he included an appendix titled "Whitman, American Poet" that, without alluding to his earlier project, appears to distill it. In it Paz argued (against Borges, whose name, except by inference, went unmentioned) that Whitman's "mask-the poet of democracy—is something more than a mask: it is his true face," while also defining Whitman's Americanism in terms of its utopian character. "America dreams itself in Whitman because America itself was dream, pure creation." And concluded: "Before and after Whitman we have had other poetic dreams. All of them—be the dreamer named Poe or Darío, Melville or Dickinson—are really attempts to escape from the American nightmare."[2]

Paz's gradual fraying away of this Americanist question, so to speak, foreshadows the course of his better-known quest after Mexican identity—one of the central themes of his early thought and a recurring subject in his essays from the 1930s and 1940s, abandoned, finally, in *The Labyrinth of Solitude* (1950). In both cases, "the history of an [American] sensibility" becomes subsumed under conceptual or imaginary constructs (Solitude, Utopia) well beyond the mirages of nationalism or geography. But Paz's two-stepped approach revealed something more than Whitman's gradual embodiment of that particular question. It actually dramatized the tensions and complications attendant to Whitman's reception in Latin America. The narrative of that reception, whose first chapter Fernando Alegría wrote over half a century ago in his *Walt Whitman en Hispanoamérica* (1954), ought certainly to include not just the bare facts of Whitman's fortunes, but also those repressed elements, internal polemics, and open misunderstandings that make up its significance—a story that Doris Sommer has rightly called "the contest for a legitimate American poetry."[3] This essay departs from Sommer's by insisting on the importance of the bibliographical details in such a story and reception. With it, however, I share a concern for the role played by the Imaginary (in its loose Lacanian sense of the constitutive role of fantasy) and modify it further as a narrative of Error—a kind of "experiment in international living" redolent of late arrivals and near misses.

By a perhaps uncanny coincidence, for example, Paz chose to spend his Guggenheim fellowship year at Berkeley, precisely where Eugene Bolton, then Professor of History at the University of California, had advocated his controversial, Hegelian views about a "Greater America" (also known as the "Bolton Theory") toward the concept of a hemispheric and geographic rather than culturally determined historiography.[4] To be sure, Paz does not mention Bolton in his Guggenheim proposal (or anywhere else, for that matter), even though the conceptual basis of his argument sounds at times uncannily like an application of the "Bolton Theory" to literary history. The resemblance was uncanny indeed since, barely two years before writing his Guggenheim proposal, in 1941, Paz had gone so far as to question, in a revealing early essay, the very continental status of America. Remarking wistfully that "because we live not in a continent but in islands, so terribly isolated, we know so little of each other that we don't even hate one another," he broached the possibility that the Americas might not, after all, have a common history—or literature, for that matter.[5] Neither does the 1956 appendix to *The Bow and the Lyre* make any mention of Alegría's study of Whitman's reception in Latin America, even though the latter had also been published in Mexico two years before. Alegría, in turn, could not have known about Paz's unpublished Guggenheim proposal, though in a stranger turn still he does not mention Bolton either. Strange, that is, because in 1944 Alegría, like Paz, was himself studying at Berkeley under Arturo Torres-Rioseco, a fellow-Chilean under whose mentorship (I suspect) Alegría first undertook his reception study of Whitman. Torres-Rioseco had, in turn, himself produced in the 1920s, as Alegría himself notes (373–377), what at the time were some of the best Spanish translations of Whitman.

The "Bolton Theory," Paz's proposal, Alegría's reception study, even the criteria for the Guggenheim Fellowship Program, all share one common source: the Pan-Americanist ideology of the Franklin D. Roosevelt era. This was the period (the 1930s and early 1940s) in U.S. history marked by the "Good Neighbor" policy as a result of feared encroachment of European powers into the American continent and its efforts to secure reliable allies to the South. Whitman, the American Poet of Democracy, thus became a convenient tag of this ideology, and it was not by accident that his cult in Latin America reached its apex then. Those were the years when noted Whitman scholar Henry Seidel Canby addressed an annual meeting of specialists on Latin American literature in order to ask, on the same subject: "Who Speaks for New World Democracy?" An echo of Canby's rhetorical question can still be heard in Alegría's quite literal introduction to *Walt Whitman en Hispanoamérica*, where, adopting Canby's motto as his own, he described the Roosevelt era as "the heroic years of the war against fascism" and his own study, implicitly, as his contribution to U.S. foreign policy toward Latin America—a kind of exercise in comparative literature as academic Good Neighbor. But just as the Latin American cult of Whitman precedes by a good many years the Good Neighbor policy, so the omissions one notes in both Paz and Alegría cannot simply be dismissed as accidents of a given political moment. Paz's transparent allusion to Borges's well-known reading of "the other Whitman"—the latter's view that Whitman's creation of his heroic *persona* compensated for his banal real life—has a greater and, in a sense, more significant precedent in the wholesale omission of Pablo Neruda from his Guggenheim proposal. Neruda had that same year published a preview of the Americanist poems he was later to gather together in *Canto general* (1950), but he and Paz had publicly and violently broken barely two years before.[6] Paz's repression of Neruda's name, his critique of Borges, as well as many other instances we will have occasion to chronicle in Borges, Neruda, and Alegría, are all part of a common discourse, a commonly shared contest or conquest of wills over the most accurate and powerful appropriation of the American bard's legacy. "*La tradición no se hereda, se conquista*" ("Tradition is conquered, not simply inherited"), Malraux's famous dictum, which became one of Paz's fighting maxims during the 1940s, could itself be viewed as the motto of that contest.

II

The Whitman cult is international, not just Latin American. And it is a poetic myth of Modernity in general, not just of the United States in particular. And yet, why Whitman, after all? To begin with, Whitman stands at the crossroads of modern literary history; both a belated romantic and a premonition of the avant-garde; a Janus-figure of that history. To this temporal duality corresponds a rhetorical convenience. Whitman's poetry embodies what has been called the Romantic Subject; only that subject dissolves conveniently into the impersonality of either pantheist or populist ideologies. Seemingly the poet for all seasons, Whitman fulfills Emerson's ideal scenario for "The Poet" and thereby dazzles equally symbolists like Viélé-Griffin, Martí, and Darío; inspires alike Pound the imagist, Marinetti the futurist, Becher the expressionist, and Claudel the neo-Thomist, not to mention the postmodern Borges and Neruda. Like the cowboy storming across *Leaves of Grass*, Whitman rides astride the last two centuries, but the dust his storm unsettles often prevents us from tracing his tracks.

In the specific case of Latin America, that crossroads is situated at a stage somewhere between *Modernismo* (Hispanic Symbolism) and modernity, a twilight zone that reflects the flux of Spanish American literary history. Often linked to post- or anti-*Modernismo*—an alleged reaction on the part of late-nineteenth and early-twentieth-century poets to a decadent French influence—Whitman actually forms part of the very mythology of *Modernismo*, a truism we can understand from Paz's remark that "the *modernistas* did not want to be French; they wanted to be modern."[7] As discovered by *modernistas* like Martí, Darío, and Lugones, Whitman became yet another emblem of modernity, one of the missing portraits in Darío's gallery of *Los raros* (1896). The initial cult of Whitman, then, did not so much mean a wholesale denial of *Modernismo* as the clustering of one of its phases: a different, critical, and, I would add, *political* phase (in the sense of a rhetorically powerful interpretation) whose real butt was not France but Spain, or at least a certain turgid Spanish poetry. It is this critical or political use of Whitman in the initial phase of its Latin American cult that explains, I believe, his emblematic use in some of the early texts of *Modernismo*-Martí's famous 1887 chronicle, for example, or Darío's plodding sonnet in *Azul . . .* (1888).[8] That is, the *modernistas* invoke, rather than imitate, Whitman. In their works, Whitman is more a theme and less a stylistic or rhetorical model, even in those particularly hostile instances like Darío's haughty dismissal ("The rest is all yours, Democrat Walt Whitman . . .") proffered at the end of his preface to *Prosas profanas* (1896). During the first decades of the twentieth century, the Whitman theme becomes gradually replaced by his *persona*, as it began seducing Latin American bards into adoption as a full-blown model. Only by the time they did adopt it, that *persona* had become fused with yet another, perhaps unlikely, kindred spirit by the name of Friedrich Nietzsche.

About Nietzsche's presence I shall have more to say later. We should first underscore, in tracing this uncanny itinerary, this collapse of the distinction between the emblematic and rhetorical uses of Whitman in most discussions about his influence in Latin America. The collapse of critical distance was noted, in a sharp 1929 essay, by no less than Borges, where he remarked that those who write about Whitman incur two fallacies, one of which was confusing poet and *persona*, while the other was "the senseless adoption of the style and vocabulary of his poems, that is, the same surprising phenomenon that aims to be explained."[9] Borges's remark may appear to underscore an isolated critical problem, but it actually has roots in Latin American historical life. For when José Enrique Rodó in his review (later to be the preface to the second edition) of *Prosas profanas*, reports to have heard that Darío was not "the poet of America," he must have said so regretting that Darío was not in fact Whitman, or at least not yet. Shortly thereafter Darío would write his ode "A Roosevelt," later included in *Cantos de vida y esperanza* (1907)— a book he dedicated to Rodó—in which he explicitly invoked "el verso de Walt Whitman" in order to address the bellicose American president. By then, of course, Darío and other *modernistas*, like the Uruguayan Alvaro Armando Vasseur, had already internalized Whitman's rhetoric, so it could be said that by invoking "el verso de Walt Whitman" Darío then marked Whitman's passage from strict theme to flamboyant *persona*. Yet despite his use of the blank verse Darío adopted as a Whitman password in his ode, what his *persona* expressed in that poem was not so much Whitman's proverbial eroticism or democratic chant as much as a turgid anti-imperialist speech that echoed Old Testament prophecy.

Indeed, Darío's equivocal gesture could be taken as an emblem of the entire erratic relationship between Latin American poets and Whitman, a link constituted by a fantasy, and namely, the fantastic disparity between what Whitman *actually was* and wrote and what those poets *imagined* he was and wrote. That is, *Whitmanism* writes not so much *from* a Whitman point of view as *about* it. This erratic relationship is based, in turn, upon a paradox of political vintage: it borrows Whitman's mask from *North* America in order to shield *Latin* America against U.S. imperialism. Whitman thus became rhetorically useful, and even politically expedient; but his usefulness and expediency were no less subject to bad faith. And while such bad faith may be explained as one more version of the paradox with which all of (Latin) American culture is fraught—being an American Self through the language of a European Other—the Whitman model in particular may yet turn out to be the tensest dramatic instance of that general cultural paradox.

The error may be explained by its unusual source. Since most Latin American poets could not read Whitman in the original English, they read him in translations, mostly French, which, as Betsy Erkkila has shown, were the result of an extremely successful continental reception.[10] Alegría himself demonstrated that idealized French biographies of the "Good Gray Poet," like Léon Bazalgette's immensely popular *Walt Whitman: L'Homme et son oeuvre* (1908), make up much of the notes and summaries of Whitman's Latin American reception beyond Martí's 1887 chronicle. In two long and densely footnoted chapters, Alegría documented the recurrence of a Whitman myth in Spanish American discussions of the poet's life. Yet missing altogether from Alegría's chapters was any discussion about the effect that such an idealized perception of Whitman's biography might have had on the actual creation of Whitmanian *personae* among Latin American poets. That is, Alegría's study on the reception of Whitman in Spanish America, crucial though it may have been, failed to articulate precisely the most crucial question of that entire subject: the relationship between the prevalence of a certain Whitman myth and actual writing. It therefore failed to show the connection between Latin American poets as *readers* of a foreign source and as *reciphers* of that source. The failure surfaces especially in Alegría's placement of his chapter on the Spanish translations of Whitman's poetry at the end rather than the beginning of his reception study, thereby skipping over the (con)sequential use of those translations by the poets discussed in earlier chapters. But this was merely one of many missed opportunities in Alegría's otherwise useful account of the Whitman cult in Latin America, a fact that further reinforces my view that it, too, forms part of the cult and as such participates in what Borges called the "senseless adoption" of a rhetoric blinded by its object.

My broad point here is that, far from the pious Pan-American chorus for which Alegría and others have argued, the production of a Whitman question in Latin America constitutes a revealing instance of an alienated colonial discourse, in the sense of a body of information filtered through the language of a foreign Other—in this case, idealized biographies and translations twice-removed from the original. And since the only sense that counts within such a discourse is what the subjects *imagine* their object to be (hence the crucial role of a Whitman Imaginary, if you will), the actual discourse appears contaminated by features that are structurally similar to (when not radically different from) those proper to the object— what biologists, using a structural term, have called isomorphic traits, as in Darío's Old Testament speech derived, allegedly, from "*el verso de Walt Whitman.*" The end-result is a literally rhapsodic text: not so much ecstatic in content (though Whitmanism certainly shows that, too) as formally heterogeneous; a porous, fractious language that magnifies its otherness in what Mikhail Bakhtin would call an instance of the carnivalesque.[11]

The point seems worth making especially in cases like Vasseur's, in whom the roles of Whitmanian poet and translator converged, and whose work (as Alegría himself took pains to show) lies at the origin of much of the Whitman cult in Latin America.[12] It is thus hardly surprising that a good portion of Alegría's chapter on the Spanish translations of Whitman (349–396) should be devoted to a detailed critique of Vasseur's contribution—what Alegría took to be Vasseur's truncated and often "incorrect" readings of Whitman's English, his "excessive liberties" in reinterpreting Whitman's poems for a Hispanic audience. Indeed, Alegría's critique of Vasseur may have been technically accurate but it was thoroughly misguided for the purposes of a reception study. Among other reasons, because Vasseur did his translations not, as Alegría claimed, from English originals, which Vasseur did not know, but from Italian translations that became available as early as 1881. Vasseur himself acknowledged this fact in his 1951 preface to the sixth edition of his *Poemas: Walt Whitman* (a text missing from Alegría's otherwise complete bibliography), and suggested as much in his use of epigraphs of Whitman verses in Italian for the different sections of his *Cantos augurales* (1904), a text Alegría did take note of.[13] Working, thus, at twice-removed from the original (and it would of course be instructive further to collate Vasseur's text with his Italian sources), Vasseur was free to turn his translation into the loose *versión* (his word) in which he rewrote Whitman according to his own idea of a certain Whitmanian voice or *persona* that was equally as valid as (and potentially more interesting than) the one at work in his *Cantos augurales* (1904).

Far, then, from Alegría's view that Vasseur's "translations" were defective or aberrant because they did not render faithfully Whitman's English original, I happen to find them most apposite. Those allegedly unfaithful versions of Whitman, foundation-texts of his Latin American cult, confirm the alienated, second-order quality of such a discourse. I suspect that much of what sounded particularly un-Whitmanian to Alegría's ears was due to Vasseur's professed admiration for Nietzsche, as a Zarathustrian title like *Cantos augurales* suggests, and the contamination of his style with Whitman's. Indeed, Vasseur's debt to Rodó's influential *Ariel* (1900)—whose verse version he may even have intended in his poetry (Rodó, in addition, also hailed from Uruguay)—cannot be discounted. And yet Nietzsche's peculiarly strident, egocentric rhetoric permeates so much of Vasseur's style (in both his own poems and his Whitman versions) that it could be said his was a truly Nietzschean mode of writing, or *écriture*. Such contamination would not be unusual. The affinity between Whitman and Nietzsche, twin post-romantic heroic figures, is a virtual cliché of late-nineteenth-century cultural history, to the point that an early essay by Borges described Nietzsche's theory of the Superman in revealing terms: "Nietzsche wanted to *be* Walt Whitman, he wanted minutely to fall in love with his own destiny."[14] Vasseur himself, in the preface to the Whitman versions that Alegría (151–154) mentions, expounded at length on the parallels between the two writers, twin "supermen" in Vasseur's heady vision.

I therefore suggest that virtually all the "distortions" that Alegría pointed out in Vasseur—particularly the general secular tone of his Whitman versions, and the *"neoclassical residue"* (285) he finds in the poetry—can be explained by Nietzsche's tacit yet powerful presence in Vasseur's versions, or else in his Italian sources. In our own terms, Nietzsche represents, with respect to Whitman, an isomorphic source that contributed decisively to a poetics of *posmodernismo*, and particularly to a new concept of the poet (or of a poetic *persona*, such as D'Annunzio's in Italy), whose dramatic traits would be Whitman's American ego, or else Nietzsche's plea for the Superman. Within the peculiar economy of that discourse, Nietzsche serves one important purpose: to hold in check, without necessarily canceling, Whitman's religious tone; a kind of secular antidote. As a historian of these dual figures once put it, "Whitman's joy envisages a transfigured rather than a perfected human nature. It is the joy of the Oversoul, not of Damocles. In contrast, Nietzsche's joy is wholly mundane and derives solely from Zarathustra's service to life."[15]

Nietzschean joy, then, not Whitmanian Democracy, provides the rhetorical basis for such Latin American *posmodernista* titles as Vasseur's *Cantos del Nuevo Mundo*, Sabat Ercasty's *Pantheos*, or Neruda's *El hondero entusiasta*, even though all of them would be simply inconceivable without Whitman. And it was Nietzsche (filtered through Italian *bravura*) who provided the tacit if raucous voice that Latin American readers overheard in Vasseur's "defective" Whitman versions. In his vitriolic though insightful 1929 essay, Borges had attributed that voice exclusively to a "French connection" that turned each budding Latin American Whitman into what Borges ridiculed then as an "insistent Hugo." Be the connection French or German, however, its sheer evidence suggests that the study of Whitman's presence in Latin America includes as well the manner and extent to which his followers may have repressed his influence, a repression attributable perhaps to the cultural paradox Whitman himself represented. Whitman, following Emerson, had urged self-reliance for Americans; to celebrate not History or Nature, but Oneself. The legacy of that urging, however, was equivocal, if not anxiety producing. To boast, as Whitman had, of having "an American Bard at last!" meant that the search for that bard was effectively over. "Of them, a bard is to be commensurate with a people," claimed the first preface to *Leaves of Grass* of that one lucky fellow, to be echoed later by his followers North and South. And yet, how could one possibly sing oneself within a tradition of self-singers and still claim uniqueness? In U.S. poetry such anxiety surfaces in what Harold Bloom has called "the American Sublime," the simultaneous desire for and resistance to influence that riddles the works of Dickinson, Crane, Frost, and Stevens.[16] We have no name for the Latin American equivalent of Bloom's term, but I suspect that it is somewhat different from its Anglo counterpart. To this difference, if indeed there is one, I now turn my attention in the exemplary cases of Neruda and Borges.

III

Neruda and Borges first read Whitman in their teens. Like Vasseur, both discovered him through indirect sources; both imitated his poetry in their early verse; and both rejected Whitman soon thereafter, only to recover him later through other creative means. For Neruda, Whitman was the Continental American voice; for Borges, one more embodiment of the idea of Literature. In keeping with the general intent of this chapter, I bring both poets together partly to oppose the common myth that Whitman influenced both simply and directly, as in a kind of Pan-Americanist rapture. I choose instead a less sentimental version of what I take to be their complicated kinship. And it is for this reason that my reading of the two concentrates on texts that may appear marginal or at least eccentric in relation to the canon that is usually invoked for the opposite purpose.[17]

Neruda once wrote he learned of Whitman as early as 1919, at the age of 15, but it was actually in 1923, at 18, that he published a review of Torres-Rioseco's translations.[18] The review itself was instructive in its contradictions. Writing as *Sachka*—one of his several pre-Pablo Neruda pennames—he praised Whitman and his Chilean translator yet objected to his example. Whitman had a vital, energetic message well enough, but that vital energy was damaging: "Lost words," *Sachka* admonished, "each poet will sing whatever he wishes without caring about Whitman's hygiene." The admonishment itself amounted to an early restatement of Bloom's "American Sublime," influence both sought and repressed. And it becomes all the more telling when compared to a second review, published a week later, on Carlos Sabat Ercasty, another Uruguayan bard, which praised his poetry effusively yet suppressed that gesture altogether.[19] A Whitman fan himself (Alegría cheerfully called him an "apostle of his message" [291]), Sabat Ercasty knew Vasseur's Whitman "versions." In turn *Sachka's* sycophantic piece demonstrated the extent to which he took in there the influence he otherwise resisted in Whitman. Within two years, the conflict reached a crisis, as soon as Neruda published *Crepusculario* (1923), his first book, and began writing, in the seductive Sabat Ercasty mode, a long poem that would be published only years later under the title of *El hondero entusiasta* (*The Ardent Slingsman*, 1933). Neruda published this poem only after acquiring just fame for *Residence on Earth*, where he found his true voice. When he did publish *The Ardent Slingsman*, the preface contained a series of revelations: 1) Sabat Ercasty's influence had led him to suppress the book; 2) the published text contained only a portion of the original poems (thus suggesting that the portions suppressed made such influence more evident); and 3) the whole thing was merely the document of "an excessive and burning youth." In another retrospective piece written 30 years after that, Neruda explained further that Sabat Ercasty's influence had been part of a broader and life-long "cyclic ambition" in his poetry. He also revealed that at the time he wrote *The Ardent Slingsman* he had even corresponded with Sabat Ercasty, and that, upon acknowledging receipt of some of Neruda's poems, Sabat Ercasty himself had confirmed Neruda's worst fears. The shock of recognition had thus led Neruda not only to withhold publication, but also to repress the Sabat Ercasty (read Whitman) model in his work. He thus turned to paring his style—"*reduje estilísticamente, de una manera deliberada, mi expresión*" ("I reduced stylistically, and deliberately, my expression"), a paring that resulted in the legendary *Twenty Love Poems and a Song of Despair* (1924). Once safely removed from a "cumulative" or "cyclic" poetry, the "love poems" succeeded in making a name for Neruda for the first time in his career.[20]

Neruda's desire for a "cyclic," "cumulative poetry" was his cipher for the Whitman model. It was by repressing, rather than giving in to that model—as forebears like Vasseur, Sabat Ercasty, and many a poetaster collected in Alegría's study had done—that he achieved his first distinctive voice, the melancholy lover's of the *Twenty Love Poems*. That the Whitman model should so thoroughly have permeated Neruda's most distinctive voice in the years to come, such as the militant prophet of *Canto general* (what counts here, let us recall, is the poet's *imaginary* relationship to Whitman)—demonstrates the persistence of that model in the constitution of his poetic voice. Indeed, nowhere does Neruda sound more like Whitman than in *Canto general*, though less so perhaps for the way in which that relationship is piously thematized (as in *Let the Woodcutter Awaken*) than for the analogy the entire book assumes. As chapter one of this book shows, *Leaves of Grass* was one of the models for *Canto general*. For this reason, I couldn't agree with Alegría's statement more than when he states that Neruda turned out to be less Whitman's disciple than his heir—someone who digested Whitman and then went on to write his own verse. But I could not agree with Alegría less than when he contends, in the course of making the same argument (317–318), that no traces of Whitman appear in *The Ardent Slingsman*, or in *Tentativa del hombre infinito*—*Venture of Infinite Man* (1925)—another of Neruda's early long poems, and that it is only in *Residence on Earth* where such traces exist. Neruda's relationship to Whitman was far more twisted. In the case of *The Ardent Slingsman*, Sabat Ercasty's imprint was enough to suggest otherwise; and *Venture of Infinite Man* happens to be the one book where, by Neruda's own admission, his "cyclic ambition" resurfaced (even if unsuccessfully) for the first time since receiving Sabat Ercasty's honest rebuff.

Borges's own struggles with the Whitman model parallel Neruda's closely, even as they show a more violent rebellion against the model. Though Borges knew English, he first read Whitman in 1917 in German translations that were filtered through his further contact with German expressionists, for whom Whitman had been a modernist hero of their own. In his *Autobiographical Essay* (1970), he reported:

> It was also in Geneva that I first met Walt Whitman, through a German translation by Johannes Schlaf ("*Als ich in Alabama meinen Morgengang machte*"—"As I have walk'd in Alabama my morning walk.") Of course, I was struck by the absurdity of reading an American poet in German, so I ordered a copy of *Leaves of Grass* from London. . . . For a time I thought of Whitman not only as a great poet but as the only poet. In fact, I thought all poets the world over had merely led up to Whitman until 1855, and that not to imitate him was a proof of ignorance. This feeling had already come over me with Carlyle's prose, which is now unbearable to me, and with the poetry of Swinburne. These were phases I went through. Later on, I was to go through similar experiences of being overwhelmed by some particular writer.[21]

Borges imposed then his peculiar stamp while acknowledging the twice-removed nature of his reception. For the young Borges, Whitman was no less than Literature incarnate, the first in a gallery of heroes-including

Carlyle, Cansinos-Asséns, and Macedonio Fernández—that throughout his career he would either choose personally or analyze impersonally as exemplary figures in the achievement of a literary destiny. Unlike the rest of his heroes, though, Whitman was the only model the young Borges went on to imitate faithfully in his poems, a fact whose anxiety he acknowledged implicitly by pointing to its "overwhelming" nature. That this was an internal disturbance and not just a superficial fancy for poetic technique is confirmed in Borges's description of "Hymn to the Sea" one of those early poems about which he later admitted: "I tried my hardest to be Walt Whitman."[22] What *being* Walt Whitman, and not simply *imitating* him, actually meant may in fact be the key to understanding Borges's troubled kinship—much as to *be* and not just *imitate* Cervantes happens to be the key to understanding the plight of that struggling minor writer "Pierre Menard." Borges offers, in other words, a *metaphysical* solution to the Whitmanian paradox, and thereby a precarious solution to his disturbing legacy, in Latin America or elsewhere. Yet in order to see clearly through the implications of this statement, we must differentiate such an alternative from two other options.

One obvious way to *be* Whitman would have been to translate his works, what Borges eventually did in his own 1969 partial translation of *Leaves of Grass*. Translating an author's work means, in effect, taking the place of that author, at least temporarily. The result is, of course, both short-lived and imperfect, for no matter the ongoing sympathy between author and translator, the otherness of the translator's task (as Walter Benjamin sadly discovered) is always a given. Borges himself echoed such melancholy in the preface to his *Leaves of Grass* translation, where, 40 years after his first attempts (and so, presumably, after that many years of trying his hand at translating), he described it as "oscillating between personal interpretation and resigned rigor."[23] Yet a second way to *be* Whitman was to identify and to write like his prodigious *persona*, much as the early Borges did in poems like "Hymn to the Sea," "Insomnia," or "Red Guard." And yet, to *become* that self-loving, romantic character meant, in turn, to be fundamentally at odds with the modernist ideal of aesthetic impersonality that Borges undertook even while writing these same early poems. The conflict, which in some ways is parallel to Neruda's early ambivalence, soon became evident and resolved itself in the following convoluted fashion.

Shortly after returning to Buenos Aires in the early 1920s, Borges attacked the growing Whitman cult in Argentina (and, by extension, in all Latin America) as a symptom of a romantic holdover that contemporary art should identify and eradicate. This militantly modernist position—whose implicit butt may have been Leopoldo Lugones, the Argentine *modernista* chieftain whom the *ultraístas* disparaged—appears in the 1925 essay "The Nothingness of Personality."[24] In it Borges argued, following Schopenhauer, that since the self is an illusion, then self and world cannot simply be coterminous, as Whitman disciples had assumed too simply. Thus focusing on the fallacy that "to try to express oneself and to want to express the whole of life are one and the same thing," Borges remarked that "[Whitman] believed he had only to enumerate the names of things in order to make their unique and surprising nature immediately palpable," and concluded, in his unique neobaroque Spanish prose: *"la egolatría romántica y el vocinglero individualismo van así desbaratando las artes"* ("Romantic ego-worship and loud-mouthed individualism are in this way wreaking havoc on the arts"(6–7)). Borges's real target, both then and later (as we shall see), was therefore not so much Whitman as Whitman's followers, including Lugones, whom Borges proceeded in the same essay to caricature at length. Yet it remains significant that Whitmanism should have been the explicit butt against which Borges defined his own modernist poetics, a fact that suggests not only the cult's prevalence but also the young Borges's personal stake in opposing and repressing it.

By then Borges himself had gone through the modernist mill of *ultraísmo* (the Hispanic synthesis of Futurism and Imagism) in Spain, where he had lived during two separate periods in the late 1910s and early 1920s. If *ultraísmo* was a cult of the impersonal image—*"agudezas imprevistas y maravillas verbales"* ("unforeseen wit and verbal marvels" [911])—Whitmanism meant an opposite cult of the self that was no longer operative, a paradoxical "new anachronism" that by then was so *démodé* not even his chic fellow-Argentines could recognize it as unfashionable. Repressing Whitman—which for young Borges meant repressing an "overwhelming" passion and an earlier Self—had already been the way to effect the self-discipline that made possible imagistic poems redolent of *"agudezas imprevistas,"* like the ones that appear in *Fervor of Buenos Aires*. With Neruda's *Crepusculario*, Borges's first book of poems shared the publication date of 1923, by which time both were sharing as well a common repression—less Whitman than Whitmanism, or at least the Whitman that lay deep within. Unlike Borges the militant *ultraísta*, Neruda the budding erotic poet had shied away from a cult of the image in *Crepusculario* and other early works. Neruda's repression of Whitman/ Sabat Ercasty had meant a self-imposed stylistic reduction; Borges's repression, by contrast, was done in the name of a more radical change in style and poetics, a different concept of poetry altogether that questioned, in effect, the very basis of the cult.

That Borges meant to attack the cult rather than Whitman became crystal clear four years later (1929), in the first of his two classic essays on the subject, where he drew the distinction further. Borges argued then that because fascination for Europe, rather than continental communication, unity, or solidarity is what binds all Americans together; and because Paris (the only Europe Latin Americans care about) cares only for the politics of literature, so our Whitman cult reflects all those prejudices. "Amazement, despite all, created a false image of Whitman: that of a merely saluting and worldly male, an insistent Hugo inconsiderately inferred time and again."[25] That is, our so-called (Latin/ North) American Whitman myth is actually a peculiarly French misreading that has ended up petrifying that sprightly American voice into a plodding institution, as plodding, that is, as the last clause of Borges's latter quotation makes it sound. To counter this myth Borges provides, in the same essay, his own translations of several passages from *Leaves of Grass* that, for him, demonstrate Whitman's contrary "trembling and sufficient laconic quality," Whitman's "denial of all intellectual schemes and appreciation for the primary senses"—that is, a discrete kind of poetics that sounds uncannily close to the very *ultraísmo* Borges was still advocating those years. For Borges, then, Whitman became ultimately an impersonal rather than a self-proclaiming poet; a heroic *persona* that compensated for a shy self but whose ultimate goal, consonant with his celebration of Democracy, was to identify with Everyone. "With impetuous humility," writes Borges in the second of his two essays, "he wants to resemble all men."[26] In so doing, however, Whitman succeeded in being not Himself, as romantic heroes, Byron to Valéry, had done, but Nobody.

Truly to *be* Walt Whitman, then, meant neither to translate nor to imitate. Translation reinforces rather than dispels Otherness; imitation, in turn, would mean incurring the very French myth being scorned. Indeed, Borges's fascination for Whitman did not exclude the knowledge that to imitate him would have meant sounding like Neruda, or at least the Neruda of *Canto general*, where Neruda had wanted to sound like Whitman: "*West of the Colorado River/ there's a place I love,*" says the speaker of *Let the Woodcutter Awaken*, turgidly. In this, Borges would have been no different from many a Whitman follower, American or other. "Numerous are those who have imitated, with varying degrees of success [*con éxito diverso*], Whitman's intonation," wrote Borges, tongue-in-cheek, in the preface to his translation; and then proceeded to enumerate, Whitman-like and with perverse vengeance, their names in a long string: "Sandburg, Lee Masters, Maiakovski, Neruda . . ."[27] Borges's solution, the third way to *be* Whitman, was therefore to elude the totalizing ambition (cyclic or otherwise) shared equally by American poets through imitation, and to realize instead that the way to *be* that "semi-divine hero of *Leaves of Grass*" was *through* none other than Walter Whitman, "man of letters," or else, as the preface to his translation put it, "the modest journalist from Long Island" (172) who wished to be that other self but could not.

Thus where Borges did attempt most fully this third way to *be* Walt Whitman was neither in an essay nor in a poem—though a late text like "Camden 1892," which re-creates Whitman's last moments, can certainly be read this way—but in "The Aleph" (1949), arguably the strangest of his bold short stories. For who, after all, is Carlos Argentino Daneri, the rambling poetaster of this tale, if not that self-conscious Whitmanesque bard whose life-ambition is to write an encyclopedic poem titled "The Earth," which, "consisting" of a description of the "planet," lacks "no amount of picturesque digression and bold apostrophes," and the "Argentine sections" of which ultimately attain the dubious "Second National Prize for Literature"? To Daneri's arrogance, Borges opposes the bumbling uncertainty of "Borges," timid admirer of the beautiful (and late) Beatriz Viterbo, who literally stumbles upon literary totalization in a cluttered Buenos Aires basement. The "Borges" of this story, an aspiring writer in his own right, is Borges's own self-projection of Walter Whitman ("modest journalist from Long Island") stripped here of *heroic personae*. He is none other than the banal "I" of the parable "Borges and I," the Borgesian passive reader. The paradox upon which the story turns, then, is that the totalization all poets seek—and the Whitman cult would be but one among several versions—obtains from accidents with the lowly and banal, and not, as Daneri fantasizes, from the self-conscious pursuit of the monumental. While Daneri—whose name, like Beatriz Viterbo's, as Rodríguez Monegal showed, conceals a parody of *Dante Alighieri*—seeks to be Whitman (like Dante, a totalizing poet), he succeeds only in achieving what even Walter Whitman had rejected as a writing method: "The laborious plotting of an ode or perhaps an allegory, complete with its vocative interjections and capital letters," says Borges in his preface.[28] "Borges," still pining after the unfaithful Beatriz, uncertain about his own literary talent and humiliated by Daneri's insufferable arrogance, stumbles upon *being* Walt Whitman and creating, in his confessional text, a totalizing allegory; Daneri, sedulously at work for years on "The Earth," mistakes literal prolixity for literary totalization and celebrates the abstract while pretending to write about the concrete. By contrast, "Borges," in his oblique elegy to Madame Viterbo, catches a glimpse of the universe (including a capsule summary of Daneri's "The Earth") while offering a personal confession. Daneri tries to sing like

Walt Whitman but fails; "Borges" cries like himself and succeeds in *being* Whitman, that is, in being *Everyone*, which is to say, *No One:* "I saw in a desk-drawer (and the handwriting made me tremble), obscene, incredible detailed letters that Beatriz had sent Carlos Argentino; saw a beloved monument in Chacarita, saw the horrendous remains of what had once, deliciously, been Beatriz Viterbo."[29] "Beatriz Viterbo," wrote the real Borges years later, as if pointing to the one central issue of this text, "really existed and I was very much and hopelessly in love with her. I wrote my story after her death" (264).[30]

IV

Is "The Aleph" a parody of *Canto general*? Such a reading would not be farfetched. We know, of course, that Borges wrote "The Aleph" at the peak of Perón's rule, its Hebrew title (lent to the book's) a dare to Perón's anti-Semitism. Under Perón, the entire Borges household endured penury and humiliation, even as Borges himself continued to write and publish. The story thus contains a veiled satire not only of the Whitman cult but also of the vulgarity of Peronist cultural tastes. Neruda, by contrast, prospered under Perón, even as his fellow-Communists were themselves being persecuted by the Argentine police, an irony that did not escape Borges when, years after *Canto general* was published, he complained that in the book's section on Latin American dictators (*The Sand Betrayed*) Neruda had conveniently skipped over Perón, possibly to obtain favor in a pending lawsuit in Buenos Aires.[31]

It matters little, of course, that Borges's story should have been published a year before Neruda's book. News of *Canto general* were known at least since the early 1940s, though what confirms that parody most may well be a typical Borgesian device—the anagram *DA-NE-RI* for *NE-RU-DA*.[32] More likely, however, what appears to be a direct parody may be a mere effect of Borges's satire of the Whitman cult. Its point was to identify the object of the cult as the desire for totalization—what could otherwise be called an anxiety of literary legitimacy or, perhaps, the contest for "encyclopedic form"—and to demonstrate instead the undeliberate, accidental nature of such status. Its lesson thus runs along proverbial Borgesian lines: at no time do we reach the Other more than when we are ourselves. Imitating Whitman in literature bears the same error as imitating our peers in real life: we succeed not in being that Other but in alienating ourselves, or else becoming a mere abstraction, like Daneri's "Earth." Only in being oneself, and in resigning ourselves to being Nobody, do we succeed in being the Other, and thus Everyone. The shortest distance between the Self and the Other, Borges seems to say, is not a straight line but a slip.

Borges's reading of the Whitman cult is also a reading of its history, a history of hidden (and, as we have seen, not-so-hidden) polemics, confrontations, and misunderstandings. Much, of course, remains to be said about that history, not the least of which is the relative lack of discussion in most studies (including this one) of Whitman's fortunes in the Luso-Brazilian world. Far from being a poet of heroic vitalism, Whitman for many of these poets—beginning, perhaps, with *Sousândrade*, the pen name for the nineteenth-century Brazilian Joaquim de Sousa Andrade (1833–1902), author of *0 Inferno de Wall Street*—was a poet of death, a writer of elegies, and of nihilist allegories like "The Sleepers."[33]

In time we have learned to view the Latin American version of the Whitman cult as one of several overarching cultural myths—like the Monroe Doctrine, Francoist "*Hispanismo*," the OAS, or the more recent globalization—that historically have meant to compensate for the fragmentation of (Latin/Anglo) American societies. As the political versions of such myths often collapse onto sheer political fronts, so the Whitman reception in Latin America contains a different story; namely, a dependent discourse whose production shows both the heterogeneity of origins and the denial of synthesis. What appears to be simple influence is actually a rhapsodic production of contradictory, often erratic effects.

Not the least of these effects is the myth, both poetic and critical, that lies at its origin. For restituting Whitman in Latin America rather meant creating him anew, contaminated either by third-removed translations or, as Borges complained, through sheer confusion with German and French would-be prophets, like Nietzsche or Hugo. Thus restitution would seem to be the faulty though no less necessary method whereby historical retrieval occurs in literary history, at least in the Latin American context; a history that, as we have seen in the last two chapters, bears important implications for the construction of specifically political myths. To an examination of that method in the exemplary case of Octavio Paz's modern restitution of Sor Juana Inés de la Cruz, the seventeenth-century Novo Hispanic nun, I devote my next chapter. Although I fear my reading may raise more questions than answers, I seek to understand there the precise workings of a dialectics of restitution as interpretive practice and, more broadly, as the basis of ethical, political, and indeed cultural judgment.

CHAPTER THREE

Sor Juana, Octavio Paz, and Poetics of Restitution

And so, different from myself
Amongst your plumes I fly,
Not as I am but rather
As you wished to imagine me.

Sor Juana, "To the Matchless Pens of Europe"

There is no meaning: there's only irony
and pity, and the pronoun that is transformed;
I am your I, the truth of writing.

Octavio Paz, "Though it is night" (1987)

I

Toward the end of *Sor Juana, or the Traps of Faith* (1988), Octavio Paz sums up his insights into the life and works of Sor Juana Inés de la Cruz (1648–1695), the seventeenth-century New Spanish poet and nun, by stating that "in the light of her work, it is her defeat that takes on a new meaning . . . her writings, especially her *Reply* and *First Dream*, are the best antidote for the moral righteousness that would make an edifying example of her fall."[1] "The moment we begin to weaken," he then adds on a more personal note, "seduced by guilt and punishment, we remember those texts and, as if questioning a mirror, we ask them, what was the real meaning of her defeat?" (488). At the heart of Paz's multifarious book—biography, critical study, and historical treatise, a work whose monumental size and range (650 pages long in its first Spanish edition) rivals classics of philology—therefore lies a moral intent. Like Phaeton, the myth of transgression that Sor Juana invokes defiantly at the end of *First Dream*, she falls defeated, but despite that defeat her last two major works still uplift us, her modern readers, with the moral strength to overcome those obstacles to which she succumbed while waging her embattled last years. Indeed, like Phaeton, for Paz an emblem of paradox—"the paradoxical image of freedom: flight and fall, transgression and punishment" (38)—Sor Juana was both transgressor and victim. Yet her actions at the end of her life openly belied, and even contradicted, her last works, thus forming an antithetical bond. In the abyss that opens between Sor Juana's final years and her two testaments one can therefore read the enigmatic text that constitutes what Paz calls the "real meaning" of her life.[2]

Paz's moral intent appears as early as his introduction, where he explains the meaning of his subtitle "The Traps of Faith": "The phrase is not applicable to all of Sor Juana's life, nor does it define her work; but I believe that it does describe an evil common to her time and our own. The recurrence of that evil is worth emphasizing, and that is why I have used the phrase: as a warning and example" (6). The effects of such "recurrent evil" is what Paz intends to combat by means of what he calls "an attempt at restitution": "I hope to restitute to their world, to seventeenth-century New Spain, Sor Juana's life and work. In turn, Sor Juana's life and writings restitutes the society of 17th-century New Spain to us, her twentieth-century readers. This restitution is historical, relative and partial, a twentieth-century Mexican's reading of a seventeenth-century New Spanish nun" (7).

One ought not miss that by Sor Juana's restitution Paz means restoring the work of this woman poet to its rightful place within the canon of Hispanic Golden Age literature alongside better-known male peers like Calderón de la Barca, Góngora, and Quevedo. But it is no less true that the view of restitution that dominates his argument is tied to a moral reading of Sor Juana's life. Such would be the elements that provide Paz, at the end of a long line of Sor Juana biographers, an exemplary story, a trenchant morality tale that is earmarked, for him, by the seeming disparity between the courage of Sor Juana's two testaments and the abjection of her last actions. The culprit in this tale, the recurrent "evil" to which Paz alludes, would be nothing less than the cooption of writers and intellectuals by orthodox bureaucracies—what in Sor Juana's case would be the Catholic Church in Counter-Reformation New Spain. "In a sense," Paz answered once to a pointed question in our 1988 interview "[Sor Juana] does embody the situation of the 20th-century intellectual, especially in totalitarian countries. Also, of course, the Latin American intellectual, understood as the one who struggles with constituted powers and with society but who is stripped of all weapons, except his or her pen."[3] Paz makes restitution for Sor Juana by identifying the causes and effects of her complicity, as a writer, with the orthodox bureaucracy of her time.

This chapter attempts its own antithetical reading of Paz's book by focusing on restitution as the central theme of an interpretive cluster, and identifying that very procedure as a cipher of both Paz's interpretive strategy and Sor Juana's poetics. The thrust of my argument derives from a confrontation of Paz's use of restitution as his avowed critical ethos, the origins of which I shall also examine, with the recurrent use of the same concept in both Sor Juana's works and the critical canon built around it. Though Paz himself would have been the first to deny it, restitution in the Sor Juana canon is not new, even as it finds in his own reading its most explicit formulation.

I therefore hope in what follows to show that restitution has always been, albeit under various guises, at the heart of the institutional reception of Sor Juana. Whether under the auspices of a Catholic orthodoxy, political liberalism, or a feminist politics, what I call the will or compulsion to restitute is determined by the convergence of several institutional strands; chief among which is the fact that Sor Juana was a Baroque woman poet. While each one of these three traits was enough cause for marginalizing Sor Juana, her successive restitutions are embodied not only in a particular critical canon, but, more pointedly, in the peculiar editorial reception of her works, or at least in the conventions at work in such an enterprise. Yet the linchpin of my argument lies ultimately not in historical proof, crucial though that may be, as in a reading of one exemplary poem of Sor Juana's that invokes restitution yet sets limits to it in ways that the critical canon has often chosen not to follow.

Beyond elucidating Paz's book, far and away the culmination of that canon, or contributing to the sexual politics of literary reception, I am interested here in reflecting upon restitution as a generalized practice in contemporary critical and cultural studies. I wish, in this ciphered reading, neither to defend nor dismiss Paz's book, at least not in any direct way, but rather use it as the grounds to inquire further into the actual workings of what Geoffrey Hartman once called, in an essay titled, "Criticism and Restitution," "the Philomela project (the restoration of voice to mute classes of people)," and which Gayatri Spivak has restated as "the foreclosure of the native informant."[4] For Hartman at least, such a project, as identified in contemporary critical and political practices, suggests that "the process of restitution (of righting wrongs) seems endless," as we face retrieving only fragments of the historical record and therefore condemning historians and critics to construct what he calls "legal fictions," to "invent, that is, a persona for absent presences" (32). Hartman protested, in the course of the same essay, the potentially negative social effects of such critical moves, and concluded that "recognition is the key to restitution" because "the end is not righting wrongs as such (there may be several rights in conflict)," but rather what he calls "a new sense of respect that is spiritually as well as politically effective" (32).

I remain skeptical of Hartman's general conclusions—the fragmentation of historical records may simply be a given of our alienated cultural legacy—but my chapter does take a useful cue from his essay by seeking to inquire into the nature of the "legal fictions" to which he refers, and which happens to provide the backbone to Octavio Paz's book. I wish to focus, instead, on the compensatory hermeneutics of restitution as a critical and cultural practice and ask, of this particular instance: precisely what sort of *persona* do we end up constructing in the process of inventing such "absent presences"? My working hypothesis is that, as a critical practice, restitution is supplementary in character—in compensating for a previous lack it exceeds rather than simply restores the original. And, further, that in Sor Juana's case such excess accounts for the construction of different *personae*—be it the "saint" of Catholic orthodoxy, the "martyr" and "dissident" of nineteenth- and twentieth-century Liberalism, or the "precursor" of contemporary feminism—that the critical canon constructs in order to domesticate the radical otherness of her work.

II

Restitution, the concept Paz invokes so insistently throughout his reading of Sor Juana, is, we may know, a moral and legal concept whose basic sense is the return of property to its rightful owner. As an instrument of commutative or exchange justice, restitution is executed through the repair of an injury or the righting of a wrong. Like restoration, restitution implies returning in kind or in value what has been unlawfully taken away; but unlike restoration, which does not presuppose a violated right and therefore falls outside the system of legal exchange, restitution always involves a means of reparation. The legal force of the term can be gathered from its etymology. Spanish *restitución* is a Latin borrowing, a *cultismo*, which is related etymologically to other cognates of Latin *statuere: estatuir, constituir, instituir, prostituir.* Corominas dates a first occurrence at the second half of the fifteenth century, and Fernández de Palencia's

Universal Diccionario Latín-Castellano (1490) also lists it. The legal roots of restitution lie in both Hebraic and Roman Law. The *restitutio in integrum*, the Roman antecedent for all modern statutes guaranteeing such a right, was an extraordinary power of the *pretor* that allowed claims on behalf of absent, demented, or minor parties. Hebrew law, in turn, outlines restitution as a corollary of the seventh commandment and is itself the basis for its further treatment in both canon law and moral theology. Aquinas's, for example, is only one of such treatments in moral theology.[5]

It is in its biblical versions, however, that we can identify most clearly the peculiar commutative logic that governs restitution as a broad cultural practice. Hebrew law points to two elements in any act of theft or damage: one, there is an imbalance of justice caused by the act; and two, there is guilt of the crime incurred by its performance. Restitution of what was taken remedies the inequity; and punishment, the exaction of *more* than was taken, intends to make amends for the guilt of the crime. As a practice, that is, restitution always assumes an accrued interest or surplus value that is meant to compensate symbolically for the transgression committed against the system of justice. As such, restitution always involves some form of expiation; indeed, if it is to restitute, and not simply restore, then the punishment *must* exceed the crime.

The Bible is full of such moments. "If what he stole is found alive in his possession, be it an ox, an ass or a sheep, he shall restore two animals for each stolen," (Ex. 22:3); "Behold, Lord, I give one-half of my possessions to the poor, and if I have defrauded anyone of anything, I restore it fourfold," (Luke 19:5). As a means of symbolic exchange, then, restitution exacts more than what was originally taken away. Yet a corollary of the same symbolic logic would be that, if such is the case, then we can never exact what was originally lost. For better or worse, restitution returns more of the same, or something else altogether. Such melancholy truth is what recent cases in U.S. federal courts, such as the one brought on by the plight of Japanese Americans interned during World War II, reveal with special poignancy. When these U.S. citizens recently won their case against the government for deprivation of legal rights under such a policy, they were made restitution, to be sure, though not so much by giving back the original time and dignity they lost—nothing could do that by then—as by a public apology, a retraction of the policy, and a hefty financial settlement.

Telling instances of the same logic can be found, though exercised with subtle differences, in actual critical practice, particularly in philology, the one discipline or method where the term restitution is most often used, though significantly as a metaphor for the procedures of textual authentication—as in the formal restitution of an original manuscript, or discussions of authenticity and attribution of authorship. Such use is authorized by the general restorative aims of the philological enterprise, philology being, in Guillaume Budé classic definition, "a means of revival and restoration." Since the Renaissance, following a well-known disciplinary pattern, philology has been an instrument in the revival of learning and, as a critical practice, the restoration of ancient meanings that are deemed true. Indeed, as part of a humanist enterprise, philology is directed at disengaging the *meaning* of a text, deemed to be a function of its linguistic structure and historical context, from the *truth* of a text, a function of its interpretation and therefore subject to the changing ideological needs of its readers. Tzvetan Todorov, in studying the role of symbolism in philological interpretation, draws usefully such a distinction by putting these two polar terms (meaning / truth) on a scale, on the former of which "there is truth, knowledge, reason, philosophy, science," while on the latter there is "faith, effect on the receiver, and, as we say today, ideology."[6] Todorov views a search for meaning to be the basis of *scientific* discourse, "in which the representative function dominates" (134), but he views the search for truth, dominated by what he calls the impressive function, as the basis of *ideological* discourse.

One need not extend further the implications of such humanist disengagement to realize that what I have called the surplus logic of restitutive practice sets in the moment the quest for "truth" exceeds "meaning" in any interpretive structure. One could of course assert that all interpretation involves some form of restitution—as, for example, when it attempts to restore in rational, discursive terms the theme or message displaced by the text's figurality. Yet Todorov's distinction does allow us to identify how certain forms of interpretation, such as the explicitly moral or ideological, strain the tension between meaning and truth so as to tilt the balance, so to speak, in the latter's favor, and render a discursive message that exceeds the text's figural language. Thus, philology would seem to exemplify the enactment of the one constant law in the surplus economy of restitution: as in litigation the punishment exceeds the crime, so in interpretation truth exceeds meaning.[7]

Such excess is what one finds most often in modern, historicized versions of philology, as in Romantic historiography (especially in Germany) whose echoes are felt strongly in Paz's book. For Romantic philologists, from Boeckh to Menéndez Pidal, philology was less a technique of textual criticism than one of decipherment whose aim was to understand and gain mastery over lost or alienated knowledge. A branch of learning with its own specific object, nineteenth-century philology had an additional ideological mission of its own: to overcome alienation and restore wholeness and harmony, viewing the past not merely as an antiquarian object but as broken pieces of a past whose reintegration into present life would restore a continuity between past and present.[8] The restitution of the founding texts of national literatures—*Beowulf, La Chanson de Roland, Poema de Mio Cid, the Nibelungenleid*—are all part of such a broad "rescue mission," combining elements from psychology and ideology no less than from linguistics or paleology, through the historical study of national languages and the piecing together of literary fragments from the medieval past. Within such broad aims, a historicized philology thus worked most often by subordinating actual knowledge of the past to the restorative needs of the present—what in Hegelian terms would be the subordination of a knowledge of the ancient Other to the mastery of a present Self. As Michel Foucault, who himself reflected upon this radical change of episteme during the nineteenth century stated: "God itself is perhaps not so much a region beyond knowledge as something prior to the sentences we speak."[9]

The shift in the aims of interpretation witnessed throughout the nineteenth century—from an understanding of the past in and for itself to one subordinated to the needs of the present—took place, as is well known, as the question regarding language changed from a concern with genealogy ("where does it come from?") to one about structure ("how does it work?"). Philology thus became, as Edward Said noted, "a way of historically setting oneself off, as great artists do, from one's time and an immediate past even as, paradoxically and antinomically, one actually characterizes one's modernity by so doing."[10]

Hence it could be said that, as a discipline, philology is riddled by an epistemological dilemma similar to the one at work in a field like ethnography: its methodology tends to *create* rather than *understand* its object. Unlike ethnography, however, which incorporates that dilemma into its methodology (even if it does not, ultimately, resolve it), a historicized philology represses that question in its efforts to gain mastery of the historical present. Rather than represent the past in its irreducible otherness, its purported goal, philology translates and reinvents it in the name of mastery of the present Self. Transposing such a historical scheme into the terms of our own inquiry, one could therefore say that philology is concerned in theory with restoration but in fact deals with restitution; "revival and restoration" is its ethical justification, its ideology, but restitution is its actual practice—giving back something other or more than what it purports to restore.

It would be tempting to press this inquiry further into the role of restitution as a broader symbolic economy whose workings have been partially revealed in, among other fields, psychoanalysis (Melanie Klein's dialectics of guilt and reparation in ego-formation, for example), ethnography (Marcel Mauss's studies of forcible exchange in his classic *The Gift*, 1925), and philosophy (Jacques Derrida's undoing of the notions of identification, attribution, and ownership in *The Truth in Painting*).[11] Such an inquiry would involve as well its most recent social expression—our ongoing national discussion about minority discourses in both the academy and society at large, a discussion which in many ways is a political debate about restitution rights for the oppressed and that, in its academic version, empowers the critical forum that Hartman calls the "Philomela project." Our age of litigation is also an age of restitution. Yet, I choose to focus on the role of restitution in philology in particular because I believe it is the one critical method closest to Paz's in this book, as indeed it is the method used or implicit in most studies of Colonial Latin American literature.

Indeed, in Latin America in particular, where the rise of Romanticism coincided with the aftermath of the independence wars from Spain and the search for political and cultural autonomy, philologists like Andrés Bello, as we saw in chapter one, provided ample justification for the specificity of a Latin American identity. Among these justifications lay the very vocabulary and even orthography of a Spanish American language, distinct from Spain's. And so, as the Middle Ages became for philologists the historical origin of modern European national cultures, so did the so-called Colonial period become for Romantic philologists, chief among them Bello, the origin of an independent Latin America whose cultural monuments—lost and alienated to the culturally autonomous present—were themselves in need of restitution. Hence Bello's authoring not only of a modern Spanish grammar, the first of its kind, but also his many studies on the classics of colonial literature, like Alonso de Ercilla's *The Araucaniad* (1569), the Renaissance epic which for Bello stood as the Latin American equivalent of Spain's *Poem of the Cid*.[12] Little did it matter, of course, that Ercilla himself had been a Spanish soldier, or that at the time he wrote his poem he was at the service of the Spanish king—hardly valid credentials for a Latin American cultural citizenship. What counted most for Bello was what he called Ercilla's "plain, reserved and natural style," which to him fit his version of Romantic literary taste, and the poem's depiction of the *araucanos* in as noble and heroic a vein as that of the Spanish conquerors, moralized traits that could serve as models for independent Latin Americans. The trouble, of course, is that since Latin America could not boast of a Middle Ages of its own, philologists set out to "invent" it, literally forge it out of the European vestiges of the colonial past. Yet too many things, not the least among which was the political nature of American societies, stood between that cultural project and historical facts. Philologists did not feel quite as alienated, for one, from the indigenous pre-Columbian origins of Latin America, whose difference was effectively repressed after three centuries of Colonial rule, as from their colonial Spanish origins. And yet it was to these origins that they actually felt closer, even as they rejected political differences that were deemed premodern and retrograde, following the drawn-out wars of independence. Abetting further that political difference was an aesthetic one—the Baroque aesthetics and rhetoric whose bankruptcy had been declared by Enlightenment critics, like Bello himself; what the Spanish philologist Menéndez Pelayo, in a bristling comment made in the course of his classic *History of Spanish American Poetry* (1901) denounced as "the atmosphere of pedantry and alienation in which Sor Juana used to live."[13] Indeed, the very attempt at the restoration of the Colonial period that philologists carried out in Latin America throughout the early nineteenth century was an enterprise haunted by the ghost of these differences. Such ghostly differences are what explain both the ambivalence with which writers like Bello (Perú's Ricardo Palma would be yet another case) viewed their task. It could be said that much of the scholarly work on Colonial Latin American literature remains, to this day, premised on the same philological will to restitution and that, with rare exceptions, its largely unquestioned premises conditions its ongoing practice.[14]

In the case of Paz's book on Sor Juana, whose entire first part is a broad revisionist reading of the colonial period in Mexico (what Paz calls by its more accurate, historical name of "New Spain"), such restitutive will is evident in two formal ways. One is mostly rhetorical and centers on the subtle use of litigation as its own "legal fiction." That much is suggested by the book's dual framing-markers—the "Prologue," whose statement of purpose I cited in my first paragraph, and the "Epilogue" (or last chapter in the original edition), titled "Towards a Restitution" ("Essay on Restitution"). The latter title had been the original one Octavio Paz had chosen for the lecture course on Sor Juana, the basis for the book we have today, he gave at Mexico's *Colegio Nacional* in 1974. The second, 1983 Spanish edition of *Sor Juana* further reinforced that code when it added an Appendix titled "Sor Juana: Witness for the Prosecution" that contained a recently discovered, astonishing letter, allegedly written by the nun, detailing her break with her confessor, the powerful Jesuit Antonio Núñez de Miranda. Known as the "Monterrey letter" (after the Mexican city where it was found), that document allowed backdating Sor Juana's dissent from the Church hierarchy to 1680, a full decade before the crisis at the end of her life. The letter surfaced while the first edition of Paz's book was in press and was restituted then.[15] Its timely discovery (with all the elements of poetic justice such timeliness can carry, or create) appeared to confirm one of Paz's working premises—that Sor Juana's so-called final conversion and renunciation of letters was a hagiographic myth that her church enemies had made up in order to justify their actions against her. Following the logic of all these structural markers, then, if Sor Juana's restitution to our time is the book's goal, then the reason must be because Paz believes that Sor Juana was unlawfully taken away from it. And if all of this makes of Paz's interpretation a clear-cut judicial argument, then pressing this argument with such force does amount to restituting Sor Juana to our present historical moment, including the Latin American time to which Sor Juana's life and work speak most directly.

Yet a second, strategic aspect of Paz's reading of Sor Juana would be the tension between what I called earlier, with Todorov's help, "meaning" and "truth," or else what could rightly be called Paz's attempt to balance the irreducible otherness of Sor Juana's past with his own perceived ideological requirements of the present—though Paz himself often insisted such requirements were moral and ethical rather than ideological. The strategic tension appears most clearly in Paz's attempt to juxtapose throughout a rigorous historicism to a demystified political reading. While historical rigor has the effect of bracketing those ideological features that Sor Juana's work elicits most frequently in modern readers—such as her feminism—the strictly *political* reading of her intellectual career is cast as an atemporal, trans-ideological moral structure: nothing less than the *exemplum* of "the traps of faith." And so, while, on the one hand, a strict historicism serves Paz's will to restitute Sor Juana, and thus facilitate a seemingly detached reconstruction of her life, works and historical context, the moral interpretation subtly stakes out, on the other, an interpretive claim that appears to avoid ideological reductions. Paz the voracious *interpreter*—in the dual sense of both translator and conveyor of meaning—is here intent on establishing nothing less than broad, atemporal truths such as the ones his moral reading would afford, not on identifying isolated meanings that could easily collapse as isolated political or sectarian debates. The entire program appears contained in "Though It Is Night," a long poem from his last book *A Tree Within* (1988), whose last lines respond uncannily to Todorov's polar terms:

> There is no meaning: there's only irony
> and pity, and the pronoun that is transformed.
> I am your I, the truth of writing.[16]

Indeed, whenever Paz stated, in his much-quoted Flaubertian *boutade*, that *"Sor Juana Inés de la Cruz, c'est moi,"* he appeared to be claiming, however ironically, that he *was*, in fact, Sor Juana, insofar as his moral biography had uncovered the *truth* regarding her life.[17]

Given the resistance of Paz's moral argument to ideology, then, it seems logical that his study should have become the butt of contending camps of the Sor Juana critical canon. Feminist critics like Stephanie Merrim, for example, complained that it provided "insufficient information, be it social or literary, regarding the *woman*'s world in which Sor Juana lived and wrote," while it contains "negligible efforts to situate the subject's works either in a female literary tradition or within the context of women's writing."[18] Arguing for what she herself called "a feminist restitution," Merrim admits that Paz did view Sor Juana as a *"feminist avant la lettre"* (18) since he took into account "the feminist ideological content" of her writings as well as those circumstances of her life "which would have inspired her proto-feminist stances," yet concluded that he viewed "Sor Juana, profoundly, in his way, as a woman, but not as a woman writer" (18–20).

The trouble with Merrim's critique was not so much that it was unjustified—Paz's omissions regarding a specifically female culture were indeed glaring—as that in issuing it with such conviction she did not seem as sufficiently historicist as she could, for example, by at least raising the possibility that the seventeenth-century Sor Juana might not herself have approved of such an exclusively "female" (or feminist) reading. Conversely, however, neither did Merrim venture far enough in the ideological claims of a feminist reading, at least not as far as a critique of Paz's historicist bias would allow. For in conceding that Paz's "work avoids the ideological blunders regarding the female subject, be they overt or implicit, so rife in other critical studies" (16), she appeared to approve of Paz's selective historicism. And yet, one could ask, why should the historicism that brackets a feminist reading not suspend as well other interpretations that Paz does press?[19]

Yet in order to gauge more fully the complications attendant to Paz's historicist bias, we must delve at some length into the origins of his interest in Sor Juana. With such a context in place, we will broach his reading of Sor Juana's final "crisis." Alongside we shall take up the challenge that his reading has elicited from other camps of the same critical canon.

III

Sor Juana herself had been a frequent subject of editions and discussion in the 1920s among Mexican intellectuals—Alfonso Reyes, for example, and some of the *Contemporáneos poets*—, but Paz himself barely mentions her in his essays between 1931 and 1943. It was in the late 1940s and early 1950s, however, while living in Paris and while writing both *The Labyrinth of Solitude* (1950) and its editorial offshoot—a UNESCO anthology of Mexican poetry—that Paz undertook a first reading of her work. Between 1948 and 1950 Sor Juana appears in no less than three essays: the famous passage at the end of the fifth chapter on the colonial period in *The Labyrinth of Solitude*, the passage on Sor Juana in Paz's introduction to the same anthology, and a full-blown essay on the tricentennary of Sor Juana's birth.[20] While in his 1950 book, Sor Juana embodied the conflicts of New Spanish society, conflicts that were expressed in the repression of New Spanish literary figures like herself, the introduction to the anthology defined her as a poet—"an intellectual [poet] . . . for whom life is an exercise of the mind" (29). Both essays point to the uniqueness and significance of Sor Juana's *First Dream*, her Baroque long poem, but in his book Paz speaks of Sor Juana's "double loneliness as a woman and intellectual," (112) of her need "to create a world in which she could live by herself," and of her image as a "melancholy loner" (116).

It was in his third essay, however, written soon after *The Labyrinth of Solitude* was published, that Paz took up again Sor Juana's status as an intellectual, shifting the focus from the poetry proper to the crisis at the end of her life. Whatever Paz will say now about the poetry is subordinated to his "crisis" thesis. "I fear," he wrote then, "that it may not be possible to understand her work and her life unless we understand first the meaning of this renunciation of the word" (4). Paz thus focuses on the telling coincidence of Sor Juana's personal crisis with the 1692 New Spanish riots, the former being but a symptom of a broader historical and political crisis of colonial order in New Spain. "Renouncing the rational word—keeping silent—and burning the Court of Justice, a symbol of the state, were acts of similar significance . . . The poet fell silent, the intellectual *abdicated*, the people rebelled" (5, emphasis mine). As in *The Labyrinth of Solitude*, where Paz had taken a shot at Sor Juana's "Catholic panegyrists" (111), so in the essay proper he presses the specifically intellectual conflict between herself and her contemporaries yet stops short of refuting the theory of Sor Juana's so-called final conversion. The essay expands upon the crisis by reexamining Sor Juana's immediate historical context and its political, rather than purely literary repercussions. "Denying this world and affirming the other were acts that could not have the same significance for Sor Juana than they had for the great spirits of the Counter Reformation" (7). Because intellectual knowledge

rather than mystical union was Sor Juana's personal portion, texts like
First Dream and her *Reply* bespeak a conflict that existed not only in New
Spanish society but within Sor Juana herself.

In a matter of two or at most three years, then, between publication of
The Labyrinth of Solitude and the homage essay, Paz shifted his entire reading of Sor Juana. The shift may be explained by one contemporary historical event that surely influenced, if not determined it altogether. I refer
to the polemic and subsequent libel suit that in late 1949 took place
between David Rousset and the Communist journal *Lettres Francaises*
over the existence of Soviet concentration camps. The polemic broke in
Paris, where Paz had been living since 1946, and it broke immediately
after *The Labyrinth of Solitude* was completed and just before, perhaps in
the very midst of, his writing of the homage essay. It was the second such
polemic regarding Stalinism—the first one had been being the famous
"Kravchenko Affair"—that broke in Paris that year. On November 12,
1949, Rousset, best known then as author of the bestseller *Les Jours de
notre mort* (The Days of Our Death) (1947), on the subject of Nazi concentration camps, appealed to former political prisoners in Germany to
join an investigating commission on Soviet camps. Rousset's appeal met
angry denials from *Lettres Francaises*, the leading Communist journal in
Paris, which in turn led him to sue the journal for slander. In the course
of the trial a number of documents and eyewitness accounts surfaced, all
related to the (then secret) Soviet penal system. Rousset's eventual success in the French courts did not, however, alter the opinion of Soviet
sympathizers, among whom figured writers like Jean-Paul Sartre and
Maurice Merleau-Ponty, who justified the existence of such camps as a
logical reaction to capitalism.[21]

For Paz's own part, years later he recalled Rousset's revelations as
"shaking, for they questioned the validity of a historical project that had
lightened up the heads and hearts of the best among us."[22] So moved
must Paz have been then that he and writer Elena Garro, then his spouse,
undertook to gather and translate into Spanish a selection of the documents from Rousset's *dossier* and had them published, along with Paz's
brief introduction, in the March 1951 issue of Buenos Aires's *Sur*.
Unsurprisingly, this was the same journal where nine months later the
essay on Sor Juana would appear. To be sure, neither Rousset nor Paz
addressed at the time Soviet cooption of artists and intellectuals in particular. (In his own brief preface, Paz even went so far as to claim that the
camps themselves were an "accident," rather than an inherent part, of the
Soviet system.) And yet what seems to have had had the greatest impact on
Paz were not so much Rousset's revelations by themselves as the reactions

of French intellectuals like Sartre and Merleau-Ponty, who dismissed them as anti-Soviet propaganda.[23] For Paz, who ten years earlier had broken with the Communists (among them Pablo Neruda, one of his early mentors) over the Hitler-Stalin Pact, had lived through Trotsky's assassination in Mexico in 1940 and, once living in Paris, became close to the André Breton wing of the Surrealist group, Rousset's revelations confirmed his own political trajectory.[24] Neither Sartre nor Merleau-Ponty, he wrote years later, "denied the facts [in Rousset's revelations], but neither were they willing to reach the logical conclusions that the existence of the camps made evident" (241). Indeed, we would search in vain to find explicit mentions of the Rousset polemic in any of Paz's contemporary texts on Sor Juana. But it would be difficult not to view the formula he used in the homage essay—"the poet fell silent, the intellectual abdicated, the people rebelled"—as the historicized version of the particular crisis he was witnessing in postwar Paris.

The year 1949, once Paz had completed the historical meditation of *The Labyrinth of Solitude*, thus marked the origin of his view of Sor Juana as a silenced dissident. That view broke through 20 years later in *Sor Juana, or The Traps of Faith*. In his "Preface," Paz tells the story of how "like an almost cyclically recurring presence, Sor Juana reappeared twenty years later" (i). Indeed in 1971, as Norton Lecturer on Poetry at Harvard, Paz was invited to teach an additional seminar, for which he chose Sor Juana and her works. "I gave the course again at Harvard in 1973, and in 1974, at the Colegio Nacional, delivered a series of lectures on Sor Juana, her life and her work" (i). The dates are again significant: 1971 was the year Paz returned to Mexico for the first time after his controversial October 1968 resignation as ambassador to India, following the Tlatelolco student massacre. And it was precisely in May of that year the infamous "Padilla Affair" broke publicly in Cuba, so called for the literary scandal wherein the Cuban Security Police arrested poet Heberto Padilla for alleged crimes against the State and forced him to recant publicly. As is well known, the "Padilla Affair" was denounced by intellectuals the world over. Among them was Paz who wrote then a brief text in which, pointing out the uncanny parallels with the Moscow Trials, he underscored "the disturbing religious tone of the confessions," since it seemed that "the self-divinization of leaders demands as a counterpart the infidels' self-humiliation."[25]

Once again, then, a crisis of intellectual dissidence coincided with Sor Juana's "cyclical recurrence" (the following Fall Paz would teach the course on Sor Juana at Harvard), only this time it was ringing close to home, next door to Mexico, rather than in the distant Soviet past. That

Sor Juana's case gradually became for Paz a synthesis of his dual concern for Mexican history and the troubled status of intellectuals in the contemporary world seems therefore evident. And that Sor Juana happened to have been a nun appeared to demonstrate, in addition, the crucial role that orthodox ideology—the Neothomist tradition in which Sor Juana had flourished—played in Mexican history and present political reality.[26] An alliance of politics and religion, what in the colonial order of New Spain had been the fusion of Catholic Church and absolute monarchy, was resurfacing 300 years later in the dogmatism of Latin American politics, much of it Marxist-inspired. The project to restitute Sor Juana, beginning in 1971, thus became part of a broader aim: to carry out the ideological and moral therapy of Mexico that, 20 years before, had begun in *The Labyrinth of Solitude*.

For his views on Sor Juana's final crisis in particular, in his book Paz built upon the archival research of Dario Puccini, a distinguished Italian Hispanist who in his own 1967 book on Sor Juana had unearthed data suggesting that her final crisis had been an offshoot of a contemporary power struggle between two church prelates over the archbishopry of New Spain.[27] Paz's further view of the crisis underscores that it occurred at a time when the departure from New Spain of Vicereine María Luisa, her personal friend and protector, had left an already insecure Sor Juana alone and vulnerable to her enemies and in search of new allies. Sor Juana chose then to become an accomplice of the Puebla Bishop Manuel Fernández de Santa Cruz in a backstage attempt to discredit Francisco Aguiar y Seijas, his more successful rival for the archbishopry, by composing a critique of a sermon delivered 50 years earlier by Antonio de Vieira, Aguiar y Seijas' Jesuit model. In turn, however, Sor Juana appears to have been betrayed by her presumed ally, who went on to publish Sor Juana's critique (without her blessing, she claimed later) along with the famous preface. The latter, authored under the penname "Sor Filotea," itself criticized Sor Juana's unusual bent for secular letters. Publication of this critique thus left Sor Juana to assume all public responsibility. As we know, it is to her pseudonymous editor whom Sor Juana addresses her famous, posthumous *Reply*, her intellectual self-defense and swan song.[28]

Sor Juana's role in this "conspiracy," according to Paz, had been a public yet veiled attack—it addressed not Aguiar y Seijas's views but rather Vieira's. That Aguiar y Seijas was also a well-known misogynist—a fact Paz underscores—could not help adding insult to Sor Juana's injury. And although in the *Reply* Sor Juana claimed she wrote her critique for private circulation, still Paz was unequivocal in identifying her complicity with Bishop Santa Cruz against his rival. Unlike Puccini, who believed that Sor Juana had been "an involuntary instrument of Fernández's [de Santa Cruz] machinations" (409), Paz asserted she "was his ally" (410), what in effect amounted to Sor Juana's gamble in a power struggle within the Church bureaucracy. It would thus be fair to say that within the legal fiction Paz constructs, Sor Juana plays a dual and not just a single role—as much accessory to the crime as witness for the prosecution. Moreover, what Paz found significant about this particular crisis was not so much its byzantine character ("it reflected one of the characteristics of Hispanic society in that period: rivalries between prelates were expressed only in veiled ways. Theology was the mask of politics" (409–410), as that it involved a woman, "the appearance of a female consciousness" (410). In such battles by proxy or indirect backstabbing, by means of which Sor Juana unwittingly set her own literal "trap of faith," Paz found a direct forebear of more recent cases of intellectual dissidence—like Zhdanov's attacks against the poet Anna Akhmatova, which were actually aimed at Grigor Malenkov, Zhdanov's rival, and Akhmatova's protector. "Less prudent than Akhmatova," Paz averred, "Sor Juana intervened in the quarrel between two powerful Princes of the Roman Church and was destroyed in the process" (403). Hence the bemused didacticism of a subtitle like "*Las trampas de la fe*," the traps of faith, which evokes those of eighteenth-century *romans philosophiques* like Sade's *Justine, or The Misfortunes of Virtue*, and which provides an ironic twist to the moral of the story.

It should come as no surprise that Paz's "conspiracy theory" should have raised eyebrows among the somewhat more sated *sorjuanistas*. Until then, the critical canon had viewed Sor Juana as either a pious exemplar or a martyred dissident, never as a betrayed accomplice. To Paz's arguments, which recast Sor Juana as an active agent, reacted Catholic scholars like Marie-Cécile Bénassy-Berling, whose own book on Sor Juana appeared the same year as Paz's. In a number of veiled responses to Paz's book, Bénassy-Berling countered the "conspiracy theory" by underscoring, among other things, that it was Bishop Fernández Santa Cruz, Sor Juana's presumed accomplice, who approved publication of her defiantly feminist *Villancicos a Santa Catarina* after publication of her Vieira critique. Her responses thus suggested that her alleged accomplice actually kept defending Sor Juana behind the scenes rather than abandoned her, as Paz claimed. The same critic disputed as well Paz's view of archbishop Aguiar y Seijas as a neurotic menace, or the instigator of the sale of Sor Juana's library and eventual capitulation, and proposed instead he was more of a "paper tiger," less a misogynist than a pious fanatic, since he personally approved Sor Juana's purchase of her convent cell (again, after publication of her Vieira critique) in open contradiction of her vows of poverty.[29]

Yet despite the philologically detailed character of such counterargu-ments, most revealing about the logic of scholars like Bénassy-Berling was that they left undisputed all the archival evidence—Puccini's research regarding the apparent rivalry between the two bishops—upon which the "conspiracy theory" rested. That is, in challenging what could be called Paz's ostensibly nonideological, *political* reading of Sor Juana's final crisis, the entire debate actually sidelined the importance that Church politics could have had on Sor Juana's crisis and veered the discussion onto Sor Juana's "conversion." The argument shifted, in other words, from the *cause* of the crisis (Sor Juana's complicity in the power struggle) to the *effects* of its final outcome (Sor Juana's conversion), or else from Sor Juana's political to religious identities. And so, it becomes less important, in such counterarguments, to disprove Paz's theory than to restitute Sor Juana *in yet another way*—an interpretive move that, not unlike Merrim's apparent sanction of Paz's historicist bias, left Paz's argument virtually intact. This line of argument seems to me important because through it I wish to redirect these questions: was Sor Juana's conversion forced, as Paz asserted, or was it instead a freely chosen decision, a natural outcome of her Catholic formation and religious vocation? And further, and more broadly: could Sor Juana's renunciation of secular letters, her pious self-abjuration, be made analogous to the contemporary self-humiliations of a Buhkarin, as Paz also claimed?

That Paz's interpretation constituted a political reading deserves to be stressed, then, if only because most reviews of his book—particularly those published in Mexico—missed it altogether, distracted perhaps by the reviewers' fascination toward Sor Juana's poetry, not to mention Paz's inspired reading. And yet, clearly, Sor Juana's specific historical and indeed moral value for Paz stemmed not only from her excellence as a poet, but from her (largely negative) exemplariness as an intellectual—as his use of the verb "abdicated," in the 1951 homage essay, had anticipated.[30]

It is at this juncture where a feminist restitution realigns itself with a Catholic one to dispute Paz's interpretation on historicist grounds. And it does so by stressing Sor Juana's fortitude and consistency throughout her final crisis. Georgina Sabat-Rivers, the one *sorjuanista* who pressed this issue furthest, cited the testimony of Dorothy Schons, Sor Juana's first feminist scholar, who upon inspecting the documents where Sor Juana foreswore her devotion to letters found "her handwriting contin-ued to be firm and clear until the very end."[31] "The factors that allow us to foresee the decision that she made toward the end of 1693," wrote Sabat-Rivers, "about a year and a half before her death in April 1695, had long been present in her writings: as a woman and nun of the seventeenth century, she put a higher value on eternity than on temporal concerns" (161). Sabat-Rivers went on to find the parallels Paz drew "between the pressure used by the Church at that time" and "the pressure used by Stalin's regime in the Moscow trials" "excessive," arguing instead that "the Church was promising the nun, in exchange for her sacrifice, a spiritual reward of eternal glory," and questioning whether we can "really establish parallels of this sort, between such different ideologies, without knowing in a direct way the mentality of the period and Sor Juana's intimate thoughts and feelings" (161). Sor Juana was not, she concluded, "the sort of woman who would let herself be terrorized" (161).

Even when one must agree with Sabat-Rivers's plea for a more sober historicist interpretation of Sor Juana's final crisis, it does appear equally as logical to concede the parallel between orthodox pressures that Paz invokes. Sor Juana may well have sought her soul's eternal salvation; and yet it would be difficult for her twentieth-century readers not to recognize at least echoes of it in cases like Bukharin's, whose prosecutors promised eternal glory in the heaven of History rather than the Christian God's. Indeed, there is good cause to believe—as the Monterrey letter shows—that "Sor Juana was not the sort of woman who could be terrorized." And yet, the handwriting Dorothy Schons detected was "firm" *despite*, not because of, Sor Juana's signing Church documents "in her own blood." I may seem to be defending Paz's interpretation against Sabat-Rivers's justified challenge, but I am actually trying to make a larger point about the Sor Juana critical canon, which encompasses both of their readings. Namely, that, as the preceding examples show, the various competing Sor Juana restitutions hold a supplementary relationship to one another; and further, that they supplement each other's lacks or omissions precisely because they are commonly built upon a series of questions, questions that in effect constitute *lacunae* in our knowledge of Sor Juana's life and times. While Paz's restitution does contain a trenchant critique of such *lacunae*—which he views less as a natural erosion of the Sor Juana archive than the result of centuries of willful censorship— this does not prevent him from constructing a "legal fiction" out of the fragments of Sor Juana's historical record and in the space left necessarily open by other restitutions. To take this latest sample of the debate: which side, one wonders, restitutes the true "feminist" Sor Juana—the one claiming she was terrorized into submission *because* she was a woman intellectual, or the one claiming she *resisted* such terror and thereby acted out of religious conviction?

If no restitution of Sor Juana ultimately is able to claim totalization, the reason for this may have to do as much with the nature of the Sor Juana archive as with the supplementary logic that governs the will to restitute. For all such surplus interpretations, which of course remain grounded on Sor Juana's biography, aim to account for her "tragic flaw"—what Paz, in his reading of *First Dream*, identifies symptomatically as her telling fascination for Phaeton "determined 'to immortalize his name in his ruin' " (384). It is this tragic flaw, either real or perceived, that triggers what can be described as nothing less than the "rescue fantasy" of the Sor Juana critical canon, that strange obsession on the part of scholars, editors, and even writers and artists, to *save* Sor Juana from mortal enemies, from oblivion, and even from herself. Indeed, the very paucity of information regarding details of Sor Juana's life and work and the subsequent "ruin" of her life records—the disappearance of most of her correspondence, for example—is one of the underlying *leitmotiven* of that rescue enterprise. Hence the speculative nature of most of the scholarship on Sor Juana, the recurrent questions about her life decisions, our ultimate uncertainty about the reasons behind her renouncing the world of letters, or her decision to become a nun; or else, the critics' perverse voyeurism regarding her sexual orientation, not to mention the frequent polemics regarding the correct attribution of her works which, to this day, continue to be the subject of spirited public debates in Mexico—*a mysterium regni* that has made of the restitutive will such a "natural" strategy in the interpretation of her works.[32]

IV

One of the first, or at least clearest, expressions of such a strategy may well have been the anxiety that Sor Juana's well-meaning editors have shown in their labors to rescue her texts. One thinks, in this regard, of Juan de Castorena y Ursúa, the colorful Bishop of Yucatán who put together Sor Juana's third and posthumous volume of poetry, the *Fama y obras póstumas* (*Fame and Posthumous Works*, 1700) and as such the man who holds the dubious distinction of being Sor Juana's first posthumous editor.[33] Indeed, soon after her death in 1695, Castorena managed to gather together Sor Juana's remaining scattered works and had them published in Spain, where they became a bestseller. The *Fama* was not exempt of problems, to be sure. Antonio Alatorre has shown that the edition angered many New Spanish bards who were incensed by Castorena's decision to exclude them from the *laudatio* section. More significant, however, is that in his lively "Prólogo" Castorena should have bemoaned the fact his edition was incomplete, owing to his leaving behind many of Sor Juana's manuscripts upon his hasty departure from New Spain—possibly in direct reaction to the troubling circumstances of her "disappearance." As Castorena put it, in his ultra-Baroque Spanish prose: "*Retirómeslo lo huraño, con noble intención de atesorarlos, o recatólos la discreción de mesurada prudencia que malogré obligar con mis instancias por la precisión de mi viaje*" (82); ["Stinginess took them away from me, thus nobly intending to treasure it; or else, discretion of measured prudence kept them, which I defeated by insisting that my trip back was imminent."] It should not perhaps surprise us that in the course of his preface Castorena should go so far as to solicit—much as in an "author's query" in the *New York Times Book Review*—readers' help in gathering Sor Juana's scattered manuscripts so as to restitute them physically in future volumes: "*así los privilegias de lo caduco del olvido, los indultas del peligro de un papel suelto, darás buenos ratos de diversión a los tertulios, y renuevos inmarcesibles al perenne nombre de la Poetisa*" (88); ["Thus you'll keep them from being forgotten, safeguard them from being attacked in a *suelto*, provide hours of pleasure at parties, and will renew the Poetess's fame."]

Little did Castorena suspect that finding that helpful reader would take literally two centuries, until 1873 to be exact, in the unlikely person of Juan León Mera, the Ecuadorian writer who is better known as the author of *Cumandá, or A Drama Among Savages* (1879). The latter was a bombastic if interesting Latin American romance whose author put together what could be called the first truly modern edition of Sor Juana's poetry.[34] Mera did not, to be sure, find Sor Juana's missing texts, but he did "rescue" them. By then, Sor Juana, along with Baroque poetics, had fallen victims to Enlightenment rationalism and the Liberal reaction against all things colonial. Between 1700 and 1873 not one single edition of Sor Juana's poetry was published. As the Brazilian poet Haroldo de Campos once rightly spoke of a "kidnapping of the Baroque" in Brazilian literary history, so we, too, can speak, in the case of Spanish American literary history, of "Sor Juana's kidnapping."[35] Where Castorena had struggled against incensed poetasters, lazy collaborators, and overzealous collectors, Mera had to contend with something worse: indifference and oblivion. Thus making use of his narrative skills, Mera's *Biografía y juicio crítico* [Biography and Critical Judgment], his long preface to the edition, reads like yet another romance, as he reconstructs his personal interest in the works of the Mexican nun, the obstacles he faced in obtaining reliable information about her, and the hunt after the texts themselves. The very "plot" of Mera's "legal fiction" consists of a pattern of downfall and redemption, loss and restitution, not so much regarding Sor Juana's texts (what one would expect normally from an editor) as the real historical author. He tells us, for example, how he first discovered Sor Juana in Ticknor's *History of Spanish Literature*, which describes her (quoting in turn Mexico's *Semanario pintoresco*, 1845) as "more notable as woman than as poet" (II). Reacting to such a comment with uncertainty at first (though barely hinting at Ticknor's sexism), Mera tells of his pursuit of the real Sor Juana, only to learn that "*el velo de la ilusión no se había rasgado del todo, aunque presentíamos que iba a desaparecer una estrella del cielo americano, y esto nos causaba enojo. La ruptura entre nuestro primer pensamiento sobre la autora y nuestro juicio posterior, entre el afecto que había anidado en el corazón y el rayo de luz que aclaraba el entendimiento, nos parecía inevitable* (V)." ["The veil of illusion had not yet been torn, though we felt that a star was about to fall from the American heavens, and this made us angry. The break between our first thought about the poet and our later judgment, between the affection nestled in the heart and the ray of light that cleared our mind, was therefore inevitable."] Mera thickens his plot further by explaining that his own "conversion" to the Sor Juana cause took place when he stumbled upon the famous "Hombres necios" *redondillas*, Sor Juana's signature feminist poem, the reading of which won him over and literally restituted her moral stature in his mind: "*La belleza poética y la belleza moral de esos versos nos entusiasmaron, y Sor Juana Inés fue restituida al honroso pedestal del que la habíamos bajado a causa de la cavilación en que nos pusieron las palabras del 'Semanario pintoresco.' Esa poesía, nos dijimos, no la produce sino un poeta; esa verdad no es hija de un alma vulgar: Sor Juana, fue, sin duda, mujer de gran talento, y sus obras deben ser dignas de ella*" (VI–VII). ["The poetic beauty and moral beauty of these poems excited us, and Sor Juana was *restituted* to the honorable pedestal from which we had lowered her because of the comment we had read in the *Semanario pintoresco*. Such poetry is written only by a poet; such truth is not the child of a vulgar soul; Sor Juana was doubtless a woman of great talent and her works worthy of her."]

Castorena and Mera's shared editorial confessions demonstrate the extent to which their common fondness for archeological metaphors, which both invoke as ways of justifying their attempts at a primitive philology, underlie their critical enterprise. Castorena, full of the rhetoric of conquest, speaks of excavating "rubies and gold" in Sor Juana's poetry; a jaded Mera, peeved by stingy bourgeois society, speaks of the same poems as "pearls taken out of the sea," along with a stronger desire still: "to shake the dust that covers the works we have been talking about, choose the most beautiful ones and hold them up to the light for the delight of all poetry lovers" (XIII). What grounds ultimately all such uncanny tropes of restitution (along with Mera's literal use of the word) is a common anxiety about editorial efficacy. One could even go so far as saying that such anxiety is but the hidden nerve of the Sor Juana critical canon, the institutional core of the rescue fantasy that underlies it. That is, under the confident language of Sor Juana's earliest editors lay the shared fear that her physical disappearance—whether by immolation, persecution, or oblivion—stood to make restitution of her work difficult, perhaps impossible. If Paz was indeed right about Sor Juana's truculent political context, then we can understand how this particular editorial anxiety is related to an unconscious fear of retaliation (still latent in Mera's time) on the part of the Church bureaucracy against a vocal dissident—as if restitution still carried the risk of transgression against some unspoken taboo.

And yet, despite our fairly clear understanding of all of these institutional constraints, what I fear we understand less is how the editorial anxiety stemming from a surplus logic of restitution has the further effect of over-determining the critical reception of Sor Juana's works, as if the need to restitute lost texts itself conditioned a restitutive mode of interpretation. Such critical anxiety, one notices further, happens to go hand in hand with the canonical signature of Sor Juana's poetics—the haunting lyrical voice intent upon the shadowy world of portraits and erotic desire. Indeed, no other formal feature defines Sor Juana's poetry more closely perhaps than this hauntingly elusive character, a point that Paz stresses repeatedly throughout his book. The contemporary Mexican novelist Sergio Fernández captured it best, perhaps, when he remarked that "even when the question does not disappear and the dilemma persists the more one reads, thinks, and interprets her, one gets the impression at each moment and at every turn that we're about to discover a latent, aggressive secret that perversely slips out of our hands."[36]

In light of all of which it would seem logical now to turn to the possible relationship of the institutional realities we have examined with Sor Juana's own poetics of restitution, such as they may be. For this purpose I wish to examine one text in particular—the famous proem and dedication to *Inundación castálida* (1689), the first volume of the first edition of her poetry—where Sor Juana herself happens to have addressed restitution as a poetic theme. My choice, as we shall see, is not all arbitrary, for it is determined by the poem's original use of restitution as a metaphor for interpretation and, as such, by the institutional privilege it enjoys, or should enjoy, within the Sor Juana canon.

A la excelentísima señora condesa de Paredes, marquesa de la Laguna, enviándole estos papeles que su excelencia la pidió y pudo recoger soror Juana de muchas manos en que estaban, no menos divididos que escondidos como tesoro, con otros que no cupo en el tiempo buscarlos ni copiarlos.

El hijo que la esclava ha concebido,
dice el derecho que le pertenece
al legítimo dueño que obedece
la esclava madre, de quien es nacido.
    El que retorna el campo agradecido,
opimo fruto, que obediente ofrece,
es del señor, pues si fecundo crece,
se lo debe al cultivo recibido.
    Así, Lisi divina, estos borrones
que hijos del alma son, partos del pecho,
será razón que a ti te restituya;
    y no lo impidan sus imperfecciones,
pues vienen a ser tuyos de derecho
los conceptos de un alma que es tan tuya.

To that most excellent lady, the Countess of Paredes, on sending manuscripts of verse that she wished retrieved from their possessors.

The child the slave girl has conceived
becomes acknowledged property
of the rightful lord and master
whom the mother serves in fealty.
    That harvest which a grateful earth
in plentiful obedience yields,
the owner's is whose mind was set
on wresting fruits from barren fields.
    Just so, fair Lysis, these poor scrawls—soul's children,
offspring of the heart—
revert to you, to be your own.
    No hindrance may their failings be,
since thoughts of one entirely yours
are rightly yours and yours alone.[37]

As is well known, the above sonnet accompanied 109 other texts that were destined for inclusion in *Inundación Castálida* (1689), Sor Juana's first published poetry collection. As its metaphorical structure would have it, all the poems in that book are the speaker-slave's children; just as the fruit of the land belongs to its rightful owner, so they rightly belong to the Countess of Paredes, the slave's master. As we know and Paz explains in his book, Sor Juana dedicated this first book of hers to María Luisa Manrique de Lara y Gonzaga, Duchess Laguna and Countess Paredes, her friend, protectress, muse, and (as it turned out) first publisher. It was to the Countess whom Sor Juana physically handed over the manuscripts for publication; thanks to her (or to her secretary, Francisco de las Heras, who acted as Sor Juana's agent and correspondent), *Inundación Castálida* was the only edition of her works Sor Juana actually got to approve. In his book Paz does not dwell on this particular poem but does refer to it as "one of the most impressive testimonies" (266) of the correspondence that the two women must have exchanged.

The proem is actually an epistle built upon an editorial allegory that provides a portico to the book and logically (this being a *first* book), to all of Sor Juana's work. It is significant, however, that despite its inherent aptness and obvious legitimacy, this sonnet was never again, until very recently, to serve as the proem to Sor Juana's works. Replacing it consistently since then (beginning with the second, 1690 edition of *Inundación castálida*) has been the innocuous (perhaps even anonymous) *romance* "Al lector."[38] It would take almost three centuries, until 1982, for this sonnet to be restored to its rightful place in Sor Juana's works in Sabat-Rivers's critical edition of *Inundación castálida*. The canonical, four-volume edition of Sor Juana's *Obras Completas* (1951–1954) does not, to be sure, suppress the sonnet, but its editor, Father Alfonso Méndez Plancarte, following the custom established since the 1690 edition, displaced it from the preface and relegated it to the section he named *Lírica personal*. By disclosing the proem's peculiar fate I do not mean to suggest we have here a case of copyright infringement; seventeenth-century authors simply did not have the sorts of rights over their works that modern authors do. And yet, the effects of this displacement are particularly telling, certainly more than the result of defective variants.

Sor Juana's proem was not only the preface to the only edition whose order and contents she got to approve; displacing that proem has had the further effect of suppressing the dedication to the Countess. An obvious hyperbole of the Countess herself, with whom Sor Juana is known to have had an intense personal relationship, such dedication is far from the ad hoc text Sor Juana's editors appear to have deemed it, and is rather an essential component of the "performative unity" that holds *Inundación castálida* together as a lyric sequence.[39] "Lysi" or "Lísida" (the Countess's poetic name) is invoked explicitly in at least eight other poems (numbers 17, 19, 20, 30, 51, 52, 63, 70) throughout *Inundación castálida*, references that structure the dramatic role this particular poetic character plays within it. More crucial, however, is that the last text in the sequence (numbers 107–110) is the *Neptuno alegórico*, the Baroque text Sor Juana was commissioned to write for Manuel de la Cerda Manrique de Lara (the Countess's husband) for decoration of the triumphal arch that was built in 1681 on the occasion of the vice-royal couple's arrival in New Spain. Thus the "arch" that ends the sequence is itself one of the two pillars of the book's "arch" extending from the proem. With Baroque symmetry, the book thus begins and ends, arch-like, with each member of the vice-royal couple presiding emblematically over the entire sequence. In reordering her works, Sor Juana's editors all but tore down this textual arch, no less than they suppressed, as we shall see, the proem's crucial statement.

Even if we took into account the unstable status of proems in Renaissance poetry (Petrarch's *Rime sparse* comes immediately to mind), one wonders whether there might not be some link between the poem's peculiar editorial history—a history of textual *de*stitution—on the one hand, and its overt thematics—textual *re*stitution—on the other.

Using restitution as its editorial conceit, the sonnet is built upon a series of legal analogies, based on courtly love conventions, which define the enclosed or ensuing poems to which this one serves as proem. In turn such analogies form part of the "affected modesty" *topos* that defines the poet's view of her own writing. Lysis (that is, the Countess Paredes) appears as the poet-slave's master who, rather than offer poems of her own, actually restitutes them to whom she properly views as rightful owner. The extended metaphors of family and agricultural law thus create the hyperbole of Lysis—lady muse and proprietor, lady and landlady—and, indirectly though no less significantly, the *litotes* or ironic understatement of the poet's achievement. This understatement is ironic, of course, because the reader knows well ahead that all of the ensuing poems are none but the author's—streams flowing out of a "Castalian Flood." And as the poems are cast as "*borrones*" (scrawls) whose "*imperfecciones*" (failings) threaten to have them rejected by Lysis, so the poet-slave's authorship, Sor Juana's *persona*, comes through as Lysis's shadow or ghost, an adoring stenographer whose second-order scripts aspire to return to their blank—because necessarily silent and therefore superior—origin. In turn, this regressive self-understatement flows against the grain, thereby creating a further chiasmus effect, of the increasing idealization with which the speaker views the poems—a great chain of being (of clear Neoplatonic resonance) from the base "child the slave-girl has conceived" of the first stanza, to the higher "fruits" of the second, on to "soul's children" in the first tercet, finally to become the idealized "soul's conceits" in the last verse. The poem's argument can be summed up thus: if my soul belongs to you, then my poems, being the soul's children, must properly belong to you, too. So rather than simply letting you have them, I actually give them back to you: I make restitution.

As a proem, the sonnet works beautifully, I think; better at least than the plodding "*Al lector*" [To the Reader] with which most editions of

Sor Juana's poetry replace it. Far from restrictive, the address to Lysis, the sonnet's implicit reader, structures an apostrophe to the reader in general and therefore sets up an ideal proem that, in addition to forming an arch with the *Neptuno alegórico*, encompasses the entire volume. How can we account, then, for the bizarre functional disuse into which this sonnet fell for the next three centuries? Sabat-Rivers (27–28) does not speculate on the matter, except to cast doubts on whether Sor Juana could possibly have revised any editions subsequent to this one—which falsely hailed them as "corrected and improved by its Authoress"—given the slowness of communication between New Spain and Madrid. Neither does Méndez Plancarte, editor of the canonical *Obras completas*, who three centuries later opted for reordering Sor Juana's poems according to theme and versification rather than chronology.

One might well question, under such circumstances, whether a text so redolent of ironic understatement and which proposes the figure of a stenographer no less as the poet's *persona* could possibly work well as a proem. How could this ghostly image, this uncomfortably ventriloquial speaker, possibly have been favored by editors eager to publicize this "Unique, Tenth Muse" (so goes the title page of *Inundación Castálida*) whose overflow threatens to drown us all in a flood of poems? In contrast, the favored *romance* "To the Reader," though still exploiting the rhetoric of false modesty, leaves little room for doubt: "*Estos versos, lector mío*" [These verses, reader of mine] reads the first line, turgidly. Even if this poem turned out (as I venture) to be not Sor Juana's but an anonymous patch, there is little question here of a concrete poet, standing on two feet, addressing the reader. And yet one disturbing question would still linger: is this Sor Juana—or better said, is this the *persona* Sor Juana wished to deploy and exploit in her poetry?

Well-intentioned editors, from Castorena y Ursúa to Mera and Méndez Plancarte, along with legions of truly noble readers, the culmination of whose efforts may well be Octavio Paz's magnificent book, have aspired to render us a strong, clear image of Sor Juana. But their separate attempts at restituting her image continue to fall short precisely in the same measure that Sor Juana, or at least the Sor Juana that comes through in the poetry, succeeds in *not* allowing this to happen—in *resisting* restitution. The effects of the editorial prejudice we have just examined, which I take to be a telling institutional decision—further evidence of a gender politics of literary history that is as old as Sappho, wishes implicitly to restitute a concrete poetic voice.[40] Yet we also witness the extent to which this decision actually works to undo Sor Juana's original choice, to the point of keeping it suppressed for almost three centuries— an institutional choice that, one might add, uncannily repeats and prolongs

Bishop Fernández Santa Cruz's unauthorized publication of Sor Juana's critique of the Vieyra sermon. The institutional effects of that suppression can be further gathered from the summary attached to the head of the sonnet (which Paz attributes correctly to Father Calleja, Sor Juana's first biographer). With a typically ambivalent logic, it betrays the canon's trademark editorial anxiety while also thrusting upon the speaker a concrete personal identity that the poem rejects explicitly—slaves having no personal identity of their own.

It would be difficult, finally, simply to collapse the sonnet's chosen rhetoric as one more instance of false modesty. Acting as both proem and dedication, the text reworks self-consciously the figure of the self-effacing slave, thus making of destitution the very source of Sor Juana's poetics, the paradoxical foundation of her language of desire. Sor Juana's *persona*, in other words, undertakes well enough the task of restitution. But it restitutes not so much the Self as much as the Other; not the poet or her *persona*, so much as her subject, and implicitly, her reader. Instead of the concrete voice her editors were so anxious to promote, she gives us back a ghost: restitution becomes *de*stitution, an emptying-out of the poetic self.[41] And in making this rhetorical choice, Sor Juana appears to be relying less on the courtly love conventions the sonnet so visibly exploits than on the hermetic myth of Isis, the one myth Paz views as central to Sor Juana's personal mythology and the one she first elaborated fully in the *Neptuno alegórico*, the text at the closing end of *Inundación castálida*. In the sonnet, we should note, the myth appears as a subliminal blueprint in the Isis homophone of "L[ysis] L[ysi]." For the myth of Isis and Osiris, the foundation myth for the cultural practice of mummification, is itself a hermetic (and therefore alternative) myth of restitution—Osiris'/ transformation into the Egyptian God of Death through his murder, his body's dispersal, and the eventual retrieval of his fragments by Isis for the sole purpose of resurrecting him magically, only to find, in the end, that an irretrievable fifteenth missing part (Osiris's phallus) fates his restitution to remain incomplete. Mummies are, in fact, restituted bodies, but they, not unlike the critical editions of restituted texts, are either more than or different from the bodies they purport to retrieve.[42] It is such melancholy truth that resonates in Sor Juana's proem and, I dare say, in all of her poetry. For instead of a secure and self-assured voice in it we find something more disturbing, perhaps even painful—what Patricia Spacks has called a "rhetoric of uncertainty," a language that, consistent with a traditional feminine discourse, denies itself both the security of legitimacy and the credit of accomplishment.[43]

V

My conclusion points therefore to one question: how do we read Sor Juana without betraying Sor Juana?

The question arises at the end of this chapter as naturally as the questions regarding Sor Juana's identity and the personal decisions she took during her life arise at the beginning of *Sor Juana, or The Traps of Faith*. It is perhaps to Octavio Paz's credit that 500 pages into his book, amidst his Epilogue "Towards a Restitution," he nevertheless admitted that the distinctive element in Sor Juana's poetry was "an elusive though clearly perceivable quality" that he could only describe by recourse to a series of questions: "Lucidity? Irony? Knowing how far to go and where to stop?" (482). Well beyond the pertinence this statement, these questions, may have for Sor Juana studies, one must admit that the honesty with which Paz himself faced them then has been infrequent among contemporary debates about restitution—those latest zealous drives toward vindications of the Other which the readings this book contains attempt in part to unearth and criticize. Suffice it to say that be they called academic exoticism, colonial tolerance, or plain tokenism, benign forms of restitution usually share one thing in common: when unchecked, they subordinate the Other to the Self's salvational perception. Rather than recognize the Other's stubborn difference—which would lead to a further humbling recognition of the Other's equality, and perhaps, superiority—our restitutions pigeonhole the Other within prescribed institutional roles that are designed to fit the Self's mystified self-righteousness. They claim to work on behalf of the Other but actually work to ease the Self's moral and historical conscience.

To questions like Paz's, and indeed our own, Sor Juana herself appears to have responded in her last unfinished *romance*, the ballad known as "To the Matchless Pens of Europe" in which she reacted, in both surprise and confusion, to the laudatory poems that were written about her and were appended to *Inundación castálida*. More than the simple note of thanks to admirers for which it has been taken, that last poem of hers constitutes one of Sor Juana's few reactions on record to the critical reception of her poetry, and underscores, in a move typical of her frequent meditations on portraiture and of Baroque aesthetics in general, the vexing disparity that mediates between the self and its representation. Sor Juana's reading—what amounts to her critical position toward her poetry—avows an antithetical view of personal identity in which the insight yielded by the poem derives in directly *inverse* proportion to the revelation of a self:

> No soy yo la que pensáis
> sino es que allá me habéis dado
> otro ser en vuestras plumas
> y otro aliento en vuestros labios.
>
> Y diversa de mí misma
> entre vuestras plumas ando, no como soy
> sino como, quisísteis imaginarlo.
>
> [I am not at all what you think
> What you've done is attribute to me
> A different nature with your pens,
> A different talent with your lips].
>
> [And so, different from myself
> Amongst your plumes I fly,
> Not as I am but rather
> As you wished to imagine me].[44]

The pointed self-denial shown both here and in the proem we have examined amounts to Sor Juana's gendered version of the paradoxical discovery made by all great writers, usually toward the end of their careers—namely, that the historical and existential self, to whose knowledge that career was largely devoted, disperses into fragments each time the writer sets pen to paper. The writer knows by then that historical, existential, and even judicial claims will eventually be made to compensate for that dispersal. But she also knows that all those well-intentioned claims, like her own earlier attempts at self-knowledge, will remain hypothetical, subject to stubbornly imaginary evidence. Not that it should simply be a matter of avoiding restitution, for it clearly cannot be, short of obliterating the writer's record—Kafka's unfulfilled wish. The writer *knows* that she will be misunderstood, her works misread. But at such late stage all that remains is to provide a critique of restitution, to demystify and set limits to its future claims, along with comforting the reader's despair at the inevitability of misunderstanding.

Sor Juana's discursive strategy, her precarious way of disclosing and concealing her self in the poem, is to urge us to reconcile ourselves to a sad but nevertheless poignant truth: that we may in fact never know who she really was, what she really thought, or indeed what was the "truth" regarding her "defeat." By resisting restitution, she preserves her difference and otherness; and by thus resisting, she urges the question about "Sor Juana," like all such important questions, to remain.

CHAPTER FOUR

Through the Grapevine: Rulfo, Garro, and National Allegory

The language of the exile muffles a cry, it doesn't even shout.

Julia Kristeva

Gossip is the opiate of the oppressed.

Erica Jong

I

My meditation on restitution as a critical practice evokes obvious conceptual corollaries, such as the twin issues with which it is associated most frequently in contemporary theoretical discussions. The first of these, nation studies, is historical, and concerns the ways in which cultural evidence is marshaled to describe the contents of a national imaginary, often buried or at least unattended. The role of the critic in such practice is to restitute cultural contents that play a role in discourses that either construct or undermine collective identities, such as those encompassed by the concept of nation. Yet clearly the gap between the original nature of those contents and its eventual critical restitution, its retrospective rendering, ought to be mediated by, or at least checked against, the primary evidence of the national archive. And, needless to say, such practice does not always work neatly in favor of encompassing all the identities that are in need of articulation. The other issue, allegory, which is rhetorical rather than historical, would seem to go to the heart of the restitutive will, in the sense that every allegorical interpretation, by its very definition and structure (allegory being literally the discourse of the other, *allos agoueirein*), attempts to translate one code or set of ciphers onto another, perhaps more accessible, set of signs. Thus allegorical reading would appear to be a primary restituting activity, as decipherment, subject to speculation or correct reading, remains a matter of constant slippage.

This chapter brings national history and allegory together in a reading of two canonical novels, *Pedro Páramo* (1955) and *Recollection of Things to Come* (1963). In returning to Mexico, I wish now to focus on narrative, and specifically the novel, the genre that traditionally most enjoys a historicist privilege. Indeed, my interest so far in texts and contexts other than narrative has been in part an attempt to correct the common view that historicist issues are an exclusive province of narrative. For close to half a century now Latin American Boom novels, part of the contemporary canon—from *One Hundred Years of Solitude* and *Three Trapped Tigers to Terra Nostra* and *The War of the End of the World*—have virtually monopolized critical attention by virtue of their alleged advantage in the critique of historical and social forces and thanks, in great measure, to our combined interest in the collective historical fate of Latin America and in what Fredric Jameson once called narrative's privilege as a "socially symbolic act." And yet, reading *Canto general*, the Latin American reception of Whitman, or else Octavio Paz's reading of Sor Juana goes to show alternatively, I think, the presence not only of a strong historicist imagination in those non-fictional (in the sense of non-novel) contexts, but of narratives of their own that piece together stories of political contest and poetic appropriation. That is, narrative in such contexts becomes ciphered in the form of (equally valid) stories of historical engagement and process, as they arrange causal accounts of actors and events that endow meaning and themselves argue for social change.[1]

Rather than better-known Boom novels, I choose here two relatively marginal canonical works that actually preceded them in time, that are credited with inspiring much of their poetics, and that, despite their common appearance, deal in oblique ways with the historical conscience otherwise flaunted by their better-known heirs.[2] Such appearance is due, in great measure, to their common narrative mode: so-called Magical Realism, a mode which would set them off, at first sight at least, as mere fantasy tales devoid of historical or contextual reference. Granted that "Magical Realism," as concept and cultural practice, has often been defended on the precise grounds of its engagement with historical issues. Such at least is the defense often mounted in the exemplary case of García Márquez's *One Hundred Years of Solitude*. But that defense has not been precise or sufficient enough, I think, to counteract the effects of canonical domestication, at least not to the extent of undoing pervasive critical habits. Indeed, whatever the actual historical content of "magical realist" texts may be, the common view persists that these two novels in particular—Borges's stories would be yet another instance—constitute the ambivalent origin of future Latin American novels that pointedly avoided the "moral pitfalls" of such ahistorical fantasies.[3]

For such allegedly damaging speculation the novels themselves provided enough fodder. After all, Rulfo's is a ghost story in two halves, in the first of which we witness Juan Preciado's fruitless search for his father, the title character, upon returning to Comala; while the second, as the reader discovers everyone in Comala is dead, offers piecemeal Pedro Páramo's personal story, a village chieftain whose frustrated love for Susana San Juan ends up destroying both town and inhabitants. *Recollections of Things to Come* is a ghost story, too, or at least much of it is, and like Rulfo's it is split into two halves, each devoted to the story of a woman; the first, to Julia Andrade, whose physical beauty overpowers Francisco Rosas, the general whose army division occupies Ixtepec. This first half ends magically when Julia betrays Rosas and runs off with Francisco Hurtado, her mysterious lover, during an elopement when time literally stands still. The second half focuses on Isabel Moncada; she, too, falls in love with General Rosas despite his having killed one of her two brothers. As in the novel's first half, then, the second one ends when the spurned woman petrifies—she literally (and magically) turns into stone. Thus Rulfo and Garro tell stories with two common themes: village life and forlorn desire. They also share a common assault on verisimilitude. In Garro's, the village itself, rather than the characters, tell the story; in Rulfo's, the narrative voices come from the dead.[4]

What interests me about these two works, however, is less that shared assault, or else the "magical realist" content they have in common—less still how that content allegedly articulates a "primitive" Latin American identity, distinct from Western epistemology—as their shared engagement with the historicist mode of national allegory. I wish to understand, through both formal examination of narrative procedure and internal historical reference, the workings of this mode in two seemingly ahistoricist narratives. But I also wish to identify in gossip, that is, in what we commonly call idle or malicious chatter, the specific content of that national allegory.

My interest in gossip, hardly a historical or even rhetorical category, may perhaps seem surprising. Gossip, rather than more formal modes of discourse and speech, would seem far from commanding analytical status in the context of more serious social and political issues often treated in canonical narrative, less so in those that aspire to the status of national allegory. But as I attempt to identify material evidence of historical life in a variety of contexts, I find myself attracted to alternative discursive modes that cipher social and historical meaning; gossip, I believe, constitutes one such privilege. In order to do this, however, we must first put aside whatever negative preconceptions we harbor of gossip as simple badmouthing and begin considering it as a form of communal discourse, or else as a form of intimacy. "Gossip as a phenomenon," writes Patricia Spacks, whose book provides one of the better guides on this subject, "raises questions about boundaries, authority, distance, the nature of knowledge, and demands answers quite at odds with what we assume as our culture's dominant values."[5] Thus starting with national allegory as a polemical term and concept, then going through the common historical context and a structural discursive model, my argument will lead up to an inquiry into why gossip is significant in these two novels, and, indirectly, how the shared use of gossip serves as a comment on Mexican historical life.

II

Fredric Jameson's "Third World Literature in the Era of Multinational Capitalism" coined national allegory as a concept in 1986 and since then underwent a polemical reception.[6] In it Jameson set out to understand, waxing bold, the difference between first and third world cultural productions by way of analyzing the alleged preponderance, in the third world, of what he calls "national allegory" and its significance. "All third world texts," he wrote, "are necessarily allegorical, and in a very specific way: they are to be read as what I will call national allegories . . . particularly when their forms develop out of predominantly western machineries of representation, such as the novel" (141). This was, Jameson admitted, a "sweeping hypothesis," and supported it with the belief that whereas in first world cultural production we find a "radical split between the private and the public, between the poetic and the political," (141) between sexuality and the unconscious on the one hand and "secular political power," on the other, in "third world texts, even those which are seemingly private and invested with a properly libidinal dynamic, necessarily project a political dimension in the form of national allegory." In such national allegories, "the story of the private individual destiny is always an allegory of the embattled situation of the public third-world culture and society" (142).

Jameson's idea was, clearly, both old and new. That certain texts within national literatures can and often do become privileged representations of national values and aspirations is an unstated cliché of literary history, as shown most often in realist narratives whose mimetic language easily represents collective values. Phrases like "the great American novel" or Balzac's "novel as the private of nations," attest to that cliché. Indeed, though often unstated, this has been the precise basis for critical interest in so-called nation studies: certain texts, particularly narrative ones, can be viewed as embodiments and promotions of national formation. Homi Bhabha, in his critical anthology *Nation and Narration* (1990), called this type of study "the nation as metaphor," and thereby proceeded to give us a list of candidates: *Middlemarch, One Hundred Years of Solitude, War and Peace, Moby Dick, Things Fall Apart.*[7] In each case, the nation— Nineteenth-century Britain, twentieth-century Colombia, *Risorgimento* Italy—is the working metaphor, and the novel its allegory. Following the same logic, then, each Latin American nation would have its own analogous list of likely candidates—as in the specific case of Mexico, *The Itching Parrot, The Underdogs, The Death of Artemio Cruz, Here's to you, Jesusa!* or indeed the two novels at hand. So, at least, was the argument behind a number of canonical studies of Latin American criticism that emerged at roughly the same time as Bhabha's legendary anthology.[8]

For national allegory Jameson himself offered three components. First, while available in all cultural zones, national allegories within the so-called third world display an overtly conscious or manifest link between psychology and collective issues: "libidinal investment is to be read in primarily political and social terms" (144). This is so, the argument goes, because in the modern first world the link between politics and the unconscious is repressed, while in the so-called third, due to its relative marginality from an alienating modernization, the same link remains conscious and overt. To summarize: "third world allegories imply a radically different and objective relation of politics to libidinal dynamics" (142).

A second, important point of the same argument is that allegories are the favored mode for representing the relationship between politics and the unconscious. This is so for two reasons: first, because all allegories are necessarily narrative, they occur in time; and second, because allegories, unlike other narrative modes, allow for tandem or parallel representation: characters or events can be deciphered through reference to ideas or concepts. Allegory's dual structure—surface or manifest and deep or latent—makes of it the kind of text that literally invites interpretation. The last point is Jameson's revision of traditional allegory, as derived, say, from medieval poetics. As a Marxist, he opts for deciphering codes having in mind History writ large; yet instead of viewing allegory as simple tandem equivalences, as traditional Marxism often does, Jameson chooses to cast it as "profoundly discontinuous, a matter of breaks and heterogeneities" that are "themselves in constant change and transformation at each perpetual present of the text" (147). This exception seems important, if only because it delineates the fundamental difference between classical and modern allegory, a distinction that was first drawn by Lukacs in his damning reading of Kafka and of modern literature in general.[9] It is also important for one practical reason: it allows for looser readings of modern allegorical codes, as it no longer limits hermeneutics to figural deciphering, as in classical allegory, and makes form itself, including formal, stylistic and technical devices, significant.[10]

The point will recur often in the course of this reading, but for now we must consider some of the troublesome epistemological assumptions posed by national allegory. Indeed, Jameson's "sweeping generalization" appears not to have been crucial enough to ward off its critique from many quarters, most prominently from scholars such as Aijaz Ahmad, the Pakistani Marxist, or of Jean Franco, the British Hispanist.[11] Ahmad's first and, I would add, legitimate complaint was that national allegory only reified the third world onto a homogenized otherness: "the enormous cultural heterogeneity of social formations within the so-called Third World is submerged within a singular identity of 'experience' . . . Peru and India simply do not have a common history of the sort that Germany and France, or Britain and the United States, have; not even the singular 'experience of colonialism and imperialism' has been in specific ways the same or similar in, say, India and Namibia." Thus, he added: "to say that all Third World texts are necessarily this or that is to say, in effect, that any text originating within that social space which is not this or that is not a 'true' narrative" (104). Yet another of Ahmad's points was that, from a strictly Marxist standpoint, the national experience (and within it national allegory) is not particularly specific to so-called third world cultural production. He argued, instead, that the allegory of the link between private and public, personal and communal, Jameson associated exclusively with the third world could also be found in the first. Hence the examples he cited—Ellison's *Invisible Man*, or Adrienne Rich's *Your Native Land*—where the private imaginations of the American writer, quoting Jameson's own statement, "must necessarily connect with experiences of the collectivity" (105).

Ahmad's trenchant critique, coming as it did from no less than a third world Marxist reader, serves to remind us of the epistemological question upon which all cultural inquiry hinges: how do I read the Other without turning that Other into a projection of Myself? Or else: can a First World critic, despite sympathy for the plight of the culture under study, actually theorize so-called third world texts without idealizing them? As a question on method there may not be a totally satisfying answer—short of the cultural relativism I advocate, following Geertz, in these readings. Yet more pertinent to our discussion of national allegory in Mexico may be the critique that Jean Franco also directed against it, as she found that model inadequate, too, when applied to a specifically Latin American context. "Not only is the nation a complex and much contested term," she warned, "but in recent Latin American criticism it is no longer the inevitable framework for a liberating ideology" (205). Franco went on to question whether national allegory could possibly be applied to a literature "in which nation is either a contested term or something like the Cheshire cat's grin—a mere reminder of a vanished body," and explained further that the category of "nation," much like "third world" for Ahmad, had little analytical status, because "nation states were in Latin America vehicles for often enforced capitalist modernization" (205). And so, just as for Franco "national allegory" did not account accurately for what she calls the "cyclical conjunction of modernity and repression in the name of national autonomy," the novel, as part of that cycle, amounted merely to the "skeptical reconstruction of past errors" (205). Thus Franco doubted seriously that canonical Latin American novels, like Fuentes' *Death of Artemio Cruz*, Rulfo's *Pedro Páramo*, Vargas Llosa's *Green House*, or Carpentier's *Lost Steps*, could possibly amount to national allegories. As those novels in general seem to have no positive content, because they constitute "the skeptical reconstruction of past errors," they also commonly "make visible that absence of any signified that could correspond to the nation. Individual and collective identity, social and family life, were like shells from which life had disappeared" (205). Thus, in Franco's view, the blatantly allegorical emblems of such titles (wasteland, cross, green house, lost steps) were actually intended more as indicators of loss or absence than as positive, material signs of allegorical reading(s).

Even as I share Franco's healthy skepticism toward Jameson's sweeping dicta, I find myself questioning her understanding of national allegory. To begin with, Franco's critique of the concept of nation, or at least of its Latin American version, seems to have had in mind more the concept of state. (Twice she refers to "nation-states," in the sense of the power structure, rather than the nation as the imaginary construct of collective values.) Extending the same argument onto *Plotting Women* (1988), her own lengthier study of Mexican women's fiction of the same year, Franco went on to argue, in specific reference to Elena Garro's *Recollections of*

Things to Come, that, "in national allegories, women became the territory over which the quest for male national identity passed."[12] Thus, for Franco, novels like Garro's actually demonstrate "an impasse." "Women do not enter history—only romance," and concludes that the problem was "rooted in the woman writer's attempt at appropriating the then-hegemonic genre—the novel as national allegory . . . it is simply not possible to retain verisimilitude and make women into national protagonists" (138, 146).

I find these arguments precarious. Both of Franco's essays date from the late 1980s, but her broad point that the nation was no longer "the inevitable framework for either political or cultural projects" simply flies against the face of the virtual avalanche of cultural projects, both political and critical, that at the time took the concept of nation as a theoretical base. Bhabha's work is a case in point, but perhaps the best evidence within Latin American cultural studies is Doris Sommer's landmark *Foundational Fictions* (1991), on the nineteenth-century romances of Latin America. And because Sommer herself glossed national allegory for her own readings, I should like to profit from its direct relevance and consider it now as an oblique road to situating my own take on this question before returning to Franco's argument.

Indeed, I do not share entirely Sommer's apparent view that national allegory is inadequate to describe the "interlocking, not parallel, relationship between erotics and politics" (43) she identifies in nineteenth-century romances. She argues, for example, that by not taking a clue from Walter Benjamin's dialectical view of allegory (in his *The Origin of German Tragic Drama*) Jameson actually fell back onto a "static structure" (43), as if arresting dialectical play, thereby reestablishing the mechanical tandem lurking at the heart of all allegorical hermeneutics and missing the "loomlike" (42) procedure she undertakes in her own readings. But if I understand Jameson's argument correctly, in the precise passage Sommer cites from, allegorical equivalences, when viewed dialectically, "are themselves in constant change and transformation at each perpetual present of the text." That is, a loomlike procedure is seemingly assured within such hermeneutic awareness. Sommer never does get around to using the term "national allegory," for reasons she never makes entirely clear, all the more odd perhaps because the whole point of her historical readings is to bear out, in nineteenth-century Latin American novels, the "relationship between the libidinal and the political components of individual and social experience" that lies at the heart of Jameson's idea.[13] Sommer does describe, instead, the "zigzagging movement" of her own hermeneutic project as the work of "metonymic associations between the family and the state" (47), a procedure I would rather pose, in my own reading, in terms of the coextensive structure of the linguistic sign. That is, I view the two levels of allegory, rather than as metonymic links, as signifier and signified; they appear simultaneously and coextensively, though each remains available to perception in radically different ways: the one, materially present, as in the plots of stories, while the other is ideationally absent but still subject to hermeneutic deciphering, as in the plots' significant commentary on social and historical life, sometimes even through nondescriptive means. Ultimately, however, the difference between Sommer's readings and mine lies not so much in our common interest in allegorical reading—particularly their dialectical, or Benjaminian strain—as in the objects of study we each choose and their determining historical contexts. Sommer concentrates on nineteenth century "foundational fictions" that foster, through reciprocal reinforcement between *eros* and *polis*, romance and nation-building, and on their wielding an optimistic rhetoric at crucial points of Latin American national development, that is, during a postindependence period before an alienating modernization set in. The content of that dialectic appears to be the stories of desire and passion in those fictions, which in turn translate onto, and reinforce, Liberal (read, optimistic) nation-building. My own interest in two twentieth-century-postrevolutionary-Mexican novels, once the national project appears spent, takes into account as much the loss of community through tales of desire and passion as the narrative structures of that loss through a cumulative, non-dialectical discourse. The characters' libidinal or passionate trajectory is not of much interest to my argument as other formal or textual components certainly are. And yet the end-effect of that entire discourse is, I submit, the subversion of the very power structures that originated that loss.

Returning to Franco's view of national allegory, then, we should note further that the aggregate of four novels—two Mexicans, one Peruvian, and one Swiss-born Cuban—with which Franco dismisses the relevance of national allegory for a Latin American context hardly amounts to a national sample. Unless, that is, the four be lumped together as "Latinamericans" and on that questionable basis claim they belong to a super-structural (and therefore unreal) "nation." Franco viewed both *Pedro Páramo* and *Recollections of Things to Come* in particular as "spaces of loss" that disqualified them, in effect, from the roster of national allegory candidates. Accordingly, the women characters there fail to engage in the stories' necessary dialectic, even when their function does appear to be crucial in both cases. And so, since "Garro escapes from verisimilitude through fairy tale but cannot insert her heroines into history" (146), this escapism demonstrates the impossibility, or denial, of a will to allegorize nationally.

I view the entire question differently, beginning with the crucial role of women characters. Susana San Juan's active spurning of Pedro Páramo, for example, is precisely what motivates, along with his son's violent accidental death, the chieftain's resentment and ultimate corruption. Similarly, Julia Andrade and Isabel Moncada do function as "heroines"— one positive, the other negative—upon whose mirror-fates the entire plot turns. In both novels, then, women play "supporting" roles to their allegedly "master" male counterparts. But this is merely surface appearance, a narrative mirage. In fact, both stories appear to be based on the common plot device of reversal as dramatized by gender conflict; in their seemingly marginal and supportive roles, women get the upper hand, at least morally—the one point of view both novels sanction—and the men against whom they react do themselves in by their own erratic power. Thus the women characters' reactions are no less significant or indeed as active as their male counterparts' power over other characters. However passive they may appear (and I would add this is hardly so), women are equally as "inserted" within the "history" they share along with their male counterparts—unless of course we choose a priori to view "History" as an exclusively male domain, as determined by circumstantial activities as military conscription or property ownership. And yet, I would argue, this is precisely what both novels deny, particularly when we consider that—less so perhaps in Rulfo than in Garro—most of the male characters are flat, that is, they undergo little if any internal transformation. This is substantially different from the women heroines, who change either for the better (Julia Andrade), or indeed the worse (Isabel Moncada and Susana San Juan).

Finally, the difference between Franco's view of national allegory and mine is based on our radically different takes on the role of oral culture in both novels. Franco views the reach of both women and marginalized ethnic groups for a script culture, as embodied in national allegory, as a guilt-producing betrayal of an "orally-transmitted culture to the nation" (132), since she views such incursions into "master narratives" based on script as implicit betrayals of the margins to which women and other minorities are relegated. Here, too, I view the matter differently. It is precisely by taking recourse in oral qualities that both novels, as we shall see, actually contend such scripted master narratives and thus subvert the latter's implicit power structures. Such copresence of orality and women characters, not to mention the marginally ethnic and poor, actually constitutes a counter-discourse to what Franco calls the "master script." I shall soon take up the actual strategies attendant to that discourse. Suffice it to say for now that where Franco sees "treachery," I see a subversion implemented through women's appropriation of both orality and a peculiar narrative fragmentation.

Thus if *Pedro Páramo* and *Recollections of Things to come* constitute national allegories—as I believe they do—these are made up of the inter-action of men and women characters whose identity is the result of a dialectic between male power and female foiling. The sum-total of that interaction, not merely one or the first of sundry components, makes up the content of the national allegory. In my view, Franco's reading arrests the dialectical play of that interaction in order to assert the broad point that women are excluded from the national allegory; in contrast, I assert that without women characters there would be no conflict, plot, or indeed moral to the stories, and thus that a so-called space of loss cannot be invoked logically to deny such allegories. Beyond all that, however, lies an even broader and more relevant point; namely, that nothing logically keeps loss itself from becoming a legitimate component of allegorical content. Allegories do not live by presence alone. Indeed, to claim that such novels are "like shells from which life had disap-peared" is not so much wrong as misguided. To the statement that allegories can only be represented positively, one could in turn respond by asking: what prevents absence or loss from providing clues to allegor-ical reading? Why couldn't a national allegory embody "skeptical recon-structions of past errors"? Why couldn't such allegories, alienated representations of a collectivity, be like "shells from which life has disap-peared"? Indeed, why not a national allegory, like *Recollections of Things to Come*, in which an abstract town, rather than its concrete inhabitants, tells its story; or another, like *Pedro Páramo*, in which all the characters are dead?[14]

III

My remarks so far should indicate that, contrary to Franco, and perhaps Sommer, too, national allegory as a concept is worth retaining, though critically so. Ultimately, I find Jameson's idea useful as a cue to hermeneutic decoding rather than as an insight into the nature of third world culture, whatever that may be. Ahmad's assertion to the effect that the alleged link between private and communal is not any more con-scious or overt in the case of the third world is closer to a truth I share. Yet my embrace of national allegory as a concept is conditioned on its ability to allow for that loose, dialectical access that Jameson himself recommends and Sommer endorses, but only so long as other textual components, such as formal or stylistic devices, not to mention historical context, are allowed to enter into dialectical freeplay.

One important initial component in that reading would be the overt link between private and communal levels operating in the two novels. Theirs are stories as much of individual characters as of entire villages acting as microcosms of the Mexican nation; as much about Pedro Páramo and Isabel Moncada as about Comala and Ixtepec. In this, they are not unique, at least within recent Mexican literary history. Their clearest precursor was perhaps *Al filo del agua* (1947) [*The Edge of the Storm*], Agustín Yáñez's critical portrait of Mexican provincial life. It could even be argued that Rulfo and Garro provide critical glosses to Yáñez's precursor text. The common aim of all three, including Yáñez, where the village actually tells the story, is to provide individual portraits within collective narrative structures. In the case of Rulfo's and Garro's, however, and unlike Yáñez's, those stories are structured around a critique of the *cacique*, the chieftain whose power destroys lives, creates human wastelands, and freezes history, and they formulate that critique by mismatching the chieftains and their chosen love objects. Their greatest difference yet, as we shall see, lies in their highly unusual structure, something far more basic than their plots, or points of view.

Conspiring against such common allegorical thrust, however, is the one formal trait that, along with the use of myth, is invoked most often in any joint study of Rulfo and Garro. I refer again to so-called Magical Realism, the culturalized term used most often to refer to fantasy elements in so-called third world texts in general and Latin American ones in particular. And I do so with the goal of reminding ourselves of the kinds of obstacles a hermeneutics of national allegory faces in the context of a historicized reading. So often do magical realist readings recur in the critical canon, in fact, that they end up absorbing critical attention and obliterating the historical and political evidence the novels share.[15] Far from wishing to dispute the presence of fantasy elements, I rather aim to identify their function within a broader historicized structure. Were it the fact that the historical content of both novels be marginal or concealed relative to its fantasy content, there would certainly be cause to justify that repression. And yet history happens to be just as dominant. For what are Pedro Páramo and General Francisco Rosas if not figures of political power? In Rulfo, in particular, incidents related to the Mexican revolution appear only sporadically. Yet the one that dramatizes its critique most, fragment 54 (166, 95), the night that insurgents show up at Pedro Páramo's ranch, happens to be key. It constitutes one of the few moments of comic relief amidst the onslaught of otherwise macabre events, which thereby highlights the incident.

—Good, Pedro Páramo said. But what can I do for you?
—As you see, we've taken up arms.
—And?
—That's all, Isn't that enough?
—But why have you done it?
—Because a lot of others have done the same thing. Didn't you know about it? We're waiting till we get instructions, and then we'll know what it's all about. For the time being, we're here. (95)

Rulfo's political satire hinges precisely on the insurgents' bumbling lack of ideology. But it would be wrong simply to claim on that basis that *Pedro Páramo* is a spooky version of the so-called Novel of the Mexican Revolution. *Rulfo and Garro* write their novels forty years after the properly military phase of the Revolution; both emerge within a later, ironic stage of the history of that novel. Thus despite the frequent allusions to the 1910 Revolution in both, the historical frame they actually share is the later social conflict of the late 1920s known as the *Cristiada* or *Cristero* Rebellion.[16] This later rebellion was, as we know, the result of a major Church and State conflict between the revolutionary government, headed then by Plutarco Elías Calles, and the Catholic Church. To government-imposed curfews and restrictions, the Catholic hierarchy countered with a boycott, and its secular soldiers, named *Cristeros*, led mostly by fanaticized priests, took arms through pillaging, sabotage, and murder. Their influence spread far and wide, but they concentrated mostly in the Western states of Jalisco (where Juan Rulfo was born), Michoacán, Colima, and Zacatecas. As we know, the *Cristero Rebellion* has inspired a number of literary treatments, among them *The Power and the Glory* (1940), arguably Graham Greene's darkest novel.

In *Pedro Páramo* the 1910 Revolution remains implicit and appears only sporadically, but the *Cristero* rebellion is discussed overtly in fragment 43, one of Dorotea and Juan Preciado's most spirited dialogues, so to speak. After relating a blow-by-blow chronicle of Comala's downfall and the chieftain's slow decline, Dorotea reports: "Not long before he died, the *Cristeros* revolted and the troops took away the few men that were left here. That was when I began to die of hunger, and I never got caught up" (79). Timing is the cipher here. Because the outbreak of the *Cristiada*, or at least its fictional incidence in Comala, coincides with

Pedro Páramo's last days, the timing identifies symbolically the ruthless *cacique* with the Jacobin regime the religious and conservative *Cristeros* rebelled against.[17] In turn, the *Cristiada* provides an important context of *Recollections of things to Come*, as it determines the political background to Ixtepec's occupation by Rosas' revolutionary (by-then Federated) troops. Like Pedro Páramo in Comala, Rosas in Ixtepec kills, destroys, and otherwise takes revenge against the town's citizens both for aiding the *Cristeros* and, indirectly, though no less effectively, for witnessing the chieftain's failure at love.

Ixtepec's (and possibly Comala's) lost ideal is in fact *zapatismo*, the traditional agrarian strain of the revolution espoused years earlier by Emiliano Zapata, which the *Cristeros* tried to vindicate indirectly through their own later rebellion.[18] To alert us of that link Garro's town of Ixtepec states: "They were really surprised at the bloody friendship between the Catholic followers of Porfirio Díaz known as Porfiristas and the atheistic revolutionaries . . . The two groups were linked by greed and the shameful origin of the mestizo. They had inaugurated an era of barbarism unprecedented in my memory" (64). We should note, however, that this blanket critique is aimed not just at the Revolution, whose Jacobin rigors the town's population endures, but also at Modernity writ large. Modernity, in this partial view at least, encompasses both nineteenth century *Porfirismo* and the "atheistic revolutionaries," both secular movements, or else symptoms of a greater historical sweep that shook the spiritual foundations of the village and indeed of Mexico itself.

It is no exaggeration to say that the *Cristero* Rebellion was the first overt, conservative critique of the Mexican Revolution. It was very much in the spirit of more recent marginal offenses within Mexico, like the *neo-Zapatistas'* in the Mexican state of Chiapas. And it was nothing less than a Catholic counter-revolution, a war in the name of orthodoxy similar in spirit to the *Canudos* rebellion in Northeast Brazil that Mario Vargas Llosa made so famous in his *The War of the End of the World* (1981). The *Cristiada* opposed not simply the anticlerical restrictions of the 1917 Mexican Constitution, but the entire modern, secular project that underlined commonly both the Porfirio Díaz dictatorship and, later as well, the Mexican Revolution. Academic summaries of the *Cristiada* tend to describe it as an isolated, temporary Church and state conflict. But the crisis the rebellion reflected actually ran much deeper, harking back at least to the 1857 Mexican Reform and its Liberal Constitution. For if we recall, the *Reforma* was the first government initiative, in the name of modernization, that granted rights to all Mexican citizens; only it did so at the cost of suppressing their indigenous and Catholic heritage. Citizens were supposed to be Mexicans, not specifically Indian or Catholic. This the Reforma did through the abolition of two age-long institutions: Catholic religious associations and, among the indigenous population especially communal landholding, the *ejido*. The effect of these so-called reforms on secular modernization is indisputable; its spiritual cost, however, particularly as it created a sense of collective alienation, was devastating. In a lengthy but useful paragraph in *The Labyrinth of Solitude* (1950) Octavio Paz summarized this ambivalent legacy of Liberalism as "a critique of the old order and as projected social pact":

> It was not a religion but a utopian ideology; it fought rather than consoled; it replaced the notion of an other world with that of a terrestrial future. It championed man but it ignored a half of its nature, that which is expressed in communion, myths, festivals, dreams, eroticism. Above all, the Reform movement was negation, and its greatness resides on that fact. But what this negation affirmed—the principles of European liberalism—was a philosophy whose beauty was exact, sterile and, in the long run, empty. Geometry cannot take the place of myth. To convert the schemes of the liberals into a truly national project it would have been necessary to win the support of the country as a whole. This would have been supremely difficult, because the reform was attacking a very concrete and particular affirmation: that all men are the sons of God, a creed permitting a genuinely filial relationship between the individual and the cosmos. In its place the Reform offered an abstract postulate: that all men are equal before the law. Freedom and equality were—and are— empty concepts, ideas with no other concrete historical content than that given by social relationships, as Marx has demonstrated. We are aware, by now, of the forms into which that abstract equality can change itself, and of the true meaning of that empty freedom. Also, the founding of Mexico on a general notion of man, rather than on the actual situation of our people sacrificed reality to words and delivered us up to the ravenous appetites of the strong.[19]

Páramo in Spanish means wasteland, a symbol that in Rulfo I take to mean, with the aid of the historical subtext described by Paz, Comala's moral devastation. Jean Franco could not have been more accurate in describing *Pedro Páramo* as a "shell from which life has disappeared"; but she could not have been more wrong, I think, in dismissing that "shell" as the cipher of national allegory. The same could be said of Garro, whose own personal vehemence regarding Mexico's revolutionary legacy was even more strident than Rulfo's.[20]

By thus harking back to the *Cristero* rebellion, Rulfo and Garro agree on and coincide in identifying that moment in Mexican history when the Mexican nation began to petrify under the oppression of a modern state apparatus allegedly created in order to liberate its oppressed citizens. Thus it could be said that to Stanley Ross' ominous question, "Is the Mexican Revolution Dead?" Rulfo and Garro answered with a resounding, "Yes."[21] It is not by chance the two novels highlight the stone as an allegorical emblem. Páramo's first name is *Pedro*, on whose name Rulfo builds not a spiritual temple but the ruin of a man. Hence the last paragraph where Pedro returns to the dust of his own name: "He leaned against Damiana and tried to walk. After a few steps he fell down, pleading within but not speaking a single word. He struck a feeble blow against the ground and then crumbled to pieces as if he were a heap of stones" (123). *Recollections of Things to Come* begins and ends highlighting the stone upon which the village is perched in order to recount its pained memory. "Here I sit on what looks like a stone. Only my memory knows what it holds" (3); "The stone, the memory of my suffering . . ." (288). Isabel Moncada, Garro's tragic heroine, turns into stone at the end of her story. Like Pedro Páramo, she, too, petrifies. Not only is her desire frustrated and unfulfilled; her stony metamorphosis is also the symbol of a spiritually sterile community; and the novel, its epitaph.[22]

IV

It would be too simple, however, to leave things as such, what for purposes of the workings of national allegory one could call the two novels' negative content. So far I have described the contours of a common critique in both Rulfo and Garro that denies almost everything and offers little in return. This move was in part necessary in order to demonstrate, against prevailing opinion, that national allegory need not limit itself to summoning a positive content for its representation. I also wanted to provide a historical context for two narratives that, with few exceptions, have been canonized as anything but historical. Now I turn to pursue somewhat of a reverse argument; namely, to identify those formal components, particularly non-figural ones, that constitute positive allegorical embodiment. Thus, instead of asking what do Rulfo and Garro commonly criticize or deny, I now turn to ask: what do they offer in return? How do their novels represent national allegory?

To answer these questions I wish to examine two passages, one from each novel, and analyze closely the one structural element, narrative fragmentation, they fully share. I begin with Rulfo's because working through his more difficult text first may smooth the way to a reading of Garro's. Indeed, the critical canon has had a field-day with *Pedro Paramo*'s fragmentation by describing it under various names: from stream of consciousness and surrealist dream language, to mythical discourse. Among all those alternatives, the one I find formally most satisfying is the narratological description that González Boixó, editor of the canonical Cátedra edition, provides in his introduction.[23] He calls it "narrative interpolation." By this he means: "the inclusion of fragments of a character's thoughts, in a way that they shape series with narrative unity" (30). Accordingly, the novel's entire text can be viewed as the aggregate of three such series: (1) Juan Preciado's memories of his dead mother's descriptions of Comala; (2) Pedro Páramo's longing thoughts of Susana San Juan; and (3) Susana San Juan's memories of Florencio, her dead husband. But while certainly detailed and accurate, González Boixó's description still seems to me insufficient. Surely, *Pedro Páramo* contains more than just three interpolated series. In fact, when examined closely, one finds that each of these three series branch out or break up, in turn, into several more of their own. Thus the entire text rests upon, or rather is made up of, a complex system of intertwined, interposed units that together make up discrete narrative sequences numbering more than just three. Within the novel's sequential order, for example, the 37th fragment contains the famous dialogue between Juan Preciado and Dorotea, or else their respective spirits. It is precisely here, as has been remarked repeatedly, well into our reading and after working through 36 successive narrative sections that we take to be description or diegesis, that we finally discover we have been overhearing all along a conversation between two dead people. In the fragment immediately following this dialogue (126–130; 56–59) we then read or hear as well the voice of Dolores (Juan Preciado's mother), transcribed in italics, as if suggesting, through the insertion of a different script, that her voice is fading in and out. J.M. Cohen, in one of the earliest readings of *Pedro Páramo*, called this technique "cross-fadings," a term he admittedly borrowed from radio to describe the effect of voices crossing each other during broadcast, as in the reporting one hears in programs like NPR's *All Things Considered*.[24] Almost as if reflecting upon the predominance of these voices, Juan Preciado himself refers to them as *"los murmullos: me mataron los murmullos"* ("the voices: the voices killed me"). While cross-fadings are overt in this particular passage, they become present as well in the dialogue that subsumes Dolorita's lament the moment we realize we are overhearing a dialogue. Formally, what actually takes place is a dialogue superimposed upon the voice of an omniscient (perhaps third-person) narrator. That much is borne out in fragment 38, following immediately which picks up the narrative from Juan Preciado in a fairly diegetic, objective tone: "At daybreak, great drops of rain fell on the earth . . ." (60). It is no exaggeration to say that Rulfo's entire text relies on such cross-fading effects. No sooner does the reader become accustomed to hearing one character's voice, thoughts, or reported speech, than she finds herself switched, unexpectedly, onto another sequence or voice. Garro's text is built upon a similar principle, as we shall see, but before examining its own workings we must first reflect upon their common general significance.

We appear, for one thing, to be before an open system. Interpolation actually means the denial of causality: any voice can cross-fade with any other at any point. Which thus means that we can make virtually endless connections among the text's different fragments or voices. The principle that appears to be at work, then, is multiplicity rather than unity, the kind of multiple or plural connection that is so evident in root-like stems, as in rhizomes like couch grass, weeds or, indeed, a grapevine: a horizontal vine rather than a vertical tree. Deleuze and Guattari, from whose meditation I borrow this model, argue that "to be rhizomorphous is to produce stems and filaments that seem to be roots, or better yet, connect with them by penetrating the trunk, but put them to strange uses."[25] They add that "the rhizome operates by variation, expansion, conquest, capture, offshoots," "an a–centered, nonhierarchical, non-signifying system without a [military] general and without an organizing memory or central automaton, defined solely by a circulation of states" (21). Rhizomes might lack a General, but neither one of these novels does; one could say at least that each posits a "General," which their respective rhizomes work to undermine.

My point here is twofold. First, it is clear both texts mobilize peculiar rhizomorphous designs whose ultimate reading-effects contend symbolically against the power structures embodied by Páramo and Rosas, those two "Generals." In other words, the novels' rhizomorphous designs operate as formal counterparts to the women's subversion of the *caciques'* male institutional power. Waxing symbolic, and recalling Deleuze and Guattari's terms, rhizomorphous procedures undermine the power of a central, "arborescent," narrative, as embodied in each "General." But my second and more important point is that, as we shall see, the specific content of that common rhizome is nothing less than village gossip. My claim is that the shared national allegory is made up of the sum-total of all these sundry symbolic and reading effects.

Garro's novel does not itself operate, like Rulfo's, on the basis of cross-fadings. But it does exploit another narrative device, digression, which I view as yet another, and equally powerful, rhizomorphous procedure. In the introduction to her translation of *Recollection of Things to Come*, Ruth L.C. Simms remarked: "this is a book that does not depend for its effectiveness on narrative continuity. It is a book of episodes, one that leaves the reader with a series of vivid impressions" (vii). And yet, the discontinuity of its narrative derives, I think, not so much from its episodic form as from its startling winding procedure.

Section VII of Part I, which proceeds in such offshoot fashion, is typical of the whole, in the sense that it makes connections that are not necessarily, and in fact seldom are, causal. The passage in question begins by reporting General Rosas' question to Julia, his mistress: "Julia, why were you afraid?" (44). One would expect an immediate response to this question; but instead the narrator proceeds in winding fashion by reporting a long series of at least ten sundry events, namely: (1) how Felipe Hurtado meets Juan Cariño, the town's mad president; (2) a flashback that fills us in on Cariño's past; (3) an unrelated conversation between Cariño and Hurtado; (4) Hurtado meets Don Joaquín; (5) Don Joaquín's house; and (6) room are described; (7) Matilde reappears at the site of the dead; (8) flash-forward to conversation between Hurtado and Don Joaquín; (9) A scene at the whorehouse; (10) Don Pepe recalls events from the night before. At long last, though several pages later, the digressions end where we began, with the same question: "Tell me, why were you afraid?" (52).

Like cross-fadings, digressions break unannounced into the narrative and create reader uncertainty. Their content is not, to be sure, unrelated to the main narrative, but, as shown in the example above, they keep the reader on edge by straying constantly from a relatively central theme or series of events and deferring or suspending necessary information to fulfill a previous expectation. Thus by constantly changing the subject, but eventually returning to it, digressions maximize entropy, that is, the discursive capacity toward randomness, disorder or chaos, without ever actually losing control. In fact, digression does all this, as Ross Chambers has argued, "within discourse from the fact of its existence in time (which in turn appears as the ultimate condition of possibility of the digressive")[26] Moreover, the sheer accumulation of seemingly trivial digressive instances, such as Garro's "episodic" plot displays, works to flaunt digressiveness itself and thus functions "at the limit-point between pleasure and something more threatening," creating "a certain modus operandi in common with what is called teasing," that is, a textual dynamic that "can at any moment 'tip the balance' and go 'over the edge' " (91).

Coextensive with this peculiar textual dynamics, then, is the characters' chatty or gossipy behavior I have pointed out and which I happen to view as one of the signatures of the shared national allegory. For if, as I have argued, each text rejects linear logic on behalf of a multiple, heterogeneous, open system of connections, it does so while engaging in the homologous (in the sense of formally equivalent) social mode of behavior we know as gossip. Statements like "The rumors got to the *Media Luna* the night before the burial while the men rested from the long walk they had taken up to the pantheon" (26, translation modified for emphasis); or else, "Life in the *Hotel Jardín* was passionate and secret. People peeked through the balconies trying to see something of those loves and these women, all of whom were beautiful and extravagant" (36) are but two of the many markers of gossip behavior, both textual and diegetic, the reader witnesses. My broad point here is that digression is the narrative technique whereby the reader actually participates in the formal equivalent of social gossip. The reader literally journeys through the grapevine of both stories, a fact that Garro's novel further underscores symbolically by making a *Hotel Jardín* (literally, "Garden Hotel") the object of the town's gossip. As these novels share a vine-like narrative approach, so we, too, have characters constantly engaged in gossip, even beyond the grave.

And yet to say that rhizome and gossip are homologous to each other may, however, simply beg the question. Is there anything intrinsic or peculiar to rhizomorphous texts to link them to gossip as a human activity? One quick response could be that while in both there appears a similar sense of danger stemming from either an unstable discourse or the simple threat of badmouthing, as if both posed threats through sheer unstoppable proliferation, there would also appear to be an "oral" quality to both rhizome and gossip and, perhaps also, a common origin in folklore. I mention textual orality—that is, speech-simulating texts—because such is yet another formal element the two novels share, and an element that links them both, in turn, to folk art. We might reflect a moment on this formal link in order to ascertain the final traces of the national allegory I seek to sketch.

In *Pedro Páramo* the reader discovers such oral quality, as Martin Lienhardt remarked once, upon realizing, a third of the way into the novel, that Juan Preciado has been having all along a conversation with Dorotea, and that all the characters are dead.[27] Earlier I identified this very scene as an exemplary instance of cross-fading; now that scene becomes doubly significant because the reader's discovery, as sudden as it is retrospective, is actually twofold: we realize the text simulates oral discourse at one and the same time we discover the novel's rhizome. In Garro's case, the text's oral principle hinges at first on Ixtepec's overt enunciation, its literal oral memory, only to yield eventually to the characters' (both men and women) chattiness.[28] The frequency with which both stories remark the characters' gossip, such as the ones I pointed out earlier, reinforces the predominance and significance of oral communication. Indeed, rumor, word of mouth, is important in both because it constitutes no less than an alternative to written, official, or else State-controlled, communication, and reinforces personal support among characters that feel oppressed, or are otherwise dead and lamenting their common fate beyond the grave. In fact, the characters' reliance on oral, as opposed to written, communication may well be a distant echo of the general climate of the *Cristero* rebellion the two novels commonly evoke. For as Jean Meyer once pointed out about Cristero communal life, "this culture was basically oral, even in the written supports that it employed. A book would be passed from hand to hand, and read standing up by someone who could so, before a circle of women working or men on guard" (181–182). On his views on the oral qualities of his novel, Rulfo himself was quoted once as saying he "did not want to speak as one writes, but rather to write as one speaks."[29] Garro, a prominent dramatist in her own right, has herself often been compared in her narrative style to a "Mexican Dostoevsky."

Thus it would not be wrong to see in this shared simulation of oral speech Rulfo's and Garro's link to what Mikhail Bakhtin called, in precise relation to Dostoevsky, the polyphonic novel; a work where "a hero appears whose voice is constructed exactly like the voice of the author himself," and in turn a voice that "sounds, as it were, alongside the author's word and in a special way combines both with it and with the full and equally valid voices of other characters."[30] Rulfo and Garro's shared polyphony therefore works in rhizomorphous fashion to fragment their respective narratives while heightening their characters' individual speech. Their characters' quiet gossip is not, to be sure, the polemical philosophizing that Dostoevsky's characters are known for, but is nonetheless "polyphonic" in the dual sense of oral and non-centered. The combined effect of orality, the characters' gossipy behavior, and rhizomorphous procedure is what explains the tendency in both texts toward narrative entropy, or else semantic confusion: sheer reading difficulty, a formal feature that would seem, in turn, to approach both novels, and perhaps even a good portion of Dostoevsky's own, to the folk tale.

Jan Mukarovsky remarked once, on this very subject, how the constructive principles of folk poetry differed from self-conscious literary works by tending to "disturb the semantic unity," often through the seemingly illogical rearrangement of plot elements. This is so, Mukarovsky explained, because "folk art in general experiences and evaluates each motif as an independent semantic unit. The folk narrator does not, therefore, care too much whether he has prepared the listener for a newly introduced motif or not."[31] That is, in folk art, "detail is much more than a subordinate structural element" and "does not proceed from an image of the whole but from an ordering of details provided by tradition, and unexpected wholes arise from the always new ordering of those details" (203). This is not to claim, of course, that Rulfo and Garro were simply sloppy folk artists, but rather that their novels set out to simulate folk discourse in order to achieve a certain oral, and thereby "gossipy," effect.

Gossip, then, or rather the sum-total of gossipy incidents, provides in these two cases "details" whose sheer unexpected order and accumulation creates a peculiar national allegory, or else, a microcosm of Mexico amidst its so-called institutionalized Revolution. It offers, in particular, a critique of the years of the Miguel Alemán and López Mateos administrations, when the media myth of "Mexico" appears to have reached its zenith.[32] It would be easy, however, to misunderstand such a national allegory—or worse my own reading of character behavior—as a form of moral degradation based on gossip. Far from it, my goal has been to revalue gossip as a metaphor for the reconstitution of communal life outside of the reaches of the State, a kind of collective salvation "through the grapevine." I realize of course that such a positive contribution flies against the face of the shared pessimism of the two novels, especially Rulfo's dark vision. By this I seek to describe, however, not so much the novels' common content as national allegory's shared intent. The formal role of gossip or rumor would seem to be especially pertinent in the study of narrative as discourse in both its structural and social implications. As a mode of exchange, gossip, universally deemed as trivial, and almost exclusively feminine, would appear to be crucial in the formation of the novel as an agent of communal bonding.

V

Faced with the spiritual wasteland, the *páramo*, of Modernity, characters in these two Mexican novels resort to gossip as a way of fostering human relations. The whispers, murmurs and babbles that Juan Preciado witnesses and engages in throughout his underground conversations, are not merely expressions of fear. They actually constitute a mode of sharing. Would it surprise us to learn that *Los murmullos* [The Murmurs] was Rulfo's working title for *Pedro Páramo*, or that the entire plot of *Recollections of Things to Come*, following Ixtepec's opening statement, can be read as an elongated long string of juicy gossip? "Only in a vague sense," writes Patricia Spacks, "can gossip be called a cultural form. But that vague sense does matter, for it calls attention to continuities of structure between one episode of gossip and the next" (13). And Spacks goes to on to pose a question that must be highlighted in this conclusion: "What do we offer in the economy of gossip, what do we receive? The answer is three things: point of view, information, reassurance. Participants in gossip reassure one another of what they share: one of gossip's important purposes" (22).

We would not be wrong to identify a politics in this national allegory. I don't of course mean politics in the sense of a concrete proposal, either by authors or characters, of sectarian action or policy formulation. I mean, rather, outlines of a symbolic relation to power. Such an allegory displays, for one thing, to quote Michel Foucault, the uncanny resurrection of a "subjugated knowledge" that mobilizes, in the interstices of textual procedure, the "capillaring techniques" and "micro-mechanisms" of a non-sovereign power, that is, a power exercised outside of the State apparatus and upon non-governmental issues.[33] What Juan Villoro has remarked of *Pedro Páramo*—that "its politics is specifically literary: the story of those who can't have History"—could also be said of *Recollections of Things to Come*. From their shared marginality as novelists, and as writers who throughout their careers remained, either by choice or accident, relatively marginal to mainstream intellectual arenas, even within Mexico, Rulfo and Garro assembled, in effect, works that take up not the political issues of the social and political macrocosm, but rather the minutiae proper to what Foucault, too, called "the specific intellectual" who meditates on local forms of power and reform. With that name, Foucault chose to distinguish between the traditional "organic intellectual," such as the "jurist or notable," who works within the institutional structure of sovereign power, from the "savant or expert," like the atomic scientist or the psychiatrist, whose specialized opinions affect the internal structure of institutions and the fate of individual subjects. And while it would certainly appear that Rulfo and Garro were the least likely candidates to such "specific intellectual" status, the knowledge that they, or actually their texts, mobilized do engage that same "local scientific truth" in which they, too, become "stategists of life and death" whose "powers . . . can either benefit or irrevocably destroy life" (125–133, passim), in the specific sense that their novels, or their common writing practice, assemble symbolic structures that affect readers' perceptions of their own social and political worlds. Such would be, properly speaking, what in a different context François Lyotard once called "narrative knowledge," the knowledge that, while working at the opposite pole from "science," is traditional in nature but also radically pragmatic, in the sense that it finds the raw material for its social bonds not only in the meaning of the narratives it recounts but in "the very act of reciting them."[34]

What Foucault refers to as the "specific intellectual," then, may well be what Julia Kristeva in turn once called "the dissident," which in her broad view encompasses not only "the rebel who attacks political powers" or even the psychoanalyst ("who transforms the dialectic of law and desire into a contrast between death and discourse"), but also the kind of writer "who experiments with the limits of identity, producing texts wherever the law does not exist outside language."[35] Indeed, the national allegory we have jointly scrutinized here, amidst the onset of a petrified Revolution—written up during the exact historical counterpart in Mexico to the period Foucault identifies between "the collapse of Fascism and the decline of Stalinism"—responds to the kind of work "that gives rise to a law that is overturned, violated and pluralized, a law upheld only to allow a polyvalent, polylogical sense of play that sets the being of the law ablaze in a peaceful, relaxing void" (296). That Kristeva should also mention "sexual difference," and specifically women ("who are least afraid of death or the law, which is why they administer both," 296) as another type of present-day dissidence, makes all that more compelling our case for attention to this joint national allegory; particularly in the case of Elena Garro, whose work continues to be equally as dismissed, as she herself was exiled at one time from her national community for expressing unpopular, indeed heretical political opinions.[36] "This female exile," says Kristeva, in comments I find uncannily pertinent, "in relation to the General and to Meaning, is such that a woman is always singular, to the point where she comes to represent the singularity of the singular—the fragmentation, the drive, the unnameable" (296). That is, in the national allegory these two texts unwittingly share, and beyond whatever pessimism their message entails, Rulfo and Garro appeal to that "small-scale work" that Vaclav Havel, arguably our time's best-known dissident, described once, amidst his nation's own struggle to combat the evils of one-Party rule, as necessary for the constitution of that "parallel *polis*," or "second culture" that, working on moral rather than on purely political principles, points "beyond itself" and only "makes sense as an act of deepening one's responsibility to and for the whole, as a way of discovering the most appropriate locus for this responsibility, not as an escape from it."[37]

The four contemporary European figures (Foucault, Lyotard, Kristeva, and Havel) I have invoked themselves call forth together a language that resonates strongly in some of the most trenchant critiques of the Mexican national project during the last century, beginning perhaps with Octavio Paz's *Posdata* (1970), his literal post-script to the mid-century *Labyrinth of Solitude*. In it, Paz identified outright, amidst the legacy of the October 1968 State crisis, the existence of, and conflict between, "two Mexicos (one developed, the other underdeveloped" (260), a duality that according to Paz could not, however, be reduced simply to a matter of modernization versus material backwardness because it was actually "a complex of unconscious attitudes and structures which, far from being survivals from an extinct world are vital constituent parts of our contemporary culture" (287). Elsewhere in the same essay Paz noted that "when a society decays," such as Mexico presumably was or is—beginning with the petrification of its so-called institutionalized revolution—"it is language that first becomes gangrenous" (263), which in turn explains why the critique of the Revolution had been started "not by the moralists, nor by the radical revolutionaries, but by the writers (a handful of the older but a majority of the younger)," whose criticism "had not been directly political . . . but verbal: the exercise of criticism as an exploration of language and the exercise of language as an exploration of reality" (263). Paz's late 1960s critique would eventually spill over to influence younger Mexican authors in a number of fields, such as Literature (Carlos Fuentes), History (Enrique Krauze), and Anthropology (Guillermo Bonfil Batalla).[38] But like Aristotle in relation to the Greek tragedians, Paz's contribution perhaps was to articulate retrospectively the vision that he and his contemporaries, among them Rulfo and Garro, had formulated of the Mexican nation at mid-century, a vision that another long but useful paragraph in *Posdata* summarized eloquently:

> The form it adopts is neither moral nor political but exploratory; it is not criticism in the name of this or that principle nor is a judgment on reality: *it is a vision*. Criticism of the language is an active operation that means digging into the language to discover what is hidden there: the worm-eaten foundations of institutions, the mire of the sub-soil, the slimy creatures therein, the endless underground galleries like prisons, those Mexican prisons in which so many of the young are now locked up . . . The advent of the critical and passionate art, obsessed with double images OF daily marvels and banalities. Of humor and passion, surprised and disturbed the new class in power. This was natural enough. That class, made up of

entrepreneurs, bankers, financiers, and political bosses, is only now taking its first steps along the path which their counterparts in Europe and the United States have been walking for more than a hundred years; it takes them at precisely the moment when the nations that have been its models and the object of its admiration and envy are beginning to suffer substantial changes in both technology and economics, in both the social sphere and the spiritual, in both thought and feeling. [265, author's italics]

Our last three chapters turn to Cuba, another national context whose own successive revolutions, since the 1895 War of Independence from Spain up to the 1959 Castro uprising and eventual Communist regime, has attracted global attention. I begin with the first of these struggles and its transatlantic projection onto the so-called Spanish *Generation of 1898* in an effort to understand the ambivalent status of Cuba as a postcolonial reality within Spain's metropolitan intellectual discourse. My interest, once again, focuses, both there and in chapter six, the book's sole section dealing with film, on the margins of historical reality and particularly with the ways in which the critical canon tends to obscure, if not obliterate altogether, crucial political evidence about emergent local knowledge. These two chapters could be viewed together, then, as an arch or parenthesis of sorts, both before and after the 1959 Revolution, that itself ciphers my critique of so-called politically radical discourse and what I view as some potential ethical alternatives. My third and last "Cuban" chapter, on Ortiz's *Cuban Counterpoint* (1940), closes the book with a move similar to the first chapter's on *Canto general*; a thick description of a mid-twentieth-century classic whose contents continue to affect, and at times determine, some of our dearest critical habits.

CHAPTER FIVE

1898: Narcissism and Melancholy

> Nobody colonizes innocently, nor with impunity.
>
> Aimé Césaire

I

What does a postcolonial reading tell us about the Spanish Generation of 1898? The question seems worth asking, and not just because of the growing importance of postcolonialism as a theoretical grid. Particularly surprising is that the question has never, to my knowledge, been asked within the history of the Generation of 1898 reception, even a full century after the *Desastre*, so-called by Spanish historiography to describe the Spanish defeat in the Spanish American War. We know by now that one of the things postcolonial readings show is the ways a dominant metropolis determines the production of peripheral texts and cultures. It would seem just as logical, then, that those readings should encompass as well the determining modes of metropolitan behavior; that is, determining the manner in which metropolitan knowledge of the periphery becomes codified for its own discursive consumption. It is therefore within such a postcolonial grid that I wish to situate the following paradox, or at least this concern.[1]

I have often noted that within the Generation of 1898 canon the Cuban theme, and by extension the theme of Spanish colonialism, is hardly if ever discussed. To put it bluntly: the literature of the so-called *Desastre* tells us little if anything about *el Desastre*. I say this because, as a Cuban reader myself, and therefore someone made hyperconscious of my colonial background by the grid of a metropolitan education, my search for this theme in the peninsular canon has not always borne fruit. Indeed, it could be said that its glaring absence frustrates minimal historical norms. *El Desastre* is the precise historical name Spaniards have given to the former empire's loss of its last colonies in the Spanish–Cuban–Puertorican–Filipino–American War at the end of the nineteenth century. Of all those colonies, Cuba was certainly the richest and most important—all the more reason to consider it here as a paradigm for the question I wish to pursue. The gravity and resistance to this historical crisis can perhaps be measured through its reflection in popular lore. For in seeking in vain to retain it as a colony, Restoration Spain spilled the most blood and spent the most money of all its colonial wars. *Más se perdió en Cuba* [much more was lost in the Cuban war]—the popular Spanish maxim and hyperbole, summarizes the collective grief stemming from that loss.

The relative absence of the Cuban theme occurs, in fact, as much in the texts written by the Generation of 1898 authors as in the critical canon devoted to them. One has only to glance through a number of those critical treatments—the works of Fox, Granjel, Laín Entralgo, López Morillas, Mainer, Ramsden, or Shaw—to confirm that the Cuban theme is barely touched upon, and when it is touched upon it surfaces *ambivalently*, with all the semantic weight, including the psychoanalytic, we grant to that concept. It is not so much, then, that the Cuban theme is never discussed; on the contrary, it appears everywhere if we only look for it. But its uncanny appearance is almost always shot through, in both the primary and secondary literature, by a dialectics of presence and absence—a kind of very subtle tease.

I would like, as part of this particular ciphered reading, to dwell on that tease. Through it I wish to interrogate the historical relevance of *El Desastre* in the common life of both nations. In fact, my hypothesis is that we haven't yet overcome the so-called *Disaster*; its effects have survived the historical traumas that caused it. The reasons for that survival have to do, in turn, with what one could call a crisis of historical memory, the origins of which were not only the Cuban War, but the very nature of the political State (the Spanish Restoration) that waged it. I should perhaps caution that my goal here is not so much to reject the 1898 canon as to resituate those texts by inquiring into their common nature. Though I retain the goal of gaining local knowledge from a given context, I depart somewhat from the aim of previous chapters, which sought thick descriptions of contexts and texts, and instead essay here a meta-historical approach halfway between philosophy of history and a psychohistorical reading. More than a Latin Americanist's, then, my reflections fall squarely on the side of an intellectual concerned for our common history. For in the end where I wish, and in a way must, arrive in this meditation is at a critique of the unconscious, harmful repetition of those historic burdens that continue to plague the life of the former Spanish colony and its people.

II

Here's Pío Baroja's description of the culminating moment of the year of the *Desastre*:

> One Sunday in Madrid we learned that the War with the U.S. was over and that Cuba and the Philippines had ceased to be Spanish. By then, we knew well the importance of these islands and their riches. But despite that the people looked calm and resigned. No demonstrations or outbursts. Everyone went to the bulls as if nothing had happened. It was then Silvela remarked that Spain had no heartbeat.[2]

Baroja's description of a Spain indifferent to the news of *el Desastre* sums up the collective attitude that permeated this entire period, or at least this particular moment. Following the jingoism of the previous three years of the conflict, Spaniards in 1898, witnessing their country's defeat in the briefest of wars, became overwhelmed by a gloomy indifference. Clearly, Baroja was reacting not so much to *el Desastre* itself as to the lack of popular reaction to the political crisis. And yet, one need only scratch the surface to learn that Baroja's reaction was not atypical among Spanish intellectuals of the time.

The Countess of Pardo Bazán for example, wrote, in reaction to an 1898 Queen Regent's speech in the Spanish Senate, the following: "And nobody felt how critical the times were, nobody so much as trembled— when everyone rightly should have. Because all that weak euphemistic language pointed to our history's darkest hour, Spain's agony." More emphatic even than the Countess was Miguel de Unamuno, who amidst one of his periodic religious crises described the downcast attitude that had spread and affected writers and intellectuals like himself: "The same day the Cervera squadron was sunk, it had been days since I had ensconced myself—so I couldn't have access to any newspapers—in a wheat-threshing farm, and I was oblivious to everything that had to do with the war. And I believe that in Spain there were more of those who worked in silence, worried only about our daily bread, than those who worried about current events." In his *Autobiography*, Ramiro de Maeztu summarized the prevailing mood in one short statement: "People were set on not feeling at all the better to live. . . ."[3]

That Spaniards would react defensively at the news of the *Desastre* seems understandable, even when it was also significant they do so. All nations react defensively before military defeat, particularly if its power elite is perceived to be distant and removed. Such was, in fact, the case of Restoration Spain. More significant still is that none of the canonical members of the Spanish Generation of 1898, famous collectively for their dissection of the Spanish soul, should have ever inquired about the causes or effects of such psychic defense, or even about the historical and public reasons—the regime's colonial policy—that fostered their common attitude. While it is true that in their works one often finds scattered remarks about the *Desastre*, such remarks are often limited, to say the most, to guarded reactions to the historical crisis, rather than any kind of reasoned or full-fledged critique. This is true even in the case of Ramiro de Maeztu, among the Generation's most reactionary members, who himself had lived and worked in Cuba as a young man during the 1890s; who was the son and grandson of sugar mill owners ruined by the 1895 war; and who wrote, upon his return to Spain, a series of articles about the Cuban war.[4]

The 1898 Generation's relative indifference to the Cuban question becomes all the more disturbing when we consider that a great deal of the canonical prestige of these writers rests upon a collective moral critique of Spain's history and traditions. But as one of the few studies devoted to the subject has remarked: "Spanish intellectuals were little concerned about the Cavite and Santiago *Desastre*, particularly, and perhaps surprisingly, after August 1898."[5] Most noteworthy in this regard is that both Baroja and Unamuno wrote their first novels during the Cuban war. But in 1897 and 1900, when *Paz en la guerra* and *La casa de Aizgorri* were published, respectively, the former mentioned Cuba only once (Puerto Rico twice), and both times solely in reference to the taking of Bilbao during the Carlist War; Unamuno avoided the subject altogether.

Such blatant indifference on the part of Spanish intellectuals—though not all, as we shall see—can be understood, in part, by the Spanish State's attitude toward the entire colonial question. I refer to attitude rather than policy or ideology because Restoration Spain never did quite have a clear-cut colonial ideology. As Spanish historian Carlos Serrano remarks: "They did have a policy—the unabashed defense of the interests of social groups that were linked most closely to the colonies; and they did develop a discourse—patriotism and national integrity—that seemed most timely. But they never actually took charge of the indispensable debate concerning national interest, or the nature of the fatherland, whose greatness and integrity were offered up as rhetorical justification of such a high-cost, low-yield policy."[6] The absence of a colonial ideology explains, in turn, why each time the Cuban crisis was brought up publicly before the Spanish *Cortes* it was, according to Serrano, "from an essentially peninsular point of view of domestic policy and with an eye to the regime's and the Crown's interests, which relied in turn on the Spanish oligarchy's interests."[7] Other historians of Spain, like Raymond Carr, add that Cánovas, then Spanish Prime Minister, micromanaged the Cuban crisis "solely in terms of steering between the various pressure groups in Madrid in order to retain the leadership of his party, threatened on the one hand by Romero Robledo and the generals . . . and on the other hand by the *Silvelista* conservatives who came to see in [Cuban] autonomy the only solution."[8]

With Spain's military defeat in 1898, which followed Cánovas's assassination almost immediately, the political crisis grew worse. From then on, the widespread opinion was that the Spanish State was unable to safeguard national interests. That is, the Enemy had ceased to be the so-called Cuban insurgency, or even the United States, and instead had become the Spanish State itself, or at least its leaders. About this very strange moment in modern Spanish history, López-Morillas remarked: "the State was left floating about like something alien to reality. The State was thought of, at the most, as the pompous disguise of a man incapable of fending for himself." And he added: "during the Restoration and the Regency, the State dragged out an untrue, ghostlike existence."[9] If to López-Morillas's telling imagery—*pompous disguise, untrue, ghostlike existence*—we add the crisis of legitimacy that affected the Spanish crown during the Restoration—a Regent Queen who was not Spanish and a pretender to the throne constantly making trouble at Spain's borders— one can gather a fairly clear picture of the collective *alienation* that affected all of Spanish society at the time. Indeed, there seems to be no other name for it. Restoration Spain was collectively *alienated*, made neurotic if you will, by the political and military events of the Cuban war. Small wonder, then, that Antonio Machado, in one of his more famous poems, should have recalled this time as one of "*de mentira, de infamia*" [lies and infamy]:

> A España toda,
> la malherida España, de Carnaval vestida
> nos la pusieron, pobre, y escuálida y beoda
> para que no acertaran la mano con la herida.[10]

[All of Spain / beaten-up Spain, dressed in Carnival / was handed us poor, squalid and drunk, / so that hand and wound would be confused.]

Even so, it is difficult to grasp the full extent of such alienated reactions, within the postcolonial reading I am here attempting, if we first don't understand its links to the unusual historical relationship between Spain and Cuba. The extent and depth to which that collective sense of alienation was spread in Spain at the time should itself alert us to the uneasy terms of the Metropolis–Periphery relationship that were then operative. One would assume, in fact, that this relationship was the traditional one that governs colonial dependency, such that peripheral Cuba was simply a virgin territory from which metropolitan Spain extracted raw materials and exploited human labor. The reality, however—particularly the *economic* reality—was much different. In the words of Cuban historian Manuel Moreno Fraginals: "Cuba was never a typical colony . . . On the contrary, it had the world's primary sugar industry, which in turn was the prime basic product of international trade . . . it was therefore impossible in Cuba to impose the norms and prejudices of European metropolises, or even the rudiments of seizure and extraction of wealth." Thus, after reviewing mountains of irrefutable statistical evidence, the same historian concluded: "In a number of ways Cuba exceeded the Metropolis . . . Spanish policy was one of survival within a system in which it did not act as economic Metropolis managing the affairs of another country, but rather as a strange mixture of a parasite that sucks up wealth and a Center that provides culture."[11] One can safely conclude from all this that at the end of the nineteenth century it was Spain that depended upon Cuba, the Metropolis upon the periphery, rather than the other (and vastly more common) way around.

From the above we may derive an alternative explanation to the one invoked most frequently to explain Spain's collective alienation during the 1898 crisis. As we know, the causes of such alienation are usually put in macro-political terms that defy reasonable cause: namely, that after losing its last colonies, the Spanish state came down with a case of inferiority complex, first because of its defeat to a young power whose moral values it despised, and second, because it faced with envy its European neighbors' more successful imperialist campaigns. One never hears, however, about the more plausible explanation and that sheer economic history happens to confirm: namely, that the collective reaction to the loss had itself been preconditioned by the unusual economic dependence of Spain upon Cuba, a dependence that, upon dissolving—or at least upon being perceived as dissolving—threw the Spanish nation onto a panic and quickened the identity crisis that today we know under the equivocal name of "Generation of 1898." In summary, to the 1898 crisis Spain reacted not like a mother after losing a daughter—believed to be *siempre fiel* [always loyal], Cuba's colonial motto—but rather like an orphan left homeless.

The collective alienation to which I have referred, itself the cause of collective indifference and pessimism, had yet another feature: historic Spanish isolationism or retrenchment. As early as August 1897 Maeztu would remark, in one of his many published reactions to the Cuban war: "We all wonder whether enough blood has been spilled upon a land that doesn't deserve it."[12] Maeztu's reactionary view, a staple of the majority of his generation, was not so much that the colonial enterprise had been unjustified or immoral—a position that would have led him logically to identify with the so-called insurgents. His point, rather, was that the colonies had become an unbearable burden for Spain, which thus turned all further efforts at retaining them a quixotic enterprise; and, by extension, that Cubans, Puertoricans, and Filipinos were all unworthy subalterns. Years before Maeztu complained about Spanish blood being spilled in vain, another Spanish intellectual, Angel Ganivet, had himself issued another isolationist warning: "we must lock up all the doors through which the Spanish spirit slipped out onto the four cardinal points."[13] Ganivet's early call to retrenchment gained currency with the loss of Cuba and Spain's military defeat, to the point that postwar intellectual groups, like Costa's *Regeneracionistas*, made it their battle cry. It even became the shared signature of the Generation of 1898 writers, a fact that did not prevent personalized versions, like Baroja's, Unamuno's or *Azorín's*, from becoming formulated.

III

From the foregoing I draw at least two conclusions. The first refers to the whole phenomenon of Spanish retrenchment to which I just alluded. As reinforced by the Generation of 1898's canonical image, there continues to be a misperception that such retrenchment occurred out of a deliberate critical effort, on the part of both the Spanish State and its intellectuals, to withdraw from the colonial project. Yet nothing could be further from the truth. Besides the fact that retrenchment is not equivalent to critical reflection, suffice it to recall Maeztu's remark to the effect that Cuba was "a land that does not deserve" Spanish blood. Not even by the late date of 1897, when Maeztu wrote this, was it a question of denying the legitimacy of the colonial enterprise. At the most, it was simply a matter of discarding Cubans and other colonial types as unworthy subalterns. Ganivet himself, whose *Idearium español* had proposed locking up the Spanish spirit that had escaped with the Conquest of Spanish America, corrected himself later in an 1895 letter to Unamuno to the effect that: "I, too, had said it would be good to lock all the doors to keep Spain from escaping; and yet, against my wish, I've left one door half-open—Africa's—thinking about the future . . . If we look at the future there are a thousand signs pointing to Africa as the field of our [future] expansion."[14] Had Ganivet been able to overcome the personal crisis that drove him to suicide, he probably would have led the *escuela de africanistas* he proposed to Unamuno in the same letter. And had he actually done so, perhaps Edward Said would have ended up devoting to him a separate chapter in *Orientalism*!

What was true for Maeztu and Ganivet applies more or less to each of the members of the Generation of 1898. Not unlike the State they criticized, their position was "essentially peninsular of domestic policy," and at no time one of *foreign* policy. Nor did they ever come around to analyzing critically Spain's colonial policy, except perhaps to protest what they perceived as the waste of human and financial investment. This was so even in relation to the more immediate and senseless Spanish resistance to the different versions of the separatist movement that had arisen in the last colonies. Not even Unamuno, the one writer who came closest to articulating such a critique, was able to state such moral judgment, particularly after 1897, the year Unamuno underwent his religious crisis and after which he grew increasingly skeptical about all politics.

My second conclusion arises from the earlier remarks on the collective alienation of Spanish society. Clearly it is not enough to say that the Spanish reaction to the loss of the colonies was preconditioned by its economic dependency, itself the result of the unusual inversion of roles. One must further view such a reaction in its full neurotic implications. To put it bluntly: alienation was the symptom of a collective defense mechanism that followed the severe blow to Spanish narcissism, or self-love, that was dealt by its military defeat. Antonio Cánovas del Castillo, the Spanish Prime Minister during the war, took this to the limit when he stated, in what was surely his most infamous speech before the *Cortes*: "Our government will not cease to make any necessary sacrifice, to spend its last coin and put up its last man (*hasta el último hombre y hasta la última peseta*) defending the fatherland, our glorious flag, our sovereignty never to be extinguished in America, because Cuba shall forever remain Spanish. . . . We shall persist in our efforts and in our attitude to deny any yielding to the rebels in arms."[15] This was, briefly put, the policy

Cánovas himself called the "war against war" or "war of extermination," a battle cry that resonates loudly today in other later, but no less deadly, twentieth-century versions, such as "Hitler's Final Solution." Indeed, Cánovas's "war of extermination" took its most extreme form in the 1896 and 1897 *bandos de Reconcentración* that were carried out by Valeriano Weyler y Nicolau, then Cuba's captain-general, whom Cánovas appointed in a desperate move to win the war. Weyler's orders, which segregated the Cuban civilian population from the insurgent rebels in isolated camps, made no provisions for food distribution and provided hardly any sanitary facilities for the imprisoned population. In time, tropical diseases spread and the camps claimed as many as half a million lives, an extraordinary figure when we consider that at the time it meant nearly one-fourth of the total Cuban civilian population.[16]

Whether it be under Restoration Spain, Nazi Germany, or the United States during the Vietnam War, policies such as Cánovas's war of extermination have one common denominator: they all share the inflation of the collective ego based on infantile fantasies of omnipotence. The collective alienation of Spanish society stemming from the loss of the last colonies results directly out of the previous inflation of the collective ego, whose cruelest and most disastrous outcome was perhaps not Spain's military defeat as the extermination, within the *Reconcentración* policy, of one-fourth of Cuba's civilians. Had no such ego inflation occurred; indeed, had the desperate "war of extermination" not been waged, then post–1898 Spanish society would most likely not have succumbed to such a crisis; at least, it would not have had the kind of existential repercussions that it took on immediately after.

The analogy with Nazi Germany, or more precisely, with post–World War II German society, is accurate, I believe, because, despite the many differences between the two historical situations—which I will be the first to acknowledge—one important fact does link the two. I call that link "the inability to mourn." I borrow this label from the title of the excellent essay by Alexander and Margarete Mitscherlich that I find so pertinent to this case. The Mitscherlichs' extraordinary study, of which I here make ample use, has as its theme the principles of collective psychic defense that were acted out by German society following the traumatic experience of World War II. Such principles included the collective denial of the terrible facts of recent German history and the consequent inability to mourn—that is, the inability to undertake the necessary internal work that would allow one to reconcile with the loss of a given object. The consequences of such inability to mourn become evident in various ways, and most importantly in the derealization or emptying out of the past, or else, in the censorship of all those facts that threaten the ego's integrity. And so, just as post–World War II Germany devoted itself, neurotically and obsessively, to attain the "German miracle" while turning its back on the past and denying responsibility for the crimes against humanity, so did post–1898 Spain succumb to melancholy impoverishment as a result of a blow to its collective self-esteem.[17]

Virtually all of the metaphors and concepts we associate traditionally with the joint vision of the Generation of 1898—*silencio, tristeza, adustez, sobriedad, austeridad, nostalgia, decadencia, ruinas, hastío, monotonía, desolación, abulia, abandono, aridez*—are actually satellite metaphors that rotate around one central concept: *melancolía*, melancholy, the melancholy that permeates the entire post-*Desastre* period and for which the 1898 literary canon is widely known.[18] One must, in fact, invoke melancholy in relation to this particular historical situation in order to situate more precisely our understanding of the collective alienation to which I have referred. For, as Freud once observed, there's Mourning, and there's Melancholy. Mourning occurs, or can take place, when the lost object was loved for itself, that is, when we feel empathy for whatever we lost. Melancholy, on the other hand, reveals that the lost object had an altogether different function for the self: what we call narcissism. If I happen to have chosen that love object in my likeness, or if that object was willing to adapt itself to my fantasy, once I lose it I am unable to mourn; instead, I feel something else: melancholy. That is, my grief will occur not for having lost the object, but for losing a part of my own self. And if, in addition, I associate any ambivalence with that love object, then its loss will be further tainted with melancholy self-hatred. My grief will be characterized not by the end of a relationship but by a partial loss of the self, a kind of amputation. Melancholy self-torture is thus, in the end, but a reproach against the object for causing *me* the loss. The inability to mourn—and its polar opposite: the ability to feel melancholy—is therefore preceded by a type of love in which we are concerned less with sharing the other's feelings than by confirming one's own self-esteem.

IV

The international crisis known in Spain as *el Desastre* implied an intimate narcissistic relationship between the Metropolis and Cuba, the richest of its last colonies. Restoration Spain's war policy made possible for the Spanish people, at a broad national level and with few exceptions, to place their faith and trust in its leaders' infantile fantasies of omnipotence.

To the irreparable loss of the Colonies, however, Spain responded not with collective mourning—which the 1898 writers certainly could have facilitated—but with denial, by which I mean a defense against the perception of harmful aspects in external reality—the missing "heartbeat" that Silvela had noted in 1898 and that Baroja later would remark.

It is no exaggeration to say, in conclusion, that the Generation of 1898 canon is shot through with a good measure of historical irresponsibility. None of its members ever facilitated a collective ability to mourn, particularly in relation to the colonial enterprise, part and parcel of Spanish historical identity. That this was so is confirmed in the common use of the term *Desastre* to refer to what was, properly speaking, not only a military defeat in an actual war, but the political incompetence of Restoration Spain. The concept of *Disaster*, which is always impersonal since it refers etymologically [*dis* + *astrum*] to a "bad star," avoids assigning responsibility and attributes evil to an anonymous source—a case of plain bad luck. Beyond whatever insight this conceptual usage should yield regarding the politics of Restoration Spain, the result is that, precisely because Spain was unable to mourn, it has since then never reconciled itself to the loss of the "always loyal" island of Cuba. To this day, its relationship to the former colony continues to be a strange mixture of narcissism and melancholy.

One could also say that the same inability to mourn has, in turn, affected Spanish historical memory. Beginning with the so-called *Desastre*, only certain acceptable aspects of the past become admissible to consciousness, with the end-result that responsibility becomes either denied or reinterpreted, always displaced onto others who, almost always, happen to be non-Spaniards. It is noteworthy, in this sense, that virtually all of those Spanish writers and intellectuals from the same period who did denounce the colonial enterprise as the ultimate cause of the so-called *Desastre*, and whose own works demanded and carried out such critical reflection—I refer to such writers as Luis Morote, Rafael Macías Picavea, Rafael Altamira, Francesc Pi y Margall, Domingo Isern, Pompeyo Gener—all were excluded sooner or later from the Generation of 1898 canon, to the point that today hardly anyone remembers them. No accident, no "bad star," here. Nor was their censorship simply a matter of so-called literary taste. In his 1900 book *La moral de la derrota* (The Moral of Defeat)—as explicit a title as one could ask for—Luis Morote, arguably one of the most honest writers of his time, remarked, on the subject of Cánovas's war of extermination, that "the facts have condemned it, although it remains to be seen if we have learned anything from it." A plethora of similar remarks abound in the works of all those unknown 1898 heroes.

They await to be restored to the canon of a generation that literally wiped them out of its historical memory.[19]

That the colonial enterprise was never an actual object of critical reflection on the part of the Generation of 1898 canon, and thus that to this day it remains subject to harmful repetition; that there never was, in other words, a healthy mourning of the 1898 loss a is proven in part by the course of Spanish history after the so-called *Desastre*. First, because after 1898 Spanish colonial expansion did spread throughout Africa, thus fulfilling Ganivet's wish, though its results were, so to speak, equally as disastrous. In the words of Carlos Serrano: Spain's desire to incorporate itself to the concert of great nations (read: colonial powers) "kept dictating a good part of foreign policy . . . in promoting in particular an extremely risky African adventurism in Morocco, which could only be understood in terms of a desire on the part of Spanish politicians not to see themselves totally cut off, despite everything, from the colonial pie."[20]

No less evident, however, is the additional fact that since 1898 Spain has not ceased to empty out the historical reality of Cuba while continuing to subject the former colony to successive projections of infantile fantasies. It is such grotesque fantasy that recently made Manuel Fraga Iribarne—former president of the Galicia Xunta, and before that, former president of Generalissimo Franco's *Instituto de Cultura Hispánica*—remark, in his 1952 preface to a collection of Cuba's political Constitutions, that Weyler's Reconcentration policy had been but "*un mito propagandístico*" [a propaganda myth], and that "the ones who actually caused all the hunger were the [Cuban] insurgents themselves with their tactics of 'burnt land.' "[21] It is that same fantasy that made none other than José María Aznar, the former Spanish president, to refer to Cánovas—the intellectual author of the Cuban war of extermination, Weyler's boss, and the culprit in the death of Cuban insurgent leader Antonio Maceo—as "an exceptional leader whose light still shines upon us."[22]

As we can see, *el Desastre* is still very much with us. Each time a new Spanish luxury hotel goes up in Cuba, each time a Spanish tourist travels to the island to have cheap sex with poor women, or needy children; the logic of "to the last man and peseta" comes to the fore. In time, the *Disaster* has turned into an attitude of retaliation against the former contender—the United States; but while the object of the rematch—the two countries' difficult historical relationship—has always been clear, the real and actual lost object—Spain's narcissistic relationship with Cuba—is most certainly not.

Who could have guessed that Angel Ganivet, the same Angel Ganivet who in 1895 had demanded both locking up Spain and expanding anew in Africa, would have been the one to criticize all those newer versions of the same colonial policy? We may not ourselves know that Ganivet also wrote: "If today we find ourselves totally defeated (and our defeat began centuries ago) because we were challenged in the name of our interests, our retaliation will come the day a new ideal will lead us on, not whenever we have as much money as our adversaries, were that ever to be the case."[23] Ganivet's ideal remains far off, for both Spaniards and Cubans alike. To reach it, we need first to work through that requisite stage of collective mourning we have always feared and denied ourselves, but that poets like Antonio Machado, in Castile, or Joan Maragall, in Catalonia, prescribed repeatedly in some amazing poems. "Save yourself, save yourself from all evil!" Maragall himself wrote once in his moving *Ode to Spain:*

> May your crying make you new, happy and alive!
> Think about all the life that surrounds you!
> Lift up your face:
> Smile at all the iris shining on clouds!

CHAPTER SIX

After the Revolution: Strawberry and Chocolate, *or the Politics of Reconciliation*

In memory of four Brothers:
Armando Alejandre, Jr., Carlos Costa, Mario de la Peña and Pablo Morales

I

The release, in 1993, of the popular Cuban film *Strawberry and Chocolate,* by directors Tomás Gutiérrez Alea and Juan Carlos Tabío and with a script by Senel Paz, occasioned a lively debate about its content and significance. The debate was in itself predictable, given both the subject of the film—the sentimental education of two Cuban men, one gay and the other straight—and the specific circumstance in which the film was produced—the so-called Cuban "special period" following the collapse of Real Socialism in Europe and thus in the middle of the worst crisis the Castro regime faced in its then 38-year history. Whereas outside of Cuba the film was hailed as further evidence that *perestroika* had reached the island and the Castro brothers were finally releasing their grip on dissidence, within the Cuban community, both in the island and among exiles, the film sparked conflicting opinions. Some viewed it as an unwitting critique of the Cuban State's long-standing repression of gays; others saw it as manipulative, further proof of the regime's ongoing deception about its actual policies, particularly at a moment when it was attempting to win over allies abroad in order to resolve an economic and political crisis. The debate appeared to reach a climax when the film was bought up by Miramax for U.S. distribution and nominated for the Oscar for best foreign film. And it appeared to resolve itself when the film lost out to no less than Russia's entry in the same contest.

One can of course only praise that a film would be capable of sparking discussion on such vital civic topics, even if the debate should have been based most often on previous political positions rather than on close readings. Indeed, contribution to civic discussion was the substance of the directors' ultimate defense of their film. Yet despite their best wishes, the equivocal nature of the debate has been especially glaring, I think, precisely among members of the Cuban community, both in and out of the island. For us the film poses not just a limited statement about the status of gays in Cuba, but, according to what the directors themselves claimed, a general plea for tolerance, and thus, presumably and by extension, a plea for the coexistence of contesting political philosophies— one-party socialism and multi-party liberalism, capitalism and state-directed economy—within the same national ethos.[1]

If we agree that in the film Diego is not just a gay protagonist but a Cuban nationalist and, in the end, a future exile, and further, that David is not just a straight foil but a reformed or newly enlightened young Communist, then it is clear that under the banner of a strong nationalism the film proposes the eventual reconciliation of the two political halves of the Cuban nation, torn asunder by the more than four decades of communism. In one of the film's final scenes, when the two friends are taking a view of Havana harbor, Diego laments that he is enjoying that view for the last time, to which David responds by questioning whether in fact it would be his last. Barring the possibility that here David refers ironically to Diego's future reconversion to revolutionary zeal, his question suggests that Diego will indeed return to Havana after the disappearance of the regime's historic intolerance, perhaps even the disappearance of the regime itself.

That reconciliation should be the ultimate ethical horizon of *Strawberry and Chocolate* should not surprise us, therefore, if we view the film within the context of the Cuban government's recent attempts to pursue that precise policy with respect to Cuban exiles. Under the general rubric of *diálogo*, Havana has encouraged and at times even sponsored sustained contacts with sympathetic groups of Cuban emigrés since at least the late 1970s. Under this policy, family reunification, money remissions, guided tours, and participation in youth camps, all under state supervision, have occurred at a sustained pace. With the onset of the special period in 1989, and the government's increased need for hard currency, these contacts, now formally organized as state enterprises, have increased still. To be sure, the ideology that sustains these contacts is reconciliation, stated in principle as a policy of mutual tolerance of differing political views and the consequent strengthening of national identity. In practice, however, reconciliation has rather come to mean acquiescence to policy interests of the Cuban State, particularly opposition to the U.S. embargo, a cease-fire of exile hostility against the regime and a consequent preservation of the status quo.[2]

The Cuban film institute (ICAIC) has at various times adopted the treatment of the theme of reconciliation, as in films like Jesús Díaz's 1985 melodrama *Lejanía* and the more recent *Vidas paralelas* by Pastor Vega and *Miel para Ochún* by Humberto Solás. But *Strawberry and Chocolate* is certainly the best dramatic articulation of the policy. My own ciphered reading takes as a point of departure this political debate, which I consider somewhat broader, though not necessarily more privileged, than the debate over gay rights in Cuba on which discussion of the film has focused most often. Paul Julian Smith has focused eloquently on that aspect of the film, but I shall not pursue that reading.[3] My own limited interest lies, briefly put, in analyzing the terms of political reconciliation that the film sets out for its reader. In order to pursue this reading, and as I have done in previous chapters, I shall first review some of the facts known about *Strawberry and Chocolate* in its different media versions. Second, I shall go on to consider two key moments of the film on which these terms of reconciliation appear to rest. In this section I attempt to understand the film's language. I close this analytical section by analyzing one text in particular that lends support to my reading, and end with some remarks regarding the film's *politics* of reconciliation, which I regard to be a far cry from the *reality* of reconciliation, a worthy if still unrealized goal.

II

First, some circumstantial facts, some of them well-known, about the film and its genesis. In 1990, Senel Paz, a Cuban fiction writer (b. Fomento, 1950) published the short story "El lobo, el bosque y el hombre nuevo" ["The Wolf, the Woods and the New Man"] in Havana. The story was a monologue told by a certain David about his relationship with a gay man, the travails between these two Havana residents, and the sad outcome of their friendship. That same year the story won the International "Juan Rulfo Prize," sponsored annually by Radio-France, the Mexican Cultural Institute and the Paris *Maison de l' Amérique Latine*. Paz's story was published the following year in both Mexico and Cuba and was widely translated. Previous to this story Senel Paz had published relatively little: *El niño aquel* [That child over there] a 1980 book of short stories, won a literary prize in Cuba; it was followed three years later by a novel, *Un rey en el jardín* [A King in the Garden]. Parallel to his fiction were Paz's screenplays: *Una novia para David* (which provides the first dramatic rendering of David, the protagonist of *Strawberry and Chocolate*) became a 1985 movie directed by Gerardo Chijona. More successful, or at least better known, was his second film, *Adorables mentiras* (Adorable Lies), directed by Rolando Rojas, which included, among other characters, Nancy, the former prostitute who reappears in *Strawberry and Chocolate*.

It was only after Paz's story won the "Juan Rulfo Prize" abroad that it became well known in Cuba, though it appears that at least at first its circulation was made scarce for reasons that are not entirely clear.[4] Be that as it may, what is certain is that in order to overcome that seeming attempt at censorship, a number of dramatic versions of the story began to proliferate in Havana's little theatres. Between 1991 and 1993 no less than four different versions of these plays were staged in Havana, sometimes simultaneously. One of them, the most popular by all accounts, retitled *La catedral del helado* (The Ice Cream Cathedral), held over several months in Havana's avant-garde *Teatro del sótano*, was a one-man show for a single actor and two characters.[5] In a 1994 interview published in Spain, Senel Paz elevates the number of such play versions to eight, not counting the one he himself was then writing for a festival in Germany.[6] Not unlike the textual history of Manuel Puig's *Kiss of the Spider Woman*, a text to which the Senel Paz story is often compared, the narrative of *Strawberry and Chocolate* was first a successful play before becoming a film.

One cannot underestimate the importance of these dramatic versions. By 1991 Cuba was already undergoing the so-called special period, an economic policy taken by the government in light of the crisis and eventual collapse of the European Socialist block, which placed restraints on all cultural activity. It is therefore plausible that the Paz story was slowly becoming the implicit protest symbol of this period—much as the *jineteras* or streetwalkers would do for Cuba's sexual tourism and the *balseros*, or rafters, for the regime's moral and economic failures. It is likely that such stage popularity caught the attention of Tomás Gutiérrez Alea, the legendary film Cuban director (his most famous film to date had been *Memories of Underdevelopment*) and member of Cuba's *nomenklatura*, though it was not until Senel Paz's tenth attempt at a commissioned script that Gutiérrez Alea finally approved the film project. This tenth and final script version—whose first title was *Enemigo rumor* [Rumor Enemy], after José Lezama Lima's first book of poems (1941)—dates between 1991 and 1992. It was the basis for the final film product, though upon comparison with the published script it is clear that the film changed it considerably.[7] Film production took place throughout 1992 and 1993, though it was halted briefly at one point because of Gutiérrez Alea's illness and in order to accommodate codirection with Juan Carlos Tabío, a younger colleague. Release came in late 1993, in time for Havana's fifteenth Latin-American Film Festival, where it won several prizes, including Best Picture. After that, the film went on to play to record crowds.

Predictably, and like the play versions that preceded it, the film became a barometer of the (Cuban) times. In 1994, *Strawberry and Chocolate* won Best Picture at both the Berlin and Gramado Festivals. After Miramax Pictures and Robert Redford bought the rights for U.S. distribution, it was nominated for Best Foreign Film Oscar. In April 1995, after a long battle with cancer, Gutiérrez Alea himself passed away in Havana. Before his death, he completed one last film, *Guantanamera*, now widely regarded as his swan song, both his and the Cuban Revolution's.

It was not the first time that a Cuban film was based on a homosexual theme, and particularly homosexual repression under the present regime. In 1983, Néstor Almendros and Orlando Jiménez Leal produced *Improper Conduct* [*Conducta impropia*], a scathing documentary on that very topic and based on a series of interviews with a number of former inmates, some of them gay, in the *UMAP* (*Unidades Mobilizadas de Ayuda a la Producción*: Mobilized Units to Aid Production) work camps. The *UMAP* was the acronym for work camps that were part of a vast network set up throughout the island by the Castro regime between 1965 and 1969. They had been created to confine and presumably rehabilitate various types of dissidents, varying from the religious to the sexual, among the Cuban population. While a full account of the *UMAP* camps has never been made, it is likely that homosexuals were the largest and most oppressed among the various inmate groups held there.[8] *Improper Conduct* documented many other incidents of repression and forced diaspora throughout the history of the regime, such as the Mariel exodus. But clearly, the *UMAP* camps were its focus and what damaged the regime's image most.

So much so, in fact, that soon after *Improper Conduct* was released, Gutiérrez Alea began a public polemic with Almendros in *The Village Voice*, which lasted between August and October 1984, in which he denounced the film as "a document through which one can arrive at an 'authentic' image of our reality here and now. But its lack of historical sense and social context determines its superficiality and turns the film into a document that reveals instead its authors' human misery." In the same text Gutiérrez Al a did mention the *UMAP* camps; he did not, to be sure, deny their exi tence, but minimized their importance, claiming that they were merely camps where "many homosexuals performed military service." Gutiérrez Alea also admitted that the camps had been a mistake and "created a scandal that fortunately resolved itself in their disappearance and a rectifying policy." Finally, Gutiérrez Alea complained that *Improper Conduct* had referred to the *UMAP* work camps "as if they had taken place yesterday or might still be taking place," when in fact they had disappeared 17 years before. In his response, Néstor Almendros seized on this very point, among others, to counter that it was hardly absurd to discuss events on film that had occurred barely 17 years before, particularly when considering that the plot of Gutiérrez Alea's then-latest film, *The Last Supper*, takes place more than a century before.[9]

I mention the details of this particular polemic between Gutiérrez Alea and Almendros not only to show that in the treatment of the homosexual theme *Strawberry and Chocolate* had an important precedent in *Improper Conduct*, but also to identify it as its likely dialectical origin. Indeed, in several interviews after the release of *Strawberry and Chocolate* Gutiérrez Alea admitted that he would have liked Almendros to see his film, thus invoking him, as Paul Julian Smith avers, as an "ideal addressee." Indeed, in an article published in *The Miami Herald* in April 1994, Gutiérrez Alea went so far as to remember Almendros fondly—"I cannot forget that Néstor and I were friends for many years and especially during those adolescent years when personalities are developed and when affections are decisive." He also disclosed then that he would have wished *Strawberry and Chocolate* to be "a response to that old polemic and perhaps a good reason for us to renew a dialogue we broke some time ago. We can't forget it's a film that argues for tolerance and for understanding those who are different."[10]

With the added benefit of hindsight, one can only wonder how *Strawberry and Chocolate*, a fictional film whose storyline takes place in 1979, a full 14 years after the *UMAP* policies were put into place, could possibly have supplied the "lack of historical sense and social context" that Gutiérrez Alea had once denounced in *Improper Conduct*. Suffice it to mention this as a revealing instance of misreading. But one need only invoke a minimum dose of common sense to realize that it was not necessary for Néstor Almendros to expire to have Gutiérrez Alea think of him and their earlier debate in connection with the production of *Strawberry and Chocolate*. Besides the explicit thematic link between the two films, there is the more crucial issue of the family romance between these two filmmakers, an issue that makes their personal relationship, and particularly their political differences, overflow the purely professional realm. It is almost as if in invoking the memory of their common adolescence—"when affections are decisive"—Gutiérrez Alea himself were suggesting we read *Strawberry and Chocolate*, in addition, as an allegory of the relationship between the two men; perhaps even view Diego and David, respectively, as symbolic stand-ins for Almendros and himself. There is no reason to speculate, finally, whether Gutiérrez Alea and Almendros were actual lovers. And yet one need go that far to view Gutiérrez Alea's testimony as a possible structural, perhaps unconscious, model of the relationship between the two films as texts. Within that model, *Strawberry and Chocolate* would appear to be a guilt-ridden response to *Improper Conduct*.

By a guilt-ridden response I mean that in *Strawberry and Chocolate* we find a ritual of repentance toward *Improper Conduct*. I caution the concept of ritual, however, because the film does not involve an actual retraction, at least on the part of David (the institutional character), due to the fact that it lacks one essential element. The ritual is evident in, among other things, Gutiérrez Alea's frequent defense of his own film not so much in terms of a gay thematic per se as in those of intolerance in general, a move which ends up short-circuiting any possible sustained comparison with *Improper Conduct*. What therefore turns *Strawberry and Chocolate* into a ritual, and an empty one at that, is the ultimate lack of ethical recognition of an Other; an Other, I might add, that could easily be made present by invoking two simple words of repentance: *forgive me*. I am of course speaking about the film *qua* film. But it should be noted, in addition, that Gutiérrez Alea never did ask forgiveness from Almendros, either as a representative of the Cuban government policy or as a friend. Indeed, Almendros (and, by extension, *Improper Conduct*) are wholly absent from his film, except perhaps in the cipher of Diego, the gay character who is exiled at the end. In that sense, Gutiérrez Alea's film, not unlike his 1994 *El Nuevo Herald* article, represses an ethical dimension of repentance and replaces it with a ritual. It is precisely that ritual of repentance what dramatizes what I referred to earlier as the "terms of reconciliation" the film offers as a cure to a sundered Cuban national identity.

III

How that ritual of repentance, that guilt-ridden response, is dramatized in the narrative of *Strawberry and Chocolate* will make the substance of my reading of two series of scenes, at the beginning and end of the film and which essentially make up its narrative frame. We begin by examining one particular thematic structure, the film's principal tale: the friendship between Diego and David. Their relationship takes place in 1979, a year before the infamous Mariel exodus that brought to the United States over 150,000 additional refugees. After overcoming a series of obstacles, that relationship reaches a climax, from all appearances at least, with a vindication of friendship above and beyond personal differences. In the case of the two main characters, their differences lie not only in sexual preference, but in ideology too, or at least in their differing positions vis-à-vis the Cuban regime. Diego is gay, religious, and a nationalist; David is straight, an atheist, and a communist. Their relationship is flawed, in addition, by jealousies, both mutual and contextual. Diego, urged on by Germán, tries to seduce David; whereas David, urged on by Miguel, tries to entrap Diego in illegal activity. In addition, Nancy, at first suspicious of David, who at the beginning of the film is portrayed as a government type, changes in the end to become jealous of Diego's amorous interest in David.

These are not the only symmetries. Paul Julian Smith has remarked how the two main characters embody other differences:"not just straight and gay but also provincial and metropolitan, domestic and cosmopolitan, atheist and religious."[11] Structurally, such overt differences sustain two separate and mutual betrayals: Diego pretends he is David's friend the better to seduce him; David pretends he is Diego's friend the better to denounce him before the government. But if it is true that neither Diego nor David succeeds in betraying the other because both end up becoming the other's real friend, or so the film would have us believe, the problem that remains is how the film actually sets out to represent their mutual disclosures of such failures. My view is that this is precisely where a break in the symmetry occurs. In the process what becomes betrayed is not only the two characters' friendship between the two characters as much as the film's interested ideology.

In order to understand the terms of that representation we must begin by establishing that David, and not Diego, is the true subject (in the sense of *focus*) of the narrative. During the initial scene we see David, who has come to a *posada*, a lover's motel, with his girlfriend, unveil two viewing gates. First, a curtain that opens onto an outside window and through which David identifies a red neon sign proclaiming the all-seeing eye of the Committees for the Defense of the Revolution, the Cuban government's block-by-block watchdogs of revolutionary zeal. The second gate is the hole in the room wall through which David espies next door a naked woman topping a man. By opening and closing both of these gates, successively, David is thus placed in firm visual control of his environment, his *posada* kingdom, so to speak, uncontaminated either by snitching (the sordid side of Revolution) or fucking (the physical aspect of Eros). David's gaze is thus made to appear as innocent as the subsequent slow pan of Vivian's smooth back and his offer to put off consummation until after marriage, an offer that comes much to Vivian's surprise, and of course bitter disappointment.

If David's point of view is the prevailing one in the film, then we can certainly confirm which is the ideology (in the basic sense of the object of focalization) that controls the narrative. In the first scene David's point of view prevails, focalizing from the outset, and thus makes of his character the film's logical narrative subject. The film reinforces this point of view not only by focusing on David from the beginning, but also, and above all, by showing him as a spectator, or at least as a voyeur. David's gaze, a gaze that is both sexually straight and revolutionary, is therefore the one that controls narrative content both because of what it makes present and what it makes absent: what it includes and excludes.

David's point of view predominates throughout the film by other means. We often see him alone, and his is the only actual voice-over. At the end of the film, the last image we see is, again, David's face, embracing Diego and crying; for it is he who has, if not the last word, certainly the last tear. This is radically different from the way Diego, the clear object to David's subject, is made to appear. Seldom do we see Diego by himself; whenever we do, he appears either as the object of David's look or as the object of the camera's overt editorializing, as in one scene where Diego appears in front of a mailbox dropping the letter that will seal his fate in Cuba, and afterward the camera slides to focus on a quotation from José Martí written on a nearby wall. Diego appears most frequently accompanied either by the subject's look or by the look of other characters, like Nancy, Germán, or Miguel.

IV

What is the sum effect of this particular objectification? When in separate interviews both Senel Paz and Gutiérrez Alea have said that *Strawberry and Chocolate* was not a homosexual film, they were not straying from the truth. Indeed, *Strawberry and Chocolate* cannot possibly be a homosexual film because its point of view takes the homosexual as its object, not its subject. The film does address homosexuality, but does so strictly from a heterosexual point of view. It is not so much a homosexual as a *homosexualist* film, in a way similar to how an *indigenist* can never actually be *indigenous*. Both the homosexual and the *indigenous* are subjects; while the homosexualist and the *indigenist* act ostensibly as their spokespeople. The latter cannot constitute such subjectivity but they certainly appropriate their representation; whether their objects like it or not, each speaks in the name of their respective Other.[12]

Beyond the politics of representation contained in this formula, I am interested in examining some of the consequences for our film. All points of view entail limits, of course, and this is no exception, particularly if we wish to understand Diego's and David's relationship; or else, to be more precise, if we wish to understand the limits of David's representation of his relationship with Diego. But to illustrate this we must refer to a series of scenes at the end of the film that makes up its dramatic climax.

We begin with Miguel, the other male character who is bothered out of his apparent lack of influence over David's snitching skills; in fact, Miguel decides to go to Diego's personally in order to incriminate both. Indeed, because Miguel represents what in Cuba we call a *cuadrado*, an orthodox Communist militant next to whom David appears like an ideological whimp, his dramatic function is important in order to establish David's focalizing reliability. But what plays out in this series of scenes, to the end of the film, seems far more revealing.

The first chosen scene refers to the moment Diego opens the door to find Miguel. In the published script, this scene is actually much longer (102–107) and involves nothing less than the attempted seduction of Diego by Miguel, who has come to offer himself as a print model. In the actual film, however, the scene is simplified, and therefore made dramatically awkward, by making Miguel seek Diego's complicity in expelling David from school because of an alleged affair. In the published script, the seduction scene between Diego and Miguel is interrupted by Nancy and David, both of whom enter Diego's apartment unannounced as Diego is about to go down on Miguel. After the ensuing fight between David and Miguel, the stage directions read as follows: "Diego está sumamente avergonzado, no se atreve a mirar de frente a David" [Diego is extremely ashamed and does not dare face David] (105). Diego is then heard saying: "David, perdona. ¿Cómo iba a imaginarme que era una trampa?" [Diego, forgive me, how was I to imagine it was all a trap?](106). A brief dialogue among the three characters ensues.

In the actual film, however, we slide from the fight among Miguel, Diego, and David to the immediate next scene where David catches Diego stepping off an embassy car, an action that leads him to suspect that Diego has returned to his old ways of illicit activity. Thus he bursts into Diego's apartment asking: "Ven acá, chico, ¿no quedamos en que las cosas iban a quedar claras entre nosotros?" [Come on, man, didn't we agree things would be straight between us from now on?] David appears to refer to a conversation that has presumably taken place between the two after the last fight scene and this one. I say presumably because we are never shown that scene. In that conversation David has, again presumably, revealed to Diego the part he played in betraying him, but this is not at all certain. From all signs, this should be the most important moment in David's relationship with Diego. Dramatically, the scene would contain the *anagnorisis*, the moment of disclosure and revelation whose pointed parallel will come in the last scene, where Diego finally discloses to David his seduction plot. But as I have said, the film treats the whole matter elliptically. Despite the explicitness with which the film treats Diego's confession at the end, to the point of making it the absolute dramatic climax, by contrast it treats David's own confession elliptically, to the point that we cannot tell unequivocally whether any disclosure and apology on his part has occurred at all. In the published script, the rain scene, David's spying on Diego, and Diego's explanation to David are all identical to the film; but there, too, Diego asks David to forgive him at least twice, perhaps three times—first, inexplicably, because he did not know that Miguel was setting him up (105); second time, implicitly, because he feels bad about being found out by David that he was leaving the country (107); and a third time, in the final scene, because he had plotted to seduce David (115). Indeed, Diego's question at the end was also supposed to be the film's final words: "¿Me perdonas?" [Do you forgive me] (116). No such equivalent question ever appears on David's part.

To have had David explain to Diego his relationship to Miguel would have forced him to reveal Miguel's motivation in going to see Diego, thereby confirming the suspicion that David had once formulated about himself at the beginning of the film and of his relationship with Diego: he has indeed become an *hijo de puta*. Diego asks for David's forgiveness—twice successively, according to the published script—and reveals to him his personal desires and his plans for a future exile. At no point, however, does David reciprocate by disclosing his own betrayal, never tells Diego he was spying on him. David avoids doing this even in the climactic scene when both men are catching a view of Havana harbor. All David reveals then is the relatively minor fact that he bedded Nancy in Diego's bed, which of course Diego knew all about since he had set it up himself! That particular scene takes place, as anyone familiar enough with this terrain knows, at the foot of

El Cristo, a gigantic Christ figure erected in Casablanca, at the entrance of Havana harbor. But not even the Christian allure of this site, which suggests the sacrament of confession, is enough to move David to open up to Diego in the same way that Diego had opened up to him.

Instead, Diego's further confession will take place in the following scene, at Diego's, or at least in the ruins of his *guarida*, his urban hideaway, which he is in the process of dismantling because of his imminent exile. It is then that Diego confesses to David, without having David reciprocate in any way, about his frustrated seduction. The film frames the point of view of this sequence with a low front shot of David's open legs, as if underscoring Diego's final humbling before David, a kind of camera fellatio. The two men embrace for the last time and we see them crying their heads off. But it is important to note that this embrace, which has so moved Cubans in the island and in exile alike, takes place at Diego's request, in the context of his confession, and as a further gesture to beg David's forgiveness. In asking for a hug, Diego remarks: "pensaba que al abrazarte me iba a sentir más limpio," (I thought that if I hugged I would feel cleaner.) The words echo pointedly Nancy's statement in an earlier scene to a *santero* about her own planned disclosure to David regarding her own past as a prostitute: "Dentro de mí hay una cosa limpia que nadie ha podido ensuciar." (He'll understand that inside me there's something clean that nobody has dirtied.)

In contrast with David's moral hygiene—a fact established as early as the first scene—both Nancy and Diego are implicitly "dirty"—*escoria*, scum of the earth, the epithet that was used by the Castro regime to denigrate the so-called antisocial elements who sought to emigrate during the Mariel exodus. Diego himself is about to become something else: a *gusano*, a worm, an exile. If David never gets to disclose any of his own betrayals, and if the film pointedly avoids representing them, then this is because making such revelations would unravel the character's personal ethical dimension and expose the politics of the system in which he is inscribed and in which he presumably will spend the rest of his life.

It would be an understatement to say, then, that *Strawberry and Chocolate*, as a Cuban film, remains very much "inside the Revolution," definitely far from being "against it," though it certainly pretends to being so. Such, however, are the ideologically determined limits of David's (the film's) point of view, and such are the film's stated terms of reconciliation. One need not be unduly demonic, in fact, to view David's tears in that final scene as an ironic emblem of the film's guilt-ridden conscience, a conscience that chooses undergoing a symbolic ritual over granting the very forgiveness for which his friend Diego has repeatedly begged.

VI

Comparing the Senel Paz story "The Wolf, the Woods and the New Man," and *Strawberry and Chocolate*, we find as well, and perhaps even more clearly, the presence of bad faith on the part of David, the principal narrator, over Diego's remarks. We are dealing here, after all, with a dramatic monologue, which rhetorically disallows any ethical reciprocity by means of the narrator's filtering of all of Diego's remarks. What is most remarkable, however, is that the exact opposite situation occurs in "El cordero, la lluvia y el hombre desnudo" (The Lamb, the Rain and the Naked Man), the parody of this story written by Cuban exiled writer Roger Salas.[13] Salas's story, which inverts terms and makes the gay character the speaking subject, portrays the character of David (now renamed Abel, a clear echo of *Senel*) as a government snitch in search of material on Cuban gays in order to satisfy government demands for a compromising story. Whether or not Salas's story is a *conte à clef* that provides insight into the historical origins of Senel Paz's tale, it does contain a pointed response to *Strawberry and Chocolate* and, implicitly, a rejection of its terms of reconciliation. At its climax, the following dialogue takes place: "They've asked me to watch over you—he told me sticking his thick and hard lips up my ear . . . I knew it, I know—now I couldn't stop shaking. Shut up, faggot. You can't know everything, you're not psychic. I knew it all along, darling . . . boy. And you'll do it, you're one of them . . . but I hope that one day, for your own good, they forget you, and let you live" (58).[14] This brief dialogue may yet be the best, and most dry-eyed, explication of *Strawberry and Chocolate*. I know it is at least the best summary of my own ciphered reading.

What makes *Strawberry and Chocolate* work ultimately if not as an ethical exemplum then at least as an entertaining film, is its deft manipulation of the rhetoric of melodrama. Melodrama is the same rhetoric that reinforces the film's interested ideology. Smith has pointed out, in addition to the two main characters' Manichaean differences, to the film's "overemphasis and demonstrativity" as signs of its "aesthetic empoverishment." He states: "*Fresa y chocolate* does not simply show (*montre*), it demonstrates (*démontre*), heavily gesticulating with its directorial hand." In this, accordingly, Gutiérrez Alea's film appears to retrograde to an earlier, pre-Rosellinian aesthetic that attempts to preserve the illusion of the studio in order to conceal a somber historical reality, which Smith himself describes darkly: "behind the seductive spectacle and public displays of the nazis and the Soviets lay another scene which could not be described and which would come to haunt later imaginations: the death camps"; and so, "while Diego is allowed to invoke the UMAP camps, David can simply dismiss them as an 'error' of the Revolution."[15]

Would it surprise us to learn, in this context, that Melodrama as a genre began with the French Revolution and its aftermath? This is the moment that marks, as Peter Brooks has explained, "the final liquidation of the traditional Sacred and its representative institutions (Church and Monarch), the shattering of the myth of Christendom, the dissolution of an organic and hierarchically cohesive society, and the invalidation of the literary forms—tragedy, comedy of manners—that depended on such a society. Melodrama does not simply represent," Brooks adds, "a 'fall' from tragedy, but is itself a response to the loss of the tragic vision. It comes into being in a world where the traditional imperatives of truth and ethics have been violently thrown into question, yet where the promulgation of truth and ethics, their instauration as a way of life, is of immediate daily, political concern."[16]

As a symptom of Cuba's special period, following the collapse of Real Socialism in Europe, *Strawberry and Chocolate* resorts to melodrama in order to represent the loss of the tragic vision that was the trademark of the epic struggle for anti-imperialist liberation during the early years of the Revolution. But in the urge to resacralize national identity the film's storyline cannot help but be faithful to the melodramatic rhetoric it adopts, stopping short of being self-critical and ultimately pressing a moral universe that is very similar to the one it attempts to replace. "The ritual of melodrama," Adds Brooks, "involves the confrontation of clearly identified antagonists and the expulsion of one of them. It can offer no terminal reconciliation, for there is no longer a clear transcendent value to be reconciled to. There is, rather, a social order to be purged, a set of ethical imperatives to be made clear"(17). In its rush to press the inevitability of Diego's expulsion the film thus resorts neither to heightened dramatic enactment nor to lyrical language but rather to music— the haunting pieces of Ignacio Cervantes and Lecuona, Benny Moré *boleros*, the framing devices of José María Vitier—as a way of suggesting that which cannot be stated outrightly but which nevertheless must take place. "The *melos* of melodrama," Caryl Flynn writes, "picks up where something else leaves off, veering in the direction of what might appear to be pure surfeit or excess it is . . . music indeed *does* take over for melodrama's linguistic deficiencies."[17]

In Spanish at least, *reconciliarse*, to reconcile, has two dictionary meanings. The first is social: reconciliation means to be friends again with those who have stopped being so. The second is theological: to return a heretic to the bosom of the Church; to make a light confession, as if to take communion. In the most recent discussions concerning the reconciliation of the Cuban nation, as supported by both the Cuban State and the Catholic Church, the meaning of reconciliation that appears to prevail is the second: the need for the heretic's return, the return hinted at in David's response to Diego's final farewell to Havana at the foot of *El Cristo* and in Diego's glowing face upon receiving David's guilt-ridden forgiveness. Beyond whatever margin for interpretation individual religious beliefs may grant us, the question for this reader remains, on the broader question of Cuban reconciliation, whether the second definition of reconciliation can ever include the first, whereby old friends can become so again. I confess, in this regard, to prefer to have true friends, new and old, even if that choice should mean that they and I remain exiled from the Cathedral of Ice Cream.

PART 2

CHAPTER SEVEN

Fernando Ortiz: Counterpoint and Transculturation

I

One of the challenges facing the future of Cultural Studies is the coherence between conceptual tools and objects of research. That an incongruity between theory and object should have emerged in such a relatively new field was to be expected, perhaps, for in little more than its two decades' worth the field has struggled to develop a vocabulary of its own while also reining in proliferating agendas. Unlike Psychoanalysis or Gender Studies, which inherited methodologies that new strategies could work through polemically, this discipline has taken on the unenviable dual task of inventing critical tools while targeting objects that have been as varied as they are elusive. The challenge appears to be particularly intense in Postcolonial Studies, whose success in the Anglo–American academy, particularly its French and English Literature departments, seems all but assured, but whose spread to other cognate fields, like German, Russian, or indeed Spanish and Portuguese, has yet to parallel the same hold it enjoys on their Anglo and French counterparts.[1]

What could be construed as a resistance to the postcolonial paradigm in these other fields may be said to stem from the paradigm itself. For one of the more disturbing caveats of most, if not all, postcolonial theory has been the broad contradiction that runs through it, being at once a grid of metropolitan knowledge and a destabilizing interpretive strategy that seeks to promote liberation at the periphery. Hence the anxious self-questioning that permeates so much of its best scholarship, as if by soliciting a redemptive self-consciousness it could neutralize whatever complicity might be at work between forces of oppression and epistemological premises. It is the kind of self-questioning that resonates in titles like Fernando Coronil's "Can Post-Coloniality be Decolonized?" or indeed in Gayatri Spivak's recent *Critique of Post-Colonial Reason*, whose running theme is nothing less than "the foreclosure of the native informant."[2]

No single twentieth-century book from Latin America perhaps gathers most dramatically the tensions and complications attendant to such "postcolonial reason" than Fernando Ortiz's Cuban *Counterpoint: Tobacco and Sugar*. First published in Spanish in 1940, its partial English translation appeared in 1947, and since then its reception has been as slow as it has been conflicted.[3] A polymath by any standard, Ortiz (1889–1969) himself is perhaps better known for his massive research into all aspects of Afro-Cuban culture—from music to cooking—and yet his huge, unruly bibliography has never been gathered into a single book-set, and translations of his work are still rare. Among Latinamericanists Ortiz's slow reception was mediated eventually by Angel Rama's influential *Transculturación narrativa en América Latina*, a 1982 collection of essays in which Rama made of transculturation, a concept Ortiz coined in *Cuban Counterpoint*, the foundation of his studies of layering and tension, particularly between European and Amerindian cultural traces, in a number of Latin American modernist and postmodern narratives.[4] It was thanks to Rama, then, that Ortiz's rediscovery by postmodern readers began; but such mediation contributed as well, unwittingly, to a fragmentary knowledge of his work.

Indeed, the attention transculturation has attracted has also displaced partially most discussions of counterpoint, Ortiz's tandem concept in the same book. But even such disproportion appears to be but a limited symptom of a more generalized problem which goes to the heart of the postcolonial paradigm and which I have tried to highlight throughout this book; namely, the erosion of local knowledge in theoretical discussions of subaltern or peripheral cultures, including Latin America's. As my comments above suggest, the epistemological problem for a postcolonial hermeneutics appears to be as insidious as it is evident. In the case of readings of Ortiz at least, it surfaces most dramatically in all those cases where the desire to theorize about an alleged postcolonial relevance breaks down before the theorist's inability to account for the local knowledge that presumably justifies it, to the point of either ignoring or distorting the most basic facts. Thus Fernando Coronil, author of the very fateful title question I just quoted, and editor of the most recent U.S. edition of *Cuban Counterpoint*, reads it as a "valuable book for these difficult times," and views the "counter-fetishism" marshaled by Ortiz's argument as the best response to the disciplinary manipulation wielded by Bronislaw Malinowski, in whose preface to *Cuban Counterpoint*, written at Ortiz's request, Coronil finds a self-serving attempt to neutralize Ortiz's "struggle against eurocentrism."[5] And yet, despite such vigorous pronouncements in defense of Ortiz's local authority, the same editor, working solely out of the abridged English translation, and therefore oblivious to the two Spanish editions Ortiz himself supervised, goes on to miscast it as having "two brief theoretical chapters and ten larger historical ones" (xii), when in the original the number of chapters is actually 26; claims that the prefatory essay is "an allegorical tale of Cuban history narrated as a counterpoint between tobacco and sugar" (xii), when it is actually an essay on the contrasts between the two commodities with little historical context, discussion of which is otherwise reserved for the latter section; and wishes, in general, to pinpoint Ortiz's "contestatory anti-imperialism" (xvii–xxiv), yet skips over, in recounting Ortiz's biography, the crucial 1929–1933 period, when Ortiz joined Cuban President Machado's reformist campaign, soon broke with him (and thus with his U.S. supporters), yet chose exile in Washington, D.C., where, during the nationalist revolution that toppled Machado, he did much of the research for *Cuban Counterpoint*. Such outright contradictions between stated theory and actual practice appears so pervasive, in Coronil's text and elsewhere in meditations on the entire postcolonial question, that it could perhaps only be explained by recourse to Paul de Man's tandem formula of "blindness and insight," according to which the paradox between critical insight and hermeneutic, sometimes defensive, blind spots lurks within all texts that aspire to some measure of theoretical lucidity.[6] In postcolonial theory in particular the paradox would appear to surface in the simultaneous, contradictory effect of gaining sympathizing insights into the colonial human experience while remaining blind to its stubbornly material details.[7]

Coronil's sources from his own field of Anthropology are of course manifold. But the one source his introduction appeals to most consistently, or which at least provides the broadest framework, is Edward Said's *Culture and Imperialism* (1993). Coronil cites in particular Said's notion of "contrapuntal reading," which he goes so far as to project onto Ortiz as a way of joining both authors in a "contrapuntal perspective" that may point us "to see how the Three World schema is underwritten by fetishized geo-historical categories which conceal their genesis in inequality and domination" (xli).[8] Clearly, those two notions of counterpoint, Said's and Ortiz's, while commonly grounded in music, were unrelated in time and substance. Ortiz had used counterpoint (*contrapunteo*) in its radically Cuban sense of "dialogue" or "discussion," thus pointedly displacing, in what was essentially a historical exegesis, psychoanalytic, or Marxist notions of conflict. He did so in order to articulate how the two commodities of tobacco and sugar, in their material and imaginary dimensions, had structured a deceptively harmonious Cuban history and identity; Said used counterpoint, by turns, in order to advocate a reading of Western canons in resonance with non-Western or peripheral texts so as to elicit, as he says, "a simultaneous awareness both of the metropolitan history that is narrated and of those other histories against which (and together with which) the dominating discourse acts" (51). Perhaps the most dramatic instance of the widespread tension I am describing appears in one of Coronil's last notes to his introduction, where he self-consciously raises the specter of "the reality of Ortiz's absence in contrast to the expectations of his presence" (lii, n. 35). There Coronil relates how in a talk at Duke University, in which he read a first version of his Ortiz essay, Walter Mignolo and Fredric Jameson remarked at how neither Said's book nor Claude Lévi-Strauss *Mythologies* showed traces of Ortiz's influence, despite the obvious resonance of his book in both. This was, accordingly, a clear case of a Western academic canon, as epitomized by *Culture and Imperialism*, persisting in its disdain toward a local, peripheral knowledge, despite Said's own pointed claims to have done the contrary.[9]

Ultimately, Said's blindness to Ortiz's use of counterpoint could perhaps be justified on the grounds that their respective arguments were indeed different, not to mention that Ortiz's work circulated mostly in Spanish, and among Latin American anthropologists. Where it could definitely not be excused is Said's (and thereby Coronil's) further blindness to the pointed contributions on the same subject that were made during the late 1950s in Cuba by poet José Lezama Lima, whose more pertinent essays advocated what he then literally called "contrapuntal form" as a way of vindicating the novelty of "American Expression" (both North and South) against the privileged anteriority of European canons. Indeed, it would be difficult to understate the extent to which Lezama Lima's "contrapuntal form" constitutes an uncanny, though unacknowledged, precursor-concept to Said's "simultaneous awareness."[10] And yet, for all its pertinence, Lezama Lima figures nowhere in Said's canonical, anti-imperialist text, not to mention in Coronil's appropriation of the Said thesis he projects onto Ortiz's.

Lezama Lima's own use of counterpoint owed itself ultimately, as we shall see at the end of this chapter, to Ortiz, and I invoke it here, at its outset, merely as part of a range of references whose sum-total ought make us aware of the repressed archive lying at the core of Ortiz's most recent postcolonial reception. Yet one cannot help noting along with this archive the irony of having all such aggressively ideological discourses defend local knowledge—or else, as Spivak puts it, in defense of the "native informant"—yet failing to account altogether for the material details of that same knowledge, or that defense; what in de Manian terms would amount to allowing the hubris of theoretical insight to blind historical substance. My own attempt, in this final chapter, is thus meant as a running corrective to such excesses. The basis for this implicit critique is my own experience as editor of the latest corrected, and only annotated, Spanish text of Ortiz's *Cuban Counterpoint*, an experience which in the chapter's last section I invoke as a source of insight into the nature of Ortiz's work, and more broadly, of Cuban culture. As in my reading of *Canto general*, then, to which this chapter corresponds as opposite arc, I follow here the minutiae of a contextual reading in order to situate, first, the polemical origins of *Cuban Counterpoint* at the intersection of the fields of History and Geography; then its conflicted relationship, through Malinowski, to Functionalism; and finally, the broad relationship, within the book's structure, between counterpoint and transculturation, particularly the latter term's debt to the transatlantic debate in anthropological circles amidst which it was coined. I end the chapter considering again the book's reception, and in particular its shared success among literary scholars and Cultural Studies specialists alike.

II

Cuban Counterpoint is arguably the most innovative Hispanic essay of the twentieth century. It is also an indispensable tool for the study of Latin American history, and Cuba in particular. Its first edition dates from 1940, a key moment in Cuban history, though Ortiz's book did not have the impact then it has now, as shown in the growing interest in transculturation as a concept, a term which Ortiz coined; in the spread of new theories of ethnography, which he also pioneered; and in the attention Caribbean studies commands today.

The book is made up of two sections: a long essay divided into 15 unnumbered subsections that gives the book its title; and a second section, four times the size of the first, of 26 chapters (25 of them numbered), entitled "The Ethnography and Transculturation of Tobacco and the Beginnings of Sugar in America." The essay offers contrasting empirical descriptions of tobacco and sugar; the second section, of marked scholarly tone, backs up the essay's conclusions with an array of historical data that is meant to show the many ways in which Cuban tobacco and sugar were inscribed upon global consciousness. In its first, 1940, edition Ortiz called the second section "complementary chapters"; beginning with the revised, 1963, edition, he called it "additional chapters." Since 1940, an "Introduction" by Bronislaw Malinowski (1882–1942), which endorses Ortiz's research and supports his coinage of transculturation, precedes the essay. Malinowski himself played an important role in Ortiz's first edition, as well as in the 1947 English translation, as shown in their correspondence.[11]

Ortiz took the title from Cuban folk music. According to Pichardo, Cuban *contrapunteo* means "dispute or saucy or colorful sayings exchanged by two or more people; and from this the vulgar reciprocal verb *contrapuntearse* (to counterpoint).[12] *Contrapunteo* is the Cuban version of *contrapunto*, English *counterpoint*—the technical term for the mix of parts or voices that result in a harmonious texture—but its original definition refers to the verbal content of a dispute. In Cuban folk music any musical dispute or debate goes by the name of *controversia*—two or more musical rivals (generally singers and guitarists) exchanging barbed tunes in improvised *décimas*, or rhymed ten-line stanzas. In the essay's first subsection Ortiz refers to "the erotic controversy in dance measures of the rumba" (4) and to "the versified counterpoint of the unlettered *guajiros* and the Afro-Cuban *curros*," (4) both of which are versions of the "dialogued composition" with which "ingenious folk muses in poetry" (4) express "the dramatic dialectic of life" (4). Briefly put, Ortiz's *contrapunteo* is a synonym for "musical dispute."

The semantic slip stems from the Cuban musical lexicon. In Cuba, rural *controversia* is based on the *punto*, a musical genre that is found equally among white *guajiros* or white peasants and urban Blacks; hence *contrapunteo* and *controversia* are synonymous. Ten-line folk stanzas or *décimas*, a favorite versification among the various forms of *punto*, were brought to Cuba by Canary Island immigrants, who in turn had adopted it from Andalusian music. Beginning in the seventeenth century, the Cuban *punto* began showing African ingredients as well. According to Argeliers Léon, "the simplest *controversia* is when two singers together take up a theme and rebuke one another spontaneously." Yet another version is having one performer sing the first section of the ten-line stanza (the first quatrain with two recurring lines), thus supplying a ready rhyme to the opponent. The other improviser then finishes off the six remaining lines.[13]

Controversia, then, is the *fiction* that presides over *Cuban Counterpoint*'s long essay. The book brings into line, as Ortiz himself points out, "the versified counterpoint of the unlettered *guajiros* and the Afro-Cuban *curros*," which "might be of educational value in schools and school festivals." Consistent with this fiction, the two commodities debate, much as in a rural *controversia*, which of the two is or has been the better one for Cuba. The object is to defeat the opponent through sheer poetic and musical virtuosity, victory going to the more skillful player. I say *fiction* rather than *format* because in Ortiz's book controversy is simply that: mere pretext. The essay upholds tobacco and puts down sugar, does not pretend to be impartial, and knows the winner's identity all along, if in fact there is one. To structure this debate, the essay turns the two commodities into "characters": *Don Tobacco and Doña Sugar* ("the two most important figures in the history of Cuba"), based on *The Book of Good Love*'s Don Carnal and Doña Cuaresma. Indeed, Ortiz's "counterpoint" is a parody of Juan Ruiz's "battle," itself a parody of medieval debate (*disputatio*).[14] From "debate" to "battle," and from "battle" to "counterpoint," the Cuban or Creole version is therefore parody of a parody: an imitation of Juan Ruiz, whose text was itself a satire of medieval theological debates. It would not, in fact, be too rash to view Ortiz's as a parody of academic or philosophical essays, as it satirizes the inflated rhetoric of title terms like "Introduction," "Reasons," or "Dialectic." *Dialectic* could, in fact, be its most likely object, since "dialectic," like *contrapunteo*, is a term of "verbal exchange," and the essay thematizes the interaction between two aspects of the Cuban economy and their social consequences. Imagining Ortiz's title as parody of an academic title like "Dialectic of Tobacco and Sugar" would therefore not be difficult, particularly if we know that Marx and what he called "the fetishism of commodities" ("*Madame la Terre*" and "*Monsieur le Capital*," which appear in *Capital*) was a source for Ortiz's allegorical personification.[15] Finally, as we shall see, counterpoint determines the structure of the book's "additional chapters" and provides the conceptual link between the two sections.

Although each of the "additional chapters" does have an explicit title, the essay's 15 untitled and unnumbered subsections do not. But despite this, one can identify the contents of each subsection, as in this makeshift list:

(1) Introduction
(2) General contrast
(3) Types of plants
(4) Moral contrast
(5) Religious–Magical
(6) Cultivation
(7) Transport

(8) Mechanical production
(9) Marketing
(10) Methods of production
(11) Sociopolitical
(12) Commercial methods
(13) Labor
(14) Labor history
(15) Conclusion.

According to Ortiz, the entire essay is "schematic," in the precise sense of a "general diagram." Indeed, each of the essay's subsections is built upon a contrast—thus providing a first counterpoint—between tobacco and sugar, even as their differences are not "as absolute and clear-cut as they would sometimes appear" (97). What the essay does discuss, then, is a *relative* contrast between the two commodities. The essay's sheer lack of titles, labels, notes, and bibliography highlights its "spontaneous" nature and tone; but its lack of rhetorical inflection signals that it is up to the reader to complete the text. Obvious as well is Ortiz's narrative style there, redolent of witty or ingenious turns of phrase (the spicy or "colorful" style Pichardo refers to in *contrapunteo*). In a letter to Melville Herskovits, Ortiz himself once described it as "a toy that explains a number of our country's social concepts to our people."[16]

The essay's style and structure thus contrast—second counterpoint—with the deliberately scholarly tone of the "additional chapters." The latter bear individual titles, their sole purpose being, according to chapter I, to provide "full and systematic documentation in the form of notes" (97) to the essay's ideas. Thus the book sets up not only a contrast between the two main sections, but also—third counterpoint—a system of mutual references. The essay projects a number of references onto the "additional chapters," the purpose of which is to document the ideas brought up in the essay. The same references correspond sequentially to the chapters' own; as noted in chapter I, all the "additions" in the second section have a "complementary" function, even as they deal "with a basic theme of their own" (97). The structure suggests that we can read the book in two ways: either we jump ahead to the second section whenever we encounter any such reference; or we can read both sections straight through. The latter reading underscores the essay's wit; the former highlights the book's erudition. All this, of course, is in addition to two other possible readings: we can read either the essay by itself, or the additional chapters by themselves.

According to Ortiz, the 25 additional chapters are arranged into two thematic groups: "History, Ethnography and Transculturation of Tobacco"

(*Sp*, 252) and "Beginnings of Sugar and Slavery of Blacks in the New World" (*Sp*, 252). This arrangement suggests, first, that *transculturation* as a concept applies more to the history of tobacco than to sugar's. That is, sugar in Cuba is not the result of transculturation, a socially homogenizing factor, but is rather the direct cause of slavery, an alienating factor. Second, it shows that the evidence the book presents on behalf of the two commodities is articulated discretely, by contrast or counterpoint. In other words, in the "additional chapters" counterpoint appears *between* subsections, as an effect of the book's structure, instead of *within* each section— as it does in the essay.[17] Although the book's second section begins with two introductions on transculturation, beginning with chapter III, and all through the end, chapters are grouped into subsections that alternate between the two commodities. Thus: III–X refer to tobacco; XI–XVIII to sugar; XIX–XXII: tobacco; XXIII: sugar; XXIV: tobacco; XXV: sugar. Excluding the first two chapters, the sum totals are as follows: Tobacco: 8 chapters; sugar: 8 chapters; tobacco: 4 chapters; sugar: 1 chapter; tobacco: 1 chapter; sugar: 1 chapter. The contents yield the following totals: 2 introductory chapters, 13 on tobacco, and 10 on sugar, for a grand total of 25 chapters. Such at least is the division implicit in the two lists Ortiz offers in chapter I; indeed, Ortiz points to the sections' two themes but does not underscore the latent counterpoint between them.[18]

In sum: in Part I, the essay, counterpoint is a function of content; its subsections articulate differences between the two commodities or "characters." In Part II, the "additional chapters," counterpoint is a function of structure: the subsections articulate differences by means of an internal organization. Equally apparent are the internal links between the two sections. The essay summarizes, in its manifest surface, the evidence the "additional chapters" provide; the "additional chapters" clarify the evidence summarized in the essay. Thus the "additional chapters" of Part II function very much like an archive, or database, of a legal summation; or else, in domestic architectural terms, they provide the "kitchen" to the essay's "front porch."

I turn now to Ortiz's biography and the years during which his work developed, leading up to 1940, when *Cuban Counterpoint* was published.

III

Fernando Ortiz's childhood ran parallel to the young Cuban Republic. Born in Havana on July 16, 1881, to a Spanish father and a Cuban mother between the two independence wars (1868–1878 and 1895–1898), he spent his first years in Menorca, where his mother took him when he was barely 14 months old. In Menorca Ortiz grew up until the age of 14. It was there he did his first letters, up to *bachillerato*. Ortiz lived in Havana, where the family returned in 1895, during the three crucial years of the second war of Cuban independence (known in the U.S. as the "Spanish–American War"), Spain's defeat, and the first U.S. occupation. Ortiz completed a doctorate, in Spain again, between 1899 and 1902, after which he became involved in Cuban life and obtained a second doctorate from the University of Havana. He soon left Cuba again, however, for diplomatic stints in Europe (La Coruña, Genoa, Marseilles) until 1905. At 24, having spent a total of 16 years abroad, he returned to Cuba to set up permanent residence.[19]

Ortiz's movement back and forth from Europe, and particularly Spain, is unsurprising if we know that it was customary for the island's colonial elites to send their children to study in the Metropolis. What was peculiar about Ortiz was that his comings and goings allowed him to internalize a double gaze, at once insular and metropolitan: from Menorca he could view Cuba as the Other; just as he could view Europe, from Cuba, as the obverse of the young nation.

Such a double gaze explains three things about Ortiz. First, his interest in describing cultures other than his own—at the age of 14 he had already published a first paper, *Principi y prostes*, on Menorcan customs; second, his choice of career in the law; and finally and uppermost, his liberal convictions. Indeed, Ortiz's liberalism stems from his deep-seated cultural relativism. Living outside of Cuba early on, yet conscious of his own native difference, Ortiz learned that different and sometimes opposite ways of living and thinking coexist in all societies, sometimes even within families, like his own. Further, Ortiz was born a "liberal" due to his status, soon made fully legal through citizenship. "Liberal" means here that in the throes of the Colony and birth of the Republic he was marginal and rebellious with respect to the Metropolis. And as a synonym for Cuban, liberal also meant, particularly within the Hispanic context of the times, anything that smacked of science and modernity. Knowledge was to be based on verifiable data, not on belief. Ortiz, who held degrees from both Spain and Havana, absorbed a Positivist in the courses he took under Manuel Sales y Ferré (1843–1910), with whom he began the then radical study of criminology.

Ortiz belongs, lastly, to the first Cuban Republican generation, a group that included such distinguished intellectuals as Enrique José Varona, Carlos Loveira, José Antonio Ramos, and Alfonso Hernández Catá, all of whom set out to lay no less than the foundations of the new nation. Theirs was a multiple mission: political, economic, cultural, social, and educational. Of his own long career, Ortiz himself stated: "I lived, read, wrote, published, always under pressure and restless, because the Cuban forest was dense and almost unexplored, and I with my weaknesses could do nothing but open a narrow path and try to plot a course."[20]

Besides being a writer, lawyer, and diplomat, Ortiz soon became a criminologist; indeed, his first scholarly articles were in that field. The time he spent in Genoa as a diplomat had coincided with the boom of that young science, and it was there he took all the relevant courses with Asturaro, Morcelli, and, particularly, Cesare Lombroso, the "father" of modern criminal science. His contacts would soon bear fruit in *Los negros brujos* (Black Wizards)(1906), Ortiz's first book, which Lombroso prefaced. In it Ortiz offered a double (and therefore ambivalent) reading of Afro-Cuban ethnicity. As suggested in the title, it criticized "witchcraft" (*brujería*)—superstitions that allegedly lead to crime—but emphasized the importance and complexity of Cuba's African cultures. What began as legal and moral condemnation ended up as scientific insight. Due to this change, and despite the ambivalence of the book's treatment of "Afro-Cuban" culture—an adjective Ortiz coined—his enlightened gesture created a rupture. At the time, anything Black was taboo in Havana society, heir as it was to the racist slave society Cuba had been. Moreover, Ortiz's book was part of a scientific study on "the low life," a fashionable theme in Spain at the time.[21]

Without intending to, then, Ortiz's first book reflected the fracture of the young Cuban Republic. In 1906, at the behest of Cuban President Estrada Palma, the United States intervened militarily for a second time, presumably to calm down internal partisan disputes. Intervention was legal then under the Platt Amendment to the Cuban constitution, which allowed it whenever there was a perceived danger to U.S. interests, and lasted two years, just as Ortiz was setting out on his "mission." In 1906, he was named prosecutor in Havana Superior Court, followed the next year by his joining the legendary *Sociedad Económica de Amigos del País*, Cuba's oldest academic and civic institution and whose guiding spirit Ortiz would become over time. Two years later he married, fathered a daughter, and won the Public Law chair at the University of Havana; and two years after that, he began publishing in *Revista Bimestre Cubana*, the journal of the *Sociedad* whose editor he became, until 1959. The roles Ortiz was playing then—jurist, professor, and editor—were manifold, not unlike the subjects he was writing on. To glance over Ortiz's vast primary bibliography between 1906 and 1910 is to marvel at his hand at studies on criminology, essays on Afro-Cuban cultures, articles on foreign customs, bibliographies on lexicography, summaries of books and art exhibits, political commentary, and a plethora of speeches. By 1910, barely 30 years old, he already enjoyed the reputation of an encyclopedist.

Cuban reality had changed by the time the second U.S. intervention ended in 1909. Elections that year handed the presidency to Ortiz's Liberal Party. Barely five years later, under the conservative administration of President Mario García Menocal, Ortiz became the Liberal Party's leader, the last step in his short-lived political career. In the meantime, a series of books would take prime of place: *Las rebeliones de los afrocubanos* (Afrocuban Rebellions) (1910), whose publication predates by two years the Afro-Cuban uprising of the Independent Party of Color and its brief war; *La reconquista de América* (Reconquest of America) (1910), his essays on Spain's neocolonial policy; *Entre cubanos. Psicología tropical* (Among Cubans. Tropical Psychology) (1913), which gathered articles on that theme; and *Los negros esclavos* (The Black Slaves) (1916), the second of the series begun by *Los negros brujos*. Only in 1917, and for a full decade, was Ortiz actually elected Representative to the Cuban Congress, of which he would eventually become vice-president.[22]

Those were also the years of World War I, which Cuba reflected in a hyperinflation economy known as the "Million-Dollar Dance," owing to sugar's gouged prices in the world markets. (By 1917, 85 percent of Cuba's exports were based on sugar and its derivatives.) The "Dance," in turn, spawned a local millionaire class that competed globally with the profits of an international elite, a fact which explains not only Havana's economic wealth at the time, but its remarkable culture. From the poorest of colonial backdrops Havana became, within less than 20 years, an ultra-modern city: booming architecture, luxury cars, railroads, telephones, American movies, and European operas. With wealth came political corruption, beginning with the island's presidency. The 1915 elections, which had favored Liberal candidate Alfredo Zayas, were frustrated by U.S. influence, which chose instead to back García Menocal. In reaction, an armed rebellion (known as "La Chambelona," title of a *conga* at the time) broke out. The status quo won out. All these events no doubt influenced Ortiz's decision to jump into the political fray. His position was reflected in an important 1919 article, "The Cuban Political Crisis (Its Causes and Solutions)," in which he analyzed the crisis, viewing it in sociological, political, international, and even psychological terms.[23] Ever the sociologist, Ortiz listed prescriptive solutions (7 of its 21 pages) for the benefit of future governments; counseled a deepening of "diplomatic and cultural relations with the United States based on mutual respect"; and stated "confidence in national strength" (16–21). The fact that Ortiz should have dedicated this piece to U.S. President Woodrow Wilson demonstrates how aware he was then of the ties that bound the two countries, his desire to press Cuban views upon the U.S. public, and, from that point on, attempt to influence American policy. It would not be a waste. That same year (1919) his Liberal Party sent Ortiz to Washington to argue for U.S. supervision of national elections—which García Menocal had won again. But it would not be Ortiz's last try.

By then, Ortiz was thoroughly identified with Cuba's Liberal Left, a relatively young faction within the Cuban Congress that sought government reform. But under all that political activity seethed the same burning "mission." By 1923 Ortiz was elected president of the *Sociedad Económica*, and the following year went on to create, as part of the same group, the *Society for Cuban Folklore*. At the same time, Ortiz kept publishing on Cuban Blacks ("The Afro-Cuban Festival of the Day of Kings," 1920; "Afro-Cuban Gatherings," 1921), and on historical themes (*Historia de la Arqueología Indo-Cubana* [History of Indo-Cuban Archaeology], 1922). The 1922 election of Liberal Alfredo Zayas hardly lessened his public advocacy, particularly in regard to the recession that was caused by the sudden drop of sugar on the world market. Indeed, the crisis grew even worse when García Menocal, who left power in 1921, also left behind a floating debt of 40 million dollars that provoked labor strikes and caused widespread unemployment.

Cuba at the time was rife with political, economic, and cultural nationalism, and produced, among other reactions, a student movement for university reform. Ortiz (now 43) joined those forces as author of "Manifesto for a Cuban Council for Civic Renovation." Repeating his earlier points, he criticized the evils of republican "non-government" and demanded protection for national industries, agriculture, and commerce, as well as renegotiation of bilateral treaties with the U.S.[24] His "manifesto" was preceded by yet another piece, known as the *Protesta de los Trece* (The Thirteen's Demand) for the 13 young intellectuals who signed it and which essentially restated the same critique. While not a member of this group, which soon organized as the *Grupo Minorista* (Minority Group), Ortiz was nevertheless close to them and became a moral mentor. In time the group came to be known as the 1923 Republican Generation.[25]

Indeed, 1923 was a crucial year—for both Cuba and Ortiz. It was then he published two of his major works: the first edition of *Catauro de cubanismos* (A Trove of Cubanisms), which collects the articles on lexicography he had published since his return from Spain; and *En la tribuna* (On the Podium), his political speeches. Both were followed the year after by two other key texts: a speech on "Cuban Decadence," and the *Glosario de afronegrismos* (An Afro Glossary).[26] By then Ortiz's growing work on Cuban Blacks had another unexpected impact, as it began to influence the work of modernist artists—a kind of Cuban Afro-Cuban Renaissance—and particularly Afro-Cuban poets like Nicolás Guillén, José Zacarías Tallet, and Ramón Guirao, among others. What stands out at this stage, apart from cultural nationalism, was Ortiz's parallel work as both social critic and cultural mentor.

Ortiz's speech on "Cuban Decadence" coincided in time with another one by General Gerardo Machado, then the Liberal Party's candidate for president. The "Regeneration Platform" was the name Machado gave to a plan for nationalist renovation that demanded, among other things, sovereignty, a revision of international treaties, and abolition of the Platt Amendment. It was as if Machado had read Ortiz. Machado enjoyed wide support, anchored as it was to a collective desire for reform. In his first term in office (1928–1932) the new president instituted important changes: he created a superfund for public works, including construction of the Cuban central highway, and supported economic diversification and a customs law. But soon after that, Machado began governing by force and even violence, due not only to demands of state security, but also increasing demands from foreign investors.[27] The political situation worsened as the price of sugar began to fall, which in turn made the government mandate cutbacks in production. What in 1929 turned out to be the Wall Street Crash and the beginning of the global Depression, in Cuba coincided with the end of Machado's first term, heir to all the historic dependence on the sugar single-crop. Such dependence caused so many domestic disasters that influential figures like historian Ramiro Guerra, in his classic *Azúcar y población en las Antillas* (Sugar and Population in the Antilles) (1927), soon began denouncing both *latifundia* (the accumulation of surplus land) and the island's unhealthy dependence on foreign economic cycles.

Ortiz's work during this time reflected the reformist trends of the 1920s. His *Project on the Cuban Criminal Code* (1926), for example, proposed reforms in civil crime and rehabilitation. The same year he created the legendary *Institución Hispanocubana de Cultura* (Hispano-Cuban Institute of Culture), Havana's cultural lighthouse for the following three decades, which sponsored public lectures on cultural themes (more than 200 alone between 1927 and 1931).[28] Yet another reflection of Ortiz's relative comfort with Machado's reforms was his official designation as representative to a number of international meetings, among them the Sixth International Pan-American Conference (1928) in Havana. It was in the latter where Ortiz succeeded in creating a *Pan-American Geographical Institute*, whose purview extended to the field of History. (The disciplinary union of these two fields, as we shall see, became crucial for Ortiz's thought.)[29] One last reformist marker was Ortiz's direction, however fleeting, of the 1929 Cuban *Legislative Bulletin*. But despite all this work, the erupting crisis at decade's end caused a break with Machado.

While Ortiz's circumstances changed as the years passed (in 1926 his wife died and he was left with a young daughter), Cuba, in turn, lost confidence in its government. By 1927 Ortiz had resigned his congressional post; this was barely a year before a controversial constitutional reform extended term limits for elected officials.[30] (The president's was extended a further four years, while deputies and senators got an additional two.) Machado himself ran unopposed. Thus by 1929, as effects of the global crash were being felt, a huge discontent befell all Cubans. Machado began governing by sheer military force and persecuting his enemies everywhere. (Julio Antonio Mella, an anti–Machado Communist student leader, was assassinated in Mexico.) The University of Havana and other institutions closed down, and the country slowly began to crumble. For his part, Ortiz reacted the way he knew best. In *Surco*, the *Hispano-Cuban Institute*'s ephemeral second journal, he penned an anti–Machado manifesto that cost him his eventual exile, which he then chose to spend in the United States.

Ortiz's refuge of choice was Washington, D.C. It was there he could best influence U.S. policy toward Cuba, which he felt was at the root of the crisis. Eventual pieces like "U.S. Responsibility in Cuba's Problems" (1930) and "What Cuba wants from the U.S." (1932) called for a political agenda that echoed his 1919 essay on the "political crisis." Recalling the time spent in the U.S., he wrote: "I spoke with anyone who listened: statesmen and intellectuals, financiers and journalists; all shades of American opinion and visible and contradictory forces, from businessmen who financed the horrors of the Cuban tyranny and justified its bloody methods, to the hopeless critics of the present social system, and the naysayers of any accommodation, or hope," Ortiz observed all this while recalling the title ("What the U.S. Owes Cuba") whose prophetic tone makes it worth citing at length:

> Conservative or liberal, reactionary or progressive, wealthy or proletarian, imperialist or communist, be it ideal or routine, base or fine, sincere or devious, backward or precipitous. Every Cuban program towards Cuba's collective life must take American factors into account. This can be loved or hated, but it cannot be denied . . . There can be

no better strategy for Cuba now than to march into the future with well-balanced institutions, a broad base, and directed by a central plan, that is, if we do not wish to fall to the left today, to the right tomorrow, or, what would be worse, to barbarity, by a series of violent despotisms and golden terrors, red, white, or black. What, specifically, do Cubans want? We're asking Washington diplomats to support closing down these *de facto* military regimes which for years and behind the backs of their people have ruled Cuba. We're asking them to help us on an immediate constitutional restoration of public freedoms, which Washington has always been obliged to guarantee, and by any adequate means, of the many convincing and civil tools that lie at their disposal; to reestablish institutional normality in Cuba, and popular sovereignty . . . Geography has made us friends, the economy has made us partners, and treaties have joined us together . . . Let us not allow a handful of renegades in either country disturb our harmony on behalf of civilization.[31]

Even if the Machado crisis were resolved, the lessons of History and Geography might not be learned. Against a nationalism of the Left, which advocated a split from the United States because of complicity with Machado, Ortiz stressed geographical realities, which dictated a moderate politics. Against conservatives on the Right, who demanded concessions to U.S. interests, he argued for national sovereignty. And to Americans, who saw Cuba's problems as foreign yet kept financing its military regimes, he reminded them how they had propped up the bad ones.

All throughout, Ortiz saw a possible solution in public institutions. Thus he asked repeatedly for the same thing: "institutions set up in stable balance," and argued for the "constitutional restoration of public freedoms." Last on the long U.S. to-do list, Ortiz asked for economic aid—the renegotiation of the U.S.–Cuba Reciprocity Treaty—and "technical and financial assistance."

Out of politics by the time of Machado's ouster, Ortiz kept on the sidelines of the instability that characterized the following seven years, known in Cuba's history as the "provisional" period. One might even say that in Ortiz's intellectual biography, as for many of his generation, life was split into two: pre- and post-Machado. Thus after 1933 Ortiz distanced himself from politics and began to devote full-time to research, particularly research on Afro-Cuban themes. It is no accident that all throughout the 1930s, as Fascist and Nazi racial theories grew in influence, so did Ortiz's call for greater attention to the Cuban version of Western racism, which he called *Negrophobia*. "Those who hate by raising the racial flag," he said in a 1942 meeting of the Matanzas' *Club Atenas*, an Afro-Cuban civic society, "will find themselves one day persecuted by racism."[32] If anything characterizes the later Ortiz is a passion for overcoming racial conflicts by means of an overarching concept of culture.

After his U.S. exile, Ortiz redefined his public life, owing no doubt to disillusionment with Machado and his reformist plank. In a 1955 national homage, he recalled: "More than thirty years ago, with surplus energy and illusions, I struggled with flag-waving politics, I went at it with great pleasure and curiosity, and left without bitterness or profit other than experience . . . I always acted on the opposition. And so, after leaving party life, I became a perennial non-conformist."[33] Despite the dizzying succession of presidents and cabinets (six in seven years), post-Machado and pre-1940 Cuba witnessed an avalanche of social advances: abrogation of the Platt Amendment; a labor strike law was put into place, as well as minimum wage and universal "Sundays off" laws; agricultural unions were legalized; women won the right to vote; a National Institute of Social Reform, a Social Security Institute for Working Mothers, and a Code of Social Defense were all created; a Sugar Coordination Law was established, and, in 1943, Cuba signed the Jones–Costigan Treaty with the U.S., thus creating a stable quota system for sugar imports. It was in such climate of relative political stability and prosperity that Ortiz was able to carry out his wide-ranging work of cultural criticism.

Thus Ortiz's "mission" in time became clear in two ways. First, he founded new institutions: a magazine, *Ultra*, which replaced the aging *Surco* as the journal of the *Hispanocubana de Cultura*; a *Cuban Alliance for a Free World*, a *Society for Cuban Ethnography*, the *Archives of Cuban Folklore*, and even a *Collection of Cuban Classics*; and second, through his research. I say "research" and not actual "publications" for good reason. Ortiz's bibliography shows that, when compared to the sheer amount of publications before his U.S. exile, his work was then undergoing a "gestation period." Thus if we compare his production between 1934 and 1940 (when Ortiz did not publish a single book) with the years following 1940, we find that in this later period Ortiz produced no fewer than seven tomes, among them the monumental *El engaño de las razas* (The Deception of Race) (1946), *Africanía de la música folklórica de Cuba* (Africanness of Cuban Folk Music) (1950), *El teatro y la danza de los negros en el folklore de Cuba* (Dance and Theater of Blacks in Cuban Folklore) (1951), and *Los instrumentos de la música afro-cubana* (The Instruments of Afro-Cuban Music)(1952), in five volumes.[34]

Ortiz's years immediately before publication of *Cuban Counterpoint* in 1940 were devoted to meditations on culture in its various strains.

Good encyclopedist that he was, he found ways to scrutinize Cuban history and identity while searching for solutions to the country's instability. Among such solutions, as we shall see, was the theoretical link between Geography and History. In 1928, as part of his work in the *Sixth International Pan-American Conference*, he had called for creation of a Geographical Institute. It was shortly thereafter that he must have begun the research that resulted in the "Antilles" chapters in two encyclopedic works: *The Universal Geography. A Modern Description of the World* (1933), and *Universal Geography*, edited by Vidal de la Blache and L. Gallois (1936).[35] These two pieces were Ortiz's contributions to what was then the relatively new field of "Human Geography," "Cultural Geography," or "Anthropo-Geography."

It is hardly by chance that *Cuban Counterpoint* was published in 1940, the same year the new Cuban constitution was adopted. Essentially a study of economic nationalism and its social reflections, *Cuban Counterpoint* had one important goal: to make "suggestions for the economic study of Cuba and its historical peculiarities." The 1940 Constitution itself had been more than just a labor of national consensus: it was the result of a yearlong constitutional congress in which political parties had reached consensus. This new constitution had mostly positive effects for the dozen years that followed, during which three liberal administrations succeeded each other, interrupted only in March 1952 by Fulgencio Batista's bloodless coup. Ortiz himself had not been a delegate to the constitutional congress that enacted the new constitution but must have been well aware of its significance, given his career as a jurist and politician, the legal grounds upon which he had based his earlier critiques, and the institutional basis he had stressed historically. And while his 1940 book worked toward those same constitutional goals, Ortiz's own contribution could not help engaging a timely critique of the Cuban economy. For, as we shall see, *Cuban Counterpoint* was part of a broader national debate that had actually begun 20 years earlier over the Cuban economy's dependence on sugar. For precisely that reason, *Cuban Counterpoint* became a polemical, indeed heretical book, since it went so far as to suggest that sugar is *not* Cuban. This it did in reaction to the scandalous wealth the sugar industry had produced exclusively for a certain class during the Machado years. Hence the relative silence that met publication of the *Cuban Counterpoint*'s first edition, itself a logical reaction to this context.[36]

Such polemical edge is what explains as well the link between Ortiz and Bronislaw Malinowski (1884–1942), whom Ortiz asked to write the "Introduction" to *Cuban Counterpoint*. Malinowski was perhaps the most famous anthropologist then living, "father" to the British school of ethnography (though he himself was Polish by birth and education) called "Functionalism."[37] Malinowski himself had moved to the United States in October 1939, after 15 years as the first chair of anthropology at the University of London. We know he visited Havana and met Ortiz in November of that year, and attended a talk "on economic nationalism" that Germán Wolter del Río gave at the *Hispanocubana de Cultura* on the 10th of the month. Doubtless it was there the two became friends.[38]

Malinowski and Ortiz's correspondence sheds light on important aspects of their relationship. Barely a few days after meeting in Havana, Ortiz wrote sending along pictures of his visit; and with a second letter (November 25, 1939) he enclosed "the first page proofs, which the publisher has sent me, of my essay on the contrasts of tobacco and sugar."[39] He told Malinowski then: "on page three I use the word 'transculturation' . . . Everything is submitted to your competent and generous judgment." It must have been during that meeting the two first discussed the idea of collaborating on *Cuban Counterpoint*, though when exactly Malinowski agreed to write his "Introduction" is not known. Shortly thereafter (December 20, 1939) Ortiz wrote again, asking "confirmation you've received the proofs and my request you look them over," announcing his visit to New York "in the first two weeks of January next," and asking "when I could come visit you at Yale . . . I would very much like to chat with you and shake hands." It must have been during this second meeting in New Haven in January 1940 the two reached agreement regarding the "Introduction." One of Malinowski's subsequent letters (February 20, 1940) tells Ortiz he was then preparing what he called "my little essay on your book . . . I'd like to concentrate principally on the relation your work has with the anthropological and sociological modern approach, which I like to call functionalism."

Conversations about the book must have included its eventual English translation and Ortiz's desire to impact upon U.S. public opinion. It seems that the manuscript consisted even then of two sections: the long essay that gave the book its name and a section of "appendices," what Ortiz later named "additional" or "complementary" chapters. The latter had been produced, as Ortiz explained in his March 1, 1940 letter, at the "publisher's request." Ortiz thought then the manuscript would "exceed 300 pages, owing to the numerous and well-fed appendices." Malinowski did not agree with that labeling however, thinking ahead to the reading habits of the Anglo reader, and proposed one important change: "the gringo reader is always likely to treat 'appendices' almost as appendages, as something, that is, which has no direct bearing on the subject.

This refers primarily to the American reading public, but I would give the same advice to anyone publishing the book in England." Malinowski's recommendations were mostly formal, but the fact Ortiz should have altered the original structure to incorporate his suggestions shows how much the book's potential U.S. distribution worried him, as much at least as the impact on U.S. public opinion he aspired to. This was hardly surprising if we recall all of Ortiz's earlier attempts in that regard.

Thereafter the correspondence shows how the ongoing dialogue kept changing the book. According to Ortiz's April 9 letter, for example, the book's structure had already changed from a long essay with "appendices" to the same two sections, the second of which "we will now call 'additional chapters.'" The revision, he noted, "has allowed me to extend my chapters considerably, and the book will go over 400 pages now." Among these additions, Ortiz expanded upon the concept of transculturation, surely the idea that most attracted Malinowski: "The most important part is the one about the use of tobacco among Caribbean Indians, from the strictly ethnographic viewpoint, and the ones about transculturation, whereby one religion-based social phenomenon goes on to become an economic phenomenon." Their dialogue extended to May 1940, when Ortiz visited the United States for the second time as a delegate to the Eighth Pan-American Scientific Congress in Washington, D.C. and visited Malinowski at Yale May 27th through the 31st. On June 9th, Malinowski finally sent Ortiz his text assuming all along it would be "the appendix to your book," a comment that shows both its original purpose and that Ortiz later turned it into the "Introduction." The letter containing this marker also shows that Malinowski wrote his text originally in English and that Ortiz himself did the translation. Malinowski also mentioned then an upcoming visit to Havana, which did not actually occur until July 6th, as mentioned in another June 30 letter. He announced then that "the Appendix is ready and I'll hand it over to you either on the dock or in the Havana Club or in Baccardí's [sic] Bar, while smoking a cigar and sipping a daiquiri (made with cane and sweetened with Cuban sugar," a reference most likely to his corrections to the Spanish translation.

It was not until October 26 that Ortiz sent a copy of the published *Contrapunteo cubano* along with a letter in which he shows interest in producing an English translation. He described then how it would take "reordering it, getting rid of the idea of complementary chapters and putting together a better organized volume out of *Cuban Counterpoint* and those chapters." Thus even after reorganizing the book to follow Malinowski's suggestions, Ortiz did not seem entirely convinced of the resulting product and planned to revise it for an American edition. In yet another letter (February 11, 1941), he reiterated that he was thinking then of "recomposing the materials in the book, that is, to put together a new book entitled 'Havana Tobacco,' so that tobacco would be the central theme and sugar would just be a comparison theme in the two or three chapters that have to do with tobacco's social conduct." The idea was to change into actual chapters all the tobacco sections while "adding to it forty or fifty new pages on tobacco's transculturation from the Indian to the black and from black to white." "I've also been thinking," he wrote further, "of adding a new chapter on tobacco and art, with a brief history and describing the features of tobacco's influence on the boxes, labels, pipes, etc." The idea was to rewrite the book with an English reader in mind. "If they accept it, I myself will do the adaptation; the English version could be a brand new book, with a new title and a new section."

The 1947 English translation turned out to be not the "adaptation" Ortiz had envisioned but merely an abridged version. In fact, there was never to be an "adaptation" like the one Ortiz envisioned. Ortiz's own revised Spanish edition, not released until 1963, 23 years after the first, did make many changes, though none of the ones the correspondence mentions. Finally, we know not whether Malinowski and Ortiz ever met again after their four encounters—twice in Havana and twice in New Haven—between 1939 and 1941. The year after the last letter cited, on May 1942, Malinowski died suddenly in New Haven, Connecticut.

Ortiz himself continued working on his research in Havana on the margins of the political convulsions of the 1940s and 1950s. In his response to the national homage paid him in Havana in 1955, he summed up his life's work:

> I've been a traveler along the routes of this world, just a tourist, as they say these days, in cities as much as forests, on mountaintops, or on hillsides or in ditches. Everywhere I found the same humanity; neither beast nor angel, dirty nor clean, painful nor happy, of infinite sorts, but all capable of love and hatred, of pulling themselves up or of tripping over, rising or falling . . . and I've always entertained myself focusing upon human scenes, full of movement and color, and then classifying their images and showing them to the curious . . . Only science, all the sciences together, can show us the stars of safest path. Only science will be able to recreate the world and assure its inhabitants plenty, health, wisdom, dignity, well being, freedom and peace.[40]

Ortiz died in Havana on April 10, 1969. He was 87 years old.

IV

In a 1936 essay that was the clearest preview of *Cuban Counterpoint*, Ortiz noted it consisted of "schematic paragraphs . . . taken from a book of human geography called *Antillas* that has just been published."[41] The preview had reordered "schematically" passages from the text of a *Universal Geography* Ortiz had edited the same year with Maximilien Sorre, a sociologist at the University of Lille. Volume 19 of the *Universal Geography*, on the Antilles, was in turn the Spanish version of a 1928 French original, edited by Paul Vidal de la Blache and L. Gallois. Because the original French had lacked an Antilles volume, Ortiz was asked to complete it with a team of eight Cuban experts. It was in chapters X and XI of the Spanish version, on sugar and tobacco, where Ortiz first wrote about the contrast between the two commodities.[42]

This was not, in fact, Ortiz's first contribution to the field of Geography. In 1922 he had devoted an entire book to the *History of Indo-Cuban Archaeology*.[43] In between the book and the essay, Ortiz had contributed a one hundred page chapter to a *Universal Geography: Modern Description of the World* (1933) published by Barcelona's Instituto Gallach, research for which he undertook during his U.S. exile in Washington.[44] Attracted by the encyclopedic character of the *Universal Geography*— the closest thing perhaps to von Humboldt's *Cosmos*, one of Ortiz's favorite books—the latter had offered a international forum for his ideas on economic nationalism.[45]

"Human Geography" was therefore the disciplinary origin of *Cuban Counterpoint*. During Ortiz's time—the years immediately following the heyday of Positivism—scientific disciplines were not so specialized, or their differences as drawn. True, Ortiz's contributions to the field of Geography have never been that well known, at least not as widely recognized as those he made in the fields of History, Anthropology, or Musicology. Indeed they were not the staid contributions one usually associates with Geography—the drawing of maps, for example, or geological sketches. For as early as 1928, with Ortiz's attendance at the Sixth Pan-American Conference, he had proposed that History be included among the purviews of a new Geographical Institute:

> The reason seems obvious . . . one should realize our institute's activities cannot be limited to the new studies of geodesics and topography. These studies must be extended in relation to all human dynamics, in space as well and time . . . A geographical institute must certainly be important because it will tell us *of the American*

world where we live. But its function will not be as important if we do not, at the same time, empower it to study *the way we live in it*. Geography and History are inextricably linked, that is, if we wish to give to the study of History a useful, human sense. [Ortiz's emphasis][46]

From 1928 on, then, Ortiz was at the forefront of the scientific rethinking of "Human Geography" as a field of inquiry. Today the term has fallen into relative obscurity; but in its heyday, Human (or Cultural) Geography was precisely what embraced the numerous disciplines that intersect in *Cuban Counterpoint*—from History and Economics to Sociology and Ethnography: a true interdisciplinary field. "Human Geography," wrote Vidal de la Blache, "is not to be contrasted with a geography from which human interests are excluded," as it provides a broad scientific platform for the study of "the physical laws governing our human society and the relations between the living beings that inhabit it."[47] Sorre, with whom Ortiz edited the *Antilles* volume, himself saw in Geography a hermeneutic totality that was unavailable in other disciplines: "Sociologists admit that geographers contribute two things: a total sense of environment, and the experience of direct observation acquired as part of research."[48]

Ortiz's *Cuban Counterpoint* thus emerged out of a popularizing context—written originally for the nonspecialized reader. But this original context also reveals Ortiz's unwavering scientific approach. When we read these two original chapters on sugar and tobacco, for example, one is struck by their detailed historical and statistical approach, redolent of tables and scientific data. Much as in the same vein as the "additional chapters" section, the two chapters abound in physical and ecological descriptions, harvests and botanical detail, observations on climate and its impact on agriculture. Their running argument is based on empirical data, and they derive insights into social realities from the historical growth of the two commodities. Lastly, Ortiz prided himself on systematizing the technological vocabulary used in sugar and tobacco production.[49] And yet, because Ortiz's contributions to Geography hardly circulated within Cuba, the impression seems to have been created, particularly among more recent readers, that *Cuban Counterpoint*'s thesis is purely speculative and has little scientific basis, an impression that might have been further reinforced by the essay's informal style. Yet nothing could be further from the truth.

The two chapters in *Universal Geography* stressed the two industries' political and economic context, but their joint argument never did make it into *Cuban Counterpoint*. The clear exceptions were the paragraphs from the second of these chapters (215–223, 231–233) which Ortiz reorganized "schematically" for the 1936 preview and which, four years later, he used again in the book. That "schematic" argument, based upon "contrast"—later called "counterpoint"—had first appeared in the *Universal Geography*, as well as in this summary statement: "Sugarcane and tobacco are all contrast. It could be said that a rivalry animates and separates them."[50]

Discussion of the political context of the two industries, so evident in the *Universal Geography*, never made it either into the 1940 book, though the context was evident in Ortiz's dual position as critic of sugar and advocate for tobacco. The original tobacco chapter, for example, resonates loudly in the defense that appears later in *Cuban Counterpoint*, while the original sugar chapter reads like a long list of complaints: *latifundia* (land concentration), absentee landlords, immigrant labor, seasonal work and, above all, U.S. capitalist exploitation and its negative repercussions. "Today more than ever, Cuba is enslaved to sugar. Sugar brought us African slaves; but today her entire population is made up of slaves. These days, the sugar industry is profoundly disturbed."[51] Indeed, Ortiz's chapter can be read as an outcry against the subjection of Cuban sugar to foreign interests: "It is believed that in 80 out of 100 cases, American capital holds sway in the Cuban sugar industry, which as we see, supplanted it. To it, then, is bound responsibility for the mistaken expansionist idea that dragged Cuban industry and its entire economy to its most thundering disaster."[52]

Ortiz's critique of sugar actually forms part of a broader national debate—the historical abuses of successive Cuban administrations, its social consequences, and the need for government control of the industry—that at the time was taking place in Cuba. The debate can be broadly summed up in terms of an exchange between two factions: a political elite in favor of sugar, and an intellectual elite dead set against it. Their bone of contention was single-crop dependency. The question itself harked back to the origins of sugar production in the island, though it only began to permeate national consciousness with the debate among prominent historians and essayists throughout the early twentieth century. If World War I had meant prosperity for Cuba, the years that followed it were disastrous. Even Cuban banks were affected by the Depression, as many of them had been created to supply the sugar industry's needs. Chaos thus determined a series of legal measures. The 1926 *Tarafa Law*, for example, attempted to stabilize international prices by mandating reductions in production and export; so did the 1927 Import Tax, which gave advantages to the agricultural sector by reducing the sugar industry's edge. But all attempts to regulate the industry failed. By 1929 President Machado had all but reinstated government protections. Only in 1934, with Machado gone and U.S. approval of a favorable schedule of import quotas, was any seeming stability reached. Meantime, chaos reigned, and war among the two factions broke out.[53]

The first shots were fired by Cuban historian Ramiro Guerra y Sánchez (1880–1970), who all through the 1920s published a series of scathing articles on the industry's crisis which he soon collected in a book, his classic *Azúcar y Población en las Antillas* (1927).[54] Guerra criticized *latifundia*—excessive land concentration—to which he attributed economic stagnation, owing to what he called "the quick disappearance of a class of independent rural landowners." *Latifundia* also explained, accordingly, "the substitution of the white population by blacks in the Antilles," a modern variant of the "black problem" that *créole* essayists like José Antonio Saco (1797–1879) had practically beaten to death during the previous century. As "the Africans and their Antillean descendants were more socially defenseless than the whites, so were they more easily subjugated by the economic pressures of *latifundia*." What is more, according to Guerra, the racial argument was secondary: "we are not dealing with a question of race, but with a system of land exploitation that divides the population into two groups: a small number of capitalist agents who direct and administer sugarcane planting and sugar manufacture and shipping, and a mass of laborers of whatever race obliged to accept a minimal wage and tolerate a reduced standard of living . . ."(4).

Latifundia had come about through "industrial concentration": sugar production increased as the number of mills replaced many small ones. Industrial concentration produced, in turn, land dispossession: small, independent landowners vanished, corporations or trusts took over, and absentee land ownership increased. Deep down, Guerra was a reformist and his position coincided, in many ways, with Machado's, during whose administration he worked briefly as chief of staff. With Machado's fall, Guerra's U.S. exile, and his eventual return to Cuba, his ideas on the subject changed; so much, in fact, that ten years later he even became a spokesman for the sugar industry.[55] Guerra's shift is already evident in the 1944, third edition of *Azúcar y Población en las Antillas*, in whose preface he noted that "all this . . . has in large part become historical" because of reforms attributed to timely and effective government regulation. "These changes have been instituted because the State . . . decided to regulate the industry's organization and activities" (8). And yet, barely ten years earlier, in the *Universal Geography* chapters, Ortiz had forewarned Guerra in a prescient passage that was later grafted onto *Cuban Counterpoint*:

> *Latifundia* were not responsible for the large Negro population of
> Cuba, but rather the lack of indigenous Indian or white workers,
> and the difficulty of bringing in labor that was as permanent and
> submissive and cheap as Africa's. Cuban *latifundia* has been nothing
> but the direct result of the beef industry and other concomitant fac-
> tors, such as the black population. One and the other have been
> almost parallel effects of the same basic cause, particularly the prob-
> lem of sugar. The African population is not a precise consequence of
> *latifundia*.[56]

According to Ortiz, Guerra had jumped over the root cause (capitalist
exploitation) in exchange for a mere symptom (*latifundia*). Industrial
concentration was derived, accordingly, from parallel "capitalist concentration," which in turn demanded the highest concentration of land,
workers, machinery, and money. "When we had land aplenty and
machinery was worthless, we already had large concentrations of African
slaves; no *latifundia* influence there" (191). Ortiz and Guerra differed,
then, on two questions: the critique of capitalism, and the historical
causes of African slavery. In their disagreement, Ortiz accused Guerra, in
effect, of complicity with interests that were not only exploitative, but
also implicitly racist, particularly because they minimized the causal
relationship between slavery and sugar.

Ortiz and Guerra agreed in identifying defects of the sugar industry, but
differed radically on the remedies. Guerra favored industry reform; Ortiz
preferred state control. Their ideas reflected differing political positions:
Guerra favored a liberal policy, what today we would call "center-right," or
laissez-faire; Ortiz favored a "center-left" position: more open to State regulation. Over time, their differences lessened, as reflected in Guerra's 1944
preface. Barely ten years before, while addressing the sugar crop restrictions
instituted after the revolution against Machado, Ortiz had praised that

> [T]he new restrictions would be joined by official measures
> favorable to small mills, tenant farmers and workers, because they
> were all Cuban, including those which regulated the distribution of
> crop quotas for mills, applicable only to large mills; forced equitable
> milling of tenants' cane, not just "the administration's"; demanded
> forcible repatriation of Haitian and Jamaican workers; and fixed the
> length of the workday, etc. Cuban sugar is entering a new historical
> phase. (153)

Clearly, all this constituted, on the part of Ortiz, a full-blown political critique, not just a timid reformist plea. For just as Octavio Paz, in 1969, had proposed a "critique of the pyramid" to denounce Mexico's one-party system and the sacrifices it demanded, so, too, in 1936 Fernando Ortiz articulated in Cuba a "critique of sugar." That is, a critique not just limited to an isolated aspect of the sugar economy, but of everything sugar meant: the industry's centralizing power and its negative effects upon the entire breadth of Cuban society.[57]

By the time *Cuban Counterpoint* was published in 1940, the debate had become intensely relevant due to adoption of the new Cuban constitution. That same year, Guerra published *La industria azucarera de Cuba* (The Cuban Sugar Industry) where he argued that if the industry was "far from having reached perfection . . . neither is it a mere instrument of hateful and pitiless exploitation."[58] Much was at stake. It is this local context that explains the passionately nationalist tone of Herminio Portell-Vilá's preface to *Cuban Counterpoint*. Not only did Portell-Vilá agree with Ortiz's historical axioms. He also disparaged, in a transparent reference to Guerra, all those "economists in the service of sugar interests" who "have encouraged the idea of an identity between those interests and the nation's, that Cuba and sugar are one and the same." Indeed, *sin azúcar no hay país* (Without sugar there's no nation), the premise that since the nineteenth century had described the symbiosis between Cuba and sugar, was guiding Cuban political conscience. Yet according to Portell-Vilá, the collapse between the two was "completely artificial, a result of men's horrors and selfishness. In truth, the sugar industry has never managed to support itself and has always lived off of others' favors and sacrifices, like a giant parasite." Sugar was responsible, the preface went on, for not only "the slavery regime," but also for "the people's growing poverty in that sector," virtual slaves of U.S. interests.[59] Portell-Vilá's arguments agreed in large part with Ortiz's, or at least with Ortiz's arguments in the *Universal Geography*. In other words, in *Cuban Counterpoint* Ortiz renewed his critique of sugar from the 1930s, but stopped short of entering into the (new) post–1940 constitution political fray; at least not in the same way Portell-Vilá did. Portell-Vilá's preface made explicit, in effect, the politics that was implicit in Ortiz's text, which opted instead for the broad historical view.[60] The two chapters from *Universal Geography* had already scripted the political argument that appears between the lines in *Cuban Counterpoint*.

One measure of the degree to which the anti-sugar front, courtesy of Ortiz and Portell-Vilá, rang an alarm among industry advocates can be gathered from the response that appeared three years later in *The Truth*

About Sugar in Cuba, a pamphlet edited by Antonio Barro y Segura and financed by the national Association of Cuban Sugar Producers.[61] The pamphlet had responded to yet another of Portell-Vilá's incendiary articles from 1942, "The Sugar Industry and its Future," published in *Revista bimestre cubana*, a journal that at the time was edited by Ortiz. In it the nationalist historian Portell-Vilá renewed his outcry against the industry's interests, and in particular the Cuban "campaign against U.S. sugar policy."[62] World War II raged then, and the U.S. government was negotiating, after purchase of the entire Cuban sugar harvest, future purchases with other Latin American countries and launching a campaign to regulate domestic consumption. Portell-Vilá concluded it was necessary to subject the sugar industry ("that Frankenstein of the Cuban economy") to "a prudent and well-calculated euthanasia . . . we must destroy it so that Cuba might live, and vindicate its 'right to exist.' " Unsurprisingly, the pamphlet defended the industry and challenged Portell-Vilá's views, all the while linking that challenge to "don Fernando Ortiz's interesting and erudite book *Cuban Counterpoint of Tobacco and Sugar*" (174). The pamhlet's reticence about Ortiz's text—the latter is its sole reference to it—is a symptom of the wider non-reception that met it. If indeed there was any dissension, particularly regarding his views on the sugar industry, it was silent; it simply would not have been good to disagree publicly, especially on as thorny a topic as sugar, with as important a figure as Ortiz.[63] But the silence underscored something else: the deep historical nature of *Cuban Counterpoint*.

Ortiz produced, then, not a book on transient political opinion, but a historical essay supported by data confirmed over centuries. Both his *Universal Geography* and the 1936 essay had put forth a critique based on "contrast." The new book adopted the form of a historical treatise based on counterpoint, that is, open debate, in terms of both content and form. If the book's contemporary relevance—or else, its political anecdote—fell onto Portell-Vilá's preface, then its theoretical implications were up to Malinowski in his "Introduction." Ortiz's lot was to concentrate on another two things: the "counterpoint" of the opening essay, and the "evidence," or else, the theory of transculturation, of the "additional chapters." In turn, Ortiz's nationalism, kept him from conceiving of capitalist economy as inevitably global. Right or wrong, he perceived that the global economy had been artificially imposed in Cuba out of inherent structural weaknesses, to say nothing of the historic mistakes made by successive Republican governments. All of these Ortiz deemed entirely avoidable. Yet basic economic theory did provide Ortiz one general premise: economic causes have social effects; Marxist "base and superstructure."

Ortiz's own concept of economics, is however, not rigidly scientific, in the way Marxist Historical Materialism is; nor is it the result of meta-economic conflicts, such as those of class struggle. His views could perhaps be dismissed as naïve, but only if we lose sight of his ultimate civic goal: he wanted to improve general welfare, not dissect economic structures.[64]

This Cuban debate over sugar contrasts sharply with the nation's relative agreement over tobacco. National interests were clearly different, since neither tobacco investments nor profits were ever as high as sugar's—such at least was Ortiz's belief. In fact, there never really was a Cuban debate on tobacco, even when, as Jean Stubbs has shown, the reality of the tobacco industry was much closer to sugar's than Ortiz believed, or at least than what his "counterpoint" put forward. Ortiz himself stressed, in a key passage of the essay, that the "economic system of tobacco is gradually approaching the one typical of the sugar industry, both strangled by heartless foreign and native tentacles" (69). Indeed, Ortiz's arguments show a partiality toward tobacco that can otherwise be questioned by historical data.

According to Stubbs, for example, during the nineteenth century a greater percentage of the land devoted to tobacco crops, particularly in Pinar del Río (*Vueltabajo*), was also operated with slave labor; increase in production during the same period itself created *latifundia*, much of it of foreign ownership; demand for land, particularly during the twentieth century, caused industrial and agricultural capital further to consolidate, thus gradually eliminating small landowners; and finally, the tobacco workers' lot was not that much better than sugar's, except for the negative effects of "dead time," the seasonal lay-off period.[65] This is a far different picture from the one Ortiz provides in *Cuban Counterpoint*. Ortiz himself recognized the methodological problems he faced when he warned, in chapter I, that "The historical evolution of economic-social phenomena is extremely complex and the variety of factors that determine them cause them to vary greatly in the course of their development; at times there are similarities that make them appear identical; at times the differences make them seem completely opposed" (97). Observations like these abound. We should add, however, that at the time Ortiz wrote this, both industries had already entered into a high capitalist phase whose extreme alienation provoked a number of conflicts throughout the entire Cuban economy, and not just within limited sectors. Such at least was Ortiz's view, as he complained: "But today this capitalism, which is not Cuban by birth or by inclination, is reducing everything to the same common denominator." It would not be Ortiz's last, or only, lament. Indeed, his views on the differences between sugar and tobacco were much more complex than a first reading would lead us to believe, as comments like these show:

> Capitalism is also establishing a parallel between the industrial aspects of tobacco and sugar, subjecting them both to increasing foreign domination, with devastating results for Cuba. Sugar has always been under foreign economic control, and Cuba's share in its returns has always been held to a minimum, to what it makes from producing the raw material; and the same is now being attempted with tobacco . . . In these last decades, since the process of mechanization and the growing power and concentration of capital have tended to synthesize and unify labor problems in all fields of production, the demands of the workers in these two industries have approached each other more closely than in past times, when their industrial set ups differed. (79, 85)

Even if Ortiz had known all the data Stubbs unearthed years later, one would still need to question whether a counterpoint reading actually creates, rather than describes, an alleged contest. The question itself prompts two corollaries. We should note, first, that the tone that permeates the front essay is, in the main, mournful, or at least nostalgic. That is, Ortiz wrote at a time when the differences between the two industries were blurring, which in turn means that counterpoint itself was dying out then, and with it, the national identity those differences sustained. *Cuban Counterpoint* is a crisis text, its nostalgia actually signaling a farewell to a national identity that was on the verge of disappearing, or at least changing radically. In this sense, Ortiz was a visionary, sensitive as he was to Cuba's historical reality. Yet a second corollary refers to what one could call the epistemology of counterpoint. For if Ortiz had to emphasize the differences between the two commodities through counterpoint, then what does such a method actually mean?

It was not the first time that counterpoint, in its broad sense of a discourse of contrast or opposition, had been used to describe Cuba's economy. At the start of the nineteenth century, for example, the Spanish Controller Alejandro Ramírez (–1821), sent to Cuba by the Spanish Crown to prepare a report on the island's development, had already come up with much of what Friedlaender later called the "small Cuba" thesis: encouragement of private property, white (and therefore free) immigration and colonization, and partition of large estates in favor of small landholders and peasantry. Ramírez's thesis, shared in its time by major political figures (like Captain-General Cienfuegos), was perceived as a diversification plan with the single goal of abolition. Ramírez thus opposed colonial development through metropolitan support of the sugar industry (what Friedlaender called "big Cuba"), as proposed by Francisco de Arango y Parreño (1765–1837), who had argued for keeping the slave trade as cost-effective labor supply. What seems important about all these precedents is that, be it in the nineteenth or the twentieth century, a "small Cuba" thesis could only be understood by logical opposition or contrast to a "big Cuba."[66]

Ortiz's *Cuban Counterpoint*—together with Ramírez as forebear—is in fact the pioneering prototype of twentieth-century economic studies in Latin America that had one method in common: the binary focus on two commodities within underdeveloped countries as the basis for analyzing national history. Such binary opposition was meant to demonstrate one commodity's "villainy" versus the other's relative "goodness." And yet, despite being a fairly common procedure, the method has proven to create differing results according to context. If, for example, for Ortiz in Cuba tobacco had been good and sugar bad, for Nieto Arteta in Colombia, by turns, tobacco was bad, and coffee good; while for Celso Furtado, in Brazil, coffee was good and sugar bad. For economist Albert Hirschman, who studied a wide spectrum of all such "counterpoints," it's all a matter of "convergence"—advantages or disadvantages converge toward one or another evaluation—and reaches into many other types of economic activity.[67] What interests me about Hirschman's analysis—which acknowledges Ortiz's pioneering importance—is that the matter poses an epistemological question: is convergence (that is, a counterpoint reading) created by the observer ("an active perception of reality, created in turn by the questions we want to answer"), or does it "exist in nature"? Is it in the object, or in the eye of the beholder? Hirschman favors the former because, "there is nothing intrinsically inconceivable about a given product acting as a multidimensional conspiracy in favor or against its development within a certain historical or sociopolitical environment" (96).

Be that as it may, the book's, and particularly the essay's "schematic" structure, based on contrast, is what must have made Malinowski claim: "Fernando Ortiz belongs to that school or tendency of modern social science known today by the name of 'functionalism' " (xiv). Indeed, counterpoints based on binary oppositions inform and delight us; but, above all, they organize; that is, they demonstrate the categories under which tobacco and sugar come both together and apart. Better put: counterpoint shows the ways in which commodities relate to each other in their differences. By relating them to each other, Ortiz added something else: he unearthed, interpreted, and structured. His book actually structures a basic historical mechanism, what the essay's first subsection refers to as the economy's "visceral systems." Thus in the essay, Ortiz provides a structural model of the Cuban economy; in the "additional chapters," however, he provides a history of how that structure came to be. Structure and History complement each other.

Without necessarily intending to, then, Ortiz's method (particularly in the essay) does link up, however precariously, with Functionalism, the school that Malinowski, among other anthropologists—almost all British—espoused throughout the first half of the twentieth century. Functionalist conviction was straightforward: cultures and societies possess an organic unity of their own which we can understand upon analyzing how their diverse "functions"—parenthood, economic life, social and sexual customs, etc.—relate to each other and how each contributes to the whole. As Radcliffe-Browne, the other "father" of British Functionalism, once remarked: "[F]unction is the part it plays in the contribution that it makes to the life of the organism as a whole. As the terms are here being used, a cell or an organ has an *activity*, and that activity has a *function*."[68] Function, then, is equivalent to a piece of the puzzle; functionalists figure out both the puzzle's design and the function each piece plays within it.

We would not be wrong to understand Functionalism as a type of Formalism applied to social science. As in Formalist literary criticism, Functionalism is, in that sense, a precursor to Structuralism, though lacking the modeling of cultural codes or linguistic structures that Claude Lévi-Strauss prescribed.[69] Thus based on an organic idea of culture, Functionalism/Formalism developed methods of interpretation that brought to the fore the latent (Ortiz's "visceral") mechanisms of cultural phenomena, be they literary texts or societies. In turn, this type of study was based on two premises. The first was that since organic phenomena coexist in the present, their study excludes, or at least minimizes, their evolution in time. As Radcliffe-Browne put it: "One explanation of the race-horse is to be found in history—how it came to just what it is and where it is. Another and entirely independent 'explanation' is to show how the horse is a special exemplification of physiological laws" (301). Demonstrating the latter is the Functionalist task.[70]

The second premise is the one underlying all social science: things are not what they seem to be; their true nature is hidden. Visible reality is actually the result of "false consciousness." Thus in order to reveal the hidden nature of things, we must not only suspect the surface, but actually develop methods—the body of which we call hermeneutics—that relate surface and depth in order to pierce through false consciousness.

If Descartes was the father of Western systematic doubt, modern hermeneutics rests upon three names: Marx, Freud, and Nietzsche. All three, as well as their progeny, work under one fundamental hypothesis, which Paul Ricoeur summed up neatly: "There is a process of false consciousness and there is a method of decipherment. The two go together, since the man of suspicion carries out in reverse the work of falsification of the man of guile."[71]

Such, then, would the general principles underlying the structure of *Cuban Counterpoint*. Essay and chapters relate to each other not only as summary and notes (*appendices* was the name Ortiz first thought up and rejected); they also relate as surface and depth, manifest and latent content, in the same way conscious and unconscious relate in psychoanalysis, ideology and economic structure do in political economy, or values and the will-to-power do in moral philosophy. The book's physical structure, its two sections, thus mirrors the structure of the social fact: surface and depth, manifestation and latency, masks and values. Within this structure, Ortiz offers us not only interpretive conclusions (as he does in the front essay), but also the varied data that led him there (the back "additional chapters"). The reader perceives that structure both successively, from essay to chapters, and deductively: from universals to facts, summary to data. In turn, the structure sets into motion a series of formal relations that betray the interpretive task. Within the essay's counterpoint structure, commodities turn into allegorical characters, thus taking to logical extremes the consequences of the "commodity fetishism" Marx had described in *Capital* as a perverse consequence of capitalist alienation: as men are degraded to the point of becoming objects, so do objects themselves acquire human attributes. Coronil rightly calls this move Ortiz's "counter-fetishism": "Without making reference to Marx, he shows how the appearance of commodities as independent entities—as potent agents in their own right conceals their origin in conflict was relations of production and confirms a commonsense perception of these relations as natural and necessary."[72] But beyond their pragmatic usefulness, Coronil's comments help us understand further how allegory works within the book's structure.

For just as commodities conceal relations of production and the labor that produced it, the essay conceals, by virtue of its schematic character, the historical data that made it possible. And yet the essay's mask not only conceals; it also *reveals*, in the sense that it points to what lies "elsewhere," in the book at least. That is, the essay reveals ciphered evidence that acts as a spur in ways that the reader is urged to keep deciphering in the book's second section, the "additional chapters." The reader thus perceives counterpoint as he perceives immediate reality: mere appearance, alienated false consciousness. It is beneath (or, as in this case, *following*) the two commodities' success and harmony that one discovers the real, and infinitely more painful, story: transculturation. In this sense, and however haltingly it may actually have been forged, the structure of *Cuban Counterpoint* is innovative. Most canonical twentieth-century essays from Latin America—Ezequiel Martínez's *X-ray of the Pampa* (1933), for example, or Octavio Paz's *Labyrinth of Solitude* (1950)—articulate their arguments inductively: evidence is presented first, followed by logical, homogeneous consequences. Ortiz's, however, works in reverse: he articulates conclusions first and then presents evidence in a separate, "additional" section in all its shocking heterogeneity, much as a quarry's raw matter. In such display, the book dramatizes (and thereby demythifies) the text's production through history's sundry substance, what the book calls *transculturation*. And in this sense, too, its structure mirrors the ways that history is actually perceived in real life: *Counterpoint* as manifest surface, *transculturation* as latent background. And more than just latent, repressed. For the "additional chapters," deal, in great measure, with the "beginnings of sugar and Black slavery in Cuba," that most disagreeable theme of historical violence, as a thick description of the nation's cultural mixture; only in the book that theme appears tucked away at the end, as in a kind of *barracón* or slave quarters that returns with a vengeance to unveil the deep structure of Cuba's wealth. We would not be wrong, in this sense, in identifying *Cuban Counterpoint* as yet another among Ortiz's many books on anti-African racism, a kind of "missing link" to the years after 1940, when Ortiz systematized the study of Afro-Cuba deliberately and passionately.

Thus the book's two sections complement each other. The essay, provides structure to the historical data that appears dispersed in the "additional chapters"; the essay, in turn, makes up the manifest structure of those latent, imperceptible data that lie buried in history's archive. The "additional chapters" should be read as a complement to the essay; the essay, in turn, is the structure that provides the chapters with sense, owing mostly to the counterpoint between the two commodities. Without all that data, the reader cannot know *transculturation*, Cuba's peculiar cultural evolution, especially in terms of the tobacco industry, which Ortiz favors as the true banner of nationality. Without the essay, however, the reader would lack *counterpoint*, the national economy's peculiar structural mechanism that "produced" history and, moreover, explains it.

Counterpoint and transculturation do have one important thing in common: antinomian or oppositional structures. Each confronts two phenomena, though in radically different ways. In counterpoint, tobacco and sugar argue, display differences, yet they avoid all conflict. "A close harmony of *sugar and sigar*," is how Cabrera Infante once put it.[73] Nor are they joined together in the end, except perhaps in that hypothetical "flirting" of the two commodities'"merging and living happily ever after" (93) that the end of the essay alludes to. In other words, counterpoint is *dialogical*: it reveals simultaneous difference but displays neither mutual contradiction (thesis versus antithesis) nor transcendence in synthesis.[74] Transculturation is *dialectical*: its antinomy is based on cultural difference and resolves itself in a synthesis that in turn differs from its sources: "the result of every union of cultures is similar to that of the reproductive process between individuals: the offspring always has something of both parents but is always different from each other" (103).

As such, Ortiz proposes, though only implicitly, a broad theoretical hypothesis. For if, in fact, the essay is logically derived from the data the "additional chapters" compile; that is, if its argument derives logically from previous evidence, then *counterpoint* is shown to be the metaphor or echo of *transculturation*: the "discussion" of the national economy is but a distant echo of a historical "dialectic." Put another way: *counterpoint* is the cloak that covers over, the surface that masks, *transculturation*, the one determining factor of Cuban national identity. And yet, following the essay's typical logic, that mutual metaphorical relationship is shown and displayed, but is neither inflected nor made explicit. It is a cipher the reader must perceive and unravel.

Much, then, like Freud, Marx, or Nietzsche—the essay mentions all three—Ortiz builds up a dynamic structure that invites his reader to participate in an expansion of consciousness, his own individual as well as a national, collective one. Marx had wanted to liberate *praxis* by assaulting the mystifications of false consciousness; Freud had substituted one consciousness for another mediated by the Reality Principle; while Nietzsche sought to increase human power by liberating morality. Ortiz wanted his reader to compare Cuba's surface economic "harmony" with the virtually imperceptible "dissonance" of its history. All four propose an expansion of consciousness by piercing through veils of illusion (*counterpoint*) and retrieving the material data of lived history (*transculturation*). And yet, Ortiz himself, the latest of the lot, chose to keep his argument from reaching conclusions that would be based exclusively on the hermeneutics of any one social science. Thus, when at the beginning of the essay he explains the existence of the two commodities'"multiform and persistent contrast" (5), he avoids pointedly raising the subject of "conflict," so charged with psychoanalytic and Marxist connotations, and opts for a far gentler circumlocution: "the concatenation of historical vicissitudes" (5). (At the end of the essay that reticence is even more explicit: "although there are differences between sugar and tobacco, there have never been any conflicts between them" [93].) In the case of Marxism, which the essay targets recurrently, one could stress the case even further; or in that of Nietzschean moral philosophy, which Ortiz also satirizes.

V

In his "Introduction" to *Cuban Counterpoint* Malinowski chose not to stress, so obvious must it have seemed, the essay's "schematic" character, the book's most formalist trait, and went no farther than alluding briefly to its "ingenious setting forth of contrasts and similarities." Instead, Malinowski found evidence of Ortiz's alleged Functionalism in how "aesthetics and the psychology of the sensory impressions must be taken into account together with the habitat and the technology" (xiii). Malinowski also noted Ortiz's attention to the "economic and ecological problems of work and skills," together with "the psychology of smoking, its aesthetics, the beliefs and the emotions associated with each of the finished products . . ." (xiv). Lastly, Malinowski remarked, "like the good functionalist he is, the author of this book resorts to history when it is really necessary" (xiv). It would be difficult, however, to find in such comments the credentials necessary to make a Functionalist out of Ortiz. As Malinowski's relationship with Ortiz's book was ridden by self-interest, so his reasons for claiming Ortiz's Functionalism were not the most convincing.

We have already seen how in their correspondence Malinowski stressed the extent to which Ortiz's work had to do "with the modern anthropological and sociological approach which I like to call functionalism" (February 20, 1940). For Functionalists, cultures are organized around a dynamics of needs. To cite from one of its dicta: "To the functionalist, culture, that is, the whole body of implements, the charters of its social groups, human ideas, beliefs and customs; constitutes a vast apparatus by which man is put in a position the better to cope with the concrete, specific problems which face him in his environment in the course of the satisfaction of his needs."[75] This is clearly different from the cultural theory permeating Ortiz's analysis. True, *Cuban Counterpoint* analyzes the economic lives of tobacco and sugar; but nowhere does it relate them to human needs. Far from it, Ortiz's position seems to have been the opposite: tobacco is a vice and sugar a luxury; both became commodities within a cycle of modern capitalist exploitation. Neither one actually serves an inherent need, at least for purposes of biological survival. Sugar itself, which Ortiz views as a foreign imposition, provides Cuba's marketable backbone but does not fulfill any such organic requirements.

Lastly, Malinowski and Ortiz differ in their views on history as an element of cultural analysis. Functionalism, as with any kind of Formalism, devalues history and favors the object's organic unity. That is, Functionalists are interested less in how objects are constituted over time than in how they function in the present. Or, as Malinowski himself noted: "instead of linking up evidence by the coordinates of time and projecting it under the heading of past, present and future into an evolutionary or historical sequence, we have to marshal the facts under categories, all of which coexist in the present, all of which and can be studied in empirical field work."[76]

Where Malinowski and Ortiz did coincide was in their enthusiasm for *transculturation* as term and concept. In his first letter to Malinowski (November 25, 1939) enclosing the book's first galleys, Ortiz pointed out his coinage and noted the passage where "I explain my preference for the neologism, and request your authority to baptize it." In that passage Ortiz states that

> I am of the opinion that the word *transculturation* better expresses the different phases of the process of transition from one culture to another because this does not consist merely in acquiring another culture, which is what the English word *acculturation* really implies, but the process also necessarily involves the loss or uprooting of a previous culture, which could be defined as a deculturation. In addition it carries the idea of the consequent creation of new cultural phenomena, which could be called neoculturation. In the end, as the school of Malinowski's followers maintains, the result of every union of cultures is similar to that of the reproductive process between individuals: the offspring always has something of both parents but is always different from each of them. (102–103)

Malinowski himself tells how during his November 1939 visit to Havana Ortiz mentioned "that in his next book he was planning to introduce a new technical word, the term *transculturation*, to replace various expressions in use, such as 'cultural exchange,' 'acculturation,' 'diffusion,' 'migration or osmosis' and similar ones that he considered inadequate" (ix). Timing could not have been better. The passage shows that by then Ortiz must have known Malinowski's earlier essay "The Anthropology of Changing African Cultures" (1938), an introductory text to a volume on culture contact in Africa where he had markedly changed his views regarding the study of native cultures in contact with Europeans, and the need to study such [native] history.[77] Malinowski himself cites this 1938 essay as a way of showing that his alliance with Ortiz was based on the shared view that "contact, clash, and transformation of cultures cannot be conceived as the complete acceptance of a given culture by any one 'acculturated' group." Such a view supported his opinion that the two races "exist upon elements taken from Europe as well as Africa . . . from both cultural storehouses. In so doing, both races transform the borrowed elements and incorporate them into a completely new and independent cultural reality" (xii). Thus Malinowski's views on "culture contact" appear to have changed even before he traveled to Havana in November 1939; contact with Ortiz confirmed them and gave them a name: *transculturation*.[78]

Both men were reacting, albeit for different reasons, to the spread of *acculturation*, the term and concept that since the 1930s the social sciences had chosen to name "those phenomena which result when groups of individuals having different cultures come into continuous first-hand contact, with subsequent changes in the original cultural pattern *of either or both groups*."[79] I cite from and emphasize the original 1936 definition by Redfield, Linton, and Herskovits not only to avoid the subsequent distortions the term has endured. My sense is that Malinowski actually distorted the meaning of acculturation when he claimed it was "an ethnocentric word with a moral connotation . . . the 'uncultured' is to receive the benefits of 'our culture'; it is 'he' who must change, and become converted into 'one of us.'" We shall see, in a moment, Malinowski's reasons for making such distortion. Suffice it to say that the point seems worth emphasizing because the latest postcolonial reading of Ortiz (though not, curiously, of Malinowski) has invested much on an alleged opposition between Herskovits's ethnocentrist claims and Ortiz's allegedly decentering challenge. And yet once we place Ortiz's coinage and Malinowski's support of it in context, the alleged opposition lessens, if not dissipates altogether.[80]

Ortiz, for his part, repeated Malinowski's error, though less angrily. Indeed, Ortiz's objections to acculturation were chiefly lexical, not conceptual; for him, it was merely a question of using the right word ("acculturation does not mean strictly acquiring another culture, which is what the Anglo-American word strictly signifies"). There is no doubt Ortiz's neologism is more analytically precise, at least in Spanish, than *acculturation*, an English term that has no exact Spanish equivalent.[81] Ortiz himself articulated an analysis of transculturation, something lacking from advocates of acculturation, and divided it into two stages: *deculturation*, partial loss of a group's culture, and *neoculturation*, partial gain. Suffice it to say that the ethnocentrism Ortiz and Malinowski attached to acculturation was groundless. The "give and take" Malinowski identified in *transculturation* as Ortiz's most original contribution was actually present in *acculturation*, at least in the original authors' proposal. Herskovits himself, upon receiving his copy of *Cuban Counterpoint*, wrote Ortiz how those who defend acculturation apply it "to studies in this field which concern the results of contact between two primitive folk," thereby setting aside any possibility of "inculcation" (October 29, 1940). All of which means that while acculturation as a term may have been conceptually imprecise, even in the original English, the alternative Ortiz and Malinowski offered up did not amount, in fact, to the trenchant rupture its authors claimed, or their forebears have pressed.

Ortiz and Malinowski had different reasons each for opposing *acculturation*. Ortiz's was the term's imprecision. His objection might also have been fueled by a critique of Herskovits' works on African culture in the New World, which, incredibly, had never mentioned Ortiz.[82] Malinowski's case was more complex. It included his personal resentment of Herskovits, and by extension of the entire American school of anthropology. In fact, by the time he and Ortiz met in Havana in late 1939 a transatlantic war raged between the two schools, American and British, over so-called applied anthropology and the ethical conflicts of anthropologists who both lived with natives and counseled colonial administrations. The differences between the two schools had persisted for at least a decade, starting with their differing stances on the importance each accorded to the study of the history of native peoples. (The British, orthodox Functionalists, disdained it, while the Americans made much of it.) In a 1936 lecture, Herskovits went so far as to accuse Malinowski's students of open complicity with British colonial policy, then known as Indirect Rule, and mentioned Malinowski as one of its architects.[83] Two years later, Malinowski publicly flipped on the matter, reacting perhaps to Herskovits's charge, not to mention his new professional circumstances in the United States, where he had begun teaching. The shift became evident in his polemical contribution to *Methods of Study of Cultural Contact in Africa* (1938), which he cites in his "Introduction," where he stressed greater attention by so-called applied anthropologists to the changing native progeny of Africans and Europeans.

Even allowing all these shifts on the part of Malinowski and his school, that same year Herskovits again accused the British school of disdaining native history. Indeed, Herskovits's thesis in *Acculturation: The Study of*

Culture Contact (1938) points out Malinowski's dramatic change, the critiques he wielded against his own students, and the defensive tone of the debates within the British School. Herskovits concluded then that everything in Malinowski pointed to a reluctant conversion to the principles of the American school. Thus by the time Malinowski and Ortiz met in Havana, the dispute between the two schools revolved around the one burning question that today is being revisited by Postcolonial studies: Which of the two schools waged a better defense of the native's rights and personal integrity?

Such is the true background of *transculturation* as term and concept; or at least, such are the facts behind Malinowski's enthusiasm for it. Beyond the conceptual benefits of Ortiz's coinage, for Malinowski its adoption meant giving the American school a taste of its own medicine. Acculturation, claimed Malinowski, in an evident distortion, concealed the same disdain toward the native of which the Americans accused the British school. And the fact that a Cuban nationalist, well known for his studies of his culture's African strain, had waged separately an intelligent critique of acculturation and its implicit racism, made for an ideal refutation. What is more, Malinowski's interest in contesting the American school was the precise reason behind his insistence on placing Ortiz firmly within the Functionalist camp, despite all evidence to the contrary. Ortiz's own alliance with Malinowski rested for the most part, more than on academic politics, on Cuban internal political interests, and particularly the repercussions emerging from his "critique of sugar." A critic of U.S. policy toward Cuba since the *Chambelona* crisis, Ortiz had returned to the fray with a new anthropological concept in order to challenge U.S. imperialism precisely during implementation of its Good Neighbor Policy and at the timely juncture of a new Cuban constitution. Malinowski's support for the concept, buoyed by his global prestige, was Ortiz's efficient way to shut down the armchair critics, respond to Herskovits at a distance and open a beach-head from which he could influence U.S. public opinion.

Herskovits's letter to Ortiz responding to the gift of a copy of *Cuban Counterpoint* (October 25, 1940) validates my reconstruction of this background. After describing Ortiz's coinage as "thought-provoking," he wondered whether acculturation "might not be so firmly established, and its meaning enough understood, that it will be somewhat difficult to substitute for it the new term which you have proposed." His other comments were directed at Malinowski's assault:

> Certainly, it is necessary for me to enter a strong demur to the implications of the term *acculturation* as stated on pages xvi–xvii by Malinowski. It is *significant*, I think, that he does not document this

passage; certainly, in our use of the term in this country there is no implication of handing down a superior civilization to a *savage* folk. The term as we use it in our scientific work is indeed entirely colorless and in my book I have stressed the need for studies in this field, which concern the results of contact between two primitive folk. One student who has worked in West Africa has investigated this problem of the results of contact between non-European cultures among the Hausa of Nigeria, while I am hoping to send soon a student to Honduras to study the cultural amalgalm resulting from and between the Carib Indians and Africans. If anybody has been guilty of discussing cultural contact in terms of *inculcation* (to use Malinowski's own word) it has been his own students writing of *culture contact*, rather than those of use in this country who are concerned with the scientific problems of acculturation.[84]

In addition to complaining about Malinowski's seeming dishonesty—or at least his failure at documenting his claims—clearly Herskovits differentiated between a North American "we," involved in "scientific problems," and "Malinowski's disciples," engaged in the allegedly dishonest "culture contact." The latter had opted for involvement in the ethically questionable administrative and political aspects of applied anthropology. Far more pertinent to Ortiz, however, must have been Herskovits' warning against the new coinage. In fact, were one to credit Ralph Beals' assertions, in his panoramic 1953 study of the field of anthropology, Malinowski himself barely used Ortiz's term in his subsequent work, even though Beals himself admitted that the great majority of acculturation studies assumed "culture contact" was unidirectional rather than reciprocal. Herskovits himself referred again to Ortiz's contribution in a 1948 survey of his own when he noted (citing the 1947 American edition of *Cuban Counterpoint*) that "every situation of cultural contact and the subsequent innovations that result from it implies cultural borrowing. The misapprehension of Ortiz concerning the term acculturation is certainly not as serious as one which would ascribe to acculturation an ethnocentric quality which it never had." Thus Herskovits expressed his disagreement, suppressed Ortiz's possible rebuttal, and reserved the heavy artillery of his argument for the British school, not to mention Malinowski's ghost.[85]

We would not be wrong to conclude, then, that *transculturation* as a concept has had a polemical history. In Spanish, its reception among anthropologists has been frankly ambivalent, at times even negative within more orthodox circles, whereas in Portuguese "*aculturação*" has been the staple term. No less polemical, though somewhat better, has been its fate within cultural studies, particularly as spread through the work of

Angel Rama's hugely influential *Transculturación narrativa en América Latina* (1982).[86] Rama applied Ortiz's scheme of cultural transformation to texts and narrative traditions as a way of counteracting the harmful, alienating effects of modernization, "a form for the promotion of cultural survival undertaken as a reactive response to modernization."[87] He thus identified stages of "partial deculturation" that can affect "various zones of cultural as well as literary practice"; a second stage that implies "reasonable incorporation of an external culture"; and lastly, "an effort at recomposition, utilizing surviving elements of the original culture and those from outside" (38). Rama's interest lay mostly in the mechanisms of cultural resistance by way of ethnic recomposition. At the same time, his book constitutes an effort to use transculturation as a metahistorical tool by sharpening readings of Latin American narrative. His reconfiguration, postulated as a utopian project and liberationist in nature, was based on ideology rather than anthropology. It also provided an allegory of cultural intermixture, which in turn explains why it centered on texts from Andean culture, and in particular on the narrative works of José María Arguedas, which reflect a strong European-indigenous transculturation. After Rama, transculturation as a term tends to be replaced by other sundry ones, like "heterogeneity" or "hybridity," of differing semantic shades.[88]

While for Rama transculturation allows him to study historical forms in narrative, Mary Louise Pratt refers to it as a "phenomenon of the cultural zone" and also as a type of reading "that avoids reproducing the dynamic of possession and innocence" of texts that narrate encounters between natives and colonizers.[89] Indeed, *transculturation* as a concept has been most successful in cultural studies, and specifically in those devoted to postcolonial research. Other uses of the term abound, though unfortunately they tend not to be rigorous. Almost all depart from *Cuban Counterpoint*'s anthropological aims, in which transculturation surfaces only after sifting through vast historical changes, particularly economic ones, as reflected in everyday uses and customs. Indeed, the majority of studies that invoke *transculturation*—or its adjective, *transcultural*—do so as a rarefied synonym of *mestizaje* (racial mixture) or hybridity, and often disregard altogether the essay or "counterpoint" section, the historical details of the additional chapters, and sometimes even Ortiz's name.[90]

VII

Yet another strain is the literary reception of *Cuban Counterpoint*. Its healthiest effect perhaps has been to do away with the solemnity with which Ortiz has often been read. Indeed it is not difficult to understand why, among Ortiz's many books, this one would elicit literary readings. Its very structure suggests, as we have seen, an aesthetic consciousness beyond factual information. The essay's counterpoint format is justified by a "fiction" whose paradigm is the medieval *Book of Good Love*. Thus for Gustavo Pérez Firmat, who pioneered this type of study, its literary character rests not only on its ambivalent or parodic link with its medieval precursor, but in its "paraleptic" character (from *paralepsis*, refusing to say what we mean), and what he calls the "trope of duplicity," particularly in the essay, where we find a "rhetoric of the incomplete." Pérez Firmat associates this rhetoric with the peculiarities of the literary essay—"an approximation, a tentative or preliminary grappling with a subject that awaits more sustained or polished treatment"—but attributes it, ultimately, not so much to the genre as to Ortiz's "writerly" nature, the literariness that is evident in the essay's collapse of subject and object.[91] For Roberto González Echevarría, in turn, the book's "literature" is rooted in Ortiz's broad connections with Cuban modernism (particularly the Afro-Cubanist movement, which Ortiz's ethnographic work inspired), and its Baroque humor—"Gracianesque, if you will . . . a witticism, a *jeu d'esprit*, typical of avant-garde art and literature; the *Cuban Counterpoint* is a long, prolix, Joycean play of words and concepts, like those found in its contemporary, *Finnegans Wake*." He concludes that poetics, rather than science, dominates the book: "Thus in *Cuban Counterpoint* a scientific wisdom and a poetic ability are mixed, but the wrapper (*envoltura* to use cigar terminology) is the second, the poetic."[92]

Lastly, for the late Antonio Benítez Rojo, whose literary reading arguably represents a pinnacle, the text "does not seek its legitimacy in the discourse of the social sciences, but rather within those of literature, of fiction." Benítez Rojo's reading, too, saw through the book's traits as an essay, but his interests centered upon its postmodern paradigm, which he associated with the identity of the entire Caribbean, and not just Cuba. Accordingly, he identified the un-hierarchical disposition of the book's two sections, and the deconstruction of the binary opposition between the two commodities; the book's "promiscuous origins," what he called its "vast heteroclitic archive," its "de-ideologized ideology"; and, in short, its "dialogic and acentric" character. If thinking in a postmodern way means thinking through difference, then *Cuban Counterpoint*, according to Benítez Rojo, thinks through the Caribbean in terms of an irreducible difference between two great "archives": "the Peoples of the Sea and the Western theorem."[93] While showing the book's affinities with other postmodern thinkers (notably, Bakhtin), Benítez Rojo demonstrated that Cubanness or Caribbeanness is hardly an essence, but rather a dialogue, or indeed a "counterpoint," that goes beyond Hegelian dialectics. Such dialectic recalls, in turn, Baroque music, and specifically the fugue—that Baroque genre par excellence, which illustrates a mode whereby "musical voices not only confront each other but also superimpose themselves upon one another in a parallel fashion, interacting with each other in a perpetual flight" (173).

It is difficult to agree, despite their richness, with all the premises of these literary readings. One need not go so far, for example, as relating Ortiz to Joyce in order to highlight the former's style. What does seem warranted is to highlight the Baroque qualities of Ortiz's style, which in the essay at least appears in its use of the same *arte de ingenio* (ingenious art) or "treaty of wit," which in 1642 Baltasar de Gracián had systematized as part of Spanish literary rhetoric. One would need to balance this view, in turn, by recalling that wit, particularly Gracián's version, has intelligence, rather than humor, as its proper object. As the moralist he was, Gracián was after worldly understanding through cerebral ingenuity, or else as he defined it: "an act of understanding that displays correspondences between two objects,"[94] hardly the same thing as humor. For Gracián, that is, understanding correspondences was a matter of confronting "disproportions," the paradigm for which was antithesis or contrast—another name for Ortiz's "counterpoint."[95] That is, in Ortiz, as in Gracián, one finds perspicacity, virtuosity and, indeed, all the qualities one associates with the language and format of Cuban *controversia*. The little humor the essay does have is merely *capa*, wrapper, to use that cigar term that also suggests a deceptive reality, as deceptive and illusory as those *trompes l'oeil* that abound in Baroque art and which, as we have seen, layer the length of Ortiz's book. In Gracián's antithetical, pessimistic world (like Martial's and Joyce's, Gracián's model and heir, respectively), discord and opposition bind the universe. Accordingly, the "ingenious" scheme of Ortiz's essay ("life's dramatic dialectic") constitutes but the illusory surface of a violent *transculturation*. True, Ortiz avoids at all costs identifying counterpoint as conflict. The book closes, in fact, with the mock "marriage" of Tobacco and Sugar and the birth of Alcohol, their lawless offspring. But even such comforts serve to lessen little the gravity of either Ortiz's mournful complaints, or the violent data contained in the "additional chapters." In fact, painful insight into the nature of identity happens to be the signature Ortiz's book shares with a number of canonical icons of Cuban culture—from José White's *La bella cubana*, to Aurelio de la Vega's *Canciones transparentes*; from José María Heredia's to Virgilio's Piñera's poetry; and from *Cecilia Valdés* to *Three Trapped*

Tigers: beauty, happiness and harmony are mere cover-ups, illusory veils cast over ugly, sad, and discordant human realities. That is, Dionysius as a mirage of Apollo; transculturation as the obverse of counterpoint. If Cubans laugh for fear of crying, then Ortiz's essay sings while the additional chapters weep. One wonders whether such a dual structure could not be a better point of departure for a hermeneutics of Cuban national identity.

Literary readings of *Cuban Counterpoint* suffer another problem still: they repress the book's scientific content. And yet, it seems difficult as well to share such a conclusion in light of all the facts this chapter unveils. We have seen, for example, how the disciplinary origins of *Cuban Counterpoint* arise from the intersection of Geography and History, and how Ortiz structured his thesis according to empirical data on the material nature of the two commodities and their social effects. There is, in addition, Ortiz's positivist training, to which he never renounced, and the taxonomic will of all his work, from Lexicology and Music through Anthropology and History. It is not simply a matter of safeguarding Ortiz's conclusions, precarious though they may be; my review of Ortiz's blind spots to the history of Cuban tobacco, for example, makes that much clear. But if we consider *Cuban Counterpoint* an essay, first and foremost, as literary readings are the first to acknowledge, then there seems to be little need to deny its scientific content in order to appreciate its literary qualities. According to Ortega y Gasset, the signature formula for any essay is "science minus proof." Thus Ortiz's book is no less "scientific" for being well written, or for showing a dazzling self-consciousness. My own view is premised on a relativized view of texts from the scientific canon. For regardless of how objective or scientific the original intentions of such texts may have been, the rhetoric and even paradigms of a scientific canon are always subject to change over time, and its referential content can always be questioned. Copernicus' allusions to Greek mythology, for instance, don't make his views any less scientific, or exclude them from the history of science. The contents of his work may, over time, appear erroneous or inapplicable, but its ultimate scientific nature is not.[96]

More disturbing perhaps, is that besides having an antiscientific bias, literary readings of *Cuban Counterpoint* are limited by a fragmentary penchant, as they pay closer, and at times exclusive, attention to the book's essay than to the "additional chapters." As unproductive as it is to gloss over the book's scientific line of reasoning simply to underscore its "literature," so it is to ignore one section for another. Literary readings thus invert Cultural Studies readings, which stress transculturation at the expense of counterpoint. And yet, it is precisely within the "additional chapters" where one finds not only the data that feeds the essay—let alone what allows for an alternate reading—but also one of the keys to understanding the book's Baroque character: the meta-chronicle. That is, just as the "fiction" that underlies the essay is parody of a parody—a meta-parody or parody squared—so the additional chapters constitute a chronicle squared, a meta-chronicle. Indeed, the "additional chapters" seam together selections from a number of chronicles and documents from sundry sources whose complex fusion reminds us of the overly ornate style of Latin American Baroque. It would be wrong simply to view these chapters as a mere "collection of documents" whose literal sense would resemble a series of "appendices"—precisely what Ortiz, following Malinowski, sought to avoid.[97] They are, rather, a conscious, deliberate construction of a long chronicle loomed out of many chronicles: texts based on other texts which successive drafts work through and revise. The "additional chapters" are themselves transcultured chronicles whose sum-total responds—counterpoints—to the essay; thus in this new light, they turn out to be no less forged, witty or worked-over than the essay they feed into.

The formal aspects we have so far described—*parody, meta-chronicle, wit,* and *fugue*—all point, then, toward a new reading of *Cuban Counterpoint* as a Baroque—or better yet: neobaroque—book. Coined by Cuban writer Severo Sarduy, the neobaroque describes a peculiar tendency in twentieth-century cultural production, and particularly the work of a group of Cuban writers and artists that included Sarduy himself and encompasses Ortiz's book.[98] Its Baroque quality has two features. First, a distinct language; and second, a distinct cultural theory—transculturation—that happens to be the *secret* source of much of the recent theorizing on the Latin American Baroque.

I emphasize secret here because, despite all the free use that has been made of these ideas, credit and acknowledgment to Ortiz is hard to find. Thus, when in a well known 1975 lecture Alejo Carpentier remarked that "all symbiosis, every racial mixture (*mestizaje*), engenders a baroque," his comment linked, in effect, the concept of *mestizaje* (racial mixture) to the Baroque, and quoted, without acknowledging as much, Ortiz's transculturation.[99] Similar instances can be found in the works of José Lezama Lima, who once referred fancifully, in an essay on the Latin American Baroque, to "plutonism that burns fragments and pushes them, metamorphosed, to their very end"; or else, in another piece, to "American man's incorporative protoplasm."[100] The common thread of statements like these, as César Salgado has shown, is the American restitution of the European conquest of the New World, a literal "counter-conquest"

(Lezama Lima's term itself echoes Ortiz's title) whose cultural effects have an ideological root.[101] Thus *Baroque* in these discussions is the trope that names the specificity of Latin American *mestizaje* in reaction to European colonization; nothing less than transculturation as Ortiz defined it: "the different phases of the process of transition from one culture to another (100).

Ortiz's *Cuban Counterpoint* acts, then, as both core theory and core practice of the (Latin) American Baroque. It is both the source of the intellectual complex that articulates *mestizaje*, and a formal sample of that complex. The best proof yet of this may well be its (neobaroque) progeny, as found not only among its multiple applications in Cultural Studies. It is also evident in the way it has inspired neobaroque books such as Guillermo Cabrera Infante's *Holy Smoke!* (1985), which prolongs "tobacco's biography" as an ironic chronicle of its representation in film; or else, to cite another offspring, Fernando G. Campoamor's *Biografía del ron cubano* (Biography of Cuban Rum) (1985), whose subtitle (*El hijo alegre de la caña de azúcar*) derives from the final image in Ortiz's front essay.[102]

Finally, I find little contradiction, against various expectations, between the science of *Cuban Counterpoint* and the baroque quality of its style, at least from the standpoint of a specifically Latin American tradition. As Lezama Lima himself argued, Baroque art in Latin America is "a firm ally of the Enlightenment," in the sense that, beginning in the eighteenth century, science itself is an important source for a Latin American aesthetic. There is, as we know, a Baroque period in the history of Philosophy, as shown, among others, in Leibniz. And the same could be said of Sarduy's brilliant neobaroque essays, which themselves show a peculiar cross between art and science.[103]

VIII

Beyond all such formal features, however, perhaps the most compelling one yet in favor of *Cuban Counterpoint's* eccentric, neobaroque character may stem from hard internal evidence, at least as it became palpable in my own experience as editor of this text. I remarked earlier that extant editions of *Cuban Counterpoint* included two original author versions (1940 and 1963), followed by an abridged English translation (1947), and another revised edition (1999) done by Ortiz's daughter. The latter, like the 1963 edition, was based, in turn, on Ortiz's corrected copy of the first. Ortiz himself had corrected, in 1963, typos and style, tightened the text, and both added and removed entire passages from the essay and from nine of the "additional chapters," for a total of 351 newfangled paragraphs. His revisions increased the size of the book but not the number of chapters.[104]

My own 2003 edition took both the 1999 edition and the corrected copy as points of departure. Besides surviving typos and howlers, the most corrections I made were of original foreign terms and quotations, book titles in Spanish and other languages, and mistaken citations, which had survived since the first edition. I thus corrected at least half of the parenthetical bibliographical citations in the "additional chapters," which either lacked citation elements or contained abbreviated or incorrect data. Among the corrected problems were textual anomalies, such as displaced or headless references, whereby, for example, reference was made to a source ahead of its actual citation.

Such peculiarities, though linked specifically to textual problems, resonate strongly with other aspects of the neo-baroque canon. As "every symbiosis, every racial mixture," according to Carpentier, "engenders a Baroque," so exceptions to the text's discursive homogeneity jump out as Baroque features. Baroque markers appear as much in discursive proliferation—as made evident, say, in semantic density or difficulty—as in the text's overall inability to tame semantic excess. "If Baroque [style] was learned," notes Harbison, "it was at the same time deliberately incorrect and aberrant, which helps make it a harder mode to define satisfactorily than its predecessors." This fact leads Harbison to reflect, in addition, how "using this conception of the style's essence, emphasizing its exuberance and incorrectness, one can say that Mexican Baroque is the most complete fulfillment of the potential of Baroque perception."[105] Harbison's comment, which I take to apply to all Latin American art, dovetails with Sarduy's reading of Lezama Lima's neobaroque Cuban sentence: "syntactically incorrect due to incompatible, illogical elements," which shows "loss of concordance."[106] Indeed, Lezama Lima's grammatical aberrations can be raised to the level of text, as shown by a novel like Lezama Lima's own *Paradiso* (1966), whose legendary errors of typography and erudition have themselves provoked a scholarly debate that is still ongoing.[107] I am not of course attempting to construct a seamless analogy between Lezama Lima's aesthetics and Ortiz's science. And yet one can certainly identify, at the level of text at least, commonly shared features, particularly if we recognize similar contexts, formal effects, and a common national culture.

Ortiz, like Lezama Lima, composed a prolific text of tensile prose that carried knowledge to logical extremes. Although *Cuban Counterpoint*'s thesis was more than two decades in the making, the actual text was, as the correspondence between Ortiz and Malinowski shows, rushed through in less than two years under the pressure of both a publisher who kept demanding "additional chapters" that would placate the protests of potential local readers and a metropolitan scholar who kept suggesting improvements that promised resonance on the international stage. If, as we have seen, the Baroque signifies an aesthetics of disproportion, a turning away from normalcy as related to classical balance and adherence to discursive norms, then *Cuban Counterpoint*'s hybrid text embodies that aesthetic, too.

First, as we have seen, because of its sheer textual asymmetry: the book's two radically disproportionate sections. Second, its style: moralistic, parodic, and meta-chronical. Third and last: its running argument regarding cultural identity. For if in contemporary discussions the adjective *Baroque* means a discourse of identity through the thorny topic of *mestizaje*, then *Neobaroque* postulates its own logical connection with cultural identity, and, indeed, with the very idea of Cubanness. Once again, the thesis that supports this particular identity, both national and aesthetic, is none other than transculturation. Thus, in a perhaps indirect but nevertheless significant way, Cuba's own "barbarian style," the concept Antonio Vera León once proposed in reference to the work of Juan Francisco Manzano (1797–1854), has also something to do with Lezama Lima and Ortiz.[108] According to Vera León, who saw in Manzano's literary project an institutional prototype of Cuban writing, the "uncouth" work of this lettered Black poet-slave must be read not only as an unwitting parody of his contemporary Creole canon, but also as an emblem of the Cuban nation in all its contradictions. Manzano's legendary writing "errors," his "barbarian style," became, for the Creole writers who both sheltered and exploited him, a useful commodity within early nineteenth-century narrative because it serviced a peculiarly "Cuban" mode of writing. Thus it is in the texts of such Creole writers—Tanco y Bosmeniel, Villaverde, Del Monte—where one can find "a narrative demography, negotiating the white man's letters alongside the Black's 'barbarian' language." That is, writing or speaking "incorrectly," full of errors, at times faking them, became for these founding fathers of Cuban literature a convenient way to stage national identity.[109]

Great differences of circumstance, style, and intention separate, to be sure, Manzano, Ortiz and Lezama Lima; little do I wish to minimize those differences here. It is remarkable, however, that in all three, or at least in all three of their texts, the same unusual feature, editorial error, happens to recur. Error is linked logically, in all cases, to speculations on national identity. Thus Manzano's errors in grammar, prosody and spelling determine an involuntary parody of the White, Creole canon, as if enacting a strategy of resistance within a minor literature. Lezama Lima's twists of a falsely erudite writing display, in his own writing, poetic and sexual facets that resist both the morals of the Cuban Republic's bourgeoisie and the European modernist canon. In Ortiz, finally, bibliographical irregularities, not to mention a mangled text, determine a broader resistance strategy in relation to both an academic canon, which his book satirized, and the ideological subtext implicit in what I have called "the critique of sugar." In all three, Baroque exceptionality marks a common impasse of the rational will before excess signification, be it the result of slavery's brutal inhumanity, the poetic image's resistance to death, or the expansion of consciousness against the limits of nationalism.

It should be clear, finally, that neither Manzano, nor Lezama Lima, nor indeed Ortiz was aware of such so-called errors. What I have called their common "aberrance" cannot be reduced to a matter of conscious intention. Error, rather, appears to constitute the enigmatic cipher of Cuban nationality. As in the case of the typos that surface throughout Neruda's chronicle in *Canto general*, such errors point to a resistance to domestication, a persistent dissatisfaction with the status quo and a rebellion against it. An ambivalent barbarism, then; exceptional both in regard to canons of rationality and culture, and in the superlative, profoundly Cuban sense of *superb*. For one can only grasp such ambivalence when we know that in Cuban Spanish the adjective *bárbaro* [barbarous, barbarian] is actually a term of hyperbolic praise—as when used to refer, proverbially, to Benny Moré, arguably the Cuban Republic's greatest Cuban popular musician and performer, who was known as "*el bárbaro del ritmo*" (the Barbarian of Rhythm). *Bárbaro*, in Cuba, happens to be a synonym of "intelligent," "able," and "outstanding."[110] Ortiz's style and work are "barbarian" in all these unusual and various senses.

"Neo-baroque," as Sarduy finally defined it, is "a necessarily pulverized reflection of a knowledge that knows itself no longer 'peacefully' self-enclosed. An art of dethronement and of discussion."[111]

In a word: *counterpoint*.

APPENDIX ONE

Latinamericanism
(1991)

For Ricardo Quinones

My subject is not so much Latin America, interesting though that is, as our *image* of it. The subject is immense, its implications encyclopedic and contentious, to say the least. I can only aspire to sketch broad outlines, raise a few questions, and advance a couple of hypotheses. Is the subject original? Probably not. One could even say that by invoking the discourse of *Latinamericanism* I am merely restating one of the fundamental principles underlying all knowledge regarding Latin America, perhaps regarding the entire so-called third world—namely, the mixture of a Western language and imagination with physical and cultural realities that are only marginally Western. Indeed, the paradoxical tension of the ontology or philosophical reality of Latin America is that it is constituted by Western languages and cultures that do not fully encompass, define, or articulate it. Yet despite all these truisms, it is my sense that in the last 500 years little or at least less attention has been paid to Latin America as a discourse, that is, as a largely imaginary construct the West has built for its own consumption and interested use, often at the expense of the realities that give rise to it. We know many facts about Latin America, but we know little or at least much less about the use to which the West puts those facts in the construction of a certain interested *image* of Latin America, an image often at odds with the reality from which those facts are derived. And yet, were we to pay attention to the discourse *about* Latin America, we could perhaps begin to take hold of a number of images, issues, stereotypes, clichés, *idées fixes*—in short, take hold of the representations and unquestioned habits we unconsciously practice in our everyday dealing with it as a subject, particularly those we repeatedly encounter in the classrooms of U.S. colleges and universities.

Latinamericanism, my concept and term, owes much to *Orientalism*, the title of a well-known book in which Edward Said studied the ways in which the imperial West built up a discourse in order to deal with—that is, name, restructure, have authority over—the Orient. Said's inspiration, in turn, was the work of Michel Foucault, the French philosopher and historian, author of important works like *Madness and Civilization*, *The Archeology of*

Knowledge and Discipline and Punish, among others, which during the 1960s and 1970s put into circulation the notion of discourse. Discourse, for Foucault, means any body of texts and traditions whose sheer cumulative material presence and weight gives shape not only to knowledge of a given reality but control over it. Foucault's insight, in other words, and one that Said easily picked up on in his study of Orientalism, was that by focusing on the notion of discourse we can reveal the relationship between knowledge and power.

Like *Orientalism*, then, *Latinamericanism* identifies the corporate institution that frames both a systematic discipline—we can in fact choose *Latinamericanism* ("Latin American Studies") as a college major as well as a professional career—and the network of political, economic, and imaginary interests that underlie that discipline. To focus on the status of each as discourses would actually mean to deal principally with their own internal consistencies, not with a supposed correspondence with given cultural or geographic realities. In other words, both *Orientalism* and *Latinamericanism* are bodies of knowledge and cumulative layers of language that hold power yet exist beyond, or despite, the real Orient or the real Latin America. Last and most important, however, is the pointed impact of such discourses upon the creation of a hierarchical perception of the West in relation to the Orient and Latin America. For *Latinamericanism*, like *Orientalism*, is never far from the collective notion that identifies Europe, and, by extension, the United States, as a superior culture in relation to all other non-European peoples and cultures. Like the Orient, "Latin America" is there to be charted, deciphered, understood, remade, and ultimately controlled by latinamericanists—by which I mean, implicitly, or at least positionally superior Western Europeans who never lose the upper hand. What creates and preserves that "upper hand" is none other than *Latinamericanism*, the discourse that guarantees a representation of Latin America and which satisfies those hierarchical requirements, quite apart from whether it has anything to do with a real, historical existence.

Pervasive Latinamericanism, beginning with its very name. Would it surprise anyone to learn that *Latin America* (Spanish *América Latina*) is *not* Latin American? Like the "Orient," which can only be perceived from the vantage point of an "Occident" or West, Latin America can only be perceived as such from outside, as if condemned to be repeatedly baptized by a colonizer. Traveling through so-called Latin America one discovers that hardly anyone uses, except in the most formal or solemn of occasions, the Spanish or Portuguese *América Latina* or *Latinoamérica*, terms that are rarefied and stem from bureaucratese. In so-called Latin American countries people don't go around calling themselves *latinoamericano/a/s* (which sounds fake), and instead use national designations: *mexicano, peruana, argentino, cubana, brasileiro*, and so forth, to describe both themselves and others like them. That in the United States and Europe we use the term constantly, and sometimes to the exclusion of any other, is a symptom that requires meditation. Nor did the Spaniards or Portuguese, for that matter, ever use the term *América Latina* to describe their colonies; they used, instead, the misnomer *Indias*, or the totalizing *Nuevo Mundo* (New World). After 1810, once the former colonies became independent, Spain resorted to a number of other clever alternatives, like *Hispano América* or *Iberoamérica*, seeking somehow to preserve their claim on the name. Even Francisco Franco, ever the resourceful *gallego*, devised a new name for the spirit that bound Spain to its former colonies. He called it *Hispanidad*, in which racist traces resonate all too loudly.

I can of course make no claim to an exhaustive inquiry into the various names by which the New World has been known for the past 500 years. I know of no such philological or historical study, still lacking from the annals of scholarship even in these well-funded days of the *Quinto centenario*—a lack which itself points to the pervasiveness of *Latinamericanist* discourse: it remains unidentified, and of course powerful, because it goes unnamed . . . Yet as far as I have been able to ascertain, the term *Latin America* is itself of relatively recent vintage. It dates from the early nineteenth century and originates, of all places, in France, to designate (with the expression "*les états latines de l'Amérique*) the French colonies of Québec and Louisiana. The term's French fortune continued when in 1836, in a travel book about the United States, Michel Chevalier, a little-known French journalist and follower of Saint Simon, counterposed a Catholic and Latin South America to the Protestant Anglo-Saxon North America. Typical of his times, Chevalier was guided by the Romantic historicist penchant for national ethnic definitions. Thus there were "Latin" and "Saxon" cultures, as there were "Germanic" and "Slavic" ones, and so forth. From Chevalier, whose book became a bestseller in France, following on the heels of de Tocqueville's *Democracy in America*, the French expression *Amérique Latine* appears to have been picked up 25 years later by a certain José María Torres Caicedo, a Colombian resident of Paris. In his book *Unión latinoamericana* (Paris, 1865) Torres Caicedo appears to have been the first to propose, reacting partly against the threat of United States "Manifest Destiny," a kind of proto-OAS, an organization of American states from which the United States would be pointedly excluded since it did not partake of a requisite "latinity." But the fact that Torres Caicedo's Latin American Union never quite made it to New World (its only offices remained in Paris and Rome) demonstrates, once again, the role that an exterior designation, a naming from the outside, plays in the formation of *Latinamericanism* as an effective discourse.

Efforts like Torres Caicedo's, to be echoed years later in José Martí's call to "Nuestra América," his well-known 1891 essay, itself written in New York, demonstrate a renewed anxiety to supplement with an overarching fiction what Simón Bolívar himself had perceived, at the origin of so-called independence, to be the fundamental lack at the core of so-called Latin America.

"For more than three centuries," wrote Octavio Paz, "the word 'American' designated a man who was defined not by what he had but by what he would do. A person who has no past, out only a future, is a person with little reality. Americans: men of little reality, men of little weight. Our name condemns us to being the project of a foreign consciousness: European consciousness." We are all familiar, of course, with the aesthetic possibilities of being, as Paz says, "the project of a foreign consciousness." Works like those of Borges, not to mention Paz's own, are but the systematic nurturing and flowering of that utopian seed. Yet, Paz's reformulation leaves unresolved the distorting consequences of such a project. What is good food for literature may be poison for historical life; Borges and Paz themselves were the first to criticize the paternalism of a foreign consciousness whose project they would appear to be. When in 1929, in an essay on Whitman, Borges complains that "the people of the diverse Americas remain so out of reach that we hardly know each other by reference, counted only by Europe," he links to Western superiority the fragmentation of which Bolívar so bitterly complained. Implicitly, Borges identifies

Latinamericanism as the only way out of such fragmentation, yet locates as well its ironic source in Europe, rather than in "the diverse Americas."

By identifying *Latinamericanism* so far as a mode of Western domination, I may seem simply to advocate the more or less traditional defense of a weak and fragmented so-called Latin America before a powerful discursive alliance between Europe and the United States. In this I appear to be following the stand of most Liberal Latinamericanists, both in Europe and the United States, whose implicit sympathy for the material plight of the people in whose countries they do research provides a moral justification for their work. I am not certain, however, that sympathy by itself would be enough to bypass the snares of as entrenched a discourse as *Latinamericanism,* or that simply by expressing lofty platitudes a Liberal European can neutralize the paternalism implicit in his perception of so-called *Latinamericans*. In this Latinamericanist colleagues often remind me of Francisco de Vitoria's arguments, in the famous 16th-century Salamanca debates over Spanish rule and the enslavement of the native Indian population, not because it was a natural right but because it was a precept of charity. . . . I tend, rather, to believe the opposite: the Liberal rhetoric of sympathy and salvation, often couched in mindless platitudes, is but one more and ever so powerful turn in the attempt to position the European in a superior relation to non-European peoples and cultures. Such "noble" efforts often work to reinforce, rather than dispel, the oppressive discourse of *Latinamericanism*. To paraphrase the Venezuelan essayist Carlos Rangel: if we once had a "noble savage," why could we not have now a "noble revolutionary"?

How aware are Latinamericanists, in the United States and Europe, of their complicity with the discourse that underlies their discipline is a question we may not be able to answer right away; but the question remains, at least to me, a source of deep concern. I wish I were able to report that I perceive in Latin American Studies, especially in that *terra incognita* we call the Social Sciences, the kind of epistemological self-questioning that is a matter of course in the physical or hard sciences, or that lately has been the stuff of such healthy research in fields like ethnology and cultural anthropology (the work of James Clifford, for example), or else in literary theory. I often perceive, instead, the same provincialism and isolationist tendencies that more than 20 years ago the Brazilian sociologist Florestan Fernandes complained about U.S. Latinamericanists: "These scholars lack both information and understanding about the Latin American scene, and they are excessively preoccupied with the academic status of Latin American studies in United States university circles . . . The intellectual effort exerted by Latin American countries to develop the teaching and application of the social sciences, as well as research in this field, is usually not fully or thoroughly described, as if this effort were a marginal activity of no great value or of no great importance . . . The margin between this and an active kind of 'scientific colonialism' is a narrow one."

I also wish I had prescriptions for this general malady. I have none, except perhaps for issuing a plea for an archeology of the discourse that I have called *Latinamericanism*. It remains a daunting task. For it means nothing less than stripping ourselves bare of the pretense to material, or indeed moral, superiority that our society reinforces at every turn through various means, including the media. Yet, one worse evil still may be not so much our need for constant comparison as our constant need to *create* traumatized cultures, monsters we behold for our delight, made all the more monstrous because they do not, in fact, exist.

APPENDIX TWO

The Neruda Whitmaniana

The summer of 1989 I had the privilege of visiting Santiago de Chile and work in the two libraries that had preserved the books of Pablo Neruda. These collections are located in a special section of the University of Chile Library and at "La Chascona," Neruda's last Santiago residence (Fernando Márquez de la Plata 0192). The former houses the books he owned until 1954, the year he donated the entire collection to the University of Chile; the latter houses the books Neruda collected since then and which he owned at the time of his death in September 1973.

Following is a list of the Whitmaniana in both collections. While doing research in the former collection I was fortunate to meet Professor Selena Millares, now a renowned Neruda scholar in her own right, who was then researching Neruda's literary sources. Professor Millares informed me then that because the collection catalogue was very incomplete, she had undertaken to tally all the Whitman books herself, and she allowed me to copy the list. Independently, I owe Ana Maria Díaz Grez, Secretary of the Santiago Pablo Neruda Foundation, for giving me permission to copy the relevant entries of the Chascona collection. I thank both of these ladies for their many kindnesses.

At the University of Chile

Leaves of Grass. Boston: Thayer and Eldridge, 1860–1861.
Leaves of Grass. New York: D. Appleton and Co., 1919.
Leaves of Grass, Including Sands at Seventy, Good Bye My Fancy, Old Age Echoes, and A Backward Glance O'er Travel'd Roads. Boston: Small, Maynard and Co., 1899.
Poems of Walt Whitman (*Leaves of Grass*). New York: T.Y. Crowd and Co., 1902.
Paul Famati, *Walt Whitman, Une étude, un choix de poèmes*. Paris: Seghers, 1950.

At La Chascona [entries 71–98 of Library Catalog]

Leaves of Grass. New York: Doubleday, Doran and Company, 1940.
Specimen Days & Collect. Philadelphia: Rees Welsh and Co., 1882–1883 (2 copies).

Leaves of Grass. Philadelphia: David McKay, 1884.

Leaves of Grass. London and New York: D. Appleton and Co., 1911.

November Boughs. Philadelphia: David McKay, 1888.

An Exhibition of the Works of Walt Whitman. Detroit: Detroit Public Library, 1955.

An Exhibition of the Works of Walt Whitman. New York City: Mrs. Frank Julian, 1939.

The Gathering of the Forces. 2 vols. New York and London: G. P Putnam's Sons, 1920.

Pictures. New York: June House, 1927.

After All, Not to Create Only. Boston: Roberts Brothers, 1871.

Autobiographia. New York: Charles L. Webster & Co., 1892.

Complete Prose. New York and London: D. Appleton and Co., 1910.

Good-Bye My Fancy. Philadelphia: David McKay, 1891.

Leaves of Grass. Philadelphia: David McKay, 1900.

The Tenderest Lover. New York: Delacorte Press, 1970.

Catalogue of an Exhibition. London: American Library, 1954.

Walt Whitman in Europe Today. Detroit: Wayne State University Press, 1972 [2copies].

Leaves of Grass. Washington, DC: Library of Congress, 1972.

Complete Prose and Works. Philadelphia: David McKay, 1892.

Walt Whitman Review. vol. 18, no. 1. Ottawa: Wayne State University Press, 1972.

Franklin Evans. New York: Random House, 1929.

Democratic Vistas and Other Papers. London: Walter Scott, 1888.

Poems. London: Chatto and Windus, 1892.

Leaves of Grass. 3rd ed. Boston: Thayer and Eldridge, 1860–1861.

Poems. London: Reviews Office, Masterpiece Library, 1895.

Walt Whitman Catalog. Washington, DC: Library of Congress, 1955.

A Whitman Portrait. Woodcuts by Antonio Frasconi. New York: Spiral Press, 1960.

NOTES

Introduction

1. La cifra

   La amistad silenciosa de la luna
   (cito mal a Virgilio) te acompaña
   desde aquella perdida hoy en el tiempo
   noche o atardecer en que tus vagos
   ojos la descifraron para siempre
   en un jardín o un patio que son polvo.
   Para siempre? Yo sé que alguien, un día,
   podrá decirte verdaderamente:
   "No volverás a ver la clara luna,
   Has agotado ya la inalterable
   Suma de veces que te da el destino.
   Inútil abrir todas las ventanas
   Del mundo. Es tarde. No darás con ella."
   Vivimos descubriendo y olvidando
   Esa dulce costumbre de la noche.
   Hay que mirarla bien. Puede ser última.

   Both Spanish and English in Jorge Luis Borges, *Selected Poems*, ed. Alexander Coleman (New York: Viking, 1999), 452–53.
2. Fredric Jameson, *Postmodernism, or The Cultural Logic of Late Capitalism* (Durham, NC: Duke University Press, 1991), 48.
3. *Pensée 426*: "*La vraie nature étant perdue, tout devient sa propre nature; comme, le véritable bien étant perdu, tout devient son propre bien.*"
4. See Robert Alter, *The Pleasures of Reading in an Ideological Age* (New York: Simon and Schuster, 1989), 15. For similar views, see George Steiner, "Text and Context," in his *On Difficulty and Other Essays* (New York: Oxford University Press, 1978), 1–17.
5. See Gayatri C. Spivak, *A Critique of Postcolonial Reason. Toward a History of the Vanishing Present* (Cambridge: Harvard University Press, 1999).
6. J.R. de J. Jackson, *Historical Criticism and the Meaning of Texts* (New York: Routledge, 1989), 39.
7. Alberto Moreiras has called attention to current writing on Latin American art and literary history, usually written by non-Latin Americans, which excludes specificity, or whatever is not "to some degree connected to political abjection or magical realism," in his *The Exhaustion of Difference: The Politics of Latin American Cultural Studies* (Durham, NC: Duke University Press, 2001), 309–310, n. 12. See also my "Latinamericanism," in appendix one.

8. In *Subaltern Studies IX. Writings on South Asian History and Society*, ed. Shahid Amin and Dipesh Chakrabarty (New York: Oxford University Press, 1996), 1–12.

9. Katerina Clark and Michael Holquist, *Mikhail Bakhtin* (Cambridge, MA.: Harvard University Press, 1984), 207. Bakhtin (or Volosinov) develops his idea of intonation in *Freudianism: A Marxist Critique*, trans. I.R. Titunik (New York: Academic Press, 1976).

10. Gayatri C. Spivak, "Can the Subaltern Speak?" in *Colonial Discourse and Postcolonial Theory: A Reader*, ed. Patrick Williams and Laura Chrisman (New York: Columbia University Press, 1994), 66–111, now substantially revised in *A Critique of Postcolonial Reason*.

11. See, for example, Mabel Moraña, "El Boom del subalterno," *Revista de crítica cultural*, no. 14 (1996–1997), 48–53, and Hugo Achugar, "Leones, cazadores e historiadores: a propósito de las políticas de la memoria y del conocimiento," *Revista Iberoamericana*, vol. LXIII, no. 180 (Julio–setiembre 1997), 379–387. The two authors' positions are criticized in John Beverley, *Subalternity and Representation: Arguments in Cultural Theory* (Durham, NC: Duke University Press, 1999), 15–19.

12. See Florencia Mallon, "The Promise and Dilemma of Subaltern Studies: Perspectives from Latin American History," *American Historical Review*, vol. 99, no. 5 (1994), 1491–1515.

13. See Jerome J. McGann, *The Beauty of Inflections. Literary Investigations in Historical Method and Theory* (Oxford: Clarendon Press, 1985), 131.

14. I have elsewhere pursued such a reading in some of my work on José Lezama Lima, notably in "Parridiso," *MLN*, 94 (1979), 343–365, now collected in my *Bienes del siglo. Sobre cultura cubana* (Mexico City: Fondo de Cultura Económica, 2002), 168–188.

15. See Hayden White, "Formalist and Contextualist Strategies in Historical Explanation," in his *Figural Realism: Studies in the Mimesis Effect* (Baltimore: The Johns Hopkins University Press, 1999), 43–65.

16. See Peter Hitchcock, "The 'Othering' of Cultural Studies," *Third Text*, 25 (1993–1994), 11–20.

17. Gareth Williams, "The Fantasies of Cultural Exchange in Latin American Subaltern Studies," in *The Real Thing: Testimonial Discourse and Latin America*, ed. Georg M. Gugelberger (Durham, NC: Duke University Press, 1996), 245. Needless to say, I invoke the titles of these two novels as suggestive paradigms of U.S. perception of Latin America, not as a critique of their fictional work.

18. See K.L. Pike, *Language in Relation to a Unified Theory of the Structure of Human Behavior* (1954; The Hague: Mouton, 1967). For a good summary see, Pike, "A Stereoscopic Window on the World," <personalwebs.Oakland.edu/~kitchens/150d/pike.html>. For critical discussions, *Emics and Etics: The Insider/Outsider Debate*, ed. Thomas N. Headland, Kenneth L. Pike, and Marvin Harris (London: Sage Publications, 1990). For a cognate development in the field of psychology, see Heinz Kohut, *The Search for the Self: Selected Writings, 1950–1978*, ed. Paul H. Ornstein (New York: International Universities Press, 1978).

19. In Clifford Geertz, *The Interpretation of Cultures. Selected Essays* (New York: Basic Books, 1973), 20.

20. Eric Kline Silverman, "Clifford Geertz: Towards a More 'Thick' Understanding?" in *Reading Material Culture: Structuralism, Hermeneutics and Post-Structuralism*, ed. Christopher Tilley (Oxford: B. Blackwell, 1990), 148.

21. See by Geertz, *The Interpretation of Cultures,* and *Local Knowledge. Further Essays in Interpretive Anthropology* (New York: Basic Books, 1983). On Geertz's program, I have found the following particularly useful: Aletta Biersack, "Local Knowledge, Local History: Geertz and Beyond," in her *The New Cultural History: Essays* (Berkeley: University of California Press, 1989), 72–96; Paul Shankman, "The Thick and the Thin: On the Interpretive Theoretical Program of Clifford Geertz," *Current Anthropology*, vol. 25, no. 3 (June 1984), 261–280; and the two essays by Alan Tongs, "Interpretive Anthropology and Thick Description: Geertz and the Critics," *Eastern Anthropologist*, vol. 50, nos. 3–4 (1997), 215–232 and "The Philosophical Basis of Geertz's Social Anthropology," *Eastern Anthropologist*, vol. 46, no. 1 (1993), 1–17.

22. See, especially, Vincent P. Pecora, "The Limits of Local Knowledge," in *The New Historicism*, ed. H. Aram Veeser (New York: Routledge, 1989), 243–276 and Melford E. Spiro, "Cultural Relativism and the Future of Anthropology," *Cultural Anthropology*, vol. 1, no. 3 (August 1986),

259–286; for Geertz's spirited self-defense, see his "Distinguished Lecture: Anti Anti-Relativism," *American Anthropologist*, vol. 86 (1984), 263–269.

23. Silverman, "Clifford Geertz," 148.

24. See Jonathan Culler, *On Deconstruction* (Ithaca, NY: Cornell University Press, 1982), 128. The Derrida–Searle debate was partially collected in Jacques Derrida, *Limited Inc.* (Evanston, Ill.: Northwestern University Press, 1988).

25. Marx, *A Contribution to the Critique of Political Economy*, ed. Maurice Dobbs (New York: International Publishers, 1970), 215–216.

26. Octavio Paz, *Sor Juana, or The Traps of Faith* (Cambridge, MA.: Harvard University Press, 1988), 471–473, passim.

27. Jonathan Culler, *Roland Barthes* (New York: Oxford University Press, 1983), 84.

28. Roland Barthes, "The Death of the Author," in his *Image, Music, Text*, trans. Stephen Heath (New York: Hill and Wang, 1977), 147. For a critique similar to mine, see Claude Bremond and Thomas Pavel, *De Barthes à Balzac: Fictions d'une critique, critiques d'une fiction* (Paris: Albin Michel, 1998).

29. In arguing for the complexity of any cultural interpretation, Geertz comments "As in any discourse, code does not determine conduct, and what was actually said need not have been," *The Interpretation of Cultures*, 18.

30. "The word *code* here signifies a system of constraints," in *Encyclopedic Dictionary of the Sciences of Language*, ed. Oswald Ducrot and Tzvetan Todorov, trans. Catherine Porter (Baltimore: The Johns Hopkins University Press, 1973), 104.

31. Thus, "**cipher**, n. f[rom] Arab *sifr*. . . . 1 an arithmetic symbol, 0, of no value by itself, but used to occupy a vacant place in decimal etc. numeration, 2 a numeral; especially an Arabic numeral . . . 3 a secret or disguised system of writing . . . ," *The New Shorter Oxford English Dictionary*, ed. Lesley Brown (Oxford: Clarendon Press, 1993), vol. I, 402. For histories and speculations, see: Robert Kaplan, *The Nothing That Is. A Natural History of Zero* (New York: Oxford University Press, 2000); Graham Flegg, *Numbers: Their History and Meaning* (New York: Schocken Books, 1983), 67–73; John McLeish, *Number* (New York: Fawcett Columbine, 1992), 139–143; Charles Seifel, *Zero: The Biography of a Dangerous Idea* (New York: Viking Press, 1998), 74–81; George Ifrah, *From One to Zero: A Universal History of Numbers* (New York: Viking, 1985), 473–483, who avers that "when it was adopted in Europe, various names were given to [zero], all of them variations of the Arabic word *sifr*, which means "zero" [literally 'void'] and is the Arabic translation of the Sanskrit word *sunya*, with the same meaning . . . The Arabic *sifr* also gave rise to such words as French *chiffre*, the German *ziffer* and the Italian *cifra*, all meaning 'numeral.' This was a later development, however. Earlier transcriptions of the Arabic word . . . , were all used with the meaning of 'zero' " (483). For a daring revision of early modern literary history in light of the introduction of zero to Western mathematics, see Michele Sharon Jaffe, *The Story of O: Prostitutes and other Good-for-Nothings in the Renaissance* (Cambridge: Harvard University Press, 1999). See also "Zero," the last entry in W.V. Quine, *Quiddities. An Intermittently Philosophical Dictionary* (Cambridge: Harvard University Press, 1987).

32. Thus "*cifra* (Del árabe sifr, vacío, cero, se aplicó primero al cero . . . 1 Guarismo, Número . . . 3 Escritura cifrada . . . 5 Compendio. Resumen. Suma"; similarly, "*código* 1 colección ordenada de leyes . . . 2 colección de reglas o normas sobre cualquier materia," *Diccionario del uso del español*, ed. María Moliner (Madrid: Gredos, 1982), A–G, 626, 657.

33. See Paul Ricoeur, *Freud and Philosophy: An Essay on Interpretation*, trans. Denis Savage (New Haven: Yale University Press, 1970), 33–34. Earlier in the same text, Ricoeur states: "No doubt a symbol is, in the Greek sense of the word, an 'enigma,' but as Heraclitus says, 'the Master whose oracle is at Delphi does not speak, does not dissimulate,' he signifies . . . Enigma does not block understanding but provokes it; there is something to unfold, to 'dis-implicate' in symbols. That which arouses understanding is precisely the double meaning, the intending of the second meaning in and through the first" (18).

34. See Doris Sommer, "Supplying Demand: Walt Whitman as the Liberal Self," in *Reinventing the Americas: Comparative Studies of Literature of the United States and Spanish America*, ed. Bell Gale

Chevigny and Gari Laguardia (Cambridge: Cambridge University Press, 1986), 68–91. A more recent essay by Sommer does make a greater concession to historicism, possibly influenced by a reading of my essay, from which she quotes liberally; see her *Proceed with Caution When Engaged by Minority Writing in the Americas* (Cambridge: Harvard University Press, 1999), 36–63.

35. See Moreiras, *The Exhaustion of Difference*, 156. I did state it implicitly, however, in bringing together passages from "Latinamericanism" with some from the Paz/Sor Juana essay in a collage from which Moreiras cites programmatically: "Latinamericanism and Restitution," *Latin American Literary Review*, vol. 20, no. 40 (July–December 1992), 88–96. Moreiras does not, however, cite the Spanish version: *Vuelta*, 210 (May 1994). I delivered "Latinamericanism" as a lecture on April 21, 1991, at the Benjamin Z. Gould Center of Claremont McKenna College, at the invitation of then-Director Professor Ricardo Quinones. In 1997, Professor Román de la Campa published *Latin Americanism* (Minneapolis: University of Minnesota Press). His argument is not only different from mine; he appears not to have known of my previous use. See also the special issue "The Cultural Practice of Latinamericanism," ed. Marcus Embry and Alberto Moreiras *Disposition*, vol. 21 (1998).

36. See Marvin d'Lugo, "Otros usos, otros públicos: el caso de *Fresa y chocolate*," *Temas*, no. 27 (octubre–diciembre, 2001), 53–63. To my knowledge, Professor d'Lugo's piece has not appeared in English. I might add that I read a first, essay version of this chapter at a conference on Cuban film at The Johns Hopkins University in October 1996. Professor d'Lugo also delivered a paper there, but to my knowledge no debate on this issue took place at the time.

Chapter One   Poetry and the
Cold War: Pablo Neruda's *Canto General*

1. See Enrico Mario Santí, *Pablo Neruda: The Poetics of Prophecy* (Ithaca, NY: Cornell University Press, 1982). A Spanish translation, based on a revised edition, is forthcoming with Fondo de Cultura Económica.

2. For Neruda's biography, I draw on the following: Pablo Neruda: *Memoirs*, trans. Hardie St. Martin (New York: Farrar Straus and Giroux, 1976); Margarita Aguirre, *Las vidas de Pablo Neruda* (Santiago de Chile: Zig-Zag, 1967); Emir Rodríguez Monegal, *Neruda: el viajero inmóvil*, revised ed. (Caracas: Monte Ávila Editores, 1977); and Volodia Teitelboim, *Neruda: An Intimate Biography*, trans. Beverly J. deLong-Tonelli (Austin: University of Texas Press, 1991). The most documented biography by far is David Schidlowsky's *Las furias y las penas: Pablo Neruda y su tiempo* (Berlin: Wissenschaftlicher Verlag, 2003). As I complete this manuscript, Adam Feinstein has published *Pablo Neruda: A Passion for Life* (London: Bloomsbury Press, 2004).

   All citations from *Canto general*, trans. Jack Schmitt (Berkeley: University of California Press, 1991); for the Spanish text, I refer to his *Obras Completas*, ed. Hernán Loyola (Barcelona: Galaxia Gutenberg/ Círculo de Lectores, 1999–2002), 5 vols., vol. I, 417–840, cited as *OC*; and for notes to the poems, my own critical edition (Madrid: Ediciones Cátedra, 1991). For additional notes, see Alain Sicard and Fernando Moreno, eds. *Diccionario del Canto general de Pablo Neruda* (Paris: Ellipses, 2000).

3. See *Latin American Poetry: Origins and Presence* (Cambridge University Press, 1974), 27–55.

4. The first editions were as follows: *Canto general* (Mexico City: Talleres Gráficos de la Nación, 1950), flyleaves by David Alfaro Siqueiros and Diego Rivera; *Canto general*. Illustrations and vignettes by J. Venturelli (Mexico City: America, 1950).

5. Cardona Peña paraphrased Neruda's responses in his *Pablo Neruda y otros ensayos* (Mexico City: Ediciones de Andrea, 1955), 36; this chapter was a longer version of his "Pablo Neruda, breve historia de sus libros," *Cuadernos americanos*, vol. 54 (1950), 257–289.

6. See *Canto general de Chile. Fragmentos* (Mexico City, 1943). This was a private and limited edition of 100 copies, signed by the author.

7. "Pablo Neruda in Mexico," *Books Abroad*, vol. 15, no. 2 (April 1941), 168.

8. I quote from "A la paz por la poesía," *El Siglo* (May 3, 1953); now in *OC*, IV, 887–894.

9. "Algo sobre mi poesía y mi vida," *Aurora* (July 1954), 10–21; *OC*, IV, 929–944.

10. See "Las entrañas de América" and "Lucha y destierro," chapters 8 and 9 of "Las vidas del poeta: Memorias y recuerdos de Pablo Neruda," *O Cruzeiro Internacional* (May 1 and 16, 1962), 35 and 36, respectively. Clearly, the editors "corrected" here the spelling for Machu Pichu (which Neruda always wrote as Macchu Picchu). For the significance of Neruda's (mi)spelling, see 62–64.

11. "Algunas reflexiones improvisadas sobre mis trabajos," *OC*, IV, 1201–1208.

12. Neruda, *Memoirs*, 139–140.

13. *Neruda: El viajero inmóvil*, 121. For the proceedings of this conference, see *IIo congreso internacional de escritores en defensa de la cultura (1937); Literatura española y antifascismo (1927–1939)*, ed. Manuel Aznar Soler (Valencia: Generalitat Valenciana, 1987), 3 vols.

14. See "La copa de sangre," in *OC*, IV, 417.

15. This is particularly evident in articles like "Arte popular," *Repertorio Americano*, 16 (September 14, 1940), 296; *OC*, IV, 397, or speeches: "La educación será nuestra epopeya," *Aurora de Chile*, vol. 3, no. 6 (December 1938); *OC*, IV, 407–416, which show an interest in Chilean folk.

16. See "Discurso," *Tierra Nueva*, II, nos. 9 and 10 (May–August 1941), 120–122; *OC*, IV, 471–474.

17. See Clemente López Trujillo, "Nerudistas y antinerudistas," *El Nacional* (Mexico City) (August 28, 1940).

18. See Schidlowsky, *Las furias y las penas*, 418, who cites the relevant incident and correspondence. The dispute actually began with Juan Ramón Jiménez's self-exclusion, who explained it in "Carta obligada sobre mí mismo," *Letras de México* (August 1944), 7; Bergamín responded in *Letras de México* (September, 1944), 8.

19. See *OC*, I, 746; *CG*, "The Rivers of Song," 317. ("*And to those who denied you in the rotten laurel/on American soil, the space that you mantle/ with your fluvial crown or bled lightning,/let me give them contemptuous oblivion/ for they tried to mutilate me with your absence.*") For Paz's version of these events, see his "Epílogo" in *Laurel*, 2nd edition (Mexico City: Editorial Trillas, 1986), especially 488–489, and my introduction to *Octavio Paz, Primeras letras (1931–1943)* (Barcelona: Seix Barral, 1988), 44–46.

20. See Schidlowsky, *Las furias y las penas*, 448–452. The assault was reported in *Así*, 61 (Mexico City), (January 10, 1942), 8. Luis Enrique Délano, also a victim, gave his own version in "Pablo Neruda en México," in his *Lenin y otros escritos* (Mexico City: Universidad Obrera, 1975), 102–104. For additional information, see Wilberto Cantón, "Pablo Neruda en México (1940–1943)," in *Anales de la Universidad de Chile*, vol. 129, nos. 157–160 (January–December, 1971), 266–267.

21. The most accurate summary appears in Schidlowsky, *Las furias y las penas*, 433–435 and 459–461. The first trip was to Guatemala during June–July 1941, taken during a leave that went unpaid because of Neruda's issuing an illegal visa to David Alfaro Siqueiros to travel to Chile. Siqueiros himself had been put in jail for alleged involvement in an attempt on the life of Trotsky and his family. Neruda's second trip to Cuba, during March–April 1942, was at the invitation of the government of then president Fulgencio Batista. See also, Luis Enrique Délano's *Lenin y otros escritos*, 93–95.

22. For the public reaction, see the Mexican newspaper *Novedades*, October 22 and 29 and November 5 and 12, 1942.

23. I paraphrase, here and below, my own discussion in *Pablo Neruda: The Poetics of Prophecy* (Ithaca: Cornell University Press, 1982), 108–118; see in chronological order, the following: Juan Ramón Jiménez, *Españoles de tres mundos* (Buenos Aires: Losada, 1942); "Carta a Pablo Neruda," *Repertorio americano*, 23 (January 17, 1942); José Revueltas, "América sombría," *Repertorio americano*, 23 (May 9, 1942), although published first in Mexico City: *El Popular* (March 13, 1942); Juan Ramón Jiménez, "¿América sombría?" *Repertorio americano*, 24 (August 14, 1943), 209–211. For the Jiménez-Neruda link, see Juan Cano Ballesta, *La poesía española entre pureza y revolución*

(*1930–1936*), (Madrid: Gredos, 1971), 202–212 and Ricardo Gullón, "Relaciones Pablo Neruda—Juan Ramón Jiménez" in *Pablo Neruda*, ed. Rodríguez Monegal and Santí (Madrid: Taurus, 1978), 175–197. In time, Neruda referred to Jiménez as "that poor great poet eaten up by envy," (*OC*, V, 262).

24. See Schidlowsky, *Las furias y las penas*, 478. According to the evidence, the girl died on March 2, but Neruda only got the news on March 19, while on a visit to New York City.

25. The response was published in the Mexican newspaper *Excélsior* (June 22, 1943).

26. See Wilberto Cantón, "Pablo Neruda."

27. *Ibid.*

28. Teitelboim, *Neruda*, 257.

29. "Palabras de Pablo Neruda," *Repertorio Americano*, 24 (October 13, 1943), 274–275; *OC*, IV, 488–490. The statement appears on 490.

30. For information on these visits, see the entries 196–207 of Woodbridge and Zubatsky, *Pablo Neruda: An Annotated Bibliography of Biographical and Critical Studies* (New York: Garland Publishing, 1988), and in particular Fernando Gómez Pérez, *Neruda y Laureano* (Medellín: Ediciones Pepe, n.d.).

31. "América, no apagues tus lámparas," *OC*, IV, 494–497. The speech was first published in Lima's *La noche* (October 22, 1943).

32. See Mariátegui's classic *Siete ensayos de interpretación sobre la realidad peruana* (1924); Neruda's "Discurso en homenaje a Uriel García," *Qué hubo* (Santiago de Chile), 30 (January 2, 1940); *OC*, IV, 441. Uriel García's *El nuevo indio: ensayos indianistas sobre la sierra peruana*, 2nd ed. (Cuzco: Rozas, 1937); also, by Uriel García, "Sumas para la historia del Cuzco (I)–(III)," *Cuadernos Americanos*, vol. 104, nos. 103–105 (1959), 133–151, 140–161, 152–186, respectively. Also of note: "Machu-Picchu," [*sic*] *Cuadernos Americanos*, 106 (1963), 161–251. John Felstiner wrote on their relationship in his *Translating Neruda: The Way to Macchu Picchu* (Stanford University Press, 1980), 143–144.

33. "Pablo Neruda habla," *El Siglo* (December 5, 1943); *OC*, V, 1075–1084. Of course, Neruda exaggerated the ruins' antiquity; hyperbole betrayed his indigenist gaze.

34. "Palabras de Pablo Neruda," *El Siglo* (June 24, 1945), and *Cuatro discursos* (Santiago: Principios, 1945), 13.

35. González Videla, *Memorias* (Santiago: Gabriela Mistral, 1975), I, 761; the doggerel is now collected in *OC*, IV, 594.

36. See Teitelboim, *Neruda*, 282. González Videla nominated him for Senate ratification on December 30, 1946 but withdrew his name after a tie vote January 7, 1947; see *Yo acuso. Discursos parlamentarios* (1945–1948), ed. Leonidas Aguirre Silva (Santiago: Editorial Antártica, 1997), 92–93. The latter is a useful compilation of Neruda's Senate speeches and related documents.

37. Paul Drake, *Socialism and Populism in Chile, 1932–1952* (Urbana: University of Illinois Press, 1978), 288. For a history of the Chilean Communist Party, see Robert J. Alexander, *Communism in Latin America* (New Brunswick: Rutgers University Press, 1957), and Carmelo Furci, *The Chilean Communist Party and the Road to Socialism* (London: Zed Books, 1984). Teitelboim, *Neruda* (285–289) gives a biased account from within the Party. For relations between Chile and the United States during that period, see Claude G. Bower, *Chile Through Embassy Windows* (New York: Simon and Schuster, 1958). González Videla, *Memorias*, I, 763 also comments on this period.

38. See "Las pequeñas hermanas olvidadas," preface to Pericles Franco Ornes, *La tragedia dominicana* (*Análisis de la tiranía de Trujillo*) (Santiago: Federación de Estudiantes de Chile, 1946); "Saludo a la delegación uruguaya de cultura," *Diario de sesiones del Senado* (June 26, 1946), 666–669; "Saludo al Paraguay," *El Siglo* (March 20, 1947); "Deber de Chile hacia el pueblo de Nicaragua," *El Siglo* (June 5, 1947); "Derrocamiento del Presidente de la República del Ecuador, Señor Velasco Ibarra," *Diario de sesiones del Senado* (August 26, 1947), 1620–1622. Most of these have been collected in *Yo acuso*, and in *OC*, IV, 613–680.

39. The same text appeared in several Spanish American newspapers (Mexico's *El Popular*, Costa Rica's *Repertorio Americano*, Chile's *La Voz del Pueblo*, Colombia's *Horizontes*) and as a booklet (Lima: Ediciones del Hombre, n.d.). See *OC, IV*, 681–702.
40. González Videla, *Memorias*, II, 76.
41. See *OC*, IV, 704–730, originally as "Exposición del Señor Neruda acerca de los hechos que han determinado la petición de desafuero deducida en su contra," *Diario de sesiones del Senado* (January 7 and 8, 1948), 977–993. Neruda stated here that even then his poem was titled *Canto general de Chile*; but this could simply reflect a desire for self-justification before his Senate colleagues, and against the immunity proceedings. See also the comments in Volodia Teitelboim, *Voy a vivirme (variaciones y complementos nerudianos)* (Santiago: Ediciones Dolmen, 1988), 109–137.
42. "Ésta era la orden: ¡Disparen contra Neruda!" *El Siglo* (August 30, 1963); fifth in a series of interviews with Volodia Teitelboim, published in the same newspaper between August 27 and September 4, 1963. In another interview at the time (*Ercilla* [February 3, 1948], 5), Neruda stated he had requested asylum because "on three occasions, the police has tried to break into my home by jumping the fence. Another time, other people unknown to me have tried to burn down my house."
43. See Jaime Torres Bodet, *Memorias*, 2nd ed. (Mexico City: Editorial Porrúa, 1981), 596. Both Torres Bodet and Gajardo are satirical objects mentioned in *Canto general*; see the notes in my edition, 362.
44. The leave was first granted on April 27, 1948 and extended for more than one year on January 10, 1950; see *Yo acuso*, 341–342. According to at least one report, Arturo Alessandri, the Chilean senate president, met Neruda more than once during his underground period; see "En clandestinidad se reunían 'El León' y Neruda," *El Siglo* (August 31, 1969).
45. "No hubo fuga precipitada: obedezco a mi partido," *Ercilla* (February 3, 1948), 5. For an opposing and anonymous point of view, see *Hoy* (Santiago de Chile, February 3, 1948), 8.
46. "Se busca a Neruda por todo el país," *El Imparcial* (February 5, 1948), 1, and "¡Disparen contra Neruda!"
47. González Videla, *Memorias*, I, 761–762.
48. The editorial was anonymous, but it was implicitly the work of Raúl Aldunate Phillips, editor of the magazine at the time.
49. "*Algo sobre mi poesía y mi vida*," 13; *OC*, IV, 934.
50. *El Siglo* (August 30, 1963).
51. "Algo sobre mi poesía y mi vida," 13, 16; *OC*, *IV*, 934, 936.
52. Teitelboim, *Neruda*, 250.
53. The clear exception would be practically all of Section III, which, according to Robert Pring-Mill, was written between July 27 and August 17, 1948; see his "*Neruda y el* original de 'Los libertadores,'" *actas del sexto congreso internacional de hispanistas* (Toronto: Department of Spanish and Portuguese, University of Toronto, 1980), 587–589.
54. For the previews' dates of first publication, see the corresponding notes to the poems in *OC*, I, 1208–1213. My estimate is based on comparison, section by section, of the number of poems published before February 1948 and the number that actually appear in the book: I, 0 of 6; II, all; III, 2 of 25; IV, 1 of 41; V, 1 of 5; VI, all; VII, 8 of 17; VIII, 0 of 17; IX, 0; X, 0; XI, 0 of 15; XII, 1 of 4; XIII, 0 of 17; XIV, 0 of 24; XV, 0 of 28; only by examining the *Canto general* manuscripts, now presumed lost, could the stages of Neruda's writing be determined with any certainty. See, however, Robert D.F. Pring-Mill, "The Evidence of the Drafts," in his *A Poet for All Seasons* (London: Institute of Latin American Studies, 1993), 32–43.
55. Joaquín Gutiérrez and Santiago del Campo, "Camino al destierro," *Ahora*, 28 (October 26, 1971), 6–9. See also "Neruda relata su fuga entre los precipicios y las tormentas cordilleranos," *El Siglo* (August 31, 1963), fifth of the Teitelboim interviews. Bellet himself wrote up the detailed itinerary: "The trip to José Rodríguez's ranch meant a car ride through Valdivia and Futrono. From there, we rowed across Lake Ranco through Lifén up to Puerto de los Yoyes, at

Lake Maihue, then cross that lake, too, and reach a timber ranch at a place called Hueinahue."
From there, the three went on to Termas de Chihuío, within the Andes range proper, crossed the
lake at the Argentine border (also called the Limpela Pass), and arrived on February 24, at *San
Martín de los Andes*, a town on the Argentine side of the border. For a fictional rendition of
Neruda's escape see José Miguel Varas, *Neruda clandestino* (Santiago de Chile: Alfaguara, 2003).

56. Cardona Peña (40–45) provides the details on the public edition and Teitelboim (306–308) the
    names of those who worked on the underground edition. On this subject see also José Miguel
    Varas, "La edición clandestina de *Canto general*: Entrevista a Américo Zorrilla," *Araucaria de Chile*,
    8 (1979), 29–34.

57. Manuel Durán and Margery Safir, *Earth Tones: The Poetry of Pablo Neruda* (Bloomington, IN:
    Indiana University Press, 1981), 82. René de Costa discussed this issue in his *The Poetry of Pablo
    Neruda* (Cambridge: Harvard University Press, 1979), 105–143. Elisabeth Siefer rendered the
    most complete such reading in *Epische Stitelemente im Canto General von Pablo Neruda* (Munich:
    Wilhelm Fink, 1970). For more recent discussions, see: Jürgen von Stackelberg, "War Neruda
    ein Epiker?" in *Das Epos in der Romania: Dieter Kremers zum 65 Geburstag*, ed. Susanne Kneller
    (Tübingen: Narr, 1988), 373–382; María José Bustos Fernández, "El *Canto general* de Pablo
    Neruda: Revitalización del género épico," *Cuadernos de Poética* (Santo Domingo, R.D.), vol. 7,
    no. 19 (September–December, 1989), 51–61; Keith Ellis, "Lo épico en la lírica de Pablo
    Neruda," *Hispanic Review*, vol. 58, no. 3, (1990), 309–323; and Mike Gonzalez and David Treece,
    The Gathering of Voices: The Twentieth Century Poetry of Latin America (London: Verso, 1992),
    218–226.

58. In one of the first reviews, Ben Belitt, one of Neruda's earliest translators, called it "a psalter of
    Isaianic salutations": *Poetry* 80 (1952), 116–118; years later, another critic described *The Lamp on
    Earth* as "almost a non-Christian book of Genesis (needing no God)"—Robert D.F. Pring-Mill,
    ed. *Pablo Neruda: A Basic Anthology* (Oxford: Dolphin Book Co., 1970), xiii; Luis Enrique Délano
    called it "a large tome, like an old Bible" ("Pablo Neruda en México," 117). For further com-
    ments, see Jean Franco, "Orfeo en Utopía," in *Simposio Neruda*, ed. Juan Loveluck and Isaac Jack
    Levy (New York: Las Américas, 1975); Gastón Soublette, *Pablo Neruda: Profeta de América*
    (Santiago: Nueva Universidad, 1980), and my *Pablo Neruda: The Poetics of Prophecy*, 55–58.

59. See Northrop Frye, *Anatomy of Criticism* (Princeton University Press, 1957), 55–58, 315–326.

60. Giambattista Vico, *The New Science*, trans. T.G. Bergin and Max Fisch (Ithaca, NY: Cornell
    University Press, 1970), 319–320. According to Vico, the term "cyclical poet" comes from
    Horace's *ars poetica* to refer to a "trivial market poet." Giuseppe Mazzota has studied this topic
    with particular care in his *The New Map of the World* (Princeton University Press, 1999), 111,
    146. On this issue, see the comments by Volodia Teitelboim, *Voy a vivirme*, 83–89.

61. Rodríguez Monegal, *Neruda: el viajero inmóvil*, 313. For a study of Bello's ideas: see, also by
    Rodríguez Monegal, *El otro Andrés Bello* (Caracas: Monte Ávila, 1969).

62. See especially *La natura delle Indie Nuove: da Cristoforo Colombo a Gonzalo Fernández de Oviedo*
    (Milan: Ricardo Ricciardi, 1975).

63. According to the catalog of the "Colección Pablo Neruda," donated in 1954 to the Central
    Library of the University of Chile, Neruda owned a copy of Barros Arana's *Historia Jeneral de
    Chile* (Santiago: Rafael Jover Editor, 1884–1907), 5 vols. This catalog of the collection, still
    unpublished, is an indispensable tool for determining not only Neruda's book collection, but
    also the "library," in the broad sense of the readings implicit in the composition of *Canto general*.

64. See Diego Barros Arana, *Compendio de Historia de América* (Santiago: Imprenta del Ferrocarril,
    1865); the "Introducción" appears in ii–iv. The "procurer" of books used by Neruda was himself
    a young historian by the name of Alvaro Jara, identified by Hernán Loyola in *OC*, I, 1206.
    On the general theme of the encyclopedia, see Giuseppe Mazzotta, *Dante and the Circle of
    Knowledge* (Princeton University Press, 1998), and Herbert Dieckemann, "The Concept of
    Knowledge in the *Encyclopédie*," *Essays on Comparative Literature*, by Dieckemann, Harry Levin,
    and Helmut Potekat (St. Louis: Washington University Press, 1961), 72–107; also, Walter Tega,

Arbor Scientarum: Enciclopedie e sistemi in Francia da Diderot a Comte (Milan: Società Editrice Il Mulino, 1984).

65. See especially *Canto general*, ed. Enrico Mario Santí (Madrid: Ediciones Cátedra, 1991), 145–182 and my notes.

66. On the ornithology of *Canto general*, Philippi's, Goodall's, Johnson's *Las aves de Chile. Su conocimiento y sus costumbres* (Buenos Aires: Platt Establecimientos Gráficos, 1946) is the key source; also, P. Rafael House, *Las aves de Chile en su clasificación moderna. Su vida y costumbres* (Santiago: Ediciones de la Universidad de Chile, 1945). Neruda owned the following works by Rodulfo Amando Philippi: *Viage al desierto de Atacama* (Halle in Saxony: Librería de Eduardo Antón, 1860), *Los fósiles terciarios y cuarternarios de Chile* (Santiago: Imprenta de F.A. Brockhaus, 1887), *Los delfines de la punta austral de la América del Sur* (Santiago: Anales del Museo Nacional de Chile, 1938), and *Figuras i descripciones de aves chilenas* (Santiago: Anales del Museo de Chile, 1902). Molina's *Saggio* (Bologna: Stamperie di S. Tommaso D'Aquino, 1782) figures in the "Colección Pablo Neruda," as well as his *Compendio de la Historia Geográfica, Natural y civil del Reyno de Chile* (Madrid: Antonio de Sancha, 1788–1795). On Molina, see Hernán Briones Toledo, *El abate Juan Ignacio Molina. Ensayo crítico-introductorio a su vida y obra* (Santiago: Editorial Andrés Bello, 1968). The "Colección" also holds numerous sources on Natural History, among them: Charles J. Cornish et al., eds., *The Library of Natural History* (New York: The University Society, 1906) and Philip Henry Gosse, *The Romance of Natural History* (London: James Nisbet, n.d.).

67. Michel Foucault, *The Order of Things* (New York: Vintage, 1970), 130, 131.

68. The texts are included in *OC*, IV, 739–760, with corresponding annotations in 1262–1267. See also the two sonnets, written in 1948, where Neruda dons the mask or voice of González Videla himself! [*OC*, IV, 759–760].

69. Karl Marx, *Economic and Philosophical Manuscripts of 1844* (Moscow: Foreign Languages Publishing House, 1961), 105. For a discussion of authorship within Marxist theory, see Raymond Williams, *Marxism and Literature* (Oxford University Press, 1977), 192–198.

70. See Alain Sicard, *El pensamiento poético de Pablo Neruda* (Madrid: Gredos, 1981), 284–285. For additional Marxist, or at least historical, readings; see: María Magdalena Solá, *Poesía y política de Pablo Neruda: Análisis del Canto general* (San Juan, PR: Prensa Universitaria, 1979) and Eugenia Neves, *Pablo Neruda: la invención poética de la historia* (Providencia, Chile: RiL Editores, 2000).

71. Hayden White, *The Content of the Form: Narrative Discourse and Historical Representation* (Baltimore: Johns Hopkins University Press, 1987), 149.

72. See, *El amanecer del capitalismo y la Conquista de América* (Santiago: Ediciones Nueva América, 1943); this book was published the same year Neruda returned to Chile from Mexico. Gonzalez and Treece (219) argue that the Marxism of *Canto general* lies in its being "the result of *labor*, the transformation of the material environment by creative imagination" which "for Marx, and thus for Marxists, is the dialectical source of historical process," thus placing "the act of production, and the force of labour, firmly at the centre of that history" (emphasis theirs). But this seems to describe only the first two sections, and it obviates the arbitrary treatment of history in the rest of the book. For alleging a Marxist reading of *Canto general*, the authors' blatant disregard of the material details of such historical narrative seems highly unmarxist.

73. See *Neruda: el viajero inmóvil*, 314; and Guillermo Araya, "El *Canto general* de Neruda: poema épico-lírico," *Revista de crítica literaria latinoamericana*, vol. IV, nos. 7–8 (1978), 119–152. Determining what exactly Neruda knew, or when, about "The Great Terror" has not been a favored subject among Neruda scholars. Teitelboim, for example, in his *Neruda: An Intimate Biography* (1984), does not so much as mention Stalin's name, though he does broach the subject in his later *Voy a vivirme*, 157–170, but only to justify Neruda's reaction in "The Episode," his long political palinode in *Memorial de Isla Negra* (1964). At least one scholar has claimed that Neruda "had no idea of the atrocities [Stalin] had committed; those were revealed later," (Roberto González Echevarría, *Canto general*, 7); but this confuses Kruschef's 1956 "secret speech" before the 20th Congress of the USSR Communist Party with the information that

years earlier had already filtered out of the Soviet Union. Neruda himself was more honest: "Knowing is painful. And we knew. Every fact that filtered from the shadows/ put us through an inevitable suffering./ These rumors turned into truths,/ the dark threshold filled with light,/ and the sufferings were put right./ Truth was the light that came out of that death," *Isla Negra: A Notebook*, trans. Alastair Reid (New York: Farrar, Straus & Giroux, 1981), 353; *OC*, II, 1305. As one historian has put it, "By the late 1940s, information about life under Stalin and his system was readily available to anyone." Cf. Tony Judt, *Past Imperfect: French Intellectuals, 1944–1956* (Berkeley: University of California Press, 1992), 101. For a refreshing critique of Neruda, but which still fails to mention the Moscow Trials, see Jean Franco, *The Decline and Fall of the Lettered City* (Cambridge: Harvard University Press, 2002), 78–81. Judt and others have detailed that those trials had taken place between 1936 and 1938; news of the "forced collectivization" campaign and the *gulag* had leaked out to the West immediately after the War, particularly in the context of the scandalous "Kravchenko Affair." See Victor Kravchenko, *I Chose Freedom: The Personal and Political Life of a Soviet Official* (New York: Scribner's, 1946) and the transcripts of the slander trial in the French courts that made it famous: *Le Procès Kravchenko* (Paris: Michel, 1949). For documents on Neruda's chronic Stalinism, see Schidlowsky, II, 724–725, 768, 773–773, 710, 842 and 1153.

On the relative absence of women in *Canto general*, see Juan Villegas, "Héroes y heroínas: el machismo de *Canto general*," *Alba de América*, vol. 4, 6–7 (July 1986), 195–204; Borges's complaint appeared in one of his interviews with Richard Burgin, *Conversations with Jorge Luis Borges* (New York: Holt, Rinehart and Winston, 1969), 95–96 (see also chapter two in this book). H.A. Murena, in one of the first reviews, remarked that "The *Canto* which for many reasons deserved to have been a portrait of all [Latin] America, is limited to an epic of a few [Latin] American men bearing a few non-[Latin] American ideas"; see his "A propósito del 'Canto general' de Pablo Neruda," *Sur*, 198 (April 1951), 58.

74. Rodríguez Monegal, *El viajero inmóvil*.
75. See "The British Rule in India," in Karl Marx and Frederick Engels, *On Colonialism* (Moscow: Progress Publishers, 1959), 41.
76. See Octavio Paz, "Re/Visions: Mural Painting," in *Essays on Mexican Art* (New York: Harcourt Brace, 1987), 162.
77. *Neruda: el viajero inmóvil*, 315; and Sicard, 234–235. For a list of essays that discuss the book's political content, see Woodbridge and Zubatsky's 356–378. See also the more recent, Manuel A. Matos Moquete, "Mito y unidad americana en el *Canto general* de Pablo Neruda," *Alcance: Revista Literaria*, vol. 3, no. 2 (1984), 5–6, Fernando Vega Mercado, "*Canto general*, la ideología y su proyección imaginaria: la epopeya actual," *Revista de crítica literaria latinoamericana*, vol. 11, nos. 21–22 (1985), 59–74; Neves, *Pablo Neruda: La invención poética de la historia*; and Teitelboim, *Voy a vivirme*, 95–100. For a sample of the ideological debate, see the polemic between critics Guillermo Sucre and Fernando Alegría with regard to the popular edition prepared by the latter: *Canto general* (Caracas: Biblioteca Ayacucho, 1976), in *Vuelta*, 4 (March, 1977), 32–33; also two reviews written about my *Pablo Neruda: The Poetics of Prophecy* (Ithaca: Cornell University Press, 1982): *Revista de estudios hispánicos* (Puerto Rico), 10 (1983), 154–162, and *Crítica* 1 (La Jolla, California, Spring 1984), 117–120.
78. See Cardona Peña, *Pablo Neruda*, 38–39. With respect to the last phrase, it may be a simple typo: where it reads *araucana*, it should perhaps read *americana*.
79. It is worth noting that the first poem of *Antología de la resistencia*, by a certain "J. Aguilera," was titled "*El pueblo te llama traidor*" (The People Call You Traitor); see *OC*, IV, 739–741.
80. White, *The Content of the Form*, 13.
81. Neruda appears to have tried out this "chronicle" technique first in his Senate self-defense (January 6, 1948), where he readily compared his own plight to earlier patriots, both Chilean (Manuel Montt, Victorino Lastarria, Francisco Bilbao) and foreign (Victor Hugo, Rómulo Gallegos); see *Yo acuso*, 254–260. "Aldunate" is mentioned disparagingly (*CG*, 90, *OC*, I, 590) within a list of names of colonial landowners.

82. See Wayne Booth, *The Rhetoric of Fiction* (University of Chicago Press, 1961), who defines it as a narrator whose version of a story or comment the reader has reason to suspect; see also Shlomith Rimmon-Kenan, *Narrative Fiction: Contemporary Poetics* (London: Methuen, 1983), 100–101. As far as *Canto general* is concerned, the issue has not been discussed since first broached by Nelson Osorio: "El problema del hablante poético en *Canto general*," *Simposio Neruda. Actas,* eds. Juan Loveluck and Isaac Jack Lévy (Columbia, SC: University of South Carolina/ Las Américas, 1975), 171–188.

83. For explications of these "errors," see the notes to my edition, *Canto general,* especially 308–366. None of these "errors" are either noted or, thankfully, corrected in the latest edition of Neruda's *Obras completas;* compare, for example, the "incorrect" epigraph by Túpac Amaru I, in *OC,* I, 448 with the editor's oblivion in I, 1248; few of them are even noted in Sicard's *Diccionario del Canto general.*

84. See White, *The Content of the Form,* 16.

85. I proposed this reading of the poem in my *Pablo Neruda: The Poetics of Prophecy,* 104–175. For a useful, though somewhat limited, review of the critical literature on this poem, see Donald L. Shaw, "Interpretations of *Alturas de Macchu Picchu,*" *Revista Interamericana de Bibliografía,* vol. 38, no. 2 (1988), 186–197. The aberrant spelling proposed by the chronicler can be gauged in part by its institutional effects. In an anthology of poems about the ruins, one editor arbitrarily "corrected" it; see Hugo Montes, *Machu Pichu en la poesía* (Santiago: Nueva Universidad, 1972). For a fascinating reading of this supplement as "the historical foundation of the Latin American poetic site, understood as what we could call an auratic practice of the postauratic," see Albero Moreiras, *The Exhaustion of Difference* (Durham, NC: Duke University Press, 2001), 222.

86. See Pablo Neruda, *Cantos de Pablo Neruda,* Illustrations by David Alfaro Siqueiros and Carlos Beltrán (Lima: Ediciones Hora del Hombre, 1943). On at least two further occasions Neruda "published" poems in the form of public posters, and even titled his farewell poem "On Mexico's Walls."

87. The pinnacle of such a reading may be Hugo Méndez's *Neruda's Ekphrastic Experience: Mural Art and Canto general* (Lewisburg, PA: Bucknell University Press and Associated University Presses, 1999). Neruda also wrote about the paintings of another Mexican artist: "Los frescos de Xavier Guerrero en Chillán," *Ars,* vol. 1, no. 5 (May, 1943), 60–62.

88. See Serge Fauchereav, *Les Peintres revolutionnaires mexicains* (Paris: Editions Messidor, 1985), 69 and 74.

Chapter Two   This Land of Prophets:
Walt Whitman in Latin America

1. Both the late Octavio Paz and Stephen Schlesinger, former secretary of the John Simon Guggenheim Memorial Foundation, were gracious enough to allow me to cite my translation of Paz's unpublished 1943 fellowship proposal.

2. Octavio Paz, *The Bow and the Lyre,* trans. Ruth L.C. Simms (Austin: University of Texas Press, 1973), 274. This translation is based on the second revised (1967) rather than the first (1956) Spanish edition. Paz was alluding to Borges's classic essay "El otro Whitman" collected in *Discusión* (Buenos Aires: M. Gleizer, 1932). Borges's other famous essay, "Nota sobre Walt Whitman," appeared in *Otras inquisiciones* (Buenos Aires: Emecé, 1960), 97–104; (English translation in *Other Inquisitions, 1937–1952,* trans. Ruth L.C. Simms [Austin: University of Texas Press, 1964]), but I prefer to cite from my own translation as it appears in *Discusión* where it has been collected most often.

3. See Doris Sommer, "Supplying Demand: Walt Whitman as the Liberal Self," in *Reinventing the Americas: Comparative Studies of Literature of the United States and Spanish America,* ed. Bell Gale Chevigny

and Gari Laguardia (Cambridge: Cambridge University Press, 1986), 68–91. Also, Fernando Alegría, *Walt Whitman en Hispanoamérica* (Mexico City: Colección Studium, 1954). In the half century since publication of Alegría's study, the following studies have been added: Hensley C. Woodbridge, "Walt Whitman: Additional Bibliography in Spanish," *Walt Whitman Review*, 12 (September 1986), 70–71; Didier T. Jaén, trans. and ed., *Homage to Walt Whitman: A Collection of Poems from the Spanish*, foreword by Jorge Luis Borges (University: University of Alabama Press, 1969); José Benito Alvarez Buyila, "Whitman: poeta ibérico," *Filología moderna*, 40–41, 43–65; Alberto Uva, "Notas para un estudio del 'Whitman' de José Martí," trans. Jean R. Langland, *Anuario de Filología* 8–9 (1969–1970), 199–212; Luis Eugénio Ferreira, *Walt Whitman: Vida e Pensamento* (Aifragide, Portugal: Galeria Panorama, 1970); "Whitman's Presence in Alvaro de Campos [Fernando Pessoa]," *Calamus*, 7 (February, 1973), 2–9; Mauricio González de la Garza, *Walt Whitman Racista, Imperialista, Anti-mexicano* (Mexico City: Colección Malaga, 1971); Hensley C. Woodbridge, "González de la Garza: Anti-Whitman," *Walt Whitman Review* 17 (December 1971), 142–143; Emilio Bernal Labrador, "El idioma de Whitman: su traducción," *Revista Interamericana de Bibliografía* 21 (1971), 46–63; Roger Asselineau and William White, eds., *Walt Whitman in Europe Today: A Collection of Essays* (Detroit: Wayne State University Press, 1972), 9–12, 32–33, 41; Sister Agnes V. McLaughlin, "Una comparación entre la poesía de Luis Llorens Torres y la de Walt Whitman," *Horizontes: Revista de la Universidad Católica de Puerto Rico*, 31–32 (1973), 73–93; Roger Asselineau, "Spanish Leaves from Argentina," *Walt Whitman Review*, 23 (June 1977), 94–96; Claire Paxton, "Unamuno's Indebtedness to Whitman," *Walt Whitman Review*, 9 (March 1963), 16–19; Debra Harper, "Whitman and Unamuno: Language for Immortality," *Walt Whitman Review*, 25 (June 1979), 60–73; Luis Benito, *Walt Whitman, Poeta lírico* (Granada, 1975); Vilma Areas, "Uma Epopea para Vozes." *Actas do 2O Congreso Internacional de Estudos Pessoanos* (Oporto: Centro de Estudos Pessoanos, 1985), 47–59; Manuel Gómez-Reinoso, "Martí and Whitman," *West Hills Review*, vol. 3 (1981–1982), 47–48; Horacio Peña, "Aproximaciones a Rubén Darío y Walt Whitman," *Káñina*, vol. 8 (1984) 165–176; José L. Caramés Lago, "Evocación de León Felipe en su centenario," *Arbor*, 118 (July–August 1984), 125–132; Neil Larsen and Ronald W. Sousa, "From Whitman (to Marinetti) to Alvaro de Campos: A Case Study in Materialist Approaches to Literary Influence," *Ideologies & Literatures*, vol. 4 (September–October 1983), 94–115; Angel Rama, "José Martí en el eje de la modernización poética: Whitman, Lautréamont, Rimbaud," *Nueva Revista de Filología Hispánica*, vol. 32 (1983), 96–135. See also Juan Ramón Jiménez's radio scripts on the subject of "El modernismo: Estados Unidos," *Alerta*, ed. Francisco Javier Blasco (Salamanca: Universidad de Salamanca, 1983), 127–135. Also, Josef Raab, "El gran viejo: Walt Whitman in Latin America," *Comparative Literature and Culture: A WW Web Journal*, vol. 3, no. 2 (2001 June), 25 paragraphs; María Angeles Castro Hidalgo, "Tenacidad poética de Walt Whitman," *Káñina*, vol. 20, no. 1 (January–June 1996), 31–37; Jorge Salessi and José Quiroga, "Errata sobre la erótica, or the Ellision of Whitman's Body," in *Breaking Bounds: Whitman and American Cultural Studies*, ed. Betsy Erkkila (New York: Oxford University Press, 1996), 123–132; Ilán Stavans, "Whitman y Darío: Un Colón, dos . . . y ninguno," *Letras Peninsulares*, vol. 5, no. 1 (Spring 1992), 107–113; Ana Redondo and Javier Azpeita, "Versiones de Whitman," *Quimera: Revista de Literatura*, 109 (May 1992), 34–37; Charles Harmon Cagle, "Walt Whitman: Un pie en la Grecia Antigua, el otro en un bar gay," *Quimera* 109 (1992), 28–39. Several Whitman translations have been done since Algería's pioneer study, notably by Francisco Alexander, Jorge Luis Borges, Leonardo Wolfson, and E.M.S. Danero. See also, by Whitman: *Una mirada retrospectiva a los caminos recorridos*, tr. María Coy and ed. Juan José Coy (Girón, León: Universidad de León, 1992); *Tres poetas norteamericanos: Walt Whitman; Emily Dickinson; William Carlos Williams* (Bogotá: Editorial Norma, 1991); *Saludo al mundo y otros poemas*, trans. Carlos Montemayor (Buenos Aires: Ediciones Colihue, 2001); *Hojas de hierba: antología bilingüe*, trans. Manuel Villar Raso (Madrid: Alianza, 1999); *Canto a mí mismo*, trans. Enrique López Castellón (Madrid: Edimat Libros, 1999); *Oh, Capitán! Mi capitán!* trans. Francisco Alexander (Barcelona: Mondadori, 1998); *Whitman, poesía completa*, trans. Pablo Mañé (Barcelona: Ediciones Hojas de hierba, 1992); *Walt Whitman*, trans. José Antonio Gurpegui, José Luis Chamosa, Rosa

Rabadán (Madrid: Espasa, 1999); *Hojas de hierba*, trans. Victoria Patea, María Coy (Girón, León: Universidad de León, 1999); *Hojas de hierba: Primera antología*, trans. Pablo Mañé Garzón (Barcelona: Ediciones 29, 1996); *Antología poética ilustrada*, trans. Javier Mirá (Valencia: La Máscara, 1996).

4. For the texts of this polemic see Lewis Hanke, ed., *Do the Americas Have a Common History? A Critique of the Bolton Theory* (New York: Knopf, 1964). O'Gorman's text, partially reprinted on 103–111, first appeared as "Hegel y el moderno panamericanismo," *Universidad de la Habana*, 22 (January–February 1939), 61–74; English version in *Points of View*, 3 (1941), 1–10. For a different and more recent critique of Hegel see the lectures by José Lezama Lima, *La expresión americana* (Havana: Instituto Nacional de Cultura, 1957), and Irlemar Chiampi's excellent introduction to her critical edition (Mexico City: Fondo de Cultura Económica, 1993).

5. I quote from "América¿ es un continente?" (Is America a Continent?)(1941), collected in my edition of Octavio Paz, *Primeras letras (1931–1943)* (Mexico City: Vuelta, 1988), 189–192. Twelve years before, in 1929 in "El otro Whitman" Borges had remarked something uncannily similar: "The people of the diverse Americas remain so out of reach that we hardly know each other by reference, counted by Europe." I should like this chapter to be an extension of Borges's and Paz's shared insight.

6. I refer to *Canto general de Chile. Fragmentos* (Mexico City, 1943); for more details, see Chapter I. For Paz's version of his quarrel with Neruda, see *Sombras de obras: Arte y literatura* (Barcelona: Seix Barral, 1983), 48–56; for his comments on the significance of their breakup, see *Primeras letras*, 44–47.

7. Octavio Paz, *The Siren and the Seashell and Other Essays on Poets and Poetry*, trans. Lysander Kemp, et al. (Austin: University of Texas Press, 1970).

8. See José Martí, "The Poet Walt Whitman," in José Martí, *Selected Writings*, trans. Esther Allen (New York: Penguin, 2002), 183–195; and Rubén Darío, *Azul* . . . (Valparaíso: Excelsior, 1888). On Martí, see Remedios Mataix, "Amor y temor de ciudad grande: Notas sobre la poética urbana de José Martí," in *Escrituras de la ciudad*, ed. José Carlos Rovira (Madrid: Palas Atenea, 1999), 75–91; Doris Sommer, "José Martí, Author of Walt Whitman," in *José Martí's 'Our America': From National to Hemispheric Cultural Studies*, ed. Jeffrey Belknap and Raúl Fernández, (Durham, NC: Duke University Press), 77–90; Enildo A. García, "José Martí y Walt Whitman: 'Literatura', libertad y democracia" *Círculo: Revista de Cultura* 25 (1996), 75–88; Sylvia Molloy, "His America, Our America: José Martí Reads Whitman," *Modern Language Quarterly: A Journal of Literary History*, vol. 57, no. 2 (June 1996), 369–379; Félix Ernesto Chávez, "Whitman por Martí: Análisis de una confluencia," *Anuario del Centro de Estudios Martianos*, vol. 24 (2001), 158–167.

9. Borges, "Nota sobre Walt Whitman," 122–123.

10. See Betsy Erkkila, *Walt Whitman Among the French: Poet and Myth* (Princeton: Princeton University Press, 1980).

11. For a discussion of carnival and the carnivalesque, see Mikhail Bakhtin, *Rabelais and His World*, trans. Hélène Iswolsky (Cambridge: MIT Press, 1968).

12. "Vasseur's work deserves a detailed analytic study because of all the Spanish translations [*sic*] of Whitman's book it is the one that has had the greatest influence on the poets and public of Spain and Spanish America . . . Vasseur's is the translation that accompanies the modernista and post-modernista movement. It is the breviary where Lugones and Chocano, Barba Jacob and Neruda, Parra del Riego and de Rokha and Mistral learned their Whitman." (Alegría, 349, my translation). Vasseur's translations of Whitman have been recently reprinted; see *Hojas de hierba*, trans. Armando Vasseur (Mexico City: Fontamara, 1996).

13. See Vasseur, *Cantos augurales* (Montevideo: O.M. Bertani, 1904), and Alegría, 284). Vasseur noted his Italian source in his preface to the sixth edition of *Poemas: Walt Whitman* (Buenos Aires: Schapire, 1950), a text he also published in *Alfar*, vol. 89 (1951), n.p., from which I translate the following: "In 1902, in Montevideo's Comini Bookstore, I found the two volumes of the Italian version of the *Leaves* edited by Sonsogno in Italy [Milan, 1896]. Some lines appear at the beginning

of one or two chapters of my *Cantos augurales*." Elsewhere in the same essay, Vasseur explained how he was never able to take in "Anglo-Saxon words and tones," and how all translations from the original English were done by his wife and son, who "took it in better" than he. Compare Vasseur's testimony with Alberto Zum Felde's recollection that "Vasseur did not know English well . . . he had a great assistant in Dr. Vitale, a well-educated doctor and author of books on Sociology and Political Economy. Dr. Vitale knew English well and did the literal translations that Vasseur then fashioned poetically." See Arturo Sergio Visca, "Conversando con Zum Felde," *Reportajes Culturales* (Biblioteca Nacional, Montevideo), 1 (1969), 36. (My thanks to Dr. Visca for this reference.) The bibliography in *Walt Whitman en Hispanoamérica* does note the sixth edition (418) of Vasseur's versions, but this appears to be an add-on (see chapter 6, no. 3, 406) where Alegría mentions that "a third edition by Schapire has been published," as if he knew none of the later ones. In 1910, when Vasseur began to work on his "versions," the best-known Italian translations were those by Luigi Gamberale; see his *Canti Scelti* (Milan: Edoardo Sonzogno, 1881–1932, several reprints and editions) and *Foglie di erba* (Milan: Sandron, 1907). The former, published by Edoardo Sonzogno Editrice, is the one Vasseur handled. As far as I have been able to ascertain, two-volume editions were published in 1885, 1891, and 1932, but Vasseur is obviously citing from (fuzzy) memory. For information on Whitman's reception in Italy see *Walt Whitman Abroad,* ed. Gay Wilson Allen (Syracuse, NY: Syracuse University Press, 1955), 187–198 and 278–279; and Gay Wilson Allen, ed., *Walt Whitman in Europe Today* (Syracuse, NY: Syracuse University Press, 1955). It is interesting that in the same text (36) Zum Felde, a sometime Whimanian poet as well as literary historian, observes that his own *El Huanakauri* (Montevideo: M. García, 1917) shows the dual influence of Whitman and Nietzsche, yet described the latter's influence as earlier: "Nietzsche's influence on me comes much earlier. When I was 20 years old I was perhaps the only Nietzschean in our intellectual circles." Zum Felde was born in 1888.

   On Vasseur, I have found the following useful: Hugo Achugar, "Modernización, europeización: el lirismo social en Uruguay entre 1885 y 1911," in his *Poesía y sociedad (Uruguay 1880–1911)* (Montevideo: Arca, 1985), 137–169; Rafael Cansinos-Asséns, "Alvaro Armando Vasseur," in his *La nueva literatura* (Madrid: V.H. de Sanz Calleja, 1927), 81–100; Emilio Frugoni, "Prólogo," in Alvaro Armando Vasseur, *Todos los cantos (1898–1912)* (Montevideo: Clásicos Uruguayos, 1955), vii–xxiii; "Tres polémicas literarias," in *La literatura uruguaya del 1900,* Ed. Arturo Ardao, et al. (Montevideo: Imprenta Nacional Colorada, 1950), 315–320; and Alberto Zum Felde, *Proceso intelectual del Uruguay y crítica de su literatura* (Montevideo, 1930), 2, 307–313. I thank Enrique Fierro for alerting me to many of these items.

14. Jorge Luis Borges, "La doctrina de los ciclos" (1934), in *Historia de la eternidad* (Buenos Aires: Emecé Editores, 1953), 84. In "Nota sobre Walt Whitman" Borges also mentions Nietzsche in connection with Whitman's blurring of personal and factual history. On Nietzsche's reception in Spain and Latin America the standard works are Gonzalo Sobejano, *Nietzsche en España* (Madrid: Editorial Gredos, 1967); and Udo Rukser, *Nietzsche in der Hispania: Ein Beitrag zur Hispanischen und Geistesgeschichte* (Bern: Francke, 1962). See especially the latter's bibliography (358–369) for a list of Spanish translations of Nietzsche, which began in full force in 1900–1901. Significantly, Sobejano's "Final" note (664) quotes Blas de Otero's sonnet "Posición," which invokes equally Whitman's "beautiful long book" and Nietzsche's "splendid, full shadow." Nietzsche's general influence on a poetics of *posmodernismo*, particularly as it affected late *modernista* poets in Argentina (Lugones and Martínez Estrada, for example), deserves of course a treatment fuller than the one I give here.

15. See C.N. Stavrou, *Whitman and Nietzsche: A Comparative Study of their Thought* (Chapel Hill: University of North Carolina Press, 1964), 193.

16. See Harold Bloom, *Poetry and Repression: Revisionism from Blake to Stevens* (New Haven: Yale University Press, 1976), as well as his *Agon: Towards a Theory of Revisionism* (New York: Oxford University Press, 1982), especially 330–336.

17. I have in mind the readings of both Fernando Alegría ("¿Cuál Whitman?": Borges, Lorca y Neruda" *Texto Crítico*, 22–23 [1981], 3–12) and Jaime Alazraki ("Neruda y Borges: Dos rostros

de Walt Whitman," *Confluencia*, 1 [Fall 1985], 37–42). The common effort of such essays is to demonstrate how two such dissimilar authors join forces under the same fascination for Whitman. For an early vigorous discussion of their contrasts, on the other hand, see the lively three-way debate by Carlos Real de Azúa, Angel Rama, and Emir Rodríguez Monegal, "Evasión y arraigo de Borges y Neruda," *Revista Nacional* (Montevideo) segundo ciclo, Año IV, no. 202 (October–December 1959), 514–531. See also, Jaime Concha, "Borges, Neruda: dos poetas, dos destinos," in *Jorge Luis Borges: El último laberinto*, ed. Rómulo Cosse (Montevideo: Librería Linardi y Risso, 1987), 17–30. For a sharp contrast, see Alexander Coleman, "The Ghost of Walt Whitman in Neruda and Borges," *Mickle Street Review*, 9 (1988), 76–89; and Alastair Reid, "Neruda and Borges," *The New Yorker* (June 24 and July 1 1996), 56–72. On Neruda, see Enrique Sandoval Gessler, "La poesía de Walt Whitman," *Revista Chilena de Literatura*, 55, (November 1999), 201–208; and Floridor Pérez, "Walt Whitman leído en el sur: Testimonios en la biblioteca personal de Pablo Neruda," *Revista Chilena de Literatura*, 55 (November 1999), 195–200.

18. Neruda reviewed Torres-Rioseco's translations, *Walt Whitman* (San José: Costa Rica, 1922) in the student magazine *Claridad* 86 (May 8 1923). For additional comments on Whitman see his *Memoirs*, trans. Hardie St. Martin (New York: Farrar, Straus and Giroux, 1976), 262, 294 and "Discurso en el Pen Club de Nueva York. Abril 1972," in his *Obras Completas* [henceforward *OC*] (Barcelona: Círculo de Lectores/Galaxia Gutenberg, 2002), V, 357–361, partially translated as "We Live in a Whitmanesque Age," *New York Times* (14 April 1972), 37-A. For comparisons of Neruda and Whitman see, in addition to Alegría (314–334) and the items noted in note 16, Djelal Kadir's "Neruda and Whitman: Shortcircuiting the Body Electric," *Pacific Coast Philology*, vol. 8 (1973), 16–22; Peter G. Earle, "Whitman and Neruda and Their Implicit Cultural Revolution," in *Proceedings of the Xth Congress of the International Comparative Literature Association*, ed. Mario J. Valdés (New York: Garland, 1985), vol. 3, 189–193; Guillermo Rothschuh, "Whitman, Darío y Neruda," *Encuentro* (September–October 1973), 59–67; and Alain Sicard, "Camerado Neruda . . . (Notes sur le 'whitmanisme' de Neruda)," *Letterature d'America*, vol. 14–15 (1982), 177–187; James Nolan, *Poet-Chief: The Native American Poetics of Walt Whitman and Pablo Neruda* (Albuquerque: University of New Mexico Press, 1994), and William Allegrezza, "Politicizing the Reader in the American Lyric–Epic: Walt Whitman's *Leaves of Grass* and Pablo Neruda's *Canto general*" (Ph.D. Dissertation, Louisana State University, 2003). For a list of the whitmaniana in Neruda's two libraries, see appendix two.

19. See Pablo Neruda, "Los libros: *Poemas del hombre: Libros del corazón, de la voluntad, del tiempo y del mar*, por Carlos Sabat Ercasty," *Claridad* 87 (May 12, 1923); *OC*, IV, 311. For Sabat Ercasty's views on Vasseur see his "La lírica de Vasseur," included in *Poesías, Alvaro Armando Vasseur* (Montevideo: Revista "Letras," 1933), 39–54. See also María Antonia García Orallo, *La obra poética de Carlos Sabat Ercasty* (Burgos: Universidad de Burgos, 2002).

20. See Pablo Neruda, "Algunas reflexiones improvisadas sobre mis trabajos," *OC*, IV, 1201–1208. For similar comments, see his *Memoirs*, 261–262, where "the tendency to stretch out in space" is linked to "Walt Whitman, my comrade from Manhattan."

21. I quote from *The Aleph and Other Stories* (1933–1969), ed. Norman Thomas di Giovanni (New York: E.P. Dutton, 1970), 217–218. At a further point in the essay (251) Borges mentions Whitman in a list of literary heroes. Besides Borges's own texts on Whitman, see Alexander A. Coleman, "Notes on Borges and American Literature," *Tri-Quarterly Review* 25 (1972), 356–377; Emir Rodríguez Monegal, *Jorge Luis Borges: A Literary Biography* (New York: E.P. Dutton, 1978), 147–149; Jaime Alazraki, "Enumerations as Evocations: On the Use of a Device in Borges's Latest Poetry," in *Borges, the Poet*, ed. Carlos Cortínez (Fayetteville: University of Arkansas Press, 1986), 149–157; Joseph John Benevento, "Self, Reader, Persona: Whitman, Borges, and Their Experimental Trinity" (Ph.D. Dissertation, Michigan State University, 1983), and "What Borges Learned from Whitman: The Open Road and Its Forking Path," *Walt Whitman Review*, vol. 2 (Spring 1985), 21–30; María Luisa Bastos, "Whitman as Inscribed by Borges," in Cortínez, *Borges the Poet*, 219–231; Daniel Balderston, "The 'Fecal Dialectic': Homosexual Panic and the Origin

of Writing in Borges," ed. Emilie Bergmann, and Paul Julian Smith, *Entiendes? Queer Readings, Hispanic Writings* (Durham, NC: Duke University Press,1997), 29–45; Carmen Valero Garcés, "Jorge L. Borges: poeta y traductor de Walt Whitman: Análisis de las estrategias en la traducción de poesía," *Torre de Papel,* vol. 5, no. 3 (Fall 1995), 19–40; Fernando Alegría, "Borges's 'Song of Myself,' " *The Cambridge Companion to Walt Whitman,* ed. Ezra Greenspan (Cambridge: Cambridge University Press), 208–219; Frances R. Aparicio: "Borges y Whitman: Un abrazo panteísta," *Discurso: Revista de Estudios Iberoamericanos* vol. 10, no. 2 (1993), 2.

22. Borges, *The Aleph and Other Stories*, 220. For Borges's early poetry, see *Poesía juvenil de Jorge Luis Borges,* ed. Carlos Meneses (Barcelona: Planeta, 1978).

23. Jorge Luis Borges, *Prólogos, con un prólogo de prólogos* (Buenos Aires: Torres Agüero, 1975), 174. Recall that in "El otro Whitman" (52–53) Borges makes his point about Whitman's reticence and laconic quality by offering his own translations of a few pertinent poems.

24. Jorge Luis Borges, "La nadería de la personalidad," in *Inquisiciones* (Buenos Aires: Gleizer, 1925), 90–93; "The Nothingness of Personality," in *Selected Non-Fictions,* ed. and trans. Eliot Weinberger (New York: Viking, 1999), 3–4. Subsequent references are cited in the text. In *Inquisiciones* (125) Borges mentions Whitman in another essay on Ramón Gómez de la Serna.

25. Borges, "El otro Whitman," 52–53.

26. Borges, "Nota sobre Walt Whitman," 125.

27. Walt Whitman, *Hojas de hierba,* trans. Jorge Luis Borges (Buenos Aires: Editora Juárez, 1969), 173.

28. Borges, "Preface to Walt Whitman, *Leaves of Grass*," in *Selected Non-Fictions,* 446.

29. Jorge Luis Borges, *Collected Fictions,* trans. Andrew Hurley (New York: Viking, 1999) 283.

30. *The Aleph and Other Stories*, 264. For Borges's parody of Dante, see Emir Rodríguez Monegal, *Borges: A Literary Biography*, 414–417, where he disputes Borges's dismissal of such an interpretation in his notes to the story included in *The Aleph and Other Stories* (263–264). In my view, however, Borges did not so much dismiss the Dante cipher as clarify that his real theme was the ultimate identity between impersonality and totalization, which included Dante as well as Whitman, among others. Hence Borges's remark, in the same notes, to the effect that "My chief problem in writing the story lay in what Walt Whitman had very successfully achieved—the setting down of a limited catalog of endless things. The task, as is evident, is impossible, for such chaotic enumeration can only be simulated, and every apparently haphazard element has to be linked to its neighbor by secret association or by contrast" (264). Borges restated these ideas on Whitman in many interviews; see Rita Guibert, *Seven Voices,* trans. Frances Partridge (New York: Alfred Knopf, 1973), 97. For a reading of Borges's complex relationship to Dante, see Jon Thiem's "Borges, Dante, and the Poetics of Total Vision," *Comparative Literature*, vol. 40 (Spring 1988), 97–121. Thiem shows that in "The Aleph" Borges arrived at "the paradoxical conclusion that a method of significant omission is essential to a modern poetics of total vision" (108), and further that " 'Borges' succeeds precisely where Daneri evidently failed, namely in giving the reader the illusion of having experienced a total vision" (112). Thiem misses totally, however, that Borges's approach has as much to do with Whitman as with Dante, despite Borges's explicit acknowledgement in his 1970 "Commentaries." On Borges and Dante see further: Maria Bonatti, "Dante en la lectura de Borges," *Revista Iberoamericana*, vol. 43 (1977), 737–744; Roberto Paoli, "Borges e Dante," *Studi danteschi*, 56 (1984), 189–212; and Ruggero Stefanini, "Dante in Borges: l'Aleph, Beatriz e il Sud," *Italica*, 57 (1980), 53–65.

31. See Richard Burgin, *Conversations with Jorge Luis Borges* (New York: Holt, Rinehart and Winston, 1969), 95–96; and chapter I.

32. I owe this insight to my friend and Borges specialist Professor Arturo Echavarría Ferrari. There remains the possibility, of course, that Daneri is merely a version of the young Borges. According to Edwin Williamson, Borges' third book of poems, *Cuaderno San Martín* (1929) was meant to be originally "a history in verse of Argentina"! See his *Borges: A Life* (New York: Viking Penguin, 2004), 136.

33. Alegría (211–224) did discuss the important work on Whitman by Gilberto Freyre; but Freyre was a sociologist, not a poet, and it would be essential to know whether Freyre's work was merely responding to an incipient Whitman cult, such as it appears in Brazilian poets like *Sousândrade*, or Portuguese ones like Alvaro de Campos (a heteronym of Fernando Pessoa). For some thoughts on this question, see especially Augusto de Campos and Haroldo de Campos, *Revisão de Sousândrade* 2nd ed. (Rio de Janeiro: Editora Nova Fronteira, 1982), the essay by Larsen and Sousa (n. 16), the study by Luis Eugenio Ferreira, *Walt Whitman: Vida e Pensamento*, and the following: George Monteiro, "Pessoa and the Whitman Anomaly," *Indiana Journal of Hispanic Literatures* 9 (Fall 1996), 171–186; María Clara B., "Walt Whitman's Brazilian Readers," in *Literature of Region and Nation: Proceedings of the 6th International Literature of Region and Nation Conference*, ed. Winnifred Bogaards (Saint John, NB: Social and Humanities Research Council of Canada, 1998), I, 368–80; María Clara Bonetti Paro, "Walt Whitman in Brazil," *Walt Whitman Quarterly Review*, vol. 11, no. 2 (Fall 1993), 57–66; Susan Margaret Brown, "Pessoa and Whitman: Brothers in the Universe," in *The Continuing Presence of Walt Whitman: The Life after the Life*, ed. Robert K. Martin (Iowa City: University of Iowa Press, 1992), 167–181; María Clara Bonetti Paro, "Ronald de Carvalho e Walt Whitman," *Revista de Letras*, 32 (1992), 141–151.

Chapter Three　　Sor Juana, Octavio Paz, and Poetics of Restitution

1. I cite from *Sor Juana, or the Traps of Faith*, trans. Margaret Sayers Peden (Cambridge: Harvard University Press, 1988); partial translation of the third, revised edition of *Sor Juana Inés de la Cruz, o las trampas de la fe* (Mexico City: Fondo de Cultura Económica, 1983). After publication of the 1982 Spanish edition, Paz published the following additional pieces on Sor Juana: "Préface," in Sor Juana Inés de la Cruz, *Le divin Narcisse, précédé de Premier Songe et autres textes*, trans. Frédéric Magne, Florence Delay and Jacques Roubaud (Paris: Gallimard, 1987), 7–21; "Foreword," *A Sor Juana Anthology*, trans. Alan S. Trueblood (Cambridge, MA: Harvard University Press, 1988), pp. ii–v; "¿Azar o Justicia?" in Sor Juana Inés de la Cruz, *La segunda Celestina* (Mexico City: Editorial Vuelta, 1990); "*Sor Juana Inés de la Cruz, o las trampas de la fe*," Part V of Video Series "*México en la obra de Octavio Paz*" (Mexico City: Televisa, 1989) and "Oración fúnebre," *ABC* (April 21, 1995), and in *Obras completas* (Barcelona: Círculo de Lectores, 2000), 14, 179–186; see 167–175 for Paz's texts on his polemic with Elías Trabulse over Sor Juana. In addition to the several interviews noted below, see also Eusebio Rojas Guzmán, *Conversación con Octavio Paz, Vida de Sor Juana: su nacimiento, su niñez, la Corte y el Convento* (Mexico City: Publicaciones Culturales, 1983). Film and stage versions of Sor Juana's life, loosely based on Paz's biography, have appeared: see María Luisa Bemberg's *I, the Worst of All* (1990), Juan Carlos Moyano's *Los ritos del retorno, o las trampas de la fe* (1991), Estela Portillo Trambley's *Sor Juana and other plays* (Ypsilanti, Mich: Bilingual Press/ Editorial Bilingüe, 1983), and Diane Ackerman's *Reverse Thunder* (New York: Lumen Books, 1988); see also Alicia Gaspar de Alba's novel *Sor Juana's Second Dream* (Albuquerque, NM: University of New Mexico Press, 1999).

2. L. 810 of *Primero Sueño [First dream]* in *Obras Completas de Sor Juana Inés de la Cruz*, ed. Alfonso Méndez Plancarte and Alberto G. Salceda (Mexico City: Fondo de Cultura Económica, 1951–1954), I. 355. All citations from Sor Juana's works, except otherwise noted, will be based on this edition and on *A Sor Juana Anthology*.

3. My translation from "'Conversar es humano': Entrevista con Octavio Paz," *La Torre*, 9 (enero-marzo 1989), 110.

4. "The Philomela Project," in Hartman's *Minor Prophecies: The Literary Essay in the Culture Wars* (Cambridge: Harvard University Press, 1991), 164–175. The essay was originally titled

"Criticism and Restitution," *Tikkun* (January–February, 1989), 29–32; Gayatri C. Spivak, *A Critique of Postcolonial Reason. Toward a History of the Vanishing Present* (Cambridge: Harvard University Press, 1999).

5. For a definitive discussion in moral theology see the "Restitution" entry in the *Dictionnaire de Théologie Catholique* (Paris: Letouzey, 1936), 13, cols. 2466–2501; see especially the bibliography on cols. 2499–2501. For a shortened, modernized English version, see the *New Catholic Encyclopedia* (New York: McGraw-Hill, 1967), 12, 400–401. For legal discussions, see Anthony G. White, *Restitution as a Criminal Sentence: A Selected Bibliography* (Monticello, IL: Council of Planning Librarians, 1977) and Gerald Henry Louis Fridman, *Restitution* (Toronto: Carswell, Co., 1982). It would be fruitful to consider restitution in the context of what James Boyd White has recently called the "translational foundations of the justice system"; see his *Justice as Translation: An Essay in Cultural and Legal Criticism* (Chicago: University of Chicago Press, 1990), especially 229–270, passim.

6. Tzvetan Todorov, *Symbolism and Interpretation*, trans. Catherine Porter (Ithaca, NY: Cornell University Press, 1982), 134–135; but see 136–162 for a longer discussion of philological exegesis. See also the essay by Jan Ziolkowski, *On Philology* (University Park, PA: Pennsylvania State University Press, 1990).

7. For a further critique of restitution as a critical practice see Alberto Moreiras, *The Exhaustion of Difference: The Politics of Latin American Cultural Studies* (Durham, NC: Duke University Press, 2001).

8. In this and what follows I am indebted to Lionel Gossman, *Between History and Literature* (Cambridge: Harvard University Press, 1990), especially Chapter 8: "History as Decipherment: Romantic Historiography and the Discovery of the Other," 257–284. For a contrasting view of philology as a critical practice during the Renaissance, see Franco Gaeta, *Lorenzo Valla: Filologia e Storia nell'umanesimo italiano* (Naples: Nella Sede dell'Istituto, 1955).

9. Michel Foucault, *The Order of Things* (New York: Random House, 1972), 298.

10. Edward Said, *Orientalism* (New York: Basic Books, 1977), 132; Said adds: "The job of philology in modern culture (a culture Renan calls philological) is to continue to see reality and nature clearly, thus driving out supernaturalism, and to continue to keep pace with the natural sciences." For further remarks on philology's role in the constitution of so-called objective judgments of non-Western cultures, see 134, 142, 147, 148.

11. See, among other works by Melanie Klein, "Love, Guilt and Reparation," in Melanie Klein and Joan Rivière, *Love, Hate and Reparation, and Other Works, 1921–1945* (London: Virago, 1988); Marcel Mauss, *The Gift. Forms and Functions of Exchange in Archaic Societies*, trans. Ian Cunnison (New York: McGraw-Hill, 1967); and Jacques Derrida, "Restitutions of the Truth in Pointing (*pointure*)," in his *The Truth in Painting*, trans. Geoff Bennington and Ian McLeod (Chicago: University of Chicago Press, 1987), 258–382. Restitution is also an important working concept in generative poetics, where it refers to the reader's citational competence; see Jean-Jacques Thomas and Daniel Delas, "Poétique générative," *Languages*, 51 (1978), 7–64; and the former's "Le coq et la perle," *Poétique*, 45 (1981), 111–125.

12. On Bello's philological career, see Emir Rodríguez Monegal's intellectual biography, *El otro Andrés Bello* (Caracas: Monte Avila, 1979).

13. Marcelino Menéndez y Pelayo, *Historia de la poesía hispanoamericana*, ed. Enrique Sánchez Reyes (Santander: Editora Nacional, 1948) I, 67.

14. For an important exception, see, Rolena Adorno, "Arms, Letters and the Native Historian in Early Colonial Mexico," in *1492–1992: Re/ Discovering Colonial Writing*, ed. René Jara and Nicholas Spadaccini (Minneapolis: The Prisma Institute, 1989), 201–224. Adorno reaches views similar to mine when she contrasts Tzvetan Todorov's *The Conquest of America* to Michel de Certeau's *Heterologies*, and finds in the former a penchant to reduce the otherness of the colonial past to present ideological debates. She does not relate this question, however, to philological practice, which I find essential, whether or not it relates to Todorov's views. For a study of the Romantic writer's ambivalence toward the Colonial past, see Juan Durán Luzio, "Ricardo

Palma, cronista de una sociedad barroca," *Revista Iberoamericana,* 140 (1987), 581–594. For a good introduction to the complex question of legal restitution of the rights and property of the vanquished, see Guillermo Lohmann Villena, "La restitución por conquistadores y encomenderos: un aspecto de la incidencia lascasiana en el Perú," in *Estudios lascasianos. IV Centenario de la muerte de fray Bartolomé de las Casas (1566–1966)* (Seville: Escuela de Estudios Hispano-americanos, 1966), 21–89.

15. An English translation of the letter is included in *Sor Juana,* 495–502; the Spanish original is included in *Sor Juana Inés de la Cruz,* 638–646. Aureliano Tapia Méndez, the editor, published it twice, first in a limited edition, *Autodefensa espiritual de Sor Juana* (Monterrey, n.p., 1981) and later in a fuller book, *Carta de Sor Juana Inés de la Cruz a su confesor* (Monterrey: n.p., 1986). (Both include a facsimile of the found text, based on an eighteenth-century copy.) For a critical edition of the text and a virtually exhaustive commentary, see Antonio Alatorre, "La *Carta* de Sor Juana al P. Núñez (1682)," *Nueva Revista de Filología Hispánica,* 35 (1987), 591–672.

16. Octavio Paz, *Collected Poems, 1957–1987,* ed. and trans. Eliot Weinberger (New York: New Directions, 1987), 527.

17. For instances of Paz's remark, see the interviews " 'Conversar,' " 117; and the earlier one with Jacobo Machover, "Octavio Paz, le poète dans la cité," *Magazine Littéraire,* 263 (1989), 105–111.

18. Stephanie Merrim, "Toward a Feminist Reading of Sor Juana Inés de la Cruz: Past, Present and Future Directions in Sor Juana Criticism," in her *Feminist Perspectives on Sor Juana Inés de la Cruz* (Detroit, MI: Wayne State University Press, 1991), 20. Merrim's collection, and her cogent introduction, is the most complete treatment I know of Sor Juana's feminism. The argument was pursued, with various nuances in the same scholar's *Early Modern Women's Writing and Sor Juana Inés de la Cruz* (Nashville: Vanderbilt University Press, 1999). Sor Juana's importance as a woman has in the past often been misperceived with a mixture of Catholic piety, as in Anita Arroyo's *Razón y pasión de Sor Juana* (Mexico City: Porrúa, 1952). For a premature (U.S.) feminist reaction to Paz's Sor Juana research, see Electa Arenal's "Comment on Paz's 'Juana Ramírez,' " *Signs,* 5 (1980), 552–555; and for the same reviewer's updated, though no less orthodox, reading, see *Criticism,* 21 (1989), 463–470. Of general interest are Marylin I. Ward, "The Feminist Crisis of Sor Juana Inés de la Cruz," *International Journal of Women's Studies,* 1 (1978), 475–481, and Judith Thurman, "Sister Juana: The Price of Genius," *Ms.* (April 1973), 14–21, as well as Sor Juana Inés de la Cruz, *Respuesta a Sor Filotea de la Cruz,* ed. Grupo Feminista de Cultura (Mexico City: FEM, 1979), including the editors' feminist defense of Sor Juana (7–21). Emilie Bergmann, "Sor Juana Inés de la Cruz: Dreaming in a Double Voice," Emilie Bergmann, ed. *Women, Culture, and Politics in Latin America / Seminar on Feminism and Culture in Latin America* (Berkeley: University of California Press, 1990), 151–172; "Ficciones de Sor Juana: Poética y biografía," in "*Y diversa de mí misma entre vuestras plumas ando": Homenaje Internacional a Sor Juana Inés de la Cruz,* ed. Sara Poot-Herrera, et al. (Mexico City: El Colegio de Mexico, 1993); Pamela Kirk, *Sor Juana Inés de la Cruz: Religion, Art, and Feminism* (New York: Continuum Books, 1998). For recent collections of essays on Sor Juana, see, besides Poot-Herrera, above, the following: Luis Cortest, ed., *Sor Juana Inés de la Cruz: Selected Studies* (Asunción, Paraguay: Centro de Estudios de Economía y Sociedad, 1989); Susanna Regazzoni, ed., "*Por amor de las letras": Juana Inés de la Cruz: Le donne e il sacro* (Rome: Bulzoni, 1996). See also the following by Georgina Sabat de Rivers: *En busca de Sor Juana* (Mexico City: Facultad de Filosofía y Letras, Universidad Nacional Autónoma de México, 1998); *Bibliografía y otras cuestiúnculas sorjuaninas* (Salta, Argentina: Editorial Biblioteca de Textos Universitarios, 1995); *Estudios de literatura hispanoamericana: Sor Juana Inés de la Cruz y otros poetas barrocos de la colonia* (Barcelona: PPU, 1992). Also, the following by Margo Glantz: *Borrones y borradores: reflexiones sobre el ejercicio de la escritura (ensayos de literatura colonial, de Bernal Díaz del Castillo a Sor Juana)* (Mexico City: Coordinación de Difusión Cultural, Dirección de Literatura/UNAM; Ediciones del Equilibrista, 1992); *Sor Juana Inés de la Cruz: ¿hagiografía o autobiografía?* (Mexico City: Grijalbo: Universidad Nacional Autónoma de México, 1995); *Sor Juana Inés de la Cruz: saberes y placeres* (Toluca: Gobierno del Estado de México, Instituto Mexiquense de Cultura, 1996); *Sor Juana: la comparación y la hipérbole* (Mexico City: Conaculta, 2000); and *Sor*

Juana Inés de la Cruz y sus contemporáneos (Mexico City: Centro de Estudios de Historia de México, UNAM, 1998). Finally, by José Pascual Buxó: *La literatura novohispana : revisión crítica y propuestas metodológicas*, ed. José Pascual Buxó, Arnulfo Herrera (Mexico City: Universidad Nacional Autónoma de México, 1994); *Sor Juana Inés de la Cruz : amor y conocimiento* (Mexico City: Universidad Nacional Autonoma de México: Instituto Mexiquense de Cultura, 1996) and *Sor Juana Inés de la Cruz y las vicisitudes de la crítica*, ed. Buxó (Mexico City: UNAM, 1998). Sor Juana was also recently the subject of a global conference: *Sor Juana y su mundo: Una mirada actual*, ed. Carmen Beatriz López-Portillo (Mexico City: Fondo de Cultura Económica-Universidad del Claustro de Sor Juana, 2002). For a useful bibliography, see Mario A. Ortiz, "Sor Juana Inés de la Cruz: Bibliography," *Hispania*, vol. 86, no. 3 (September 2003), 431–462.

19. "Sor Juana después de Paz: Una restitución feminista," was the title of the Spanish version of Merrim's introduction to her essay collection [Cf. *Insula*, 522 (June 1990), 20–22]. On the question of whether Sor Juana's "abdication" reflects negatively on her feminism (see n. 27 below), Merrim takes no sides; in 14, 95, and especially 119–120, n. 3, she broaches the "conspiracy" theory without mentioning Paz's name. But she does engage a running critique of Paz's reading of Sor Juana in her more recent *Early Modern Women's Writing and Sor Juana Inés de la Cruz*. The question has been recently revisited in Rosa Perelmuter's *Los límites de la femineidad en Sor Juana Inés de la Cruz: estrategias retóricas y recepción literaria* (Madrid: Iberoamericana Verwuert, 2004). In Paz's defense, it should be said that much of the research regarding a specifically female culture and literary tradition was at most contemporaneous to *Sor Juana*, and that earlier competent research was the exception, as was Asunción Lavrin's "Values and Meaning of Monastic Life for Nuns in Colonial Mexico," in *Catholic Historical Review*, 58 (1972–1973), 367–387, or Josefina Muriel's *Conventos de monjas en la Nueva España* (1946). Today we count with a voluminous bibliography on convent culture. See also by Lavrin: (with Edith Coutourier), "Las mujeres tienen la palabra. Otras voces en la historia colonial de México," *Historia Mexicana*, 31 (1981), 278–311; "Women and Religion in Spanish America," in *Women and Religion in America*, ed. Rosemary Radford Ruether and Rosemary Skinner Keller (New York: Harper & Row, 1983), 2, 42–77; "Female Religious," in *Cities and Society in Colonial Latin America*, ed. Louisa Schell Hoberman and Susan Migden Socolow (Albuquerque, NM: University of New Mexico Press, 1986), 165–196; "In Search of the Colonial Woman in Mexico: The Seventeenth and Eighteenth Centuries," ed. Asunción Lavrin, *Latin American Women: Historical Perspectives* (Westport, CT: Garland Press, 1978), 23–25, and "La celda y el convento: una perspectiva femenina," in *Historia de la literatura mexicana*, ed. Raquel Chang-Rodríguez (Mexico City: Siglo XXI, 2002), 372–410. Also of interest, *Literatura conventual femenina: Sor Marcela de San Félix, hija de Lope de Vega. Obra Completa*, ed. Electa Arenal and Georgina Sabat-Rivers (Barcelona: PPU, 1988). A bibliography of more recent scholarship on New Spanish women would include, among others, Pilar Gonzalbo, *Las mujeres en la Nueva España. Educación y vida cotidiana* (Mexico City: El Colegio de México, 1987), Electa Arenal and Stacey Schlau, *Untold Sisters: Hispanic Nuns in Their Own Works* (Albuquerque, NM: University of New Mexico Press, 1989), Jean Franco, *Plotting Women: Gender and Representation in Mexico* (New York: Columbia University Press, 1989). Solange Alberro's *Inquisición y sociedad en México, 1571–1700* (Mexico City: Fondo de Cultura Económica, 1988) contains valuable comments on the specific pressures on women in New Spain under the Inquisition. For a historicist revision of feminism see Constance Jordan, *Renaissance Feminism. Literary Texts and Political Models* (Ithaca, NY: Cornell University Press, 1990). And for a recent treatment of a "proto-feminist" poetic tradition see Ann Rosalind Jones, *The Currency of Eros: Women's Love Lyric in Europe, 1540–1620* (Bloomington, IN: Indiana University Press, 1990).

20. See *El laberinto de la soledad* (Mexico City: Cuadernos Americanos, 1950), 113–118; *The Labyrinth of Solitude and other Writings*, trans. Lysander Kemp, et al. (New York: Grove Weidenfeld, 1985), 111–116, from which I quote; *Anthologie de la poésie mexicaine*, ed. Octavio Paz, trans. Guy Lévis Mano, prologue by Paul Claudel (Paris: UNESCO, 1952); "Homenaje a Sor Juana Inés de la Cruz en su tercer centenario (1651–1695)," *Sur*, 206 (1951), 29–40; "Introduction to the

History of Mexican Poetry," in *An Anthology of Mexican Poetry*, ed. Octavio Paz, trans. Samuel Beckett (Bloomington, IN: Indiana University Press, 1958), 28–30; and "Sor Juana Inés de la Cruz," in *The Siren and the Seashell and other Essays on Poetry and Poets*, trans. Lysander Kemp and Margaret Sayers Peden (Austin, TX: University of Texas Press, 1976), 3–16.

21. The most succinct account of the affair I know appears in Herbert Lottman, *The Left Bank* (Boston: Houghton Mifflin, 1982), 273–274, along with the relevant bibliography in the chapter's notes (306); see also my chapter one.

22. Octavio Paz, *El ogro filantrópico. Historia y política, 1971–1978* (Barcelona: Seix Barral, 1982), 242; all citations refer to this edition.

23. See "David Rousset y los campos de concentración soviéticos," *Sur*, 197 (1951), 48–76. Paz further refers to Sartre and Merleau-Ponty in *El ogro*, 241–242 where he revises his views. For further bibliography, see chapter one, n. 70.

24. See, by Paz, *Itinerary: An Intellectual Journey*, trans. Jason Wilson (New York: Harcourt, 1999), 65–66.

25. For the texts of the "Padilla Affair" the standard sources are *El caso Padilla*, ed. Lourdes Casal (Miami: Ediciones Universal, 1972) and *Libre*, 1 (1972). Paz's text, originally titled "La autohumillación de los incrédulos," first appeared in ¡*Siempre!* (May 19, 1971), now in *El ogro*, 239–240. Padilla himself published his memoirs: *Self-Portrait of the Other*, trans. Alexander Coleman (New York: Farrar, Straus & Giroux, 1990).

26. On this subject, see Constance M. Montross, *Virtue or vice?: Sor Juana's Use of Thomistic Thought* (Washington, DC: University Press of America, 1981).

27. See Dario Puccini, *Sor Juana Inés de la Cruz. Studio di una personalità del barocco messicano* (Rome: Edizioni dell'Ateneo, 1967). Puccini himself reviewed Paz's book, praising its conclusions; Cf. "La Sor Juana de Octavio Paz," trans. Fabio Morábito, *Vuelta*, 187 (June 1992), 30–34. For Puccini's latest research on the matter, see his *Una mujer en soledad: Sor Juana Inés de la Cruz, una excepción en la cultura y la literatura barroca* (Mexico City: Fondo de Cultura Económica, 1997).

28. See Paz, *Sor Juana*, 389–437 and Puccini, *Sor Juana Inés de la Cruz*, 511–565, for Paz's proposal of the "conspiracy theory." Merrim avoids taking sides on the question of whether Sor Juana's "abdication" at the end of her life reflects negatively on her feminism; see *Feminist Perspectives on Sor Juana Inés de la Cruz*, 14, 95; in 119–120, n. 3, she pointedly avoids associating Paz's name to the "conspiracy theory" and instead attributes it to what she calls "another trend" of scholarship. For a contrary reading, see Emil Volek's astute essays: "Las letras de los signos: Teoría y crítica de Sor Juana," in *Sor Juana Inés de la Cruz y las vicisitudes de la crítica*, ed. José Pascual Buxó, 321–340; "Silogismos en la sangre escritos: Sor Juana, testigo de cargo (1693–1694)," in *De palabras, imágenes y símbolos*, ed. Enrique Ballón Aguirre and Oscar Rivera Rodas (Mexico City: UNAM, 2002, 533–556; and "La señora y la ilustre fregona: las trampas de la comunicación," in *Sor Juana Inés de la Cruz y sus contemporáneos*, ed. Margo Glantz (Mexico City: UNAM/CONDUMEX, 2001), 333–357. On the *Response*, see, in addition to *Sor Juana*, 411–424 and Montross, above: Silvana Serafin, "La *Respuesta sorjuanina*: Ipotesi interpretativi," *Rassegna Iberistica*, 13 (1982), 3–15; Rosa Perelmuter Pérez, "La estructura retórica de la *Respuesta a sor Filotea*," *Hispanic Review*, 51 (1983), 147–158; Josefina Ludmer, "Tricks of the Weak," in Merrim, *Feminist*, 86–93; also Merrim, "*Narciso desdoblado*: Narcissistic Stratagems in *El Divino Narciso* and the *Respuesta a Sor Filotea de la Cruz*," *Bulletin of Hispanic Studies*, 64 (1987), 111–117; and Franco, 23–54; Elena Feder, "Sor Juana Inés de la Cruz, or The Traps of (con)(tra)di(c)tion, in *American Images and the Legacy of Columbus*, trans. René Jara and Nicholas Spadiccini (Minneapolis: University of Minnesota Press, 1999), 473–529; and Margo Glantz, *Sor Juana Inés de la Cruz: ¿hagiografía o autobiografía?*

29. See Marie-Cécile Bénassy-Berling, *Humanisme et religion chez Sor Juana Inés de la Cruz. La Femme et la culture au XVIIème siècle* (Paris: Editions Hispaniques/Publications de la Sorbonne, 1982); Spanish edition: *Humanismo y religión en Sor Juana Inés de la Cruz* (México: UNAM, 1983). See also, by the same author: "Más sobre la conversión de Sor Juana," *Nueva Revista de Filología Hispánica*, 32 (1983), 462–471; "Frutos del olmo de la fe," *Nexos*, 90 (June 5, 1985), 45–49; and "Sor Juana Inés de la Cruz, Dixième Muse," *La Quinzaine Littéraire*, 501 (January 16–31, 1988),

13–14. In "Frutos" (48, n. 4) the author mentions that in 1974 she "told Octavio Paz my ideas regarding Sor Juana's conversion" and that "with the exception of two aspects of it, our dialogue got sidetracked" [my translation]. The wholesale absence of Bénassy-Berling's work from Paz's book suggests their disagreement was open. For a critique of Bénassy-Berling's scholarship, see Alatorre "La carta de Sor Juana al P. Núñez." The issue permeates the arguments of Elías Trabulse in his archival study *La muerte de Sor Juana* (Mexico City: Centro de Estudios de Historia de México Condumex, 1999).

30. See, for example, Frederick Luciani, "The Convent as Prison and Salon," *The New York Times Book Review* (December 25, 1988), 12–13, as opposed to Michael Wood, "The Genius of San Jerónimo," *New York Review of Books* (October 13, 1988), 39–43, who avers that Paz's political "point is not as strong as it looks." The one reviewer who took the political reading most seriously was Juan Goytisolo: "Una heroína de nuestro tiempo (Notas sobre *Sor Juana Inés de la Cruz o las trampas de la fe*, de Octavio Paz)," *La Torre*, 2 (1988), 527–539. In Mexico, where Paz was known as much for his political views as for his poetry, the majority of the reviews made, however, little mention of the "conspiracy theory" or its implications. See, on the other hand, the interview "Sor Juana: política sagaz," *Excélsior* (March 14, 1989), 1, 12, 14. In one of the more lucid reviews, Anthony Stanton did question soberly whether "Sor Juana is actually our contemporary. Are the conflicts with the powers of her time due to her nonconformity with the ideological foundations of her society?" in *Literatura mexicana*, 1 (1990), 242–248. For a critique of Paz's historical scholarship, see Asunción Lavrin's review in *The Americas*, 40 (April 1984), 589–591; for another critique, this time of his reading of Sor Juana's classical sources, Tarsicio Herrera Zaipén, *Buena fe y humanismo en Sor Juana* (Mexico City: Editorial Porrúa, 1984), 9–51. See also Luis Hermosilla, "La convicción de la verdad de Sor Juana Inés de la Cruz como motivo esencial de la Respuesta a la muy ilustre Sor Filotea de la Cruz," *RLA: Romance-Languages-Annual*, 9 (1997), 529–532; Pablo A.J. Brescia, "El 'crimen' y el castigo: La *Carta Atenagórica*, de Sor Juana Inés de la Cruz," *Caravelle: Cahiers du Monde Hispanique et Luso-Brésilien*, vol. 70 (1998), 73–96; Franco Meregalli, "Sor Juana Inés de la Cruz e Antonio Vieira," *Rassegna Iberistica*, vol. 57 (June 1996), 37–38; and the entire special issue of *Tinta*, "Sor Juana & Vieira, Trescientos años después," ed. K. Josu Bijuesca, et al. (University of California, Santa Barbara, 1998); and Ludwig Schrader, "Reconquista del pasado: El ensayo de Octavio Paz sobre Sor Juana," *Iberoromania*, 7 (1978), 44–49, and by the same author, "Octavio Paz und Sor Juana Inés de la Cruz: zu den Bezugen zwischen Modernität und Barock," in *Texte, Kontexte, Strukturen: Beiträge zur Franzosischen, Spanischen und Hispanoamerikanischen Literatur: Festschrift zum 60 Geburstag con Karl Alfred Buhler*, ed. Alfonso del Toro (Tübingen: G. Narr 1987), 425–433.

31. Georgina Sabat-Rivers, "*Sor Juana: Or, The Traps of Faith*," *Siglo XX/ 20th Century*, 8 (1990–1991), 160. All citations are based on this edition. See also, by the same author, her review of the original Spanish edition in *MLN*, 100.2 (1985), 417–423; and her essays, "Biografias: Sor Juana vista por Dorothy Schons y Octavio Paz," *Revista Iberoamericana*, 32–133 (1985), 927–937; and "*Ejercicios de la Encarnación*: sobre la imagen de María y la decisión final de Sor Juana," *Literatura mexicana*, 1 (1990), 348–371. Paz and Sabat-Rivers debated the question vigorously in two 1984 Mexico TV programs devoted to Sor Juana's life and works within the series "Conversaciones con Octavio Paz" produced by Televisa, Mexico City; see her memoir: "Conversaciones con Octavio Paz: crónica y anécdota," *Anales de literatura hispanoamericana*, 28 (1999), 1441–1451.

32. For such a debate, regarding the authorship of *La segunda Celestina*, a work attributed to Sor Juana, and its recent alleged restitution, see the following: Alejandro Toledo, "Por diversos caminos, Antonio Alatorre y Guillermo Schmidhuber llegaron a 'La Celestina' de Sor Juana," *Proceso*, 710 (June 11, 1990), 50–55; Guillermo Schmidhuber, "Las trampas de la investigación literaria: el descubrimiento de *La segunda Celestina*," *Proceso*, 714 (July 2, 1990), 56–57; Antonio Alatorre, "Algo más sobre Sor Juana y 'La segunda Celestina,' " *Proceso*, 715 (July 9, 1990), 56–57; "La segunda Celestina ante sus jueces" (including essays by Luis Leal, Antonio Alatorre, and Guillermo Schmidhuber) *Vuelta*, 169 (1991), 44–53; Alatorre, "Tercer repaso a 'La segunda

Celestina,' " *Proceso*, 740 (January 7, 1991), 56–58; José Pascual Buxó, "Las vueltas de Sor Juana," *La Jornada Semanal* (November 25, 1990), [no page], and by the same author, "Sor Juana Inés de la Cruz entre el autoritarismo y la frustración," *Proceso*, 745 (February 11, 1991), 56–57; also, Buxó's most recent edition of a manuscript attributed to Sor Juana, *El oráculo de los preguntones* (Mexico City: UNAM/El Equlibrista, 1991), and Guillermo Schmidhuber, "*La segunda Celestina*. Sor Juana y la estilometría," *Vuelta*, 174 (1991), 54–59; Thomas A. O'Connor, "Los enredos de una pieza: el contexto histórico-textual de *El encanto es la hermosura o La segunda Celestina*," *Literatura mexicana*, 3 (1992), 283–202; Alfonso Sánchez Arteche, *La segunda Celestina: una comedia que no escribió Sor Juana* (Toluca: Litomex, 1991). The latest debate concerns attribution of the so-called *Carta de Serafina de Cristo*, recently unearthed by historian Elías Trabulse: *Carta de Serafina de Cristo, 1691*, ed. Elías Trabulse (Toluca: Instituto Mexiquense de Cultura, 1996); on that subject, see Sara Poot Herrera, "Una carta finamente calculada," *Tinta*, 127–142; Antonio Alatorre and Martha Lilia Tenorio, *Serafina y Sor Juana (con tres apéndices)* (Mexico City: El Colegio de México, 1998); and Volek, "Silogismos. . . . " Sor Juana has also been viewed as both a closet theologian [George H. Tavard, *Juana Inés de la Cruz and the Theology of Beauty* (Notre Dame, IN: University of Notre Dame Press, 1991), and as a "Creole writer of protona-tional feelings"; Cf. René Jara and Nicholas Spadaccini, "Allegorizing the New World," in *1492–1992*. Perhaps the smartest of such latest readings is Yolanda Martínez San-Miguel's *Saberes americanos: subalternidad y epistemología en los escritos de Sor Juana*. (Pittsburgh: Instituto Internacional de Literatura Iberoamericana, 1999).

33. All citations based on the Library of Congress copy of *Fama y obras Pósthumas* (Madrid, 1700). See also the detailed study by Antonio Alatorre, "Para leer la *Fama y obras Pósthumas* de Sor Juana Inés de la Cruz," *Nueva Revista de Filología Hispánica*, 29 (1980), 428–508.

34. *Obras selectas de la célebre monja de Méjico, sor Juana Inés de la Cruz, Precedidas de su Biografía y Juicio crítico sobre todas sus producciones*, ed. Juan León Mera (Quito: Imprenta Nacional, 1873).

35. See Haroldo de Campos, *O Sequestro do Barroco na Formação da Literatura Brasileira. O Caso de Gregório de Matos* (Salvador, Bahia: Fundação Casa de J. Amado, 1989).

36. "Y aun cuando no se despeje la incógnita, sino más bien se acentúe el dilema en la medida en que más y más se insista en leerla, en meditarla, en interpretarla, se tiene la impresión de que a cada instante y a cada golpe de página va a descubrirse un secreto latente y agresivo que bur-lonamente . . . se escapa siempre de las manos. . . . " Sergio Fernández, *Retratos del fuego y la ceniza* (Mexico City: Fondo de Cultura Económica, 1968), 28–29. For a similar view, see the same author's "La doble vida histórica de Sor Juana," in *Homenajes: a Sor Juana, a López Velarde, a José Gorostiza* (Mexico City: Sep-Setentas, 1972), 20–102.

37. I follow the Spanish text as established in Sor Juana Inés de la Cruz, *Inundación Castálida*, ed. Georgina Sabat de Rivers (Madrid: Editorial Castalia, 1982), 89–90; all further references to this edition; also, *A Sor Juana Anthology*, 65.

38. For a summary of these variants see Pedro Henríquez Ureña, "Bibliografía de Sor Juana Inés de la Cruz," *Revue Hispanique*, 40 (1917), 161–214. For a partial summary, see Sor Juana, *Obras completas de Sor Juana Inés de la Cruz*, 361 and 543, for the "Romance" and the proem, respec-tively. See also the comments by Sabat de Rivers, *Inundación castálida*, 28.

39. I borrow this useful term from Roland Greene's *Post-Petrarchism: Origins and Innovations of the Western Lyric Sequence* (Princeton: Princeton University Press, 1991), especially 3–62.

40. On this question, see Joan de Jean, *Fictions of Sappho, 1546–1937* (Chicago: University of Chicago Press, 1989).

41. It is revealing that Sor Juana's only other explicit use of the term *restitución*, in the dedication of the *Ejercicios devotos* (ca. 1684–1688) to the Virgin Mary, invokes a similar emptying-out of the self, doubly reinforced in this instance by the fact that the first edition of the *Ejercicios devotos* was published anonymously. Cf. *Obras completas*, IV, 475–507.

42. Paz pursues Sor Juana's fascination with Isis in his reading of *Neptuno alegórico* (155–179) and of Sor Juana's Egyptomania. His principal source is Jurgis Baltrusaitis's classic *La Quête d'Isis* (Paris: Gallimard, 1967). For parallels between the myth of Isis and the Virgin Mary's, see Marina

Warner, *Alone of All Her Sex: The Myth and Cult of the Virgin Mary* (New York: Random House, 1976), 208–209.

43. See Patricia Meyer Spacks, "Selves in Hiding," in *Women's Autobiography: Essays in Criticism*, ed. Estelle C. Jelinek (Bloomington, IN: Indiana University Press, 1980), 112–132.

44. Sor Juana, *Obras completas*, I, 159. My translation.

Chapter Four   Through the Grapevine: Rulfo, Garro, and National Allegory

1. Jameson's statement is the subtitle to his influential *The Political Unconscious* (Ithaca: Cornell University Press, 1980). On the alleged primacy of narrative in historical understanding, see Hayden White, "The Value of Narrativity in the Representation of Reality," and "The Question of Narrative in Contemporary Historical Theory," in his *The Content of the Form* (Baltimore: The Johns Hopkins University Press, 1987), 1–57, and by the same author, *Figural Realism* (Baltimore: The Johns Hopkins University Press, 1999); *On Narrative*, ed. W.J.T. Mitchell (Chicago: University of Chicago Press, 1981); Michel de Certeau, *The Writing of History*, trans. Tom Conley (New York: Columbia University press, 1988); Dominick LaCapra, *History, Politics and the Novel* (Ithaca: Cornell University Press, 1987). Jean Francois Lyotard contrasts "scientific" and "narrative" knowledge in an argument from which I profit at the end of this chapter; see his *The Postmodern Condition: A Report on Knowledge*, trans. Geoff Bennington (Minneapolis: University of Minnesota Press, 1984).

2. I cite from these editions: *Pedro Páramo*, ed. José Carlos González Boixó (Madrid: Cátedra, 1993) and *Pedro Páramo*, trans. Lysander Kemp (New York: Grove Weidenfeld, 1959); *Los recuerdos del porvenir* (Mexico City: Joaquín Mortiz, 1987) and *Recollections of Things to Come*, trans. Ruth L.C. Simms (Austin, TX: University of Texas Press, 1969).

3. On this question, see *Magical Realism: Theory, History, Community*, ed. Lois Parkinson-Zamora and Wendy B. Faris (Durham, NC: Duke University Press, 1997), particularly its Section III, 267–406; Rulfo and Garro are discussed together in 497–550; Dolores Solveig-Hinson, "Juan Rulfo y su realismo mágico," (Ph.D. Dissertation, University of Georgia, 1999); Alicia Llarena, *Realismo mágico y lo real maravilloso: Una cuestión de verosimilitud* (Gaithersburg, MD: Hispamérica, 1997). For a gendered comparison of the two authors, see Ute Seydel, "Desmitificación de la historiografía oficial y del discurso nacionalista en *Los recuerdos del porvenir* de Elena Garro y *Pedro Páramo* de Juan Rulfo," in *Escrituras en contraste. Femenino/masculino en la literatura mexicana del siglo XX*, ed. Maricruz Castro et al. (Mexico City: Aldus, 2004), 43–86. For a position opposite from mine, see Wendy B. Faris, *Ordinary Enchantments: Magical Realism and the Remystification of Narrative* (Nashville, TN: Vanderbilt University Press, 2004).

4. For basic bibliography and general introductions to these authors, the best I know are the entries by Luis Leal and Adriana Méndez Rodenas in *Latin American Writers*, ed. Carlos Solé and Klaus Muller-Bergh (New York: Charles Scribner's Sons, 2002), I, 1227 and Supplement I, 269–288. For general questions on Mexican narrative, see *Antología de la narrativa mexicana del siglo XX*, ed. Christopher Domínguez Michael (Mexico City: Fondo de Cultura Económica, 1989), 2 vols.; on Rulfo and Garro, see II 1029–1041; and Lanin A. Gyurko, "Twentieth Century Fiction," in *Mexican Literature: A History*, ed. David William Foster (Austin: University of Texas Press), 263–267; Peter Beardsell, "Juan Rulfo: *Pedro Páramo*," in *Landmarks in Modern Latin American Fiction* ed. Philip Swanson (London: Routledge, 1990), 74–95. See the recent biography by Reina Roffé, *Juan Rulfo: las mañanas del zorro* (Madrid: Espasa Calpe, 2003) and the collection of essays by various hands: *La ficción de la memoria: Juan Rulfo ante la crítica*, ed. Federico Campbell (Mexico City: Era, 2003). See, also, Patricia Rosas Lopátegui, *Testimonios sobre Elena Garro* (Monterrey: Ediciones Castillo, 2002), the closest we have to a biography. Also, *Elena*

Garro: Lectura múltiple de una personalidad compleja, ed. Lucía Melgar and Gabriela Mora (Puebla: Benemérita Universidad Autónoma de Puebla, 2002).

5. Patricia M. Spacks, *Gossip* (New York: Alfred Knopf, 1988). For another source on the subject see *Good Gossip*, ed. Robert F. Goodman and Aaron Ben-Ze'ev (Lawrence: University of Kansas Press, 1994). Ranajit Guha has studied "rumor" as one of the modes of transmission in circumstances of insurgency, or else of "subaltern politics"; he calls it, "an attempt on the part of its interlocutors to make sense of a challenge to an established authority by matching their perceptions of the by then inevitably strained or already modified relations of power with a 'pre-formed scheme' or code of political thinking"; see his *Elementary aspects of Peasant Insurgency in Colonial India* (Delhi: Oxford University Press, 1983), 264. My argument on "gossip," or at least the ways gossip works in these two novels, runs along similar lines as Guha's on rumor in India's historical life. It would of course be useful to extend this meditation on gossip onto Mexican historical life, not just its literature. See, also, Patricia Turner, *I Heard It Through the Grapevine: Rumor in African American Culture* (Berkeley: University of California Press, 1993), and Turner and Gary Alan Fine, eds. *Whispers on the Color Line: Rumor and Race in America* (Berkeley: University of California Press, 2004).

6. See *Social Text*, 15 (Fall 1986), 65–88; though I cite from its revised version, "World Literature in an Age of Multinational Capitalism," in *The Current in Criticism: Essays on the Present and Future of Literary Theory*, ed. Clayton Koelb y Virgil Lokke (West Lafayette, IN: Purdue University Press, 1987), 139–158. For some of the latest discussions, see Michael Sprinker, "The National Question: Said, Ahmad, Jameson," *Public Culture*, vol. 6 (1993), 3–29; Imre Szeman, "Who's Afraid of National Allegory?" *South Atlantic Quarterly*, vol. 110, no. 3 (2001), 803–827.

7. Homi Bhabha, *Nation and Narration* (London: Routledge, 1990). On the same subject, see Benedict Anderson, *Imagined Communities: Reflections on the Origin and Spread of Nationalism*, revised edition (London: Verso, 1983); and Partha Chatterjee, *The Nation and its Fragments* (Princeton University Press, 1993).

8. See Doris Sommer, *Foundational Fictions: The National Romances of Latin America* (Berkeley: University of California Press, 1991).

9. On this question, see Lukacs' "The Ideology of Modernism," in *Realism in our Time*, trans. John and Necke Mander (New York: Harper & Row, 1964).

10. Jameson himself took up the question of dialectical allegory, as articulated especially in the work of Walter Benjamin, in his *Marxism and Form* (Princeton University Press, 1971), 60–82; on classical allegory, see Angus Fletcher, *Allegory: The Theory of a Symbolic Mode* (Ithaca: Cornell University Press, 1964); and Maureen Quilligan, *The Language of Allegory: Defining the Genre* (Cornell University Press, 1979).

11. See Aijaz Ahmad, "Jameson's Rhetoric of Otherness," in his *In Theory: Classes, Nations, Literatures* (London: Verso, 1992), 95–122; and Jean Franco, "The Nation as Imagined Community," in *The New Historicism*, ed. H. Aram Veeser (New York: Routledge, 1989), 204–212. See also Jameson's "A Brief Response," *Social Text*, 17 (Fall 1987), 26–27.

12. Jean Franco, *Plotting Women: Gender and Representation in Mexico* (New York: Columbia University Press, 1988), 131.

13. See *The Origin of German Tragic Drama*, trans. John Osborne (1925; London: NLB, 1977). Without aiming to make up for Jameson's seeming ellipsis of a dialectical approach to national allegory, see, however, his *Marxism and Form*, particularly 72–73, where the impulse toward allegory is viewed as "the painful attempt to restore a continuity to heterogeneous, discontinued instants" (72).

14. In another book on Mexican women's fiction, Debra Castillo writes, a propos of Garro's novel: "The indeterminacy between substantiality and unreality is an essential component of the aggressively feminized voice in this text." See her *Easy Women: Sex and Gender in Modern Mexican Fiction* (Minneapolis: University of Minnesota Press, 1998), 89. For similar views, see Julie A. Winkler, *Light into Shadow: Marginality and Alienation in the Work of Elena Garro* (New York: Peter Lang, 2001).

15. Among notable exceptions, see Daniel Balderston, "The New Historical Novel: History and Fantasy in *Los recuerdos del porvenir*," *Bulletin of Hispanic Studies*, vol. LXVI (1989), 41–46; and Sharon Sieber, "Elena Garro's New Synthesis: Epic and History in *Los recuerdos del porvenir*," *Selecta: Journal of the PNCFL*, vol. 18 (1997), 101–111.

16. The indispensable study on the *Cristero* Rebellion is Jean Meyer's *La Cristiada* (Mexico City: Siglo XXI, 1974), 2 vols.; I cite from the abridged English version: *The Cristero Rebellion: The Mexican People Between Church and State, 1926–1929*, trans. Richard Southern (Cambridge University Press, 1976). See also the more recent collection *Los Cristeros* (Mexico City: CONDUMEX, 2001). On the "literature" inspired by the *Cristiada*, see Alvaro Ruiz Abreu, *La Cristera, una literatura negada (1928–1992)* (Mexico City: UAM-Xochimilco, 2003) and Angel Arias, *Entre la cruz y la sospecha (los Cristeros de Revueltas, Yáñez y Rulfo)* (Madrid: Ibseroamericana/Verwuert, 2005).

17. "The *cacique*," writes Jean Meyer, "was at the heart of the system . . . The really important person in this context was the rich man, Don Fulano, the only man who could employ and help those whose system of tenure was insufficient to provide an adequate income; from him they expected the establishment of the conditions of mortgage, a monetary loan, an advance in kind, of any favor. Clienteles were formed around him, and he was the apex of a pyramid of hierarchies, for the craftsman and the farmer rarely enjoyed adequate income and security. Class relationships had lost all their paternalistic overtones, and the hard times accentuated the process: in the Altos and the Cañones, the democratic appearance of a society in which there were numerous small proprietors was an optical illusion; in consequence, antagonisms were more violent than elsewhere . . . The *cacique*, a rich man supported by the other rich men, in order to mobilize his clientele, made use of a structure which, in practice, turned out to be ambivalent and ill-equipped to resist the shock of the religious crisis—namely, the clan. The body of relations was formally defined by ties of kinship, but only functioned effectively in common action." *The Cristero Rebellion*, 102–103. Clearly, this social context forms the imaginative core of Rulfo's Comala.

18. Jean Meyer notes: "When Zapata entered Mexico City, he carried the standard of the Virgin of Guadalupe and reopened the churches, and the church bells rang out to welcome him. The quarrel between his followers and those of Carranza was symbolized by the practice of devotion to the Virgin of Guadalupe," *The Cristero Rebellion*, 12.

19. *The Labyrinth of Solitude, and Other Writings*, trans. Lysander kemp et al (1950; New York: Grove Weidenfeld, 1985), 128.

20. For further samples, see Garro's play *Felipe Angeles* (1979), on the famous revolutionary general, and *Revolucionarios mexicanos* (Mexico City: Seix Barral, 1997); her scathing series of newspaper articles written and published in Mexico during the 1960s; also her interviews in Emmanuel Carballo, *Protagonistas de la literatura mexicana* (Mexico City: Editorial Diógenes, 1989), 490–518 and in Michele Muncy, "The Author Speaks," in Anita K. Stoll, *A Different Reality: Studies on the Work of Elena Garro* (Lewisburg: Bucknell University Press, 1990), 23–37. Further on this same issue see Patrick Dove, *The Catastrophe of Modernity: Tragedy and the Nation in Latin American Literature* (Lewisburg: Bucknell University Press, 2004).

21. See Stanley Ross, ed., *¿Ha muerto la revolución mexicana?* (Mexico City: Secretaría de Educación Pública, 1972).

22. One must agree with Lucía Melgar when she views Isabel Moncada's petrification as an "expulsion out of time," which in effect confirms the character's radical marginality; see her "Relectura desde la piedra: ambigüedad, violencia y género en *Los recuerdos del porvenir* de Elena Garro," in *Pensamiento y crítica. Los discursos de la cultura hoy* (Mexico City: Casa Lamm, 2000), 58–72.

23. Again, citing from *Pedro Páramo*, ed. José Carlos González Boixó (Madrid: Ediciones Cátedra, 1993).

24. See *Latin American Writing Today*, ed. J.M. Cohen (Harmmondsworth: Penguin, 1967), 6.

25. See Gilles Deleuze and Félix Guattari, *A Thousand Plateaus: Capitalism and Schizophrenia*, trans. Brian Massumi (Minneapolis: University of Minnesota Press, 1987), 15. For a discussion see

Bernard Cowan, "The *Nomos* of Deleuze and Guattari: Emergent Holism in *A Thousand Plateaus*," *Annals of Scholarship*, vol. 11, no. 3 (1997), 213–289.

26. Ross Chambers, *Loiterature* (Lincoln: University of Nebraska Press, 1999), 93. On the subject of digression I have also profited from Derek Attridge, "The Backbone of *Finnegans Wake*: Narrative Digression and Deconstruction," *Genre*, vol. XVII, no. 4 (Winter 1984), especially 381–389.

27. See this author's "El sustrato arcaico de *Pedro Páramo*: Quetzalcóatl y Tláloc," in *Homenaje a Gustav Siebenmann,* ed. José Manuel López de Abiada (Munich: Wilhelm Fink, 1983), I, 473–490, where he observes that in this scene "the text directs (in imaginary terms) its own production onto orality . . . the irruption of an interlocutor (Dorotea) acts retrospectively to turn everything we have read so far into something oral." The oral qualities of Rulfo's works, and particularly *Pedro Páramo*, have commanded attention since its publication; the first one to notice it was Carlos Blanco Aguinaga, who remarked that in this text: "nobody writes: someone speaks" ["nadie escribe alguien habla"]; Cf. his pioneer essay, "Juan Rulfo: Realidad y estilo de Juan Rulfo," *Revista Mexicana de Literatura*, 1 (1955), 59–86; since Blanco Aguinaga, the bibliography on Rulfo's use of speech has multiplied: Julio Estrada, "Murmullos," *Alfil*, vol. 4 (1989), 26–29; Evodio Escalante, "La voz colectiva y el problema de la enunciación en Juan Rulfo," in *Palabra crítica: Estudios en homenaje a José Amezcua,* ed. Serafín González (Mexico City: Fondo de Cultura Económica, 1997), 354–363; Sonia Mattalia, "Espacio, tiempo y memoria: Los sonidos del silencio en Juan Rulfo," in *Studi di Lettere iberiche e ibero-americani offerte a Giuseppe Bellini,* ed. Giovanni Batista di Cesare, (Rome: Bulzoni, 1993), 659–669; Silvana Serafin, "La prosopopea in 'Pedro Páramo' di Juan Rulfo," *Rassegna Iberistica*, vol. 61 (1997), 51–54; Michael S. Joran, "Noise and Communication in Juan Rulfo," *Latin American Literary Review*, vol. 24, no. 47 (1996), 115–130; Juan Manuel Díaz de Guereñu, "*Pedro Páramo*: Murmullos de entre las grietas," *Iberoromania*, vol. 35 (1998), 98–108; Joseph Tyler, "Speech Acts, o las voces del discurso en Juan Rulfo," *Texto Crítico*, vol. 14, nos. 40–41 (1989), 3–11; Françoise Pérus, "En busca de la poética narrativa de Juan Rulfo (oralidad y escritura en un cuento de *El llano en llamas*)," *Poligrafías*, no. 2 (1997), 59–86; Carlos Pacheco, *La comarca oral* (Caracas: La Casa Bello, 1992), 65–104, and its generous bibliography, 179–191; and Juan Villoro, "Lección de arena: *Pedro Páramo*," in his *Efectos personales* (Mexico City: Ediciones Era, 2000), 15–27.

28. The clear exception would be the soldiers in General Rosas' occupying army, who remain relatively silent and offstage; but that exception itself proves the rule that the townsfolk, rather than the occupying army, use gossip as a mechanism of defense and resistance.

29. I cite from Luis Harss, "Juan Rulfo, o la pena sin nombre," *Los nuestros* (Buenos Aires: Sudamericana, 1966), 355.

30. Mikhail Bakhtin, *Problems of Dostoevsky's Poetics,* tr. and ed. Caryl Emerson (Minneapolis: University of Minnesota Press, 1984), 7.

31. Jan Mukarovsky, "Detail as the Basic Semantic Unit in Folk Art," in his *The Word and Verbal Art,* trans. John Burbank and Peter Steiner (New Haven: Yale University Press, 1977), 202.

32. On this subject the best guide is Gilbert M. Joseph, ed., *Fragments of a Golden Age: The Politics of Culture in Mexico since 1940* (Durham, NC: Duke University Press, 2001).

33. Michel Foucault, *Power/Knowledge: Selected Interviews and Other Writings, 1972–1977,* ed. and trans. Colin Gordon et al. (New York: Pantheon Books, 1980), 81.

34. Lyotard, *Postmodern Condition*, 22.

35. See "A New Type of Intellectual: The Dissident," in *The Kristeva Reader*, ed. Toril Moi (New York: Columbia University Press, 1986), 295.

36. On this controversy, see the summary provided by Méndez Rodenas; also, the excellent essay by Lucía Melgar Palacios, "¿La escritora que no quería serlo? Hacia un perfil de Elena Garro a través de su correspondencia (1947–1968)," *Torre de Papel*, vol. X, no. 2 (2000), 78–101; and, by the same author, "Conversaciones con Elena Garro," in *Elena Garro: lectura múltiple*, 237–277.

37. See Havel's essay "The Power of the Powerless" in *The Power of the Powerless*, ed. John Keane (Armonk, NY: M.E. Sharpe, 1985), 23–96, and particularly, 75–94; and *The Art of the Impossible: Politics as Morality in Practice* (New York: Alfred A. Knopf, 1997), 95–96; 110–114.

38. See, among other works, Fuentes' novel *Terra Nostra* (Mexico City: Joaquín Mortiz, 1975); Krauze's essay *Biography of Power* (New York: Harper-Collins, 1997); and Guillermo Bonfil Batalla's *México Profundo. Reclaiming a Civilization* (Austin: University of Texas Press, 1989).

Chapter Five   1898: Narcissism and Melancholy

1. On the postcolonial question see: Patrick Williams and Laura Chrisman, eds. *Colonial Discourse and Post-Colonial Theory* (New York: Columbia University Press, 1994); for a good summary, Shaobo Xie, "Rethinking the Problem of Postcolonialism," *New Literary History*, vol. 28, no. 1 (Winter 1997), 7–20.

2. "Un domingo se supo en Madrid que la guerra con los Estados Unidos se había terminado, y que Cuba y Filipinas dejaban de ser españolas. Ahora se conocía muy bien la importancia de estas islas y su riqueza; pero a pesar de ello, la gente se mostraba tranquila y resignada. No hubo protestas ni agitación. La gente acudió a los toros y al teatro como si no pasara nada. Fue por entonces cuando dijo Silvela que España no tenía pulso." Pío Baroja, "La decadencia de los pueblos," *Ensayos, Obras Completas*, VIII, 577, as cited by Luis de Llera Esteban and Milagrosa Romero Samper, "Los intelectuales españoles y el problema colonial," in *1895: La guerra en Cuba y la España de la Restauración*, ed. Emilio de Diego (Madrid: Editorial Complutense, 1996), 285.

3. "Y nadie sentía lo crítico de la hora; nadie temblaba—cuando todos debieran temblar—porque aquellos períodos endebles y llenos de eufemismos señalaban el momento más negro de nuestra historia, la agonía de España"; "El mismo día de la escuadra de Cervera, hallábame yo acordon-ado desde hacía días para no recibir diarios en una dehesa en cuyas eras trillaban en paz los labriegos su centeno, ignorante de cuanto a la guerra se refiere. Y estoy seguro de que eran en toda España muchísimos más los que trabajaban en silencio preocupados tan sólo del pan de cada día, que los inquietos por los públicos sucesos"; "La gente se empeña en no querer sentir para poder vivir. . . ." All cited in Javier Figueroa and Carlos G. Santa Cecilia, *La España del desastre* (Madrid: Plaza y Janés, 1997), 224, 155, 141.

4. On Maeztu and his Cuban years, see E. Inman Fox's introduction to his edition of Maeztu's *Artículos desconocidos, 1897–1904* (Madrid: Editorial Castalia, 1977), 11–12; on Maeztu's opinions on the war, see his first book *Hacia otra España* (1899; Madrid: Biblioteca Nueva, 1997), particularly the essays collected in section II, "De las guerras."

5. See de Diego, *1895*, 267.

6. Carlos Serrano, "Aspectos ideológicos del conflicto cubano," in De Diego, *1895*, 73. See also Serrano's *Final del imperio. España, 1895–1898* (Madrid: Siglo XXI, 1984). One of the appendices to the latter (246) gathers one of the exceptional documents of the Generation of 1898: a memorial of Antonio Maceo's death by José Martínez Ruiz, later to be known as *Azorín*. For an alternative view to Serrano's, see Elena Hernández Sandoica, "La política colonial española y el despertar de los nacionalismos en ultramar," in *Vísperas del 98. Orígenes y antecedentes de la crisis del 98,* ed. J. P. Fusi y A. Niño (Madrid: Biblioteca Nueva, 1997), 133–149.

7. De Diego, *1895*, 74.

8. Raymond Carr, *Spain, 1808–1939* (Oxford: Clarendon Press, 1975), 382.

9. See Juan López Morillas, "Preludio del 98 y literatura del Desastre," in his *Hacia el 98: Literatura, sociedad, ideología* (Barcelona: Ediciones Ariel, 1972), 235.

10. "A una España joven," in Antonio Machado, *Obras*, ed. Oreste Macrí (Madrid: Espasa Calpe, 1988), 2, 190.

11. All citations from Manuel Moreno Fraginals, *Cuba/España, España/Cuba: Historia común* (Barcelona: Grijalbo Mondadori, 1995), 293–194, passim.

12. See "¿Qué se debe hacer de Cuba? Cuatro palabras con sentido común," in Maeztu, *Artículos desconocidos*, 64. The article dates from August 6, 1897.

13. My translation from *Idearium español. El porvenir de España* (Madrid: Espasa-Calpe, 1966), 124.

14. *Ibid.*, 169. A few pages before this particular passage, Ganivet himself remarks: "The Arabs, dispersed all throughout Africa, are seemingly obscured and annulled by the Europeans, because they don't know how to deal with them; but we certainly could" (166).

15. "El gobierno está dispuesto a no detenerse ante ningún sacrificio, a gastar hasta la última peseta y a disponer hasta el último hombre en defensa de la patria, de nuestra bandera gloriosa, de nuestra soberanía que jamás se extinguirá en América, porque Cuba será siempre española . . . , persistiremos en nuestro esfuerzo y en nuestra actitud de negarnos a toda concesión a los rebeldes en armas," cited in Luis Morote, *La moral de la derrota* (Madrid: G. Juste, 1900), 31–32. For a view on the subject on the part of the current Cuban State, see Raúl Izquierdo Canosa, *El último hombre y la última peseta* (Havana: Ediciones Verde Olivo, 1997).

16. To date, no exhaustive research on the *Reconcentración* has been done. See, however, the following: Emilio Roig de Leuchsenring, *Weyler en Cuba. Un precursor de la barbarie fascista* (Havana: Editorial Páginas, 1947); Francisco de P. Machado, *¡Piedad! Recuerdos de la Reconcentración* (Havana: 1917); José Antonio Medel, *La guerra hispano-americana y sus resultados* (Havana: F. Fernández y Cía, 1932); Enrique Piñeyro, *Cómo acabó la dominación de España en América* (Paris: Garnier Hnos., 1908), 98–110; Fernando Portuondo, *Historia de Cuba*, 4a ed. (Havana: Editorial Minerva, 1950), 545–546; Jorge Ibarra, *Historia de Cuba*, 3rd ed. (Havana: Dirección Política de las FAR, 1971), 412–413; Louis A. Pérez, Jr. *Cuba Between Empires: 1878–1902* (Pittsburgh, PA: Pittsburgh University Press, 1983), 53–56; and Francisco Pérez Guzmán, *Herida profunda* (Havana: Clio, 2001). Raymundo Cabrera actually wrote a novel based in part on the Reconcentration; Cf. *Episodios de la guerra. Mi vida en la manigua (relato del Coronel Ricardo Buenamor)* (Philadelphia: La Compañía Levytype, 1898). For a list of U.S. sources, see Carlos M. Trelles, *Biblioteca histórica cubana* (Matanzas: Juan F. Oliver, 1922), I, 454–456.

17. See *The Inability to Mourn. Principles of Collective Behavior*, trans. Beverley R. Plazek (1967; New York: Grove Press, 1975). My argument, in what follows, is merely a paraphrase of Chapter I: "The Inability to Mourn—With which is Associated a German Way of Loving," 3–68. Of course, the bibliography on post-traumatic memory is much broader; see Geoffrey Hartman's *état présent*, "On Traumatic Knowledge and Literary Studies," *New Literary History*, vol. 26, no. 3 (Summer 1995), 537–563. Among the best books on the subject, see Lawrence L. Langer, *Holocaust Testimony: The Ruins of Memory* (New Haven: Yale University Press, 1991), and Shoshana Felman and Dori Laub, *Testimony: Crises of Witnessing in Literature, Psychoanalysis and History* (New York: Routledge, 1992).

18. Silence, sadness, austerity, sobriety, nostalgia, decadence, ruins, weariness, monotony, desolation, boredom, abandonment.

19. See Luis Morote, *La moral de la derrota,* 35.

20. Serrano in de Diego, 73. On Spanish colonial policy in Africa see Shannon Fleming, "North Africa and the Middle East," in *Spain in the Twentieth-Century World: Essays on Spanish Diplomacy, 1898–1978*, ed. James W. Cortada (Westport: Greenwood Press, 1980), 121–154; and James A. Chandler, "Spain and her Moroccan Protectorate, 1898–1927," *Journal of Contemporary History*, vol. 10, no. 2 (April 1995), 301–322.

21. See *Las Constituciones de Cuba* (Madrid: Ediciones Cultura Hispánica, 1952), XXIV. Fraga Iribarne's infamous remarks simply repeat Valeriano Weyler's in his five-tome *Mi mando en Cuba* (1910), preceded in time by his equally infamous preface to D. Fernando Gómez, *La insurrección por dentro. Apuntes para la historia* (Havana: M. Ruiz y Cía, 1897), VII–IX. But to my knowledge

none of the Generation of 1898 canonical writers ever reviewed, much less criticized or rebuked, Weyler's actions, or views.

22. See José María Aznar, "Pérdida de un político excepcional," *El Nuevo Herald* (Miami), August 3, 1997, 16-A. Aznar's essay was published in the same newspaper together with Frank Fernández's refutation, "Razón y consecuencia del magnicidio."

23. Ganivet, *Idearium español*, 178. On this subject see Carlos Ripoll's essay, "Castro y la España del desquite," in his *Escritos cubanos* (New York: Editorial Dos Ríos, 1998), 260–268.

Chapter Six   After the Revolution: *Strawberry and Chocolate*, or the Politics of Reconciliation

1. All references are to *Strawberry and Chocolate* [Fresa y chocolate], a film by Tomás Gutiérrez Alea and Juan Carlos Tabío. A production of the Cuban Institute of the Arts and Films Industry (ICAIC), coproduced by IMCINE and Tabasco Films-Mexico, Telemadrid and SGAE-Spain; 104 minutes. The film is based on a story by Senel Paz, "El lobo, el bosque y el hombre nuevo," *Unión* (Edición Continental), I (1991), 25–35; all citations based on *Fresa y chocolate* (Navarra: Xalaparta, 1994) and *Strawberry and Chocolate*, ed. Peter Bush (London: Bloomsbury, 1995); the latter includes "the script the writer gave the director as the final fruit of his literary endeavours" (73) and an interview with Senel Paz. My references in Spanish are taken directly from the film and I prefer to do my translation over Bush's, which is by and large unreliable.

    For a sampling of the debate and various interviews with the two directors, see the following: "Una película contra la hipocresía castrista gana el festival de La Habana," *El País* (December 12, 1993), 40; "Flirtation Across the Borders of Cuban Ideology," *The New York Times* (September 24, 1994), 8; "I Scream, You Scream: Lawrence Chua Talks with Tomás Gutiérrez Alea," *Art Forum,* vol. 33, no. 4 (1994), 62–64; Nedda G. de Anhalt, "Erótica, exótica y estrambótica," *Voces y reflejos*, vol. 3, no. 9 (1994), 51–56; Stephanie Davies, "A Rainbow Revolution," *Gay Times* (March 1995), 13–16; Dennis West, "*Strawberry and Chocolate*, Ice Cream and Tolerance. Interviews with Tomás Gutiérrez Alea and Juan Carlos Tabío," *Cinéaste*, vol. 21, nos. 1–2 (1995), 16–20; José Yglesias, "*Strawberry and Chocolate*," *Cuba Update* (November/ December 1994), 33–35; Roberto Cazorla, " 'En Cuba existe la represión, pero la gente lucha activamente,' " *Diario Las Américas* (June 12, 1994), 11-B; Michael Z. Wise, "In Totalitarian Cuba, Ice Cream and Understanding," *The New York Times* (January 22, 1995), 26-H; Kenneth Freed, "Artists and Homosexuals: 'Non-Persons' in Castro's Cuba," *Los Angeles Times* (February 7, 1995), H-4; Patrick Pacheco, "*Cause Célèbre* or Just Propaganda?," *Los Angeles Times* (January 27, 1995), F-10; José María Espinasa, "*Fresa y chocolate:* un cuento de hadas," *Nitrato de Plata*, 20 (1995), 49–52; "Fresa, chocolate y algún humor político," *La Nación* (Buenos Aires), (October 1, 1994), 3–1; "Cultural Revolution," *The Washington Blade* (February 10, 1995), 49–51; María Cristina, "Un triunfo para Cuba: *Fresa y chocolate,*" *Claridad* (San Juan, PR) (March 24–30, 1995), 27–28; Gina Montaner, "De fresas y chocolates," *El Nuevo Herald* (March 13, 1994), 15; Luis Rumbaut, "*Fresa y chocolate* tiene un tercer sabor: la censura," *El Diario de la Nación* (February 24, 1995), 11, 12; Carlos Monsiváis and Jesús Barquet, "*Fresa y chocolate*," *Fe de erratas* (Chicago), 10 (May 1995), 82–86; Roberto Madrigal, "¿Un Oscar para el cine cubano?" *El Nuevo Herald* (February 24, 1995), 16; Belkis Cuza Malé, "Ni fresita ni chocolate," *El Nuevo Herald* (April 9, 1995), 17. Echoes of the Cuban government's view of the film can be heard in the following: Ann Louise Bardach, "Conversations with Castro," *Vanity Fair* (March 1994), 130–135, 166–170, and particularly 135; Sandra Levinson, "New Cuban Film Breaks Taboo, Sweeps Awards at the Havana Film Festival," *Cuba Update* (February 1994), 23–24; Reynaldo González, "Meditation for a Debate, or Cuban Culture with the Taste of *Strawberry and Chocolate*," trans. William Rose, *Cuba*

Update (May 1994), 14–19. For an interesting discussion of the film from the point of view of Catholic orthodoxy, see Carlos M. de Céspedes, "*Fresa y Chocolate* en Adviento," *Palabra Nueva* (Havana), vol. II, no. 20 (1993), 6–7. For a partial reaction to readings of the film, including this one, see Marvin d'Lugo, "Otros usos, otros públicos: el caso de *Fresa y chocolate,*" *Temas*, 27 (octubre–diciembre, 2001), 53–63.

2. For an overview of these issues, see Grupo de Trabajo, Memoria, Verdad y Justicia, *Cuba: la reconciliación nacional* (Miami: Centro para América Latina y el Caribe, Universidad Internacional de la Florida, 2003).

3. See his "The Language of Strawberry," in *Sight and Sound*, 12 (1994), 30–33; and also the chapter "*Fresa y chocolate (Strawberry and Chocolate)*: Cinema as Guided Tour," in his *Vision Machines: Cinema, Literature and Sexuality in Spain and Cuba, 1983–1993* (London: Verso, 1996), 81–100. On the general subject of homosexuality in Cuba, see: Allen Young, *Gays Under the Cuban Revolution* (San Francisco: Grey Fox Press, 1981); Marvin Leiner, *Sexual Politics in Cuba: Machismo, Homosexuality and AIDS* (Boulder, CO: Westview Press, 1994), and Ian Lumsden, *Machos, Maricones and Gays; Cuba and Homosexuality* (Philadelphia: Temple University Press, 1996); Emilio Bejel, *Gay Cuban Nation* (Chicago: University of Chicago Press, 2001), and particularly 156–168, which deals with the film. To these one should add the following lesser known documents: the *dossier* on Cuban homosexuality, "Los cubanos y el homosexualismo," *Mariel*, II, 5 (1984), 9–15; Gail Reed, "AIDS, Sexuality and the New Man," *Cuba Update* (May 1994), 21–22; Chris Bull and Jorge Morales, "Crisis in Cuba," *The Advocate* (January 24, 1995), 48–50; and the ongoing research by Sonja de Vries, among which see, "Thoughts in Flight," *Cuba Update* (February/March 1993), 19–20 and "Homosexuality, Socialism and the Cuban Revolution," *Cuba Update* (May 1994), 11–13.

4. For contrasting readings of the story see Emilio Bejel, "Senel Paz: homosexualidad, nacionalismo y utopía," *Plural*, 269 (February 1994), 58–65; and Eduardo González, "La rama dorada y el árbol deshojado: Reflexiones sobre *Fresa y chocolate* y sus antecedentes," *Foro hispánico*, 10 (May 1996), 65–78. Of interest, too, is Stephen Wilkinson, "Homosexuality and the Repression of Intellectuals in *Fresa y chocolate* and *Máscaras,*" *Bulletin of Latin American Research,* vol. 18, issue 1, (1999), 17–34.

5. I owe this information to my friends Mario García Joya ("Mayito"), *Strawberry and Chocolate's* excellent photography director, his wife, Cuban actress Yvonne López Arenal, and Cuban actor and director Jorge Folgueira.

6. See "Conversando con Senel Paz," *Viridiana*, 7 (1994), 157. But see also in the same issue Gilda Santana's "*Fresa y chocolate,* el largo camino de la literatura al cine," 133–142, which describes the various drafts of the film. For an English translation of the Toledo interview, see *Sight and Sound*, 12 (1994). The *Viridiana* issue contains the film's published script, as distinct from the transcript of the actual film, which to date is still unpublished. (Henceforward references to the published script will be to this edition.) The script was also published in Cuba in a small, private press: (Matanzas: Ediciones Vigía, 1994). I thank Professor María Donapetry for alerting me to some of these sources.

7. See "Conversando con Senel Paz," *passim.*

8. See *Conducta Impropia*, ed. Néstor Almendros and Orlando Jiménez-Leal (Madrid: Editorial Playor, 1984); the text includes excerpts from interviews not used in the final cut. For a reading of the film, see Smith, *Vision Machines.* Former victims of the UMAPs have been slow in offering their testimony, but recently have organized as a group in Miami. For unusual records, see Nelson Noa, *UMAP: Cuatro letras y un motivo, destruirnos* (Miami: Senda Publishing, 1993), the recent novel by Félix Viera, *Un ciervo herido* (San Juan: Editorial Plaza Mayor, 2002), and Enrique Ros, *La UMAP: El gulag castrista* (Miami: Ediciones Universal, 2004).

9. See Tomás Gutiérrez Alea, "Cuba sí, Macho No!" *The Village Voice* (July 24, 1984); Néstor Almendros, " 'An Illusion of Fairness': Almendros Replies to Alea," *The Village Voice* (August 14, 1984); "Cuba sí, Almendros no!" *The Village Voice* (October 2, 1984).

10. See Tomás Gutiérrez Alea," *'Fresa y chocolate'* y una aclaración," *El Nuevo Herald* (April 27, 1994), 14A.
11. Smith, *Vision machines*, 87.
12. In a brilliant essay, José Quiroga has demonstrated that Gutiérrez Alea's ideological control of the film turns the homosexual subject into an emblem "within a repressive circumstance." What Quiroga, basing himself on a Foucaultian analysis of power relations in the film, calls Diego's becoming an "emblem of the repressed taxonomy," is equivalent to what I call the film's "homosexualist" frame; see his "Homosexualities in the Tropic of Revolution," in *Sex and Sexuality in Latin America*, ed. Daniel Balderston and Donna J. Guy (New York: New York University Press, 1997), 133–151.
13. The story has been collected in the author's *Ahora que me voy: Leyendas cubanas de ayer y de hoy* (Madrid: Libros del Alma, 1998). I thank director Roberto Fandiño for alerting me to this text.
14. "Me han pedido que te vigile—me dijo pegando sus gruesos y duros labios a mi oreja . . . Lo sabía, lo sé—yo no podía dejar de temblar. Cállate, maricón. No lo puedes saber todo, no eres adivino. Lo supe siempre, darling . . . muchacho. Y lo harás, eres uno de ellos . . . pero espero, por tu bien, que un día te olviden. Y te dejen vivir."
15. *Vision machines*, 87–88.
16. Peter Brooks, *The Melodramatic Imagination. Balzac, Henry James, Melodrama and the Mode of Excess* (New Haven: Yale University Press, 1976), 14–15.
17. Caryl Flynn, *Melodrama: Stage, Picture, Screen*, Ed. Jacky Bratton, Jim Cook, Christine Gledhill (London: British Film Institute, 1994), 108. For Paul Julian Smith, the film's constant resort to music is part and parcel of its rhetoric of overemphasis, which reinforces "particular shots or plot points which are then in the redoubling characteristic of cultural tourism alluded to explicitly in the dialogue"; see *Vision Machines*, 95.

Chapter Seven   Fernando Ortiz: Counterpoint and Transculturation

1. For discussions pertaining to Latin America and the Hispanic world, see *El debate de la postcolonialidad en Latinoamérica: una postmodernidad periférica o cambio de paradigma en el pensamiento latinoamericano*, ed. Alfonso de Toro, Fernando de Toro (Madrid: Iberoamericana/Verwuert, 1999) and *Postcolonial Perspectives on the Cultures of Latin America and Lusophone Africa*, ed. Robin Fiddian (Liverpool University Press, 2000).
2. See *Public Culture*, vol. 5, no. 1 (Fall 1992), 89–108; Gayatry C. Spivak, *Critique of Postcolonial Reason: Towards a History of the Vanishing Present* (Cambridge: Harvard University Press, 1999).
3. *Contrapunteo cubano del tabaco y el azúcar (Advertencia de sus contrastes agrarios, económicos, históricos y sociales, su etnografía y su transculturación)*. Introduction by Bronislaw Malinowski, Preface by Herminio Portell-Vilá (Havana: J. Montero, 1940). See also the revised and expanded edition (Santa Clara: Universidad Central de las Villas, 1963), and *Cuban Counter Point: Tobacco and Sugar*, trans. Harriet de Onís (New York: Alfred A. Knopf, 1947); the latter, based on the first edition, is an abridged translation. Ortiz retained Malinowski's essay in the second revised edition, as well as in the 1947 translation, but not Portell-Vilá's Preface. Thirty years after Ortiz's death, his younger daughter, María Fernanda Ortiz Herrera, revised the text again and produced yet another edition (Madrid: EditoCubaEspaña, 1999). The basis for this third edition was the author's hand-corrected copy of the first, which was used as well, though not efficiently, for the second revised Cuban edition (Havana: Consejo Nacional de Cultura, 1963). My own critical and annotated edition (Madrid: Ediciones Cátedra, 2002), also based on the corrected copy, follows all these. For the Spanish text, I refer to the latter as *SP*; for the English, I refer to the recent reprint, based on the same Harriet de Onís abridged translation, *Cuban Counterpoint: Tobacco and Sugar*, Introduction by Fernando Coronil (Durham, NC: Duke University Press, 1996). For the significance of these textual corrections as an insight into Ortiz's book, see the end of this chapter.

4. See *Transculturación narrativa en América Latina* (Mexico City: Siglo XXI, 1982).

5. "Transculturation and the Politics of Theory: Countering the Center, Cuban Counterpoint," in *Cuban Counterpoint: Tobacco and Sugar* (1995), passim.

6. See Paul de Man, *Blindness and Insight. Essays on the Rhetoric of Contemporary Criticism* (1972; Minneapolis: University of Minnesota Press, 1983).

7. Catherine Davies ("Fernando Ortiz's Transculturation: The Postcolonial Intellectual and the Politics of Cultural Representation," in Fiddian, 141–168) casts Ortiz as a "postcolonial intellectual" who "theorized about Cuban popular cultural resistance," but her ideological zeal makes her incur numerous errors of fact. Ortiz never did theorize about "popular cultural resistance" (143), terms he never used and were not current during his working life; by the 1930s the United States was scaling back, not forward, its purchase of Cuban land, and specifically of sugar mills (143); Ortiz was an "organic intellectual" during 1917–1930, when he served in the Cuban Chamber of Deputies, before President Machado's regime; but after that experience he decided to drop out of politics altogether (143); transculturation as term and concept never enjoyed a "level of success" because it never did enjoy currency among anthropologists (143); Ortiz never did practice "the kind of functionalism practiced by the founder of twentieth century social anthropology" (147), and Coronil, whom Davies cites as source, does not claim as much; Ortiz was interested as much in the dialectical process of transculturation as in "the resulting syncretism" (149), which in fact is the whole point of his coinage; in coining "transculturation" Ortiz was not after "accounting for the Cuban situation," which he had already done in his work before 1940, as much as making a contribution to analytical precision lacking in the more current term "acculturation" (150–151). Finally, and countering elementary notions of Spanish grammar, Davies claims that "Ortiz . . . challenged the concept 'acculturation' by deconstructing the word. In Spanish the Latin prefix 'ac' means 'hacia' [toward], whereas in Anglo-Saxon [*sic*] 'a' may mean 'on' or 'and,' implying supplementation. Thus 'acculturation' means 'a tendency towards culturation' with, as Malinowski points out, a 'terminus ad quem,' a finishing point" (149). Davies apparently does not know the difference between the Spanish preposition *a* and the prefix *a-;* the latter means "lack of." As such, *aculturación* would more properly mean "lack of culture," all the more reason to justify Ortiz's critique of the (illogical) English borrowing.

8. See *Culture and Imperialism* (New York: Alfred A. Knopf, 1993).

9. For a telling critique of Said's blindness to the work of Victor Segalen, and thereby to a substantial archive of local knowledge, see Charles Forsdick, "Edward Said after Theory: The Limits of Counterpoint," in *Post-Theory: New Directions in Criticism*, ed. Martin McQuillan et al. (Edinburgh University Press, 1999), 188–199; and generally, Aijaz Ahmad, *In Theory* (London: Verso, 1992), especially 159–220, where the question of "metropolitan location" is discussed in detail.

10. On this subject, what Lezama Lima called counteracting "the American inferiority-complex, as the result of sterile studies of influence that turn American writers into mere witnesses to foreign births," see Ben A. Heller, *Assimilation / Generation / Resurrection. Contrapuntal Readings in the Poetry of José Lezama Lima* (Lewisburg: Bucknell University Press, 1997).

11. For a reprint of the entire correspondence, the originals of which are currently stored in the British Library of Economic and Social Science, see my *Fernando Ortiz: Contrapunteo y transculturación* (Madrid: Colibrí, 2002), 241–316; I quote from this edition throughout this chapter.

12. Esteban Pichardo, *Pichardo Novísimo, o Diccionario provincial casi razonado de vozes y frases cubanas*, ed. Esteban Rodríguez Herrera (1862; Havana: Editorial Selecta, 1953), 204.

13. See his *Del canto y el tiempo* (Havana: Editorial letras Cubanas, 1984), 107. For further discussions of *punto*, see Olavo Alén Rodríguez, *Géneros musicales de Cuba. De lo afrocubano a la salsa* (San Juan: Editorial Cubanacán, 1992), 108–111; María Teresa Linares, "*The Décima and Punto in Cuban Folklore*," *Essays on Cuban Music. North American Perspectives*, ed. Peter Manuel (New York: University Press of America, 1991); Alexis Díaz Pimienta, *Teoría de la improvisación: primeras páginas para el estudio del repentismo* (Oiartzun: Sendoa, 1998). Cuban *controversia* is, of course, but one version of the *certamen*, or contest tradition in Spanish (American) poetry and music, as witnessed, among other samples, in the River Plate *payada*. In U.S. folk music the closest equivalent would be the South's "dueling banjos."

14. For discussions of Juan Ruiz's parody, see Félix Lecoy, *Recherches sur le Libro de Buen Amor* (1938; Farnborough, UK: Gregg International, 1974); Kemlin M. Laurence, "The Battle Between Don Carnal and Doña Cuaresma in the Light of Medieval Tradition," *Libro de Buen Amor Studies*, ed. G.B. Gybbon-Monnypenny (London: Támesis, 1970, 159–176; A.N. Zahareas, *The Art of Juan Ruiz, Archpriest of Hita* (Madrid: Estudios de Literatura Española, 1965); and Dayle Seidenspinner-Núñez, *The Allegory of Good Love: Parodic Perspectivism in the Libro de Buen Amor* (Berkeley: University of California Press, 1981).

15. See *Capital*, Book I. Fernando Coronil was the first to identify this conceptual link; see his "Transculturation and the Politics of Theory," xxvi–xxx. Marx's "commodity fetishism" refers to the mystification of the relationship between labor and value as created by private ownership of the means of production.

16. See Santí, *Fernando Ortiz: Contrapunteo y transculturación*, 307.

17. "It should be noted that the contrapuntal form does not just organize the text of the 'Contrapunteo,' but also that of the complementary chapters [*sic*], which intercalate the themes of tobacco and sugar in a dialogic format." See, Antonio Benítez Rojo, *The Repeating Island. The Caribbean and the Postmodern Perspective* (Durham, NC: Duke University Press, 1992), 285, n. 21; a similar point is made in Celina Manzoni, "El ensayo ex-céntrico: el *Contrapunteo* de Ortiz," *Filología*, vol. 29, nos. 1–2 (1996), 151–156.

18. The lists are not included in the abridged English translation; see, however *SP*, 252 and n. 1, 253.

19. My capsule biography is based on the following sources: Juan Comás and Berta Becerra, "La obra escrita de Don Fernando Ortiz," *Miscelánea* (Havana: Revista Bimestre Cubana, 1955), 347–371; Salvador Bueno, "Don Fernando Ortiz: al servicio de la ciencia y de Cuba," *Temas y personajes de la literatura cubana* (Havana: Unión, 1964), 209–218, and by the same author, "Aproximaciones a la vida y la obra de Fernando Ortiz," *Casa de las Américas*, 113 (1979), 119–128; Oscar Fernández de la Vega, *Fernando Ortiz: Biografía y bibliografía* (1973); Julio Le Riverend, ed., *Orbita de Fernando Ortiz* (Havana: Unión, 1973), 4–51; the same author, "Tres observaciones acerca de la obra de Fernando Ortiz, *Revista de la Biblioteca Nacional José Martí*, Año 72, vol. XXIII, no. 3 (septiembre–diciembre 1981), 37–44; Jorge Ibarra, "La herencia científica de Fernando Ortiz," *Revista Iberoamericana*, vol. 56, nos. 152–153 (1990), 139–151; Thomas Bremer, "The Constitution of Alterity: Fernando Ortiz and the Beginnings of Latin American Ethnography in the Spirit of Italian Criminology," *Alternative Cultures in the Caribbean*, ed. T. Bremer and Ulrich Fleischmann (Frankfurt: Verwuert Verlag, 1993), 119–129; Miguel Barnet, *Fernando Ortiz y el Contrapunto [sic] del tabaco y el azúcar . . .* , (San José: Universidad de Costa Rica, Centro de Investigación en Identidad y Cultura Latinoamericanas, 1995) [Serie Conferencias, #9]; Jorge Castellanos, "Fernando Ortiz y la identidad cultural cubana," *Apuntes Posmodernos/Postmodern Notes*, vol. 6, no. 2–no. 7, no. 1 (Spring–Fall 1996), 23–29; Antonio Fernández Ferrer, "Introducción" to his edition of *La isla infinita de Fernando Ortiz* (Alicante: Generalitat Valenciana/Instituto de Cultura Juan Gil-Albert, 1988), 11–35; Angel Puig Samper and Consuelo Naranjo Orovio, "La formación intelectual de Fernando Ortiz en España" and José Antonio Matos Arévalo, "Fernando Ortiz: cubano entre cubanos," both in *Cuban Counterpoints: The Legacy of Fernando Ortiz,* ed. Mauricio Font et al. (Lanham, Md.: Lexington Books, 2005). For Ortiz's bibliography, see the indispensable *Bio-bibliografía de Don Fernando Ortiz*, ed. Araceli García Carranza (Havana: Instituto del Libro, 1970); and by the same author *Don Fernando Ortiz: Suplemento* (Havana: Biblioteca Nacional José Martí, 1994). A revised edition of the chronology has been made available recently: *Cronología Fernando Ortiz*, ed. A. García Carranza et al. (Havana: Fundación Fernando Ortiz, 1996). *Miscelánea II* (New York: Inter-Americas, 1998) reorders the entire active bibliography chronologically. See also the CD-ROM *Cuban Culture. A Bibliographical Approach—Cultura cubana. Una aproximación bibliográfica* (Havana: Biblioteca Nacional José Martí, 1996).

20. "Más y más fe en la ciencia," *Revista Bimestre cubana*, vol. LXX (1955), 47.

21. See Fernández Ferrer, *La isla infinita*, 19, ns. 10 and 11, where he refers to the influence of *La mala vida en Madrid* (1901), among other works, on Ortiz.

22. Catherine Davies alleges that Ortiz was a "post-colonial intellectual" because he was opposed to the U.S. presence in Cuba, and views his coinage of "transculturation," as opposed to "acculturation," as a strategy of resistance to American hegemony. Davies does not refer either to Ortiz's postcolonial stance regarding Spain's belated pan-Hispanism, as exemplified by his essays in *La reconquista de América* (1910), let alone the complex history of "acculturation" as a concept in Anthropology; see Davies, "Fernando Ortiz's Transculturation," in Fiddian, 141–168.

23. *La crisis política cubana (sus causas y remedios)* (Havana: La Universal, 1919), 6. On this period see Louis A. Pérez, Jr., *Cuba Under the Platt Amendment, 1902–1934* (University of Pittsburgh Press, 1986), 167–170; and Herminio Portell-Vilá, *Nueva historia de la República de Cuba* (Miami: La Moderna Poesía, 1986), 197–212.

24. The manifesto was published in *El Heraldo de Cuba*, April 4, 1923, 1, 13. See *Biobibliografía*, 80, entry 378.

25. For studies of this moment, see Ana Cairo Ballester, *El Grupo Minorista y su tiempo* (Havana: Editorial de Ciencias Sociales, 1979), and Carlos Ripoll, *La generación de 1923 en Cuba* (New York: Las Américas Publishing, 1973).

26. See *Revista Bimestre Cubana*, vol. XIX, no. 1 (enero–febrero, 1924), 17–44; Ortiz gave the speech on February 23, 1924 at the *Sociedad Económica de Amigos del País*; see also *Glosario de afronegrismos* (Havana: Imprenta de El Siglo XX, 1924); in *Bio-bibliografía*, 39.

27. See Pérez, *Cuba Under the Platt Amendment*, 289–317 and Portell-Vilá, *Nueva historia*, 341–398.

28. On this subject, see Carlos del Toro González, *Fernando Ortiz y la Institución Hispanocubana de Cultura* (Havana: Fundación Fernando Ortiz, 1996).

29. See the proceedings in *Diario de la Sexta Conferencia Internacional Americana* (Havana: Imprenta de Rambla, Bauza y Cía, 1928); also collected in my *Fernando Ortiz: contrapunteo y transculturación*. Ortiz's proposal appears on 124.

30. See Pérez, *Cuba Under the Platt Amendment*, 269–272 and Portell-Vilá, *Nueva historia*, 354–82. The legislation was known in Spanish as the "Ley de Prórroga."

31. "El deber norteamericano en Cuba," *Revista Bimestre Cubana*, vol. XXXIII, no. 1 (enero–febrero, 1934), 75–86, a speech before the *Sociedad Económica de Amigos del País*, January 9, 1934.

32. "Por la integración cubana de blancos y negros," *Revista Bimestre Cubana*, vol. LI, no. 2 (marzo–abril, 1943), 269–270.

33. "Más y más fe en la ciencia," *Revista Bimestre Cubana*, vol. LXX, no. 1 (enero–diciembre, 1955), 48.

34. Compare, for example, the number of entries in Ortiz's *Bio-bibliografía*, 41–42 with 43–45.

35. Fernando Ortiz and Rafael A. Fernández, "Antillas," in *Geografía Universal. Descripción Moderna del Mundo* (Barcelona: Instituto Gallach, 1933); Max Sorre and Fernando Ortiz, "Antillas," in *Geografía Universal*, ed. Paul Vidal de la Blache and L. Gallois (Barcelona: Montaner y Simón, 1936), vol. XIX. The title page lists Ortiz's Cuban collaborators and their statement of purpose.

36. On this historical period, see Portell-Vilá, *Nueva historia*, 498–500.

37. For Malinowski's biography, see: *Man and Culture. An Evaluation of the Work of Bronislaw Malinowski* ed. Raymond Firth (London: Routledge and Kegan Paul, 1957). Among studies devoted to Functionalism, see Malinowski, "The Functional Theory of Culture," in his *The Dynamics of Culture Change. An Inquiry into Race Relations in Africa*, ed. Phyllis M. Kaberry (New Haven: Yale University Press, 1945), 41–45, and "The Functional Analysis of Culture," in his *A Scientific Theory of Culture* (New York: Oxford University Press, 1960), 67–74, 147–154; A. R. Radcliffe-Browne, "On the Concept of Function in Social Science," *American Anthropologist*, vol. 37 (1935), 394–402; and, by the same, "Functionalism: A Protest," *American Anthropologist*, vol. 51 (1949), 320–323.

38. The news of Malinowski's visit to Havana and his picture were published together in *Ultra*, then under Ortiz's direction; see vol. VII, no. 42 (December 1939), 564.

39. See my *Fernando Ortiz: Contrapunteo y transculturación*, 243.

40. "Más y más fe en la ciencia," *Revista Bimestre Cubana*, vol. LXX (1955), 45–52.

41. The quotation goes on: "(volume 19 of *Universal Geography*, directed by Vidal de la Blache, Spanish translation), edited by me with collaborations by several colleagues, well-known

specialists all in meterology, geology, botany, zoology and geophysics." Cf. "Contraste económico del azúcar y el tabaco," *Revista Bimestre Cubana*, vol. XXXVIII, no. 2 (setiembre–diciembre, 1936), 250; also published in *Revista Tabaco*, vol. IV, no. 38 (julio, 1936), 11–12, 14, 21–22.

42. The contrast is particularly evident in Ortiz and Fernandez, *Geografía Universal*, 215, 216, 219, 222–223, 232–233. Systematic collation might reveal additional grafts onto the essay.

43. The second edition of *Historia de la arqueología indocubana* appeared as part of Mark Harrington, *Cuba antes de Colón* (Havana: Cultural, 1935), 2 vols.

44. In a letter dated Washington, DC (September 20, 1932), to Sarah Méndez Capote Ortiz wrote: "I am very busy at the library trying to finish work on my Antillean Geography, and at the same time gathering materials for a tome that, depending on what comes out in breadth and length, will be something like *Sugar in the History of Cuba* or *Economic History of Cuba*, or *A History of the Cuban People*," in *Papelería de Renée Méndez Capote*, Sala Cubana, Biblioteca Nacional José Martí, Carpeta No. 5, Folder II, "Fernando Ortiz." I thank Nivia Montenegro for sharing this letter with me.

45. For Ortiz's interest in von Humboldt, see his edition of the latter's *Ensayo político de la isla de Cuba* (Havana: Cultural, 1930).

46. *Diario*, 124.

47. See Vidal de la Blache's *Principles of Human Geography*, ed. Emmanuel de Martonne, trans. Millicent Todd Bingham (New York: Henry Holt and Co., 1926), 3, 5; the original French edition dates from 1921.

48. Maximilien Sorre, *Rencontres de la Géographie et de la Sociologie* (Paris: Librairie Marcel Rivière et Cie., 1957), 9.

49. "These are the times of technological vocabulary. Scientific progress obliges us to be more precise about the meaning of words . . ."; see Ortiz's "Prólogo," in *Léxico tabacalero cubano*, José E. Perdomo (Havana: 1940, facsimile edition) (Miami: Ediciones Universal, 1998), XI–XII. (Ortiz's "Prólogo" is not an entry in the *Bio-bibliografía*.) For an interesting comparison, see Bonham C. Richardson, *The Caribbean in the Wider World, 1492–1992. A Regional Geography* (Cambridge University Press, 1992), which refers broadly to *Cuban Counterpoint*; see 83, 85–86.

50. Ortiz and Fernández, *Geografía Universal*, 215, and *Cuban Counterpoint*, 6.

51. Ortiz and Fernández, *Geografía Universal*, 205. This statement comes at the end of a passage that discusses Leland H. Jenks, *Our Cuban Colony* (New York: Vanguard Press, 1928).

52. *Geografía Universal*, 205. Further in the same text Ortiz makes one exception by adding, "the sugar industry is now entering a new phase of its history." Time would prove him right. In 1925 there were only 26 sugar mills in Cuba, of which all, except two, were in foreign hands; by 1939, however, 28% of them had Cuban owners. In 1952, according to Julio Le Riverend, who cites these figures, "more than 50% of sugar production was derived from Cuban-owned sugar mills"; see his *Historia de la nación cubana*, ed. Ramiro Guerra, et al. (Havana: Editorial Historia de la Nación Cubana, 1952), IX, 316. According to Manuel Moreno Fraginals, however, this gradual property transfer had more to do with the decreased attraction of sugar as an investment potential on the global market. What at first sight appeared to be the effects of Cuba's nationalist struggles were actually the interested workings of a globalized economy. See the latter's "Economías y sociedades de plantaciones en el Caribe español, 1860–1930," in *Historia de América Latina*, ed. Leslie Bethell (Barcelona: Editorial Crítica, 1991), 7, 188.

53. For the details of this history, see Jorge F. Pérez-López, *The Economics of Cuban Sugar* (University of Pittsburgh Press, 1991), 3–19, and Alan Dye, *Cuban Sugar in the Age of Mass Production* (Stanford University Press, 1998), especially 2–66; Portell-Vilá, *Nueva historia*, 68–89, 187–195, 333–340, and Pérez, *Cuba Under the Platt Amendment*, 20–27, 63–64, 187–189, 265–269.

54. See *Sugar and Society in the Caribbean. An Economic History*, trans. Marjorie Urquidi (New Haven: Yale University Press, 1964), whose text is based on the third Cuban edition (Havana: Cultural, 1944); the latter original includes all of Guerra's previous prefaces plus the 1942 appendix by his son, economist José Antonio Guerra. Guerra's book was followed by a plethora of responses; see Raúl Maestri, *El latifundio en la economía cubana* (Havana: Editorial Hermes [Ediciones Revista Avance, 1928]); and Emilio del Real y Tejera, *La industria azucarera de Cuba: superproducción,*

consumo y estabilización del precio (Havana: A. Dorrbecker, 1928). These, plus Luis Araquistáin's *La agonía antillana* (Madrid: Espasa, 1928), and Jenks make up the intellectual context for Ortiz's critique.

55. See *La industria azucarera de Cuba* (Havana: Cultural, 1940), and "Sugar: Index of Cuban American Cooperation," *Foreign Affairs*, vol. 20, no. 4 (julio 1942), 744–756. According to Portell-Vilá, "La industria azucarera y su futuro," *Revista Bimestre Cubana*, vol. L (julio–diciembre, 1942), 161–179, in 1940 Guerra (whom he calls "a careful scholar") was "an advisor to the Sugar Institute," 168.

56. Sorre and Ortiz, *Geografía Universal* (1936), 181 and Ortiz, *Cuban Counterpoint*, 34. I have adapted my rendering here to echo more pointedly the 1947 English translation; for a point of view similar to Ortiz's, see Maestri, *El latifundismo*.

57. Ortiz's concern for sugar industry abuses dated back to his first years in the Cuban Congress; see, for example, his "Regulación de las ventas de azúcares al extranjero," *Revista Bimestre Cubana*, vol. XII, no. 6 (noviembre–diciembre, 1917), 361–371; now collected in my *Fernando Ortiz: Contrapunteo y transculturación*, 93–104; also, Paz's *Posdata* (1969). My parallel with Paz's critique here assumes an untranslatable pun from Cuban Spanish, wherein "*caña*" (sugarcane) is a synonym for "force" or "strength." Thus a "critique of sugar" means a critique of power. Neither Pichardo nor indeed Ortiz registers "*caña*" as a lexical cubanism; see, however, Argelio Santiesteban, *El habla popular cubana de hoy* (Havana: Editorial de Ciencias Sociales, 1982), 81; and José Sánchez Boudy, *Diccionario mayor de cubanismos* (Miami: Ediciones Universal, 1999), 142. These and other related themes are treated in Roland T. Ely's classic, *Cuando reinaba su majestad el azúcar: estudio histórico-sociológico de una tragedia latinoamericana: el monocultivo en Cuba, origen y evolución del proceso* (Buenos Aires: Sudamericana, 1963). For a meditation on the links among the discourses of sugar, power and the formation of Cuban literature, see Antonio Benítez Rojo, "Power/Sugar/Literature: Towards a Reinterpretation of Cubanness," *Cuban Studies*, vol. 16 (1986), 9–31. See also the collection of essays by Michele Guicharnaud-Tollis, ed. *Le Sucre dans l'espace caraï be hispanophone* (Paris: L'Harmattan, 1998).

58. Guerra, *La industria azucarera de Cuba*, VI. The same argument appears in José Antonio Guerra, in *Sugar and Society*, "Appendix I: Recent Evolution of the Sugar Industry," 171–192.

59. I cite from the first edition (1940) of *Contrapunteo cubano*, XX.

60. In his "Introduction," Malinowski had cautioned: "With reference to the political implications inherent in the basic problem of this book, Dr. Ortiz has refrained from any unwarranted judgments," xv.

61. Barro y Segura's complete English title was *The Truth About Sugar in Cuba. Corrections to and Explanation of the Pamphlet entitled "The Sugar Industry and its Future" by Mr. Herminio Portell-Vilá* (Havana: Ucar, García, y Cía, 1943). According to the preface, the pamphlet "has been translated into English at the request of Sr. José M. Casanova, President of the National Association of Cuban Sugar Producers not as propaganda which it isn't, but to contribute towards an understanding of Cuban sugar industry by the U.S. and the world" (4). Portell-Vilá's essay is the same as the one in my n. 55, cited earlier.

62. Portell-Vilá, "La industria azucarera," 174.

63. One of the few reviews of *Cuban Counterpoint* to appear in Havana did so under the pen name of *Diplomaticus* and was signed "Washington, D.C."; see "Sobre un interesante contrapunteo," "Contrapunteando," "Contrapunteo doloroso," and "Final del contrapunteo," *Diario de la Marina* (January 15, 19, 23, 24 January, 1941), respectively. According to José Antonio Matos Arévalo, *La historia en Fernando Ortiz* (Havana: Fundación Fernando Ortiz, 1999), 69, the review's author was, in fact, Ramiro Guerra. Four years later, Guerra himself refuted Ortiz's thesis between the lines of his *Filosofía de la producción cubana* (Havana: Cultural, 1944); there he poses what he calls the "fundamental law of Cuban production": "The only means at Cuba's reach is to export its staples, sell them at foreign currency in the greatest quantities and then purchase and pay off its debts," 25–26. For a discussion of sugar and tobacco exports during the 1934–1941 period, see 157–171. By 1944, however, Guerra's position was much closer to Ortiz's; see 177. See also José

Antonio Matos Arévalo, "Ramiro Guerra y Fernando Ortiz: Polémica entre historiadores," *Revista de la Biblioteca Nacional José Martí*, vol. 93, 1–2 (enero–junio, 2002), 111–115. My thanks to Professor Ana Cairo Ballester, of the University of Havana, for alerting me to Guerra's book, and to Duanel García Infante for information on Guerra's reviews and Matos Arévalo's contributions to this debate.

64. For a refutation of Ortiz's Marxism, see, Julio Le Riverend, "Fernando Ortiz y su obra cubana," in *Orbita de Fernando Ortiz* (Havana: Unión, 1973), 38; in another context Le Riverend stated: "His knowledge of Marxism, as a student of Asturaro's and an early reader of some Marxist texts . . . would not be enough to place him squarely within historical materialism," in "Ortiz y sus contrapunteos," in Fernando Ortiz, *Contrapunteo cubano del tabaco y el azúcar* (Caracas: Biblioteca Ayacucho, 1978), XXII.

65. See Jean Stubbs, *Tobacco on the Periphery. A Case in Cuban Labour History, 1860–1958* (Cambridge University Press, 1985), passim.

66. On Ramírez, see Leví Marrero, *Cuba: Economía y Sociedad: Azúcar, Ilustración y Conciencia (1763–1868)* (Madrid: Editorial Playor, 1979) I, 153; and H. E. Friedlaender, *Historia económica de Cuba* (Havana: Jesús Montero, 1944), 160–161. For a short biography, see *Cuba en la mano* (Havana: Ucar, García y Cía, 1940), 990–991; for pertinent comments on the counterpoint between "small" and "big" Cuba, see Benítez Rojo, "Power . . .," *passim*.

67. See Albert O. Hirschman, "A Generalized Linkage Approach to Development with Special Reference to Staples," *Economic Development and Cultural Change*, vol. 25 (Suppl. 1977), 67–98, especially 94–96. Hirschman cites, in turn, the following: Luis Eduardo Nieto Arteta, *El café en la sociedad colombiana* (Bogotá: Breviarios de orientación colombiana, 1958; William P. McGreevey, *An Economic History of Colombia* (Cambridge University Press, 1971), 217–241; and Celso Furtado, *The Economic Growth of Brazil*, trans. R.W. de Aguiar and E.C Drysdale (Berkeley: University of California Press, 1968). According to William Luis, Ortiz lessened the importance of coffee in the Cuban economy, but later acknowledged it in his preface to Juan Pérez de la Riva, *El café: Historia de su cultivo y explotación en Cuba* (1944); see, Luis, "Cuban Counterpoint, Coffee and Sugar: the Emergence of a National Culture in Fernando Ortiz's *Cuban Counterpoint: Tobacco and Sugar* and Cirilo Villaverde's *Cecilia Valdés*," *Palara*, 2 (1998), 5–16.

68. I cite from Radcliffe-Browne, "On the Concept of Function . . .," 295.

69. On this subject, the best discussion remains Octavio Paz, *Claude Lévi-Strauss: An Introduction* (Ithaca: Cornell University Press, 1972).

70. On Functionalism, see, among other sources: Robert H. Lowie, *The History of Ethnological Theory* (New York: Farrar, Straus & Giroux, 1937); Alexander Lesser, "Functionalism in Cultural Anthropology," *American Anthropologist*, vol. 37 (1935), 386–393; Adam Kuper, *Anthropologists and Anthropology. The British School, 1922–1972* (London: Allen Lane, 1973), 9–12 and 239–241; Marvin Harris, *The Rise of Anthropological Theory. A History of Theories of Culture* (New York: Columbia University Press, 1968), 514–567; Michael W. Young, "Malinowski and the Function of Culture," in *Creating Culture*, ed. Diane J. Austin-Broos (London: Allen & Unwin, 1987), 124–140; S.N. Eizenstadt, "Functional Analysis in Anthropology and Sociology: An Interpretive Essay," *American Review of Anthropology*, 19 (1990), 243–260; Leslie A. White, *The Concept of Cultural System* (New York: Columbia University Press, 1975), 147–158; Héctor Tejera Gaona, "A.R. Radcliffe-Browne y el estructural-funcionalismo de la escuela de Oxford," *Boletín de Antropología Americana*, vol. 21 (1990), 129–144.

71. *Freud and Philosophy. An Essay in Interpretation* (New Haven: Yale University Press, 1970), 33.

72. Fernando Coronil, *Cuban Counterpoint*—Introduction, xxvi.

73. *Holy Smoke!* (London: Faber & Faber, 1985), 43.

74. Ortiz's "counterpoint" is remarkably close to Mikhail Bakhtin's "dialogism." "Bakhtin's views on Dostoevsky cannot be separated from Bakhtin's general theory of discourse, in which I am never free to impose my own unobstructed intention but must always mediate that intention through the intention of others, beginning with the otherness of the language itself in which I speak. I must enter a dialogue with others. This does not mean that I cannot make my own

point of view understood; it simply means that my point of view will emerge through the inter-action of my own and another's words as they contend with each other in particular situations." Michael Holquist and Katerina Clark, *Mikhail Bakhtin* (Cambridge: Harvard University Press, 1984), 245. On the conceptual relations between Ortiz and Bakhtin, see Miguel Cossío Woodward's unpublished dissertation, "Transculturación y literatura en el Caribe," Mexico City, Universidad Iberoamericana, 2003.

75. "The Functional Theory of Culture," in his *The Dynamics of Culture Change*, 41, where he also observes: "Function always means, then, the satisfaction of a need."

76. *The Dynamics of Culture Change*, 32. On this subject, see Leslie A. White, "The Three Types of Interpretation of Culture," *Southwestern Journal of Anthropology*, 1 (1945), 221–248.

77. See "The Anthropology of Changing African Cultures," in *Methods of Study of Culture Contact in Africa* (Oxford University Press, 1938), vii–xxxvii.

78. On transculturation, the best discussions I know are: Diana Iznaga, *Transculturación en Fernando Ortiz* (Havana: Editorial de Ciencias Sociales, 1989); Antonio Fernández Ferrer, "Fernando Ortiz, explorador de la isla infinita," in 29–32, and its generous bibliography; Alberto Moreiras, *The Exhaustion of Difference: The Politics of Latin American Cultural Studies* (Durham, NC: Duke University Press, 2001), 185–187, 264–67; Arnaldo E. Valero, "La transculturación en el marco de una antropología latinoamericana (1928–1940)," *Catauro. Revista Cubana de Antrolopogía*, Año 1, no. 1 (enero–junio, 2000), 58–67; John Beverley, *Subalternity and Representation* (Minneapolis: University of Minnesota Press, 1999), 41–64; Luis Duno Gottberg, *Solventando las diferencias: La ideología del mestizaje en Cuba* (Madrid: Iberoamericana-Verwuert, 2003).

79. "A Memorandum for the Study of Acculturation," *American Anthropologist*, vol. XXXVIII (1935), 149–152. Herskovits restated the concept in "The Significance of the Study of Acculturation for Anthropology," *American Anthropologist*, vol. XXXIX (1937), 259–264, as well as in his *Acculturation. The Study of Culture Contact* (New York: J.J. Augustin, 1938).

80. The idea stems principally from Angel Rama's influential *Transculturación narrativa en América Latina* (Mexico City: Siglo XX, 1982), which applied Ortiz's concept to culturally layered modernist narratives from Latin America, such as José María Arguedas'. See below for a fuller discussion. For a useful critique of Rama, see Beverley, *Subalternity and Representation*.

81. One must agree with Diana Iznaga when she observes that *aculturación* turns out to mean the opposite of its original English meaning, since in Spanish the prefix *a* means "absence of" and therefore "falsifies the essence of culture contact," 55.

82. As suggested by Iznaga, *Transculturación*, 49–50.

83. See Melville J. Herskovits, "Applied Anthropology and the American Anthropologists," *Science*, vol. 83, no. 214 (marzo 6, 1936), 215–222, a speech before the *American Association for the Advancement of Science* on January 3, 1936. It would be unfair, however, to make the blanket claim, as Julio Le Riverend once did, that "the absence of historicism is an important fact about Malinowski's work" ("Ortiz y sus contrapunteos," XXIV). As shown by Lucy P. Mair, Radcliffe-Browne's and Malinowski's Functionalism rejected any sort of "conjectural history" based on hypothetical or impressionistic reconstructions of the past ("Malinowski and the Study of Social Change," in *Man and Culture*, 240–243). Malinowski himself viewed tribal history not as an "objective document but as one of several facts in the present social situation, in the same category as myth," Mair, *Man and Culture*, 241. In contrasting Malinowski's views with Ortiz's, however, Le Riverend represses this important passage in order to attribute an ahistoricist bias to Malinowski: "But to the student of culture change what really matters is not the objectively true past, scientifically reconstructed and all-important to the antiquarian, but the psychological reality of today. The former is an order of events dead and buried, even to the length of having disappeared from men's memories; the latter a powerful psychological force determining the present behaviour of the native African. People are swayed by the errors they feel, not by the truth they ignore. The distinction between the two anthropologies is plain and fundamental. To the antiquarian what really matters is the past, true and objective, with all the retrospective glorification and obloquy carefully removed. To the student of culture change, the bias, the contrast and the false colors are all-important, because they are the

forces which foster change or retard it respectively." ("The Anthropology of Changing African Cultures," XXX.) Le Riverend elides most of this passage, and neither documents it nor includes it in his bibliography (453–463). Functionalist skepticism over so-called conjectural history is more a matter, in my view, of rigorous empiricism than colonialist prejudice. Malinowski's shift had occurred precisely in 1938 with "The Anthropology of Changing African Cultures," the essay that most likely caught Ortiz's attention and that Malinowski cites in his own "Introduction."

According to Firth, *Man and Culture* (4–5), Malinowski visited the United States for the first time in 1926, returned in 1933 (to Cornell University), and lived there from October 1939 until his death in 1942 in New Haven. I agree with Le Riverend that radical methodological differences separated Ortiz and Malinowski; but that does not justify denigrating the latter's reputation by calling him "a colonized Pole, subjected to Austrian foreigners" (XXVII). This is particularly unfair to Malinowski, whose views after 1938 on the gradual decolonization of Africa demonstrate he was the precise opposite of a colonizer.

84. See *Fernando Ortiz: Contrapunteo y transculturación*, 307. It should be noted that none of the latest theoretical discussions of transculturation distance themselves from Malinowski's questionable distinction. For a sample of these, see *Literary Cultures of Latin America. A Comparative History*, ed. Mario J. Valdés and Djelal Kadir (New York: Oxford University Press, 2004), III, 129–267, *passim*.

85. See Melville Herskovits, *Man and his Works: The Science of Cultural Anthropology* (New York: Alfred A. Knopf, 1948). Herskovits' professional rancor, years after Malinowski's death, reached the bitter end of linking his work to Wilhelm Muhlmann's, a German ethnologist who, in Herskovits' view, "had translated in the sphere of culture, the Nazi culture of racial superiority," *Ibid.*, 529.

86. "In Rama's refashioning of the concept, which was based on the coincidence between the literary practice of the 'boom' writers and the new political energies released by the impact of the Cuban revolution, it became something like an ideologeme for Latin American intellectual and cultural work in general. As such, transculturation posited the providential role of a 'lettered' vanguard of social scientists, pedagogues, artists, writers critics and a new type of politician to represent subaltern social classes and groups by developing new cultural and political forms in which the formative presence in Latin American history and society could be made manifest." Beverley, *Subalternity and Representation*, 43. For further discussions of Rama's ideas, see Moreiras, *The Exhaustion of Difference*; Jesús Díaz Caballero, "La transculturación en la novela regionalista: el caso sur-andino peruano y la obra de Arguedas," *Revista de crítica literaria latinoamericana*, vol. XIII, no. 25 (1987), 155–172; and *Angel Rama y los estudios latinoamericanos*, ed. Mabel Moraña (Pittsburgh: Revista Iberoamericana, 1997).

87. Moreiras, *The Exhaustion of Difference*, 185.

88. On hybridity, see Homi Bhabha, *The Location of Culture* (London: Routledge, 1994); for brief descriptions, *Key Concepts in Post-Colonial Theory*, ed. Bill Ashcroft et al. (London: Routledge, 1998), 118–121; and the special issues of *Journal of American Folklore*, vol. 112 (1999) and *Critical Studies*, vol. 13 (2000). On heterogeneity, see Antonio Cornejo Polar, "Mestizaje, transculturación, heterogeneidad," *Revista de Crítica Literaria Latinoamericana*, vol. XX, no. 40 (1994), 368–371; David Sobrevilla, "Transculturación, heterogeneidad: avatares de dos categorías literarias en América Latina," *Revista de Crítica Literaria Latinoamericana*, vol. 27, no. 54 (2001), 21–33.

89. Mary Louise Pratt, *Imperial Eyes. Travel Writing and Transculturation* (London: Routledge, 1992).

90. See, among others, *Transcultural Joyce*, ed. Karen R. Lawrence (Cambridge University Press, 1998); *Tropicalizations: Transcultural Representations of Latinidad*, ed. Frances Aparicio et al. (Hanover: University Press of New England, 1997); David MacDougall, *Transcultural Cinema*, ed. L. Taylor (Princeton University Press, 1998); Linda Pratt, *Transcultural Children's Literature* (Upper Saddle, NJ: Merrill, 1999).

91. See *The Cuban Condition. Translation and Identity in Modern Cuban Literature* (Cambridge University Press, 1989), 50. For another defense of the book's literary character, see Ricardo Castells, "Ficción y nacionalismo económico en el *Contrapunteo cubano* de Fernando Ortiz," *Journal of Interdisciplinary*

Literary Studies, vol. 4, nos. 1–2 (1992), 55–70. See also Curtis Lincoln Barrett, "Fernando Ortiz and the Literary Process" (Ph.D. Dissertation, Columbia University, 1994).

92. "*El Contrapunteo y la literatura,*" *La Gaceta de Cuba*, 2 (April–May, 1996), 23–26. The author's use here of "*envoltura*" (wrapper), not a tobacco term, may intend the more precise "*capa*": "Hoja exterior del torcido"; see Perdomo, *Léxico tabacalero cubano*, 17; or else, Ortiz's essay.

93. Benítez Rojo, *The Repeating Island*, 152–158.

94. See *Arte de ingenio. Tratado de la agudeza* (1642); *Agudeza y arte de ingenio*, ed. E. Correa Calderón (Madrid: Castalia, 1969), I, 55.

95. "De la agudeza de improporción y disonancia," *Agudeza*, Discurso V, 74–88. On Gracián and wit, see Santos Alonso, *Tensión semántica (lenguaje y estilo) de Gracián* (Zaragoza: Institución "Fernando el Católico," 1981), especially 105–108; Arturo Zárate Ruiz, *Gracián, Wit and the Baroque Age* (New York: Peter Lang, 1996), 181–214; and Emilio Hidalgo Serna, "The Philosophy of *Ingenium*: Concept and Ingenious Method in Baltasar Gracián," *Philosophy of Rhetoric*, vol. 13 (Fall 1980).

96. The first to indict Ortiz's alleged non-science was perhaps Manuel Moreno Fraginals' sweeping, unfair statement: "many of his claims are brilliant; others still cannot sustain the least critical analysis," in his *El Ingenio* (Havana: Editorial de Ciencias Sociales, 1978), III, 246.

97. The claim is made, mistakenly in my view, by González Echevarría, 25.

98. Severo Sarduy, "Baroque and Neobaroque," in *Latin America in its Literature*, ed. César Fernández Moreno, trans. Mary Berg (New York: Holmes and Meier, 1980). Among the Cuban writers Sarduy includes in his international list are: Alejo Carpentier, José Lezama Lima and Guillermo Cabrera Infante. For further sources, see: *Le Néo-baroque cubain* (Paris: Presses de la Sorbonne Nouvelle, 1998); *Le Roman Néo-baroque cubain*, ed. Daniel Meyran et al. (Montpellier: Centre d'etudes socio-critiques, 1997); María Isabel Acosta Cruz, *The Discourse of Excess: the Latin American Neobaroque and James Joyce* (Ph.D. Dissertation, SUNY Binhgamton, 1984); Irlemar Chiampi, *Barroco y modernidad* (Mexico City: Fondo de Cultura Económica, 2000; and Corey Shouse, "Barroco, neobarroco y transculturación," in *Barrocos y modernos. Nuevos caminos en la investigación del Barroco iberoamericano*, ed. Petra Schumm (Frankfurt am Main and Madrid: Iberoamericana Verwuert, 1998), 321–335. For a recent overview of Baroque art, which stresses the "perverse" commentary on Renaissance norms, see Robert Harbison, *Reflections on Baroque* (University of Chicago Press, 2000), 166.

99. See "Lo barroco y lo real maravilloso" in his *Tientos y diferencias y otros ensayos* (Barcelona: Plaza y Janés, 1987).

100. See Lezama Lima's *La expresión americana*, ed. Irlemar Chiampi (1957; Mexico City: Fondo de Cultura Económica, 1993), 83, 177. For an overview on Lezama's views on the Baroque, see *Diccionario. Vida y obra de Lezama Lima*, ed. Iván González Cruz (Valencia: Generalitat Valenciana, 2000), 40–45. Antonio Benítez Rojo attributed the Baroque character of Cuban literature to what he called the island's "cultural density"; see the interview with Ilán Stavans, *Apuntes posmodernos/Postmodern Notes*, 16.

101. See César Augusto Salgado, "Hybridity in New World Baroque Theory," *Journal of American Folklore*, vol. 112 (1999), 316–331, and in particular 324, where Ortiz is identified as a direct source for Lezama Lima.

102. See Fernando G. Campoamor, *Biografía del ron cubano. El hijo alegre de la caña de azúcar* (Havana: Editorial Científico-Técnica, 1985). Cabrera Infante's book is divided, not unlike *Cuban Counterpoint*, into two sections, but provides a parodic, inverse structure: a long essay and a brief anthology. *Puro humo* (Madrid: Alfaguara, 2000); the Spanish version of *Holy Smoke!* offers itself as a counterpoint to Ortiz's; see "Nota Beníssima," 10; and also "Ortiz o el arte de la fuga," where he calls Ortiz "excesivo, retórico, barroco," 472. In *Holy Smoke!* see "Ortiz or Lezama?" 443–444.

103. See Lezama Lima, 84–85, and Gilles Deleuze, *Le Pli. Leibniz et le Baroque* (Paris: Minuit, 1988). The affinity between the Baroque and (premodern) science appears everywhere, as in Omar Calabrese, *Neo-Baroque: A Sign of the Times*, trans. Charles Lambert (1987; Princeton University

Press, 1992), and notably in Severo Sarduy's prose essays, which reflect his work for French radio, where for years he was a science and technology correspondent; see, among others, his *Barroco* (1976), in *Ensayos generales sobre el barroco* (Buenos Aires: Fondo de Cultura Económica, 1995); and his *Antología*, ed. Gustavo Guerrero (Mexico City: Fondo de Cultura Económica, 2000).

104. Basing himself on the abridged English translation, Coronil misstates that "for the 1963 edition, published by Havana's Consejo Nacional de Cultura, Ortiz added twelve chapters (more than two-hundred pages)," Coronil, xlviii, n. 3. Ortiz did add that number of pages but did not alter the number of chapters. Also, there were two, and not just one, 1963 editions: (Havana: Editora del Consejo Nacional de Cultura), and (Santa Clara: Universidad de Las Villas). Finally, in simply reprinting the abridged 1947 English translation, Duke University Press failed to incorporate Ortiz's changes for the revised 1963 edition. Ortiz's English readers deserve a complete rendering of the final, corrected text.

105. See Harbison, *Reflections on Baroque*, 167.

106. Sarduy, "Baroque and Neobaroque," 131.

107. For a summary of this polemic, surrounding my "Parridiso," *MLN*, 94 (1979), 343–365, now collected in my *Bienes del siglo. Sobre cultura cubana* (Mexico City: Fondo de Cultura Económica, 2002), 168–188, see César A. Salgado, *From Modernism to Neobaroque: Joyce and Lezama Lima* (Lewisburg, PA: Bucknell University Press, 2001), especially 181–206 and 243–248.

108. See Vera León's "Juan Francisco Manzano: el estilo bárbaro de la nación," *Hispamérica*, vol. XX, no. 60 (December 1991), 3–22. Of course, Manzano's access to writing signifies his self-constitution as a free subject; hence his status as prototype of the Cuban nation.

109. *Ibid.*, 16. Elsewhere I have proposed that the staging of Cuban national identity finds yet another "aberrant" version in the French text of La Comtesse Merlin, particularly as studied in Adriana Méndez Rodenas, *Gender and Nationalism in Colonial Cuba: The Travels of Santa Cruz y Montalvo, Condesa de Merlín* (Nashville: Vanderbilt University Press, 1998); see my "Habanera," *Crítica* (Puebla, Mexico), vol. XXII, no. 85, Nueva época (enero–febrero, 2001), 71–81; also in my *Bienes del siglo*, 38–44.

110. "It has the academic connotation of 'daring' and 'rash,' but its meaning is broadened to include anyone capable or outstanding in any discipline," *El habla*, 51; "A very intelligent person," *Diccionario mayor de cubanismos*, 72.

111. "Baroque and Neobaroque," 131.

INDEX